Access 2000 Programming from the Ground Up

Whil Hentzen

Osborne/**McGraw-Hill**

Berkeley   New York   St. Louis   San Francisco
Auckland   Bogotá   Hamburg   London   Madrid
Mexico City   Milan   Montreal   New Delhi   Panama City
Paris   São Paulo   Singapore   Sydney
Tokyo   Toronto

Osborne/**McGraw-Hill**
2600 Tenth Street
Berkeley, California 94710
U.S.A.

For information on translations or book distributors outside the U.S.A., or
to arrange bulk purchase discounts for sales promotions, premiums, or
fund-raisers, please contact Osborne/**McGraw-Hill** at the above address.

Access 2000 Programming from the Ground Up

1234567890 AGM AGM 90198765432109

ISBN 0-07-882575-X

Publisher
Brandon A. Nordin

**Associate Publisher and
Editor-in-Chief**
Scott Rogers

Acquisitions Editor
Wendy Rinaldi

Project Editor
Janet Walden

Editorial Assistant
Monika Faltiss

Technical Editor
Rima Regas

Copy Editor
Jan Jue

Proofreader
Linda Medoff

Indexer
David Heiret

Computer Designers
Ann Sellers
Mickey Galicia
Gary Corrigan

Illustrators
Beth Young
Robert Hansen

Series Design
Peter Hancik

Cover Design
John Nedwidek

Cover Illustration
Jude Maceren

About the Author...

Whil Hentzen is president of Hentzenwerke Corporation, a 17-year-old firm that specializes in strategic database applications for Fortune 2000 companies in the manufacturing, financial, and health care industries. Hentzenwerke has commercial products and custom applications in use throughout the U.S. and in nearly two dozen foreign countries. Since 1994, Hentzenwerke has hosted the semi-annual Great Lakes Great Database Workshop.

Whil has written and spoken extensively about software development. He is a multi-year Microsoft MVP; editor of *FoxTalk*, Pinnacle Publishing's high-end technical journal on FoxPro; and the author of books about Visual Studio (*Visual FoxPro 6.0 Fundamentals*), Visual FoxPro (*Programming Visual FoxPro 3.0*), FoxPro (*Rapid Application Development with FoxPro 2.6*), and custom software development (*1999 Software Developer's Guide*). He has presented over 50 papers at conferences throughout North America and Europe, including the Microsoft Visual FoxPro DevCon, the German National DevCon, the Spanish National DevCon, Database & Client/Server World, FoxTeach, the FoxPro Users Conference, and the Mid-Atlantic Database Workshop.

He spends his spare time with his kids and volunteers for the local school districts. He is also an avid distance runner, hoping for one more shot at a sub-15 minute 5,000 meter clocking before age and common sense close the door on that activity.

You can reach Whil on the Internet at **whil@hentzenwerke.com**.

To my dad.

'Nuff said.

Contents at a Glance

Contents

IV ▭ Advanced Capabilities

Acknowledgments

You might think that the coolest part of writing a book on a piece of software is getting to play with new software before the general public sees it. I hate to burst your bubble, but actually, the best part is getting to meet new people during the project.

First, I have to mention (or blame? <s>) Lysa Lewallen, whom I've worked with several times over the years and who started me on this project over a year ago. Even after leaving Osborne, she's kept in touch regarding this book.

Next is Wendy Rinaldi, who took over the project as it gathered steam last summer, and who became more than simply a voice on the phone as we spent an evening in a downtown Seattle video arcade owned by Paul Allen (co-founder of Microsoft) shooting at Jurassic Park dinosaurs and racing Indy cars.

Janet Walden and Monika Faltiss provided the "mother-hen" nurturing and scolding necessary to turn a directory full of .DOC files and screen shots into the gorgeous work you have in your hands.

And then there's Rima. Wow. Rima Regas, my technical editor, has been a delight to work with since the first lightning-fast exchange of e-mails during Chapter 1. She not only read every word of each chapter—sometimes several times as I composed draft after draft—but did so while battling the same monsters lurking deep inside our PCs that come forth during a typical beta cycle. Together we rebuilt a half-dozen machines and commiserated about kids, bad ISP connections, and leaky ceilings, and she kept my spirits up throughout the whole process. I'm looking forward to working with her on another project.

Finally, it's time for attributions of the bands that kept me awake in the wee hours during this winter and spring while I was experimenting with this feature or that, or performing yet another NT install due to the vagaries of the beta-testing process. Although they'll never see this, nor would they care if they did, I must mention Blues Traveler, Gravity Kills, The Poor, Queensryche, Supertramp, and, proving that the truth isn't always very pretty, Rob Zombie. Software is always better when written at 105 decibels.

Whil Hentzen
Milwaukee, WI

Introduction

The purpose of this book is to get you, an intelligent computer user who has possibly used other tools or languages, up to speed in developing Access 2000 applications quickly. I've read dozens of books that try to do this, and have come to the conclusion that the best way is a four-step approach. And that approach is what this book follows.

How This Book Is Organized

Part I introduces you to Access 2000's interface and how to use it interactively.

Part II provides an explanation of each of the tools you'll use in Access 2000 to build an application. I'll cover the Form Designer, the Report Writer, the Query Builder, and others.

Part III teaches you how to build an application with the tools you learned about in the previous section. When you've finished, you'll have the fundamental components necessary to deliver a complete and working Access application.

Finally, Part IV serves as a teaser for advanced features. As with any complex tool or process, you can't possibly learn everything in one sitting, but at the same time, you want to be aware of what is possible in the future.

Here are short descriptions of the chapters:

Chapter 1 covers the Access 2000 interface. You'll learn how to navigate through each of the specific interface objects.

Chapter 2 talks about data. Unlike many other development tools that can be used for a variety of tasks, Access 2000 is strictly a database management tool, and thus, you'll want to know about how data in Access is structured. You'll also be introduced to the database used in this book's sample application.

Chapter 3 covers data manipulation. Now that you know where the data is, how do you work with it? I'll go into depth with datasheets, showing you how to add, edit, delete, search, and sort data in a variety of ways.

Chapter 4 is the beginning of Part II. In this chapter, you'll learn how to build queries—objects that allow you to select certain data from one or more tables.

Once you can create a query that represents a specific set of data, you'll probably want to develop an interface so that others can manipulate that data set—and that's what you'll do in Chapter 5. You'll learn how to create and run a form, and how to use a variety of controls.

Chapter 6 shows you how to build reports so you can get data out of an application once it's been put in.

Chapter 7 introduces the first programming tool in Access: macros. A macro is a collection of actions that can be played back automatically, saving time and ensuring consistency.

Chapter 8 extends your reach of programming tools by discussing Visual Basic for Applications. A true programming language, VBA allows you to build full-featured applications with Access.

An application is made up of more than forms and reports, and in Chapter 9, you'll learn how to build menus and toolbars that can be included in your application.

Chapter 10 introduces two important topics, database maintenance and security, and Chapter 11 winds up Part II with a discussion of the Access Object Model and Collections—necessary concepts you'll use when programming with Macros and VBA.

The excitement begins in Chapter 12, as you start to develop an application with the tools you've learned in Part II. This chapter discusses how to go about the process of designing a software system.

Chapter 13 then provides a framework for a standard Access application.

Unfortunately, the world isn't perfect, and neither will be your programming. Chapter 14 discusses how to debug your programming efforts when problems occur, while Chapter 15 covers the creation of an error handler that you can incorporate into your application to trap for errors that may occur as users work with the application.

Chapters 16, 17, and 18 delve into advanced queries, forms, and reports.

Once you've built and tested your application, you're not quite done. Chapter 19 discusses a number of finishing touches you can add to your application to give it that professional, polished look.

Chapter 20 then shows you how to deploy your application, packaging it and sending it out into the wild, as it were.

Part IV begins with Chapter 21's introduction of client/server techniques. You'll learn how to use Access as a front end to connect to a back end, such as Microsoft SQL Server.

Chapter 22 discusses the use of ActiveX controls to extend the functionality of your application.

Chapter 23 covers the integration of other applications with Access, and Chapter 24 wraps up by talking about the Internet and how you can include features to take advantage of the Web in your application.

PART I

Interactive Use of Access

CHAPTER 1

The Access 2000 Interface

Welcome to Access 2000. I'm assuming that you've got Access 2000 installed and ready to run, but that's all. Although the title of this chapter is "The Access 2000 Interface," I'll start by quickly describing what Access is and where it fits with other Microsoft applications. Once you have an idea what to expect from Access, I'll tour through the Access interface and describe each of the components and tools.

What Is Access?

A strict definition of Access often ends up being either a circular reference, or one so chockful of specialized terminology that it's of no use. So let's define Access by what it can do and where it fits in the scheme of personal computer software. In the early days of personal computers, there were three general uses for a PC: word processing, spreadsheets, and database management. Word processing had to do with the production of text documents; spreadsheets involved the manipulation of rows and columns of numbers and formulas applied to those numbers. Both tasks were end-user oriented—the person who wanted the results actually used the tool to do the work.

Early in the development of the personal computer, Microsoft produced word processing (Microsoft Word) and spreadsheet (Microsoft Excel) applications that competed with other popular applications, such as WordStar, MultiMate, WordPerfect, Lotus 1-2-3, and QuattroPro. Since then, a couple of other types of applications, including those for making visual presentations, have become popular. Microsoft introduced a tool called PowerPoint in this arena that competed with other tools like Harvard Graphics. Over the past few years, Microsoft's applications have dominated the market in each of these areas. Furthermore, Microsoft has offered these applications as a suite, Microsoft Office. Office is a bundled set of applications commonly used to perform tasks in the typical office.

Database management is the manipulation of data that can be organized or categorized into lists of one form or another. For example, a list of customers, a list of students, or a collection of invoices (both header information and specific item detail) could all be considered groups of data that would be handled by a database management application. Often, there are common tasks performed with all or part of the data. The user might want to add, update, or delete certain data; produce reports that display certain data; or combine data from different areas. These operations usually are performed on a subset of the entire database. While these operations could be performed manually by an end user, they were often complex enough to require automation. Thus, database management applications came with programming languages to enable the creation of programs that performed increasingly sophisticated automation routines.

The database management application market for personal computers was long dominated by a product called dBASE. In the late 1980s, dBASE was challenged and superseded by FoxPro. Early in the lifetime of these applications, end users could use these tools to perform database management tasks, much as they used word processors and spreadsheets. However, both applications included programming languages that eventually became sophisticated beyond the grasp of most end users. Specialists who used these tools to write database management applications for end users became common.

Yet the rise of these specialists didn't satisfy the need for end users to be able to manage data on their own. In the early 1990s, Microsoft bought FoxPro and included the next version, Visual FoxPro, along with Visual Basic and Visual C++, as part of their suite of development tools intended specifically for programmers. At the same time, Microsoft introduced a database management tool intended for end users—Access—and made it part of the Microsoft Office suite of applications.

Not that Access is exclusively the domain of end users. As is the case with Word and Excel, Access contains a powerful macro language that can be used to easily automate repetitive tasks. Furthermore, Visual Basic for Applications can be used to automate database management operations with Access to produce moderately sophisticated database applications that can be distributed to others.

The Access Interface

Access, as part of the Office suite, sports an interface similar to that of Word, Excel, and other Office applications. When you load Access, you'll encounter a modal screen, called a *dialog box*, asking you to create a new database, choose one to open, or to cancel, as shown in Figure 1-1.

For the time being, I'll select Cancel. Doing so results in a rather sparse environment (shown in Figure 1-2) with a title bar, a menu, a toolbar, and a status bar. The rest of the screen is blank.

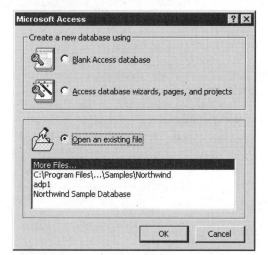

Loading
Access
presents a
dialog box that
allows you to
create or open
a database

Figure 1-1.

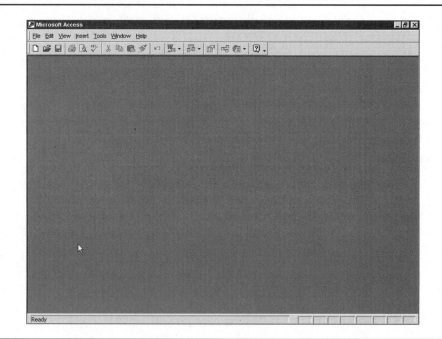

The Access
environment
without an
open database
is nearly empty

Figure 1-2.

A Windows 9*x* or Windows NT window has a strip of color at the top called the *title bar*. It contains an icon and a text string on the left, and has controls at both ends. Clicking the icon opens a menu called the *Control menu*. The menu options in the Control menu allow you to manipulate the window. The controls at the right of the title bar allow you to (from left to right) minimize, maximize, and close the window, effectively duplicating the Control menu options.

Menus

The string of words across the top of the screen below the title bar is called a *menu*. Each word is called a *menu pad*; clicking on a menu pad or pressing ALT and the underlined letter in the menu pad displays a drop-down menu. Each line in a drop-down menu is called a *menu bar* and can be executed by clicking it, moving the highlight to the desired menu option and pressing ENTER, or by pressing the underlined letter in the menu option.

If a menu pad has an exclamation mark in front of the word, selecting that menu pad won't cause a drop-down menu to display; instead, it'll launch a function directly. If a menu bar has a series of three dots (an ellipsis) following the text string, selecting that menu option will open a dialog box, prompting the user for additional information.

Menu pads may appear and disappear according to the current state of the environment and which components are open. For example, when a table is open, two additional menu pads, Format and Records, appear between the Insert and Tools menu pads.

Menu bars may be enabled and disabled as is appropriate for the current state of the environment. For example, if you pull down the File menu when there is no open database, the only enabled bars are New, Open, and Exit. The rest of the menu bars are disabled; after all, if nothing were open, why would you use the Save command?

Toolbars

The string of buttons below the menu is a toolbar. The gray vertical bars between groups of buttons are *separator bars*, and are used to visually cluster like functionality for the user. Access has 29 different toolbars, each of which has buttons that relate to a specific area of functionality. Moving the mouse over a button in a toolbar displays a small rectangular box with a description of what the button does; this box is called a *ToolTip* (also known as *Screen Tip*).

ToolTips appear after a short delay and can be turned off. I'll discuss customizing later in the chapter in "Customizing Your Environment."

You can display a toolbar either by selecting View | Toolbars or by right-clicking in an empty region of any open toolbar, which will cause a toolbar context menu to display the list of all available toolbars. The toolbars already displayed will be listed with a check mark next to them.

Just as is the case throughout the Windows interface, pressing the right button on the mouse (*right-clicking*) will open a drop-down menu at the location of the mouse pointer in many but not all areas of Access. For example, as I described earlier, right-clicking in the empty space of a toolbar will open a drop-down menu with menu bars for each available toolbar and a menu bar that brings forward the Customize dialog box. What to call the menu that drops down as a result of right-clicking is a subject of heated debate at industry conferences. I've heard it referred to as the "shortcut menu," the "right-click menu," and the "context menu." I'll use the last term because it describes most clearly what the menu does—provide menu options in context to the current mouse position. You can use a black marker and write in your own preference throughout this book if you like.

Customizing Your Environment

You can customize toolbars, adding buttons to and removing them from existing toolbars, and you can create your own toolbars as well. If you're adventurous, you can try this now; otherwise, bookmark this page and come back after you've gotten deeper into Access. To customize toolbars, open the Customize dialog box by selecting View | Toolbars | Customize, or by right-clicking on an empty spot in a toolbar and selecting Customize from the context menu, or by selecting Tools | Customize. The Customize dialog box is shown in Figure 1-3.

Selecting Active Toolbars and Setting Toolbar Properties

You can display toolbars that aren't already active by selecting the Toolbars tab in the Customize dialog box, clicking the check box for the desired toolbar, and selecting Close. You can choose more than one toolbar before selecting Close, if you like.

You can set properties of a toolbar by selecting the Properties button in the Customize dialog box. The Toolbar Properties dialog box displays, and the name of the toolbar that was currently highlighted in the Customize dialog box is displayed in the Selected Toolbar drop-down menu at the top of the dialog box.

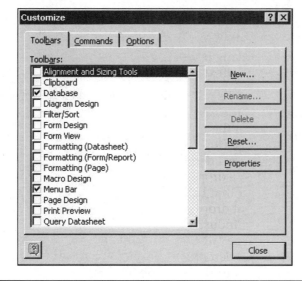

The Customize
dialog box
allows you to
modify
toolbars and
set other
environment-
related options
Figure 1-3.

The first two options in the Toolbar Properties area are only available if you're
working with a custom (user-defined) toolbar. You can change the toolbar name
and its type. A toolbar can be a Menu Bar, a Toolbar, or a Popup.

Normally, a toolbar is *docked*, which means it's lined up underneath the
menu bar, flush to the left side, much like a boat is docked next to a pier. You
can change the permitted docking attributes of a toolbar with the Docking
drop-down menu. You can restrict a toolbar's docking from being changed at
all, to only being docked vertically or horizontally, or to allow any type of
docking.

Custom toolbars can also be flagged to display on the Toolbars menu, while
Access toolbars have a setting that can't be changed. For both user-defined
and Access toolbars, you can also choose whether to allow customizing,
resizing, moving, and showing/hiding of a specific toolbar.

Customizing a Toolbar
There are two types of customization. First, you may decide to move or
delete buttons from a toolbar. To customize an existing toolbar, open the
Customize dialog box as described earlier, and select the toolbar to display it.

NOTE: In earlier versions of Microsoft applications, toolbars that were being customized could not be docked—this is no longer the case.

After selecting the toolbar button that you want to move or remove, proceed as follows:

To *move* the button to a different place on the toolbar, click and hold the mouse button down. You'll see a dark border appear around the toolbar button, indicating that it's selected. Next, drag (move the mouse without releasing the mouse button) the button to the new location on the toolbar. Once the toolbar button is in place, release the mouse button. You may have to play with the exact positioning a bit to get the hang of it.

To *remove* the button from the toolbar, drag it off the toolbar to an empty spot in the Access window, and release the mouse button. The toolbar button will now be gone from the toolbar.

NOTE: If you regret a toolbar modification, you can return the toolbar to its default state (the way it was when Access was installed) by selecting the toolbar in the Toolbars tab of the Customize dialog box and choosing the Reset button.

The other type of customization is to add buttons to an existing toolbar:

1. Activate the toolbar as described earlier.
2. Select the Commands tab (see Figure 1-4), and choose the appropriate item from the Categories list.
3. Select the menu bar that corresponds to the button you want to add to the toolbar by choosing the appropriate command from the Commands list.
4. Drag the command from the Command list (you've actually dragged a copy of the command—so you could put the same button on 50 different user-defined toolbars) to the toolbar, and position it as desired.

Creating a New Toolbar

You may decide you want buttons from a number of toolbars available, but you don't want all the toolbars open at the same time. You can create your own toolbar as well—much as you would throw a couple of favorite tools

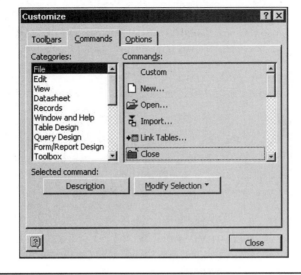

Dragging a
button from
the File | Close
menu bar to
the Database
toolbar adds a
new button

Figure 1-4.

into a small toolbox to carry with you in the car. The difference is that with
toolbars, you're actually putting a copy of the toolbar button on the new
toolbar, while with tools, you're taking the original with you in the car.

Here's how to create a new, empty toolbar:

1. Select the Toolbars tab in the Customize dialog box and press New.
   A dialog box asking for the name of the new toolbar appears, as
   shown here:

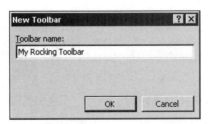

2. The name defaults to "Custom 1" (or a variation thereof if you've
   already got a toolbar named "Custom 1"). Accept the name or enter a
   new name. A toolbar with the title that you gave it and that's wide
   enough for a single button appears.

3. As you did to add a button to an existing toolbar, select the Commands tab. Choose from the Categories list, and then select the appropriate command from the list of Commands. Drag the command (a copy) from the Command list and position it on the new toolbar.

You can add separator bars to a toolbar by dragging a button ever-so-slightly to the right, until a separator bar displays.

REMEMBER:　You can also set additional properties for a user-defined toolbar that you couldn't for an Access toolbar by choosing the Properties button in the Toolbars tab.

Setting Environment Options

You can control how other aspects of menus and toolbars work by making choices in the Options tab of the Customize dialog box.

You can choose to have the most recently used commands first, and, optionally, display the full menu after a short delay. If you choose this option, Access will track your usage of the menus and adjust the bars accordingly. You can reset the menus to their default if you clear your usage history by pressing the Reset My Usage Data button. You can also choose how menus open with the Menu Animations drop-down list at the bottom of the Options tab.

You can display all toolbars with large icons, turn ToolTips on or off, and include the keyboard shortcut in the ToolTip description (along with the original ToolTip description).

There is another location for setting options. The Tools | Options menu bar displays a dialog box with tabs in which you can set options for both the general Access environment and for specific Access components like tables, reports, and so on. I'll cover those in "Options," later in this chapter.

Interface with Databases and Projects

Access uses two types of containers—databases and projects—for manipulating databases. I'll talk about databases now and projects later.

The Database window has a toolbar, a vertical item pane on the left, and, on the right, a pane that contains a list of items that have to do with the selected item on the left, as shown in Figure 1-5.

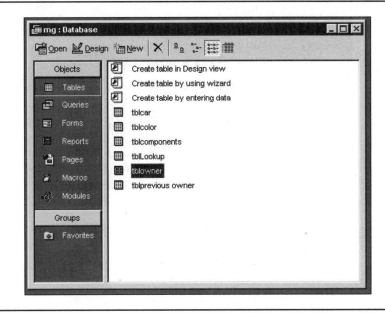

The Database window contains a toolbar on the top, a left pane that lists types of objects, and a right pane that lists all of the objects of a specific type

Figure 1-5.

Selecting an item in the left pane changes the list on the right. The selected item in the left pane retains *focus*—a "pushed-in button" appearance. Dragging the Objects and Groups separators will resize the different sections of the left pane; in fact, if you drag far enough, the Objects and Groups separators will take each other's place.

Selecting an item in the right pane displays a second window. The Database window is still open, but may be hidden by the new windows.

As you are probably aware, there are about five ways to do anything in Microsoft products, and since they all share common interfaces, Access is no different. For example, you can open a table in a database by selecting the Open button, or by selecting the table in question in the right pane. You can create a new table by selecting any of the three Create Table commands in the right pane, or by selecting the Open button, or by selecting certain combinations of the Design button and an item in the right pane, or even by selecting a certain combination of items under the File | New menu option. I would argue that this many methods is overkill, but I guess it means you can make something happen in the exact way you want.

The contents of the toolbar change according to type of item selected in the left pane of the Database window. Most items show Open, Design, and New buttons. However, the Reports item replaces the Open button with a Preview button, and the Macros item replaces the Open button with a Run button.

The Open button on the toolbar generally opens up an item as it would be used by an end user. For example, a table is opened so that data can be viewed or modified. Opening a query actually executes that query and displays the results.

The Design button, on the other hand, opens an item as a programmer would use it. A table opened in Design mode actually displays a list of each field in the database, as well as other information about the fields—how long they are, what type of data is permitted to be entered, and so on. A report opened in Design mode shows the layout of the report and allows the user to modify the report to reflect different needs.

The toolbar button in between the separator bars on the toolbar is the Delete button and is enabled when an item in the right pane is available to be deleted. Commands that create a new item, for example, can't be deleted.

The last four buttons on the toolbar operate much like those in Windows Explorer—they allow you to change the display of the items in the right pane. The first button on the left, Large Buttons, displays the items in the right pane as large icons, much like the Control Panel looks by default. The second button, Small Buttons, displays the items as small icons. The third button, List, displays the items in a List view; and the fourth, Details, displays the items in List view, but with details like description, and dates created and last modified.

TIP: When you're in Details mode, clicking the column header (for example, the Name label) will display the list sorted by that column. Clicking a second time will reverse the order—from ascending to descending or vice versa.

Options

The options available in the various tabs of the Tools | Options screen have to do with how various components of Access work. For example, the items in the Keyboard tab control how keystrokes work during data entry in a table. It's always annoyed me that the Tools | Options menu is dimmed until one of the components is open. However, all of the tabs in the Tools | Options dialog box are then available, regardless of which component you opened.

Why am I annoyed? First, in every Microsoft application I've used, there's always been at least one tab (if not more) that has contained options that apply to the application as a whole, or that I'd like to change without having to go through an intermediary step first. Second, the behavior is not consistent. If they're going to require you to open a component before gaining access to the Tools I Options dialog box, why give you access to all the tabs—should you be restricted to just the tab (or tabs) that contain options for the component that was opened? Anyway, that's the way it works. Let's look at what's available for personalizing how Access works. I'll cover the items that you'll find useful immediately, and bring up more advanced options when it's appropriate later in the book.

View

The View tab contains options for controlling how Access works in general. You can turn the status bar (the bar at the bottom of the Access window) on or off and choose whether you want to encounter the dialog box that asks which database to open when you first load Access. You can also specify whether to display the commands in the Database window for creating new objects, any hidden objects, or any system objects. In addition, you can choose whether to use a single click or a double click to open items in the Database window.

General

The General tab contains options for controlling how specific features in Access work, but still outside of any specific component. You can set the print margins, where new databases will be created, how many items will be shown on the Most Recently Used list in the File menu, whether to consider compacting a database when closed (and under what conditions to perform the compacting), and which AutoCorrect features should be turned on.

You can also determine the appearance (colors and underlines) to be used for web hyperlinks.

Edit/Find

The Edit/Find tab contains options for controlling edit and find features throughout Access. You can choose to have searches in the Edit I Find dialog box use a Fast search, a General search, or a Start of field search. Note that this is just the default—you can choose any other option when you're actually in the Find dialog box.

You can also choose to have Access notify you in the event of changes to a record, deletion of a document (such as a query or a form), or action queries.

In addition, you can set options for the currently selected database, including whether forms should display a list of values for local indexed and nonindexed fields, and a record count threshold for displaying lists.

Keyboard

The Keyboard tab contains options for controlling how the cursor or focus moves within a table or form. You can control what happens when the cursor enters a field (select the contents of the entire field, or go to the start or end of the field) after you press the ENTER key (keep the cursor in the current field, move to the next field, or move to the next record), and what arrow keys do (move to the next field or the next character). You can also choose to have the cursor stop at the first and last fields instead of wrapping around and moving to the other side of the table.

Datasheet, Forms/Reports, Advanced, Tables/Queries

The options on these tabs are all germane to specific components in Access. I'll revisit the options available to be set when I discuss the component.

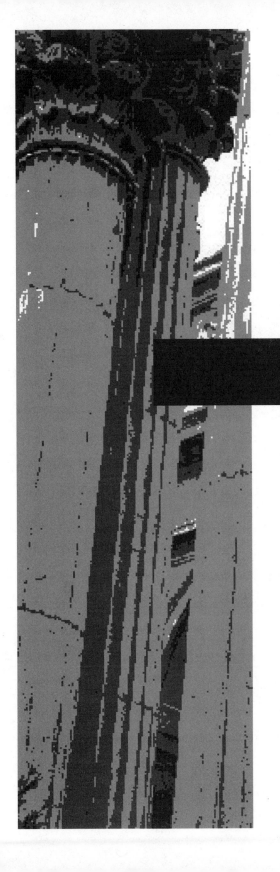

CHAPTER 2

Where Is the Data?

W ith some programs, you can go through life and never worry about where your data is. You might be only vaguely aware that there is "data" in the applications. For example, e-mail programs contain two types of data—the preferences you set up during configuration so that the program operates the way you want it to, and the actual messages you send and receive. You can use an e-mail program indefinitely without knowing exactly where the preferences or messages are stored.

Database users and programmers are different. Because their work is so heavily data-centric, they are deeply interested in knowing where the data is stored, what it looks like, and how it is formatted—after all, it is *their* data. In this chapter, I'll cover each of these topics.

Structured Data

Data comes in varying sizes and shapes, and one of the primary challenges for programmers has been to store data in an organized fashion. The first widespread attempt, still in use on many mainframes and minicomputers, jammed many types of disparate data into a single file. This methodology, called an *ISAM file structure*, would store a couple of invoices with a header record and detail lines like so:

```
H JONES CONSTRUCTION       JULY 15, 1980     N1200949
D   4    YELLOW WIDGET           $   500.00
D   1    GREEN THINGAMABOB       $    12.45
D  12    RED WHATCHAMACALLIT     $1,250.00
H ABC BUILDING CORP        MAY 4, 1980       N1200950
D   6    BLUE THINGAMABOB        $    12.65
```

Computer programs had to parse out each line from this file, and perform different operations depending on whether the line was a *header* (because it began with an "H") or a *detail* (lines that began with "D"). Doing this was processor intensive and rather slow. Furthermore, it was very difficult to make changes—suppose the name of the company had to be changed from 35 to 40 characters? Or another element of data had to be included with the header? The rest of the line had to be moved or extended, and the program that handled the file had to be adjusted to accommodate that change—in addition to all the programs that relied on the old data definition. And those are pretty minor changes. What if the relationship between customers and orders were to change? Or perhaps another level in the hierarchy between order headers and detail lines were introduced? No wonder it took years for seemingly trivial changes to be made in programs.

As a result, computer scientists labored long and hard to find a better way to handle data. In the early 1970s, E.F. Codd and C.J. Date proposed a theoretical model for designing data structures. Their work—the *relational model*—has been the foundation upon which new database applications have been created.

It's important to note that the relational model is a description of the organization of data—not a representation of how the data is stored. Furthermore, the relational model is not a panacea for all data organization. It's excellent for data that has a repetitive format and is highly structured, such as the accounting and sales records of a company. It's not appropriate for data that has unusual or unstructured characteristics. The contents of all the CDs of a radio station; a group of multimedia presentations that include sound, video clips, and images; or e-mail (many blocks of widely varying free-form text) are examples that are currently shoehorned, usually with haphazard results, into a relational system.

Before you can appreciate the data structures that Access and other relationship databases use in their day-to-day operations, you'll need to understand the relational model of Codd and Date.

The Relational Model

Related data is contained in a *database*. This related data might encompass a single application, such as the inventory management system for a retail store. Or the related data might be for a whole company, such as the accounting, sales, production, and human resources data—or anywhere in between.

A database is made up of *tables,* each of which looks like a spreadsheet—a two-dimensional grid of data elements, as shown in Figure 2-1. Each table stores zero or more instances of an entity—in other words, one or more rows (also known as *records* or *tuples*) of the spreadsheet. An *entity* is the generic description of what's being stored in the table; an *instance* is a single specific version of the entity.

For example, an inventory management system for a music store might have one table that contains each stock item—CD, tape, or album—that they carry or can order, and another table that contains each distributor from which they buy music. The distributor table's entity is "distributor," and each individual distributor is an instance. If there were 200 distributors, there would be 200 instances in the table.

Each column in a table is called a *field* (or an *attribute*), and contains a single data element of a single type. This data element must be *atomic*—that is,

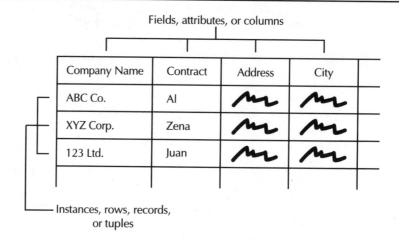

Fields, attributes, or columns

Company Name	Contract	Address	City
ABC Co.	Al	〰	〰
XYZ Corp.	Zena	〰	〰
123 Ltd.	Juan	〰	〰

Instances, rows, records, or tuples

A database table has a structure similar to a spreadsheet

Figure 2-1.

unable to be broken down into smaller pieces—and all the data elements in a field must be of the same type and contain the same sort of information. For example, fields in our Distributor table might include Company Name, Contact Name, Address, City, State, Zip, Voice Phone, Fax, and Email. You wouldn't place Name, Address, and City in a single field.

The definition of "atomic" varies according to how the database will be used. The State is an excellent example of an atomic data element—it can't be broken down any further. If you need to store a County of the State, you would use a separate field, but you could still include the State. The Voice Phone, on the other hand, might be stored in a single field, or it could be broken out into three fields—Area Code, Exchange, and Number. The latter solution, while strictly adhering to the definition of atomic for a U.S. and Canada phone number, might not be appropriate if the Distributor table were to contain Voice Phones for different countries, because different countries have different structures.

How you define "same sort of information" also can vary. For example, the Email field might contain any kind of e-mail address—Internet, CompuServe, MCIMail, and so on. If it were important, you might need to define different types of e-mail addresses and store them in different fields. However, you wouldn't store ZIP codes, e-mail addresses, and hat sizes in the same field.

The set of possible values of a field is called the *domain* of that field. The domain for the State field would be the list of all 50 states in the United

States, but could also include the provinces in Canada and the states in Mexico if the Distributor table were going to include companies throughout North America.

All the fields in a single row of a table make up a *record* (or a *tuple*). Each record represents a unique instance of that entity. This last point begs repeating. In a properly designed table, each instance in the table—each record—must be unique, by definition. If there are multiple records that are completely identical, then the table was designed incorrectly. There must be a value in at least one of the fields—or a value from a combination of fields—that distinguishes each record from any other record. If this were not the case, it would be impossible to retrieve that specific record.

2

The other important point about an instance is that it can't span more than one record in the table. In the past, people would use more than one row in a spreadsheet to store all the data for a single instance. This is not permitted in the relational model. Instead, use more fields so that the entire instance can be stored in a single record. You wouldn't put the Name, Address, City, State, and Zip in one row, and then all of the Phone and Email fields in a second row.

Tables are related to each other through the use of fields called *keys*. Each table must contain at least one field or group of fields that uniquely identifies each instance. In fact, if there isn't a field or group of fields that does so, the table is constructed incorrectly. The unique identifier is called a key if it consists of just one field, and if the unique identifier consists of more than one field, this group of fields is called a *superkey*. There can be more than one key that uniquely identifies each instance. For example, there are many ways to uniquely identify a record in a name and address table. One way would be a combination of Name, Address, City, State, and Zip; another way would be the combination of Phone Number and Zip Code. Each of these groups would be a superkey.

A *primary key* is the key—either a key or a superkey—used to relate one table to another. The choices for a primary key are called *candidate keys,* and the possible candidate keys may include several superkeys, as well as several single-field keys. Not all candidate keys are superkeys—a candidate key might be a single field. For example, in a parts table, the part number, contained in a single field, might be a primary key, while the superkey of Description and Manufacturer would be a secondary key. A candidate key must contain the minimum number of fields necessary to make it unique. For example, if Phone Number and Zip Code make up a candidate key, Phone Number, Zip Code, and State do not make up another candidate key, since State is superfluous. If a single field is used to create a key, it is called a *single key*; if two or more fields are used, the key is called a *composite key*. The Phone Number/Zip Code field combination would be an example of a composite key. A Company ID Number would be an example of a single key made up of a single field.

One of the basic rules of the relational model is the transference of duplicate data out of a table into a second table where it only has to exist in a single record. For example, the Stock table needs to know which distributor a specific CD came from—but you wouldn't want to repeat the company and address information in every stock record. Instead, all the Stock items are placed in one table, and the Distributors are in another table. The Distributor's primary key, such as the Distributor ID number, is placed in the Stock table as an attribute. When a primary key for a table appears in another table, it's referred to as a *foreign key*. Thus, the Distributor ID is called a primary key when it's in the Distributor table and a foreign key when it's in the Stock table, as shown in this illustration.

2

Obviously, a table can have only one primary key, but can contain several foreign keys. For example, to expand our music store example, we might have a table that defines a particular CD—the title, the artist, the price, the publisher, when it was released, and so on. The Stock table would contain a record for every copy of that CD—if the music store has 17 copies of "Purple Rain," then the Item table would contain one record whose attributes contained the values Purple Rain, Prince, $11.99, Warner Bros, and 1984. It would also have to have a primary key, which might be a randomly generated unique number, like 6509-4009. The Stock table, on the other hand, would have 17 records, each of which contained the Item primary key, 6509-4009, as well as a specific value for the bar code and the primary key for the distributor from whom the specific CD came. The Item primary key and the Distributor primary key are both foreign keys in the Stock table. (It's possible that the music store gets the same CD from more than one Distributor, and they want to track where each CD is coming from. Suppose that a particular CD had a high return rate—the music store would want to contact the Distributor.)

Remember that the primary key must contain a unique value for each record in the table. This means that it may not be empty or null, and that the method for creating the key for new records must guarantee unique values forever. It is also important to note that while you may view records in tables as having "record numbers" much like the row numbers in a spreadsheet, the primary key is the only way a record should be accessed. It is possible to change the "record number" (the relative position) of a record through any number of operations (such as deleting records, rearranging the table, and so on), but those operations do not change the value of the keys. In other words, the record number is only a physical convenience and has no meaning in the relational world. Suppose the first CD entered into the table was Led Zepplin's "Zoso," but later the table was physically sorted on CD title in order to provide faster searching. Zoso would now be near the end of the table, and its record number would have changed from 1 to, say, 56,788. Relationally, however, Zoso can still be located as when it was physically the first record in the table.

Designing Your Database

It's good to understand the terminology of a relational database model, but what can you do with this knowledge? Suppose you have a hodgepodge of likely data—names, addresses, clubs, purchases, and so on—in a single table. How do you get from this mess to a well-designed database structure? The process is called *normalization,* and, again, it was the same two fellows—Codd and Date—who defined how to normalize a database.

You can think of normalization as "the data, all the data, and nothing but the data."

While normalization is based on a great deal of mathematical theory, and indeed, can be described in a series of terse rules, it's easier to follow along with an example. Let me describe the sample database that I'll use throughout this book.

The Sample Database Application

Around the world there are automobile clubs for nearly every make and model of car manufactured. You can find organizations for Ferraris, Studebakers, Rolls-Royces, Corvettes, Mustangs, and for prewar and postwar MGs. Some clubs boast thousands, tens of thousands, or hundreds of thousands of members. However, the larger the number of members, the less complex the amount of information that can be gathered about the club membership and vehicle makeup. With a smaller club, one devoted to a make and model that wasn't manufactured in large quantities, a great deal of information can be gathered.

MGs, in particular the prewar 1937, '38, and '39 models, constitute a small enough run that a lot of information has been collected about various models. Usually, though, this information is stored on handwritten, typed, and mimeographed pages and passed along from club president to club president. MG owners are particularly loyal—their annual meetings are called "GOFs" (Gatherings of the Faithful), and they travel worldwide with their cars.

About the time I graduated from high school, my dad started combing the want ads for cars—not just any car, but a 1950-era MG. He found a '51 TC up for grabs just about the time I left for college, coincidentally vacating a parking spot at home. As he negotiated with the seller, a 25-year-old needing to get rid of his classic car so that he could get a car for his soon-to-be bride, my dad said, "I sold my MG TC when I got married 20 years ago and have regretted it ever since. Trust me, you don't want to make the same mistake. But since I can't talk you out of it, here's the check for the car—my car, now. <grin>" That spawned a resurgence of a hobby that has lasted him 20 years, and one of the results has been a deep involvement with both the local and international MG community.

As a result, it made sense to automate the collection and maintenance of this data—and a directory of MG owners will be the application used for this book. The original design was a listing of owners, usually couples, that included additional information about cars they owned. Big deal, right? Actually, it was complicated.

First of all, there were the usual issues that accompany a name and address database. Some owners were married and shared a last name; others had different last names. Some owners had more than one address; snowbirds maintained their primary residence in the north, often the Midwest or Northeast, but wintered in the South. Many owners lived outside the United States—these are British cars, after all. So their addresses didn't fall into the United States "City, State, Zip Code" format. Even with one address, owners had one, two, or more phone numbers. And they had one or more cars.

An often-repeated wish was the ability to track previous owners of a car. This seemed simple at first, but posed additional complexities. "Previous Owners" didn't just consist of a name; that individual might have owned more than one car, at different times, and might even own a car now. Another wish was the ability to track major components of a car—the chassis, the engine, and so on. Occasionally, a car would be sold for parts, and different parts would end up being melded into an existing car that had fallen into disrepair and was being rebuilt.

While this level of detail is appropriate for an MG club, it might not be for an organization with a larger membership, such as the Mustang or Corvette owners. However, this same application can be used for larger clubs as well.

Problems

The initial solution, handled by the various clubs on an individual basis, was to collect information about each owner on a 3"×5" card, and then transfer that information to a listing typed on 8½"×11" sheets. This is about as primitive as data collection gets, so there were many problems. The first problem, of course, arose from the manual nature of data collection. Handwritten changes would soon fill listings with scribbles so that they had to be retyped.

Next, the information couldn't be rearranged. The manually typed list was organized alphabetically by owner, and sorting and searching in any other way was impossible. Producing other output like mailing labels was similarly impossible.

Because the data on each car was tied just to an owner, any kind of reporting or statistics on items like number of cars, prices, or mileage was also impossible to produce except by the most laborious means. How about being able to list cars currently for sale, including the seller's name? Likewise, being able to quickly find a car using a variety of criteria like mileage or location wasn't feasible with the current list.

Since this is a new application, it's probable that new uses will be found for it, such as new reports from the existing data. Additional changes will undoubtedly be made to the data. Given these constraints, using a single table is not the answer.

Normalization Is the Solution

As I said, the solution is normalization. From a single table (which, after all, is what the printed list resembles), I'm going to create a series of tables and fields, with relationships between each table, with primary and foreign keys set up in each table to handle those relationships, and with the data structured properly.

Normalization consists of about 20 rules, or *forms,* each of which relies on the rule before it and more tightly structures the data. For instance, our alphabetical listing can be said to be nonnormalized. After we apply the first rule of normalization, the database will be "in first normal form." After we apply the second, third, and fourth rules, the database will be "in fourth normal form."

As a matter of practicality, the huge majority of normalized databases never get much past the third normal form, and there is some argument whether the rules past the sixth or seventh normal form, while intellectually engaging, are of any real use in the day-to-day world. I've built applications with millions of records spanning hundreds of tables, and I've never gone past the fifth normal form.

First Normal Form:
Remove repeating or multivalued fields to a second table

Repeating or *multivalued fields* are fields that store the same types of information. The typewritten owner listing had several repeating or multivalued fields, the first being the list of cars per owner; clearly, those fields needed to be moved to a second table. Some owners had a half-dozen or more cars. Furthermore, tracking previous owners per car ended up creating a third table, since one car can have multiple previous owners.

2

Designing Tables

After reading the discussion in "First Normal Form," you might wonder why tracking previous owners per car ended up creating a third table, when there was already a table for owners, some of whom might be both previous and current owners. Strictly speaking, the third table shouldn't be created—there should be just one table for Owners and another for Cars. But then how are the Owners and Cars tables related, since an Owner could be tied to one or more Cars, but a Car could have belonged to one or more Owners? Remember, an Owner might be tied to one or more Cars, but a single Car might have one or more previous Owners. Obviously, you can't put multiple Car primary keys in the Owner table—one for each Car the Owner owns, since that's violating the first normal form just as much as putting all the car information in the Owner table. Likewise, you can't put the primary keys for each previous owner in the Car table. Not only would this violate the first normal form, but it also would be impractical, since a Car might have dozens of owners over time.

The solution is to use an intermediate table called a *join table,* which holds primary keys for every combination of Car and Owner. Suppose Al owned two cars, a TC and a TD. He was the original owner of the TC, but purchased the TD from Dave, who had purchased it from the original owner, Donna. And further suppose that Dave currently owned a TA, and Donna didn't currently own a car. Thus, there would be three records in the Owner table: Al, Dave, and Donna. There would be three records in the Car table: the TA, the TC, and the TD.

The join table, however, would be more complex. It would have two columns, one for the primary key to the Car table, and another for the primary key to the Owner table. It would contain one record for each current owner–car relationship, and would also contain one record for each car–previous owner relationship. Thus, the table would look like this (I've used the name of the Owner and the Car to represent their primary keys):

Car	Owner
TC	Al (original and current owner)
TD	Al (current owner)
TA	Dave (current owner)
TD	Dave (second owner)
TD	Donna (original owner)

This table might not be complete. I never said whether Dave was the original owner of the TA; if he weren't, there would be one or more records for the TA as well. The important point is that each of these keys serves as a placeholder to a complete record in either the Car or Owner table. When Dave moves, his address has to be changed in only one place. When the mileage for the TD is updated, it also has to be changed in only one place.

Strictly speaking, this join table would contain additional information, such as the time span that the previous owner was attached to the car, but I'll hold off on that for a while, just to keep things understandable.

Second Normal Form:
Remove fields that are not dependent on the whole primary key

In some tables, the primary key is composed of multiple fields. This rule requires that any fields that are not dependent on the entire primary key should be moved to a table where they are. For example, you could construct a primary key for the Car table that consists of the VIN (Vehicle Identification Number), make, model, year, and color. However, the make—MG—is really redundant—if the model is a TC or a TD, it's an MG. It's not going to be a Ford or a Porsche.

Choosing a Primary Key

I always make up a number for the primary key for the table instead of using a field that the user has access to, and with Access, it's easy to do. This "made up" primary key is called a surrogate key, and using one has several benefits. First, you're guaranteed that the primary key is always unique—you don't have to worry about imposing made-up conditions, like "no two owners can have the same name." As obscure and complex as you make the condition, the real world is always more obscure and complex. Sooner or later (often around 5 P.M. on a Friday before you're going out of town on a long weekend), the rule will be broken and the application will stop working.

Second, a single key always provides better performance than a composite key. Customers always want applications to run faster— never slower.

Third, even if you are able to find a field or collection of fields in a table that is unique, there is no guarantee that the environment or business rules won't change to invalidate that uniqueness. For example, many people mistakenly think that a social security number (SSN) is unique, and thus is a good candidate to uniquely identify an individual. But what about people without social security numbers, for example, babies and nonnaturalized citizens? And there have been documented cases of duplicate numbers being issued.

Furthermore, suppose the Social Security Administration decides someday that they're going to reuse numbers that were first issued over 150 years ago. If you're tracking active employees at a company or investors in a mutual fund, that's probably OK. But if you're running a genealogy application and you've used social security numbers in the belief that they would always be unique, then your application is doomed.

Third Normal Form:
Remove fields that depend on other, nonkey fields

If a field doesn't depend on the primary key in the table, but instead can be tied to another field in the table that isn't the primary key, move it out of the table. The classic example of this is the inclusion of the city and state in a table that also includes Zip or Postal Code. While the Zip Code of an address relies on the primary key (the person or company in the record), the City and State don't. They rely on the Zip Code. Thus, they could be moved out of the table into a Zip Code lookup table. After all, once you know the Zip Code, you can use that as the primary key in the Zip Code lookup table to find the City and the State.

An example in the Owner table is this exact situation, in which the City, State, and Zip Code are all included in the address. I'll discuss why these fields are left in the Owner table, in apparent violation of the third normal form, at the end of this section.

Fourth Normal Form:
Remove any independently multivalued components of the primary key to multiple new parent entities

Yeah, this one is a bit much to handle. Essentially, if you are using primary keys composed of multiple fields, you don't want to select those keys composed of fields where those fields may have multiple values independent of each other. In plainer language, you don't want to create a situation in which changing data in a field also requires a change in another field.

If you use single-field primary keys, this isn't a problem; and, once your table is in third normal form, it's also in fourth normal form.

Fifth Normal Form:
Remove pair-wise cyclic dependencies (appearing within composite primary keys with three or more component fields) to three or more new parent tables

This rule is somewhat an extension of the fourth normal form. This form describes a situation in which you have a primary key with three or more fields, and those fields are interdependent for their values. Again, if you use single-field primary keys, your fourth normal form database will also be in fifth normal form.

Denormalization:
Consider physical (real-world) issues of implementation and performance, and break the normalization rules knowingly to meet real-world requirements

Now that you've gone to so much work to normalize your table, it may seem heretical to talk about denormalizing. Why go through all the work in the first place?

2

The answer is that normalization is theory, and theory doesn't always play well in the real world. For example, look at the situation in which the City and State were pulled out of the Owner table because they can be looked up in a separate table using the Zip Code. The Owner table should just contain the Zip Code, and another table, perhaps called City, would contain a list of every City and State for every Zip Code.

The problem with this is twofold. First, there is a possible performance penalty. Suppose you wanted to sort a list by city. Instead of simply sorting on the City field in the Owner table, you'd have to construct some sort of query or program that would connect the Owner table and the City table, and then sort the result. The second potential problem is one of maintenance. There are 45,000 ZIP codes in the United States alone. Since the membership is international, postal codes from Canada, Mexico, Europe, and other parts of the country need to be included. This 45,000-record table is now getting really large. Does it make sense to keep this huge table around for a database of perhaps 500 cars?

It may well be that the possible problems posed by keeping the City and State of the Owner in the Owner table are trivial when compared with the performance gain realized.

The key point is it's acceptable to break the rules of normalization. Just be sure that there's a good reason to do so, that you know why you're doing it, and that you've documented what you've done so that those who come later don't cause problems by trying to "fix" the broken rule.

Why the Work of Normalization Is Worth It

You may be thinking that, for the MG directory, this is an awful lot of work—wouldn't it have been easier to have done the redundant data entry? You could possibly argue that case successfully with this application, but if the database suddenly were to grow to 10,000 records, it would be unworkable. There are four specific reasons to normalize a database, and they are valid for any but the most trivial and inconsequential applications.

Minimize Storage Space Requirements
Imagine if your database application were to track the orders for a business. If the database were not normalized, you'd have to store the name and address for every customer in each order record. If the company were to do a lot of repeat business, you'd be entering the same information over and over, which would take up a lot of unneeded space. Furthermore, because each record would have to have a space for each item the customer could order,

there could conceivably be many unused fields that were created just in case someone ordered a large number of items.

Eliminate Data Inconsistencies

Taking the previous example one step further, imagine if you did indeed enter the customer's name and address over and over for each new record. Eventually you'd find a raft of differences—one order has the customer on 100 East Main Street and another has 100 E. Main St. Yet another has 100 E. Main and a fourth has 100 East Main Avenue. A fifth has a P.O. Box address. And then, after the company moves to a new location, variations on the new address start to appear. Later, when you look up a couple of orders, you find two different addresses. Which is current?

By storing a data element in exactly one place, there's never a question as to which entry is correct. As the saying goes, "A man with a watch always knows exactly what time it is. A man with two watches is never quite sure."

Minimize Update and Delete Problems

Again using the previous example, suppose you had taken into account the fact that a customer was stored in multiple records, and you had written a routine to update the address in every record when it was changed. First of all, that is a lot of unnecessary work. Second, and more importantly, what if a problem occurs during the execution of that routine? Suppose the power goes out or the hard disk crashes or some other event interrupts the program? Now the data is updated in only some of the records—and you're back to where you were before—with inconsistencies in the data. The same problem can occur during deletions if there are redundancies or possible inconsistencies in the data.

Maximize the Robustness of the Structure

In the previous example, I've assumed a place for a customer name and address. Suppose that requirements change—in ways that couldn't possibly have been foreseen? The space for the customer name and address also included a field for the phone and a second field for the fax number, and these have served the company well for decades. Suddenly, more phone numbers need to be tracked—mobile, pager, toll-free, 900-pay-per-call, and even mobile fax. And perhaps this even goes further—with an e-mail address—or multiple e-mail addresses. If the database had been normalized properly, there would have been a separate table with phone numbers and a description of each type, so that an unlimited number of phone numbers and other types of contact numbers could be stored. By doing so, you didn't have to change the database structure, which means the application didn't change, either—the forms, reports, queries, or programs.

Again, remember that the physical representation of these elements—databases, tables, indexes, and so on—doesn't have to have a one-to-one relationship with their logical cousins. For example, a database might be stored in more than one file, or a group of (logical) tables might all be stored in the same physical structure. However, the logical and physical representations often do map to each other. Let's look at how Access physically stores relational data.

Access Database Structures

Now that you understand the theory behind designing a database, how do you apply it to Access?

I've worked with a number of different database management programs, and one of the challenges with each of these is keeping track of all the files in an application. The project is in one file; each table is in a separate file; each form, report, and program is in yet a different file—indeed, a reasonably simple application can end up spanning a couple hundred files. Contrast this with Access, where everything—data, programs, forms, reports, and other objects—is contained in a single file.

Within this single physical file, however, there are still a number of different objects, as shown in the left pane of Figure 2-2. First, there are *tables*—the structures that contain the data that you're going to work with. Next are *queries*—definitions of subsets of the data in the database. *Forms* are the user interface for working with data in a friendlier manner than a simple, row-and-column view of a table. *Reports* are the primary mechanism for outputting data from the database to a printer or other device. *Macros* are a mechanism to save and replay keystrokes and other actions in order to automate repetitive tasks. Finally, *modules* are programs, sort of like "super macros," that can automate complex formulas, tasks, and procedures. This chapter covers the data—I'll address each of the other objects in subsequent chapters.

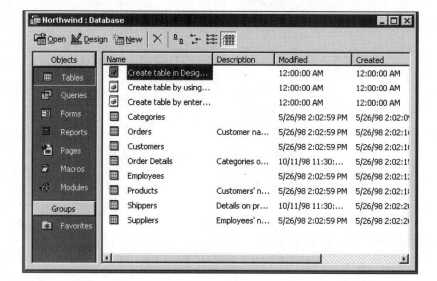

An Access
database
contains
tables, queries,
forms, reports,
pages, macros,
and modules

Figure 2-2.

Field Types and Properties

As discussed earlier, tables consist of one or more columns, called *fields*. The
proper construction of a table's fields is of paramount importance to a
well-designed database, and you need to know what options are available to
you when doing so.

Field Types

There are nine types of field data types in Access, and each is used for a
specific reason. More importantly, there are specific things that each should
not be used for.

Text

The Text data type is used for alphanumeric data that will range up to
255 bytes long. This will be one of the most commonly used data types in
your applications.

Memo

The Memo data type is used for alphanumeric data that will range up to
64,000 bytes long, or approximately 32 double-spaced typewritten pages.

This data type is best used for data such as long descriptions, sentences, paragraphs, and even small text files.

Number

The Number data type is used for numeric data that will be used in calculations. The field size can be one of several values. These are

◆ **Byte**   A single-byte integer that can contain values from 0 to 255

◆ **Integer**   A two-byte integer that can contain values from –32,768 to 32,767

◆ **Long Integer**   A four-byte integer that can contain values from approximately –2 billion to 2 billion

◆ **Single**   A four-byte floating-point integer than can contain values from -3.4×10^{34} to 3.4×10^{34}

◆ **Double**   An eight-byte floating-point integer than can contain values from -1.8×10^{308} to 1.8×10^{308}

◆ **Replication ID**   A 16-byte integer used in a database that is maintained by the Access Replication Manager

The Number field type should not be used for numeric values that aren't going to be used in calculations. For example, while ZIP codes, social security numbers, and purchase order (PO) numbers may all contain just numerals, they aren't used in calculations, and problems can arise by treating them as numeric. For example, if you were to enter a ZIP code for Boston in a Number field, the leading zero would disappear, and you'd be left with a four-digit ZIP code. Defining the Zip Code field as Text would keep the leading zero in the Zip Code field.

Date/Time

The Date/Time field type is used for calendar or clock data. Fields that are defined with this type can be used in calculations that involve years, months, days, hours, minutes, and seconds. Ever wonder how many seconds old you are? Simply subtract your birth date and time from today's date and time in an Access calculation, and the result will be expressed in seconds.

Currency

The Currency field type is used for storing monetary values. You can think of Currency as being a Number field with a fixed number of decimals (up to four places).

AutoNumber

The AutoNumber data type is used for automatically creating values for primary keys in tables.

Yes/No

The Yes/No field type is used for storing logical values—when the value is either TRUE or FALSE. This data type is used when a question can be answered: Is the student enrolled? Has the invoice been paid? Has the boat been returned? Note that, in many cases, you may wish to use a different field type because a simple Yes/No answer isn't enough. For example, you may wish to store the date that the student enrolled, assuming that an empty date field means they're not enrolled. In this type of situation, though, remember that you have to take into account whether you know the answer. You may know that the student has been enrolled, but not know the date.

Another usage to be wary of is when a No answer might be misinterpreted. A Yes/No data type for "Has Attended CPR Training" presumes that Yes means the individual has, and a No means he or she hasn't. What happens if you don't know? Better to use a field in which there are three allowable answers: Yes, No, Don't Know. The same holds for gender: don't use a Yes/No field type with a prompt like "Is Male," when the No value assumes that the individual is Female. What if you don't know? Again, better to use a field in which the user can select, "Male," "Female," and "Unknown" (or perhaps "Can't really tell" if you're feeling wicked).

OLE Object

The OLE Object data type allows you to store files that include complex data, such as .WAV files, Word documents, image files, and other data that can be maintained by a dynamic link to another Windows application. You could store an .AVI file in Access, and then automatically call up a video viewer when displaying the contents of that field. OLE Objects can be as large as a gigabyte.

Hyperlink

The Hyperlink data type allows you to store a 2,048-character text string that points to a document or file on the World Wide Web on an intranet, or to a file on a local area network (LAN) or local hard disk. The file can be stored in Hypertext Markup Language (HTML) or an ActiveX format.

Lookup Wizard

You can also define a field as a link to a lookup table using the Lookup Wizard. This will be discussed in Chapter 5.

Field Properties

In the olden days (about five years ago), you had to write code to control a number of attributes for a field. Access was one of the first database tools to change that requirement. All you have to do is enter or select options on a pair of tabs available when you are creating the field definition in order to define a wide variety of behaviors for the field. The following properties are all available on the General tab (see Figure 2-3) in the Design view of a table.

2

Field Size

You can specify the maximum number of characters allowed in the Text and Number fields. I already described the variety of field sizes available for the Number field type. Be careful to select the largest value that will be required without unnecessarily wasting space. Field sizes for other field types, such as Date/Time and Yes/No, are predefined and can't be changed.

Format

You can specify how data is displayed to the user in forms and reports by selecting the appropriate format. The available formats depend on the field type.

Decimal Places

You can specify how many decimal places display with a Number type field.

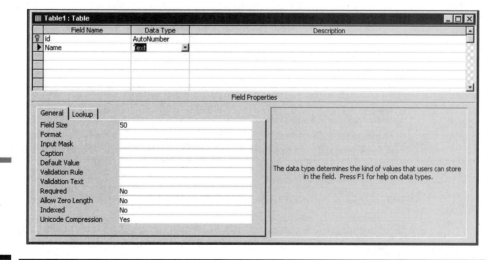

The General tab contains properties for each field

Figure 2-3.

Input Mask

You can control how data is entered into Text, Number, Date/Time, and Currency fields through the use of an Input Mask. Similar to the Format property in reverse, the *Input Mask* acts as a filter for specific characters that can be entered, or that are automatically entered around the keystrokes the user enters. An example of the latter would be hyphens automatically entered as the user types in a phone number.

Caption

The field name you use for the table might not mean as much to a user; you can provide a descriptive name that is displayed in forms and reports instead.

Default Value

You can specify a value that is automatically entered in new records for all data types except AutoNumber, Replication ID, and OLE Object. If you don't specify a default value, Access uses 0 for number fields and No for Yes/No fields.

Validation Rule

You can control what is entered into a field by use of a validation rule. A *validation rule* is a logical expression, such as "> 0," that must evaluate to true for any value that is entered (or changed) in that field. You can also create a series of values from which the entry must find a match in order to be valid.

Validation Text

If the validation rule fails, what do you tell the user? You can provide your own custom message in the Validation Text property.

Required

You can force the user to enter a value in a field by setting the field's required property to Yes. See "Empty? Blank? Null? Zero Length?," later in this chapter for more information.

Allow Zero Length

You can allow the user to indicate that the value of a field is known, but that it's empty (0), by allowing zero-length strings. See "Empty? Blank? Null? Zero Length?," later in this chapter for more information.

Indexed

You can have Access automatically create an index on a field in order to provide faster queries based on values in a field. See "Empty? Blank? Null? Zero Length?," later in this chapter for more information.

Unicode Compression

One of the significant features in Access 2000 is the ability to support the character sets of a variety of languages around the world. Unlike the U.S. language, which only uses 256 characters, other languages need an extended set of characters. *Unicode* uses a double-byte character, allowing 65,000 combinations. However, data stored in Unicode takes a lot of space. You can have this space compressed by selecting Yes—do so if you're going to be writing applications for single-language use. If your application will be used in several languages, you'll want to set this to No, so that moving data from one language to another is faster.

2

Empty? Blank? Null? Zero Length?

One issue that regularly confounds users and programmers is that of handling nonexistent data. In early database management programs, there was usually no facility to differentiate between unknown data and zero-valued data. And there is a difference.

For example, consider a database that tracked the daily high temperature in a number of cities around the country. Each day, the high temperature is reported for each city in the database. On Monday, Houston reports 67, Miami reports 58, San Francisco reports 43, Juneau reports 13, and International Falls reports –6. On Tuesday, Houston reports 71, Miami reports 55, San Francisco reports 49, and International Falls reports –12. But Juneau doesn't report anything. What value is put in the table for Juneau on Tuesday? Zero? Certainly not. Zero is a temperature, just like –5 and 47. It might have been zero, but it also might have been any other temperature in a range of values.

In this same database, the meteorologist for each city might be recorded. In Houston, it's Al; in Miami, it's Barb; in San Francisco, it's Carl; and in Juneau, it's Dave. But the field for International Falls is blank. Does this mean that there is no meteorologist? Or that there is one, but we don't know who? (Yes, you could be strict and enter the value NONE if you know there isn't a meteorologist in International Falls, but bear with me for a moment.)

What is needed is a way to say, "I don't know what the temperature was" and "I don't know who the meteorologist is" or, more generically, "I don't know what the value in this field is." The term *null* is used for this situation. When a field contains a NULL, it means that you don't know what the value in that field is. And this is not the same as a number field being zero, or a text field being blank.

In Access, the mechanism to specify these types of information—whether a field is empty or contains a NULL—involves the Zero Length String property.

You can allow empty values as well as NULL values in Text, Memo, and Hyperlink fields by setting the Allow Zero Length property to Yes and the Required property to Yes. Then, if you don't enter a value, Access will store a zero-length string if the user enters nothing or blanks in the field. If you don't set those two properties, Access will automatically convert a zero-length string to a NULL when saving the value.

Field Lookups

You can define characteristics of a foreign key that links this table to other tables. This is a really slick mechanism, because when you are relating two tables, you don't want to display the actual foreign key value—for example, a value in one of those AutoNumber fields. Instead, you want to display other data from the other table. Furthermore, you want to be able to select allowable values from the other table, and automatically have the foreign key value placed in the table. Access' field lookups, as shown in Figure 2-4, allow you to do just that.

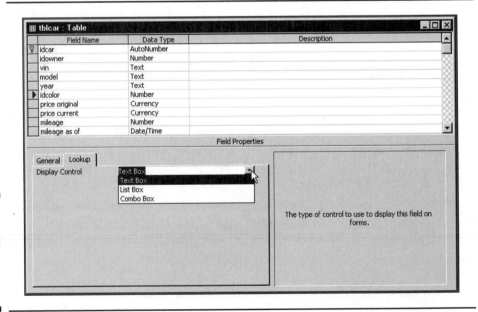

The Lookup tab allows you to manually set properties for a lookup

Figure 2-4.

For example, the Car table has a foreign key that points to a color. The Color table actually has a primary key in a field of type AutoNumber, and that primary key value is stored in the Car table as a foreign key. However, on the Car data-entry form, you don't want to see that foreign key value—you want to see the name of the color. Furthermore, for new cars being added, you want to be able to select from a list of allowable colors—instead of having to memorize a bunch of cryptic foreign key values, or having some people type in "gray" and others use the "grey" spelling.

I'll discuss how to use field lookups later in Chapter 5.

Creating Data Components

Don't confuse "data components" with "data*base* components"—remember that an Access database contains much more than just data. In this section, I'll discuss how to create the various data structures that Access uses to store data: the database itself, as well as tables, fields, indexes, and relationships.

Creating a Database

To create a new database, simply select File | New to open the New dialog box. You'll see that you can either create a Blank Database or use an existing database template as a starting point instead of starting from scratch. In either case, you'll be asked for a name of the database file—enter it and proceed. Note that the extension for the database file is MDB—and further note that as soon as you select the Create button (for a blank database), the file is created. You don't have to add tables or other objects before it's created.

I'm not going to spend much time explaining how to use the wizards that come with Access. After all, the whole point of a wizard is that you don't have to read a book or attend a training class to use it.

That's about all there is to it—a database is simply a container for more entertaining things, like tables and such. So let's move on.

Creating a Table

The empty database appears with the Tables page initially selected. An Access database without tables is terribly uninteresting. Select the New button to create a new table. Unlike a Database, which can be completely empty, you have to have at least one field in a table—you can't create an empty table and keep it in the database. However, you can create a table, again, in several different ways. First, select Design View.

There are three columns in Design view: one for the field name, one for the field type (which we already know all about), and one for the description. For each field, enter the name of the field and select the type. Then enter a description of the field. This may seem either trivial or too hard, but it will help you in the long run. If you were to run into a table with the following fields, what would you make of them?

```
PriceAmount
ValueAmount
CostAmount
CostPlusAmount
AmountAdded
```

Would you know the difference between Price Amount and Value Amount? It might have seemed obvious six months or two years ago when you were creating the application—after all, you lived with it for weeks or months on end. But not now, and not to someone who's modifying the database.

PriceAmount	Price offered to customers
ValueAmount	Price used for Customs Declarations for overseas shipments
CostAmount	Cost of Materials
CostPlusAmount	Total Cost, including overhead and sales
AmountAdded	Legacy field, not used in version 2.3 or later

Doesn't this make a lot more sense? Use the description fields. Next, select the General tab, set properties as necessary, and do the same for the Lookup tab.

Table Properties

Just as you can define properties for each field, you can define similar properties for a table. These properties are described in the following sections.

Table Description

The table description is similar to a field description—information about what the table is. Use this to define what the entity being stored in the table is.

Validation Rule

Again, as with fields, you can define a validation rule that controls whether a record is added (or saved) to the table. Remember that a field validation rule is evaluated when you enter or change the value in a single field. What if you needed a rule that controlled the interaction between fields in a record? You would use a table validation rule to do so.

For instance, suppose that different MG models were only manufactured in certain years. Perhaps TDs were not manufactured before 1950. You could enter a table rule that checked which model was entered, and that then made sure a valid year was entered for that model. A validation rule is evaluated both when a new record is added, and when an existing record is saved.

2

Validation Text

If the table fails to follow the validation rule, you can define the validation text message that Access displays in response to the failure.

Filter

A *filter* is a condition that restricts the records displayed to those that meet the condition. You can define a filter condition that is automatically applied when the table is opened. You can create additional filters to use once the table is open.

Order By

By default, the records in the table are displayed in the order they are entered, or in primary key order if a primary key is defined. You can choose to use a different order when the table is initially opened.

Creating Indexes

An *index* is a hidden table contained in the database that allows rapid searching on a value that matches an indexed field or index expression. For example, if a table has an index on one field but not on a second field, searches for values in the indexed field will return results considerably faster than searches on the nonindexed field. An index does not have to be built on a single field, however—it can use multiple fields or consist of expressions that include a variety of components, including fields, functions, and other operators.

Once an index has been created on a field or expression, you don't have to do anything special to take advantage of the increased speed an index provides. Access will automatically use the index when appropriate.

To create an index on a single field, select Yes in the Indexed field in the General tab of the Design view of the table. There are two Yes choices:

◆ **Yes (Duplicates OK)**   Allows duplicate values to be entered into the field—which is the case most of the time. For example, you would typically index on the last name field, and there are often duplicate last names in a table.

◆ **Yes (No Duplicates)**   Ensures that duplicate values are never allowed in the field. This is the value used for primary key fields, of course, but can be handy for other fields as well. For example, you might want a customer number or student ID field to be unique.

In larger tables, you might perform searches on values that span multiple fields. For example, searching on last name might provide a large number of matches if you're searching for a common name. In this case, you might want to include a value in a second table—such as first name or city—in order to narrow down the number of records returned in the result set.

To create an index based on multiple fields:

1. Open the table in Design view, and then select View | Indexes. You can also select the Indexes button on the toolbar. The Indexes dialog box, shown here, will display, listing all the existing indexes.

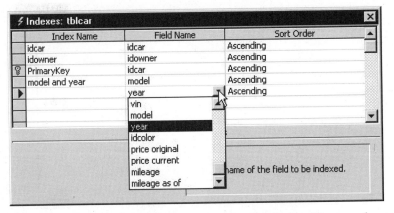

2. Place your cursor in the first empty row in the Index Name column, and enter the name for the multiple-field index.

3. Enter or select the field name in the Field Name column. In the next blank row, enter the second field name that is part of the multiple field index, leaving the value under the Index Name blank in the second row.

2

When you then search using an expression that matches a multiple-field index, Access does not require that you enter data for all fields, as long as you provide values for consecutive fields starting with the first field. For example, if your multiple-field index was based on Fields 1, 2, 3, and 4, you could search on Fields 1 and 2, leaving 3 and 4 empty.

Creating Relationships

A *relationship* is a definition that tells Access how tables should be associated in forms, queries, and reports. Simply having a primary key in one table and a foreign key in another isn't enough—you have to tell Access about the relationship between those two fields.

To create a relationship, you'll need at least two tables with a field in each of them that represents that same value (such as a primary key in one table containing the same values as the foreign key in a second table).

1. Open the Relationships window by selecting Tools | Relationships. The Show Table dialog box will appear, shown here, and you can add the appropriate tables to the Relationships window with the Add button.

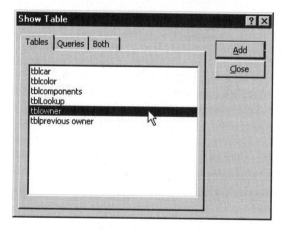

2. Once you have added the tables to the Relationships window, close the Show Table dialog box, or move it out of the way. You can resize the table windows to see the fields you need.

3. In one of the tables, highlight the field that represents one of the common values, and drag it on top of the corresponding field in the other

table. When complete, a Relationships dialog box will display, as shown here, allowing you to set a variety of properties for the relationship.

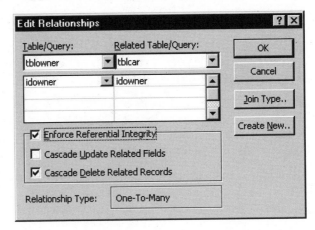

You can change the fields in the relationship, or include additional fields, and even modify the join type (see Chapter 4 for more information on join types). By the way, if you accidentally close the Relationships dialog box, you can open it again by double-clicking on the *relationship line* (see Figure 2-5) or by right-clicking on the line and selecting the Edit Relationship menu bar.

One important attribute of a relationship is whether it relates one record in one table to a single record in another table (one-to-one), relates one record in one table to many matching records in another table (one-to-many), or relates multiple records in one table to multiple records in another table (many-to-many). I've already described what each of these is, but it's not immediately obvious how to define the type of relationship. You'll see the type of relationship in the bottom of the dialog box. This is automatically determined based on the types of indexes created for the fields that are related.

For example, in the Car table, the Indexed property for the foreign key to the Color table is defined as Yes (Duplicates OK) because more than one Car record will be pointing to the same Color record. However, in the Color table, the primary key for Color is defined as Yes (No Duplicates) because the primary key better be unique. This also means that each Car will have only one Color. As a result, this relationship is a one-to-many.

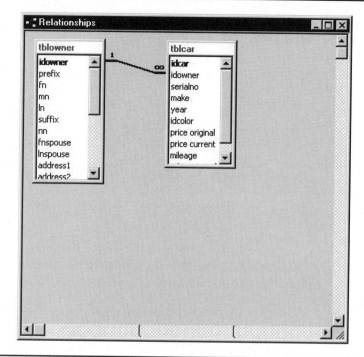

The Relationships window displays a line between the fields that make up the relationship

Figure 2-5.

The MG Database Structure

Now I've discussed how to normalize a flat file and how to create a variety of tables that obey the rules of normalization. I've also covered the tools available in Access to structure tables. It's time to construct the MG Database Structure.

NOTE: The online source code files for this book are separated by chapter. The files for this chapter are located in the CH02 directory, for example, and can be used independently of files in any other chapter. This means that you can open up Chapter 12 and immediately use the source code files, instead of having to wade through Chapters 1 through 11 and follow along with all the instructions to get to the proper place in Chapter 12.

Naming Conventions

You'll notice that I'll usually name each table with a singular name, rather than the plural form of the instance it's representing. For example, instead of a Cars table, it will simply be named Car—and there's a good reason for this convention.

The name indicates what a single record represents—and in most cases, it represents a single instance of the entity. A record represents a car, or an owner, or a ZIP code. However, in some cases, the record's instance actually represents a plural. An example is Components. A single Components record contains information about a variety of components—the engine, the chassis, the radio, and so on. So, while each Components record is related to just one car, each Components record deals with multiple components for that car.

The other thing you'll notice is that I prefixed each table with a "tbl" prefix. Eventually, you'll see that there will be a list of objects to select from—and it will be important to be able to distinguish between their different types. "tblCar" is clearly the Car table, while "Car" might be a table, a query, or something else.

The Owner Table

The Owner table consists of records, each of which represents one owner of a car. This owner may be a single individual or may be a couple. The couple may share a last name or may have different last names. Because people across a wide range of countries may be more or less concerned about their names, I've included a prefix (such as Dr., Mr., Mrs., Ms., Miss, or Sir); First, Middle, and Last Names; and a Suffix. The Middle Name is a full-sized text field—not just a single-character field—so that people who use their full middle name, as in "J. Barrington Thornmeister" or "Phillip Michael Thomas," aren't shoehorned into a badly designed structure. Suffix includes appendages like "Sr.," "Jr.," and "III." The next field, Nickname, is used for salutations—"Bob" instead of "Robert"—particularly for individuals who have complicated names. Two additional fields allow inclusion of a spouse's first and last names—in this case, I decided that middle names could be included with the First Name for the spouse. However, Last Name was made separate so as not to offend the many couples with differing surnames.

Address, City, State, and Postal Code are all typical fields—the more generic Postal Code is needed for a variety of countries. The Country is used not only for addresses, but could also be used to format the City, State, and Postal Code properly depending on which country the address is in.

2

Four phone numbers allow a voice and a fax number both at home and at work. I thought about including a fifth number for a mobile phone, but evidently the type of individual who rebuilds and drives a 50-year-old car isn't likely to put a car phone in it—if room could be found. However, since e-mail is an increasingly common tool for enthusiasts around the world to stay in touch, I've included a field for that contact information. Finally, the Holy Octagon is a "lifetime achievement" award that was created so that I could put a Yes/No field in this table for demonstration purposes.

The Owner table holds records for current owners only. Note that the Owner is the "parent" record for the rest of the application, so it contains no foreign keys.

The Car Table

The Car table consists of records that each represent one automobile. While you could define "an automobile" in a variety of ways (particularly since these types of automobiles are often found in pieces in garages, attics, and basements), I'll consider a complete automobile to be a mechanism that contains the majority of parts—either assembled or in close proximity (like the walls and floors of a garage).

The Car table contains information about the car as a whole. This includes the VIN (Vehicle Identification Number), Model (such as TA, TB, and so on), Year, original sales price and current price, mileage, and date that the mileage was last recorded (the mileage isn't necessarily current, but at least it's known how recent the figure is). There's also a foreign key for color that links the car to the Color table. As mentioned earlier, this is done because it makes a good illustration for a lookup type of table, and because it logically ensures that different users don't enter colors spelled differently.

There is a one-to-many relationship between the Owner and Car tables, since an Owner might have more than one car, but a Car can only be owned by one Owner at a time (at least, one primary owner). Thus, the Car table will have an Owner foreign key to tie it to the Owner table.

The Components Table

The Components table contains information about the major components that make up a car. These include the Engine, the Chassis, and the Body. Each of these has a manufacturer and a serial number. There is a one-to-one relationship between a Car and a Components record. Thus, the Component table will have a Car foreign key to tie it to the Car table. Note that the serial numbers are text fields—not numeric—because it is highly likely that the serial number will have dashes, spaces, or alphabetic characters embedded in it.

The Previous Owners Table

The Previous Owners table holds simple records for the previous owners of a car. Each record contains name and time span of ownership. After a couple of years of use, this table might expand, or the previous owners might be merged into the Owners table. For now I'm keeping it simple.

There is a one-to-many relationship between the Car and Previous Owner tables, since a Car might have more than one previous owner. A Previous Owner might have owned multiple cars; but, for the time being, I'm going to assume that the ease of use of a one-to-many relationship outweighs any disadvantage duplicate copies of a Previous Owner record might introduce. Thus, the Previous Owner table will have a Car foreign key to tie it to the Previous Owner table.

The Color Table

The Color table is simply used for storing standard names of colors. While perhaps a trivial example here, it will serve to show how to use a lookup table to ensure that certain data is entered into the database correctly. This table could be expanded to include color schemes (two-tone paint jobs, interior colors), as well as primary body colors.

Modifying Database Components

"Life isn't fair." It could have been uttered by a software developer after meeting with a group of users who have reversed their earlier proclamation that "this will *never* change!" It's inevitable. No matter how carefully you plan your design, you're going to have to change something—add new fields, add tables, get rid of fields, change field types, or even move fields from one table to another. There are dozens of different kinds of changes that you might run into.

Before you plunge into making changes, consider a couple of things. First, you need to make a backup copy of the database. It's always possible that you will make a change that has, er, unexpected results. Some of the changes described here don't have an undo mechanism, and so you'll want to be able to get back to a previous, known state.

2

Second, you need to know that changes made in a table are not automatically also made in other objects in the database. If you change the name of a field in a table, you'll need to make the same change to any queries, forms, reports, or other objects that reference the original field name.

Third, you'll also have to close all objects to which changes are going to be made, and delete relationships before changing the data type of a field involved in that relationship.

A particularly cool feature of Access is the ability to make a duplicate of a table within the database. You can do this in two ways. The quick-and-dirty way is to right-click the table, select the Save As option, and enter a new name. The more involved but more flexible method is to highlight the name of the table, select Edit | Copy, and then select Edit | Paste. You'll be presented with the Paste Table As dialog box. Here you can enter a name for the copy of the table, and also choose whether to copy just the structure; copy the structure and the data; or, if you've used the name of an existing table, to append the data of the original table to the copy of the table.

Modifying a Table

There are three types of modifications you can make to a table. The first is deleting it—admittedly, a rather drastic modification. Just select the table, and press DEL or choose Edit | Delete. You will be asked to confirm your deletion. If there are any relationships associated with that table, you will be asked to confirm the deletion of the relationship as well. If you decide that deleting the table wasn't such a good idea, you can immediately select Edit | Undo to reverse your action. Immediately selecting Undo will also restore the deleted relationship.

The second type of modification is to rename a table. You can use Edit | Rename, or simply select the table name, wait a bit, and then click a second time (like in Windows Explorer) to place the name in Edit mode. If you enter a name already in use, you will be asked to confirm the replacement of that table with the one you are renaming.

Modifying Fields

The third type of table modification is to change the structure of the table. This is more involved, so I've broken out each operation here.

Changing Field Names

To change the name of a field in a table, open the table in Design view, highlight the field name, and enter the new field name for the field. You may want to also change the Caption in the General tab.

Changing Field Types and Lengths

Changing data types is a simple operation, but can be a complex issue because the data in a field may not easily convert to a different type. For example, what should be done when a text field is changed to a number field? Access will do the best it can, but you should be aware of a few limitations.

First, to change the data type of a field, open the table in Design view, and choose a new data type in the field. What happens to existing data? The rules span many pages, because each data type could possibly be changed to every other data type—resulting in nearly a hundred combinations. In general, here are the rules:

◆   OLE Object and Replication ID types can't be converted to any other type.

◆   Any field can be converted to Text, but will be truncated to 255 characters.

◆   Any field except Hyperlink can be converted to Number or Currency, but the value must contain valid digits and separators.

◆   Any field except Hyperlink can be converted to Date/Time, but the value must contain a recognizable date or time.

◆   Any field except Hyperlink can be converted to Yes/No, but only the following values are converted: YES, NO, TRUE, FALSE, ON, OFF.

◆   Fields can't be converted to AutoNumber if there is data in the table.

◆   Any field can be converted to Memo.

◆   Any field can be converted to Hyperlink, but invalid text strings won't work properly.

2

◆ You can always lengthen a field; but, if you shorten a field, you may generate error messages about losing data or validation rules being broken due to lost data.

◆ You will be warned if changes to the data type or length will cause errors, and the contents of fields that can't be converted will be deleted.

Inserting Fields

To insert a field, open the table in Design view, and highlight the field that will follow the new field. In other words, if you want to insert a field between Fields 4 and 5, highlight Field 5. Then select Insert | Rows, or choose the Insert Row button on the toolbar. A new, empty row will be added to the table. Enter a name, choose a data type, and set other properties in the General and Lookup tabs as desired.

Duplicating Fields

You might find yourself creating a number of field definitions that are identical or similar. If each field has a lot of properties to set, it can be time-consuming, not to mention tedious, to specify the same definitions over and over again. You can duplicate a field, taking with it all the field properties and other attributes.

Select the row to duplicate, select Edit | Copy (or select the Copy button on the toolbar), and move the cursor to the field that will follow the duplicated field. (Again, if you are going to copy a field and place it between Fields 4 and 5, highlight Field 5.) Select Edit | Paste, or choose the Paste button on the toolbar. Finally, change the field name of the new field.

Deleting Fields

To delete a field, select the field (or fields) you want to delete, and select Edit | Delete or press DEL. If there is data in the table, you will be asked to confirm your choice.

CHAPTER 3

Manipulating Data

Working with the data structures of a database may be stimulating intellectually, but you're probably anxious to get to the good stuff: the data itself. While an end user can use Access without any real programming, a programmer can use it to create applications that are more user friendly than the raw interactive tools. In this chapter, I'm going to show you how to use the *datasheet,* the spreadsheet-like tool that you can use to interactively work with data.

Working with a Datasheet

Datasheet view is the easiest way to work with Access data. It's simply a spreadsheet-like view of the contents of a table. I find Datasheet view useful for quickly scanning large amounts of data. On a 21" monitor displaying a small font, a lot of data can be packed into a single screen. It's also useful for quick-and-dirty data entry for testing, and for making sure that what you thought happened during the use of a form reflects reality.

To use a datasheet, open the database, select the table of interest, and choose the Open button. You'll see a window full of rows and columns. The window follows all standard Windows functionality—the Minimize, Maximize, and Close buttons on the right side of the title bar and the Control menu icon on the left side of the title bar all behave as expected. You can resize the window, and double-click the title bar to maximize the window (see Figure 3-1).

Navigating a Datasheet

A datasheet has scroll bars that can be manipulated to view other portions of the table. One set of scroll bars is on the right side of the window if there are more rows than fit in the window as it's currently sized. The other set of scroll bars is on the bottom. However, if you don't look carefully, you may think you're seeing double, because of the record number bar.

Using the Record Number Bar
A second set of controls that also looks like a scroll bar is positioned on the left of the status bar of the window. This set of controls is the *record number bar* and allows you to easily navigate through the table. The two buttons with an arrow and a vertical bar allow you to move to the first (left button) or last (right button) record in the table. The arrows pointing left and right move a record at a time either backward or forward, respectively. The text box in the middle shows the current record number. The total number of records in the table (if a filter is not applied) is displayed to the right of the controls. You can enter a number in the current record number text box and press ENTER, and the highlight will be positioned at that record in the datasheet.

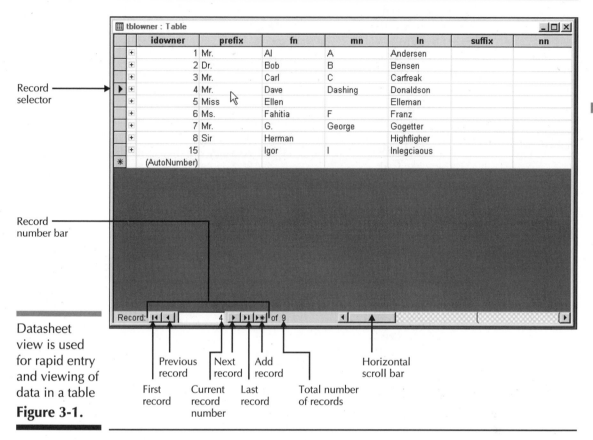

Record selector

Record number bar

Datasheet view is used for rapid entry and viewing of data in a table

Figure 3-1.

First record
Previous record
Current record number
Next record
Last record
Add record
Total number of records
Horizontal scroll bar

The current record number and total number of records appear on the surface to be simple concepts, but there is more than meets the eye with these. Suppose your table has 100 records, and you've navigated from the first row of the table down to the tenth. The current record number will be 10, and the record number bar will display "of 100." However, if you apply a filter to the table, the datasheet will not display all 100 records—it will only display those that meet the filter criteria. This subset of records is called a *recordset*. Suppose the filter produced a recordset in which records 11 through 25 out of the original 100 resulted. As you scrolled through the recordset in the datasheet, you would see the numbers 1 through 15 appear in the record number box, and you would see "of 15" appear next to the record number bar. If you attempt to enter a record number outside the range of the recordset, Access will display a warning. Fortunately, the word "Filtered" will also show up next to the "of 15" count in the record number bar.

As you move from row to row, you'll see a right-pointing arrow in the gray box on the left side of the datasheet. This arrow points to the selected record and is called the *record selector.*

Using Keyboard Shortcuts

You're probably accustomed to there usually being more than one way to accomplish a function in Access, and navigating through a datasheet is no exception. You can also use Edit | Go To, and you can scroll through the datasheet fields themselves with the cursor keys. There are a number of keyboard shortcuts, listed in Table 3-1, that you can use to move anywhere in the datasheet.

If you've noticed that these keystrokes are similar to those used in Excel, that was by design—Access is part of Office Professional.

Keypress	Action
TAB	Moves the cursor from field to field, left to right.
SHIFT-TAB	Moves the cursor from field to field, right to left.
UP ARROW	Moves the cursor up a row.
DOWN ARROW	Moves the cursor down a row.
HOME	Moves to the first field in the current record. If the first field is not visible in the window, the datasheet will automatically be scrolled so that the field is visible.
END	Moves to the last field in the current record. If the last field is not visible in the window, the datasheet will automatically be scrolled so that the field is visible.
PGUP	Scrolls the datasheet up a complete page. (If the datasheet has 100 rows, and rows 20 through 39 are visible, pressing PGUP will display rows 1 through 20—keeping one common row visible for each scrolling action.)
PGDN	Scrolls the datasheet down a complete page. (If the datasheet has 100 rows, and rows 1 through 20 are visible, pressing PGDN will display rows 20 through 39—keeping one common row visible for each scrolling action.)

Keyboard Shortcuts to Navigate the Datasheet

Table 3-1.

Keypress	Action
CTRL-PGUP	Scrolls the datasheet left a complete page.
CTRL-PGDN	Scrolls the datasheet right a complete page.
CTRL-HOME	Moves to the first field in the first record (what is known as "home" in some spreadsheets).
CTRL-END	Moves to the last field in the last record (what is known as "end" in some spreadsheets).
CTRL-UP ARROW	Moves to the first row while keeping the cursor in the current field.
CTRL-DOWN ARROW	Moves to the last row while keeping the cursor in the current field.
F5	Moves the cursor to the record number box (a feature I love!).
F2	Toggles between selecting all the data in the field and positioning the cursor between two characters in the field. All the standard Windows editing features apply—you can click in the leftmost part of a cell to select the contents of the entire cell, double-click a word to select the whole word, and click and drag through a field to highlight a block of text.

3

Keyboard
Shortcuts to
Navigate the
Datasheet
(continued)

Table 3-1.

Changing the Layout and Formatting

Across the top of the window, below the title bar, the field names (or captions, if you've used them) display in the column header (or *field selector*) of every column. You can resize columns by positioning your cursor in between two column headers and dragging, as shown here:

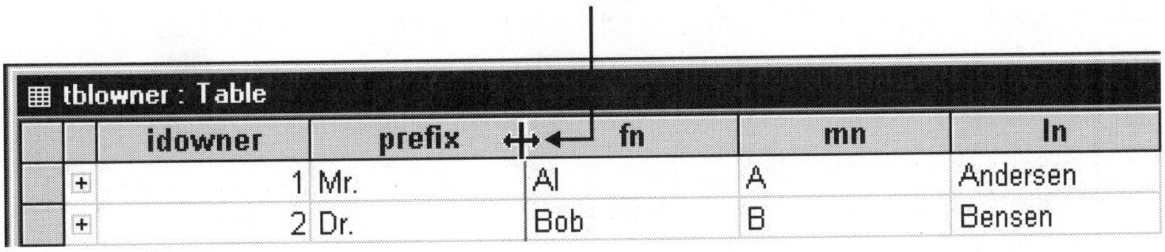

Cursor

idowner	prefix	fn	mn	ln
1 Mr.		Al	A	Andersen
2 Dr.		Bob	B	Bensen

tblowner : Table

or by selecting Format | Column Width. Check the Standard Width check box in the Column Width dialog box, shown next, to size each column to the same width (about an inch, depending on what the font is for the datasheet).

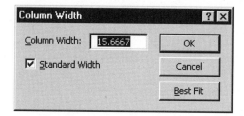

Choose the Best Fit button to have Access resize each column according to the widest data currently visible in the datasheet. Access will not search every row in the table to determine what the best column width would be, since that could take a long time on a large table.

You can resize the height of all the rows in the datasheet by positioning your cursor in between two row selector bars and dragging. Note that, unlike resizing columns, changing the height of one row changes all the rows to the same size. You can also use Format | Row Height to change the row height. Check the Standard Height check box in the Row Height dialog box, shown here, to size each row to the same height (about 1.3 times taller than the current font).

You can change the font of the datasheet by selecting Format | Font. Fonts listed with a TT (for TrueType) to the left of the name will appear the same both on the screen and when printed. Those with a Printer icon are printer fonts, and those with no icon are screen fonts. If you select a screen or printer font, Access will use the closest match it can find when performing the other operation (printing when a screen font is selected, displaying on screen when a printer font is selected).

Moving Columns

You can select multiple columns by highlighting one and, while the cursor is in the shape of an arrow, dragging the cursor to highlight additional columns.

To deselect columns, move the cursor into the header of a column that doesn't adjoin a highlighted column, or click in a field in the datasheet.

You can move one or more columns so that the columns *appear* in a different order than they actually exist in the table:

1. Highlight the columns you want to move.
2. Release the mouse button, leaving the column(s) highlighted.
3. Click and hold the mouse button down again, so that the cursor changes to a light rectangle. Then drag the columns to the desired position, and release the mouse button.

3

Hiding and Unhiding Columns

If you find yourself moving columns around a lot, but don't want to permanently change their order, you can hide columns (and show them again) by using Format | Hide Columns and Format | Unhide Columns. To hide a column (or columns), either select the column(s) by clicking on the column header(s) and then select Format | Hide Columns, or select Format | Unhide Columns and uncheck the columns you want to hide in the dialog box (see Figure 3-2).

The Unhide Columns dialog box can be used both to unhide hidden columns and to hide them in the first place

Figure 3-2.

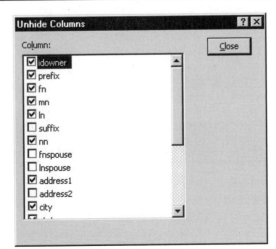

To show columns again, select Format | Unhide Columns, and check the columns you want to show. Note that Format | Hide Columns is not available unless you have selected one or more columns in the datasheet.

You can also "lock" one or more columns on the left side of the window so that scrolling to the right doesn't make those columns disappear. This effect is similar to when you scroll down in a table that has more rows than can fit in the window. The column headers stay visible all the time to provide a frame of reference.

Freezing Columns

To freeze a column, highlight it and select Format | Freeze Column. You can freeze consecutive columns by highlighting them all, and then selecting Format | Freeze Column, or by freezing each column one at a time. You'll see a thicker line in between the frozen columns and the nonfrozen columns, as shown here:

	idowner	prefix	fn	mn	ln
+	1	Mr.	Al	A	Andersen
+	2	Dr.	Bob	B	Bensen
+	3	Mr.	Carl	C	Carfreak
+	4	Mr.	Dave	Dashing	Donaldson
+	5	Miss	Ellen		Elleman
+	6	Ms.	Fahitia	F	Franz
+	7	Mr.	G.	George	Gogetter
+	8	Sir	Herman		Highfligher

You can also freeze nonconsecutive columns by freezing each column one at a time. Note that columns in between frozen columns will be pushed over to the left. If you don't want to see them, use Format | Hide Column to hide them. Format | Unfreeze will unfreeze the column(s).

Formatting the Datasheet

You can control a number of effects that have to do with the display of each cell in the datasheet. For instance, you can turn both horizontal and vertical gridlines on and off, change the color of the gridlines and datasheet background, and even "raise" or "lower" the cell with respect to the gridlines. Select Format | Datasheet to open the Datasheet Formatting dialog box, shown in Figure 3-3, which controls each of these attributes. Note that if you select Sunken or Raised cells, you won't be able to remove the gridlines—they are intrinsic to the effect.

3

Finding Data

Finding data is perhaps the most common task performed in a database application. After all, it's fairly common for data entry to be done by just a couple of persons, but everyone who uses a database wants to retrieve that data.

Simple Find

The easiest way to find specific data is to select the field that the data will be in, and then to use Edit | Find. The Find And Replace dialog box, shown in

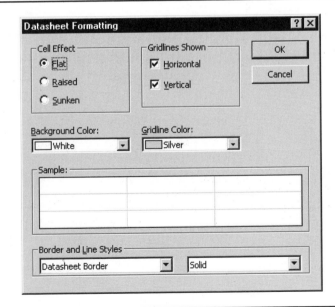

The Datasheet Formatting dialog box allows you to control the appearance of various attributes of the entire datasheet

Figure 3-3.

Figure 3-4, works just like it does in other Windows applications. Enter a value to find, and choose the Find Next button. If that data is found, the record selector will be moved to that record. The Find And Replace dialog box stays on the screen until you close it.

If you want to find additional records with the same value, open the dialog box again and choose the Find Next button. You'll see that the value of your last search is still entered in the Find What text box.

The Find And Replace dialog box has several very useful capabilities. First, you can choose what records you want to search—all records, just those from the current record to the end of the table, or from the current record back to the beginning of the table. Select the desired choice from the Search drop-down list at the bottom of the dialog box.

You can also choose how much data to match. Suppose you're searching for the string Smith. Selecting Whole Field in the Match drop-down list will find all the records that contain exactly Smith in the field, but will not find a record that contains Smithson or Smith & Wesson. Selecting Start Of Field in the Match drop-down list will find all the records that begin with Smith, regardless of what else comes after those five letters. Selecting Any Part Of

The Find and Replace dialog box allows quick searching through a datasheet

Figure 3-4.

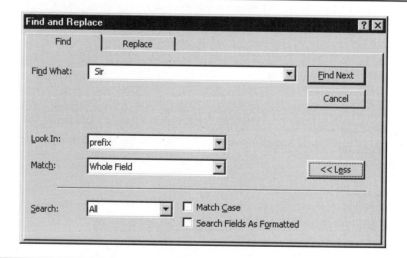

Field in the Match drop-down list will find any record that contains Smith anywhere in the field.

You may be wondering whether the field has to have the "S" capitalized for a match to occur. As with so much in life, it depends. If you've checked the Match Case check box, then yes, the operation will only find records that have Smith with a capital "S" and lowercase "mith." If you don't have the Match Case check box checked, Access will find both upper- and lowercase instances.

You can choose to have every field in the table searched—simply select the name of the table (for example, tblOwner : Table) in the Look In drop-down list. Of course, if you have a large table with many rows or many fields, this may take a while.

Remember that you can display data in a different format than it is actually stored internally by Access. For example, you may enter dates in the format 1/1/80 but have Access display them in the format 01-Jan-80. Suppose you entered all 31 days of January into 31 records, and formatted the field as 01-Jan-80. Normally, searching for the value 1 would find all 31 records. However, if you check the Search Fields As Formatted check box, only those fields that actually are displaying a 1—01-Jan-80, 10-Jan-80 through 19-Jan-80, 21-Jan-80, and 31-Jan-80—would be found. By use of the Search Fields As Formatted option, you could search for all records in February simply by looking for the string Feb anywhere in the field. If you looked for 2, you'd get a lot of values you weren't interested in.

3

IN DEPTH

Using Wildcards to Find Data

You can use special characters called *wildcards* to create more flexible and powerful search strings. A question mark will be interpreted as a single unknown character, an asterisk will be interpreted as zero or more unknown characters. A search string of Sm?th will find not only Smith but also Smyth, while a search string of Sm*th will find Smith, Smyth, Smiith, SmTOIWYEIUEYRIEWUYRIWYth, and even SMTH—when the asterisk is interpreted as zero characters.

Setting a Filter by Selection

You can restrict the datasheet to displaying only records that meet a particular condition (or a set of conditions). This mechanism is called a *filter* and can be created two ways.

The easy way, although somewhat limited, is Filter By Selection. First, find a record that contains the value upon which you want to filter. For example, you might highlight the prefix Dr. if you want to see only the doctors in the datasheet. Then click the Filter By Selection button in the toolbar or select Records | Filter | Filter By Selection, and only those records that match the highlighted value will be displayed, as shown here:

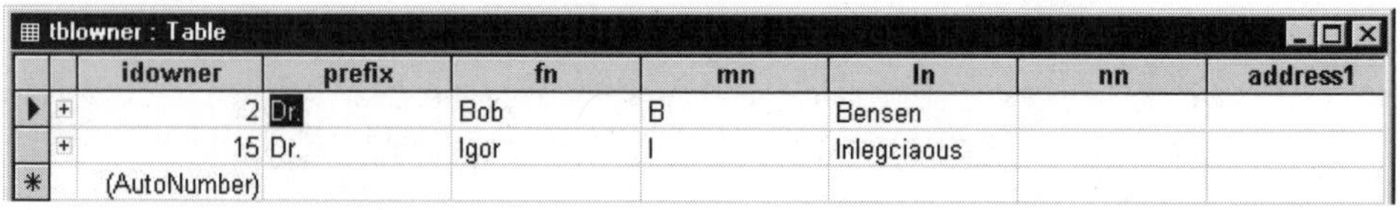

idowner	prefix	fn	mn	ln	nn	address1
2	Dr.	Bob	B	Bensen		
15	Dr.	Igor	I	Inlegciaous		
(AutoNumber)						

To see all the records in the datasheet again, click the Remove Filter toolbar button or select Records | Remove Filter/Sort.

Setting a Filter by Form

The other method of creating a filter allows you to set up multiple conditions and then view records that meet any of those conditions.

First, open the Filter By Form window, shown in Figure 3-5, by selecting Records | Filter | Filter By Form, or click the Filter By Form toolbar button. Enter values in one or more fields for the first condition. Note that values in each field form an AND condition—if you enter TB in the Model field and 51 in the Last Name field, only '51 TBs will be selected.

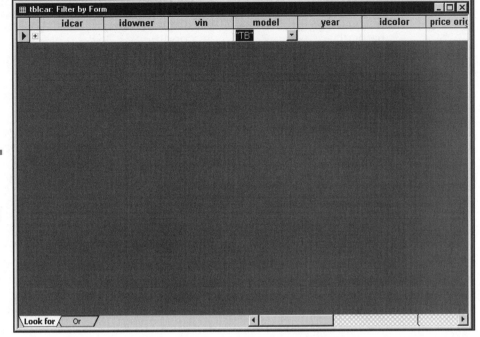

The Filter by Form window allows you to create a record with one or more entries that you are using to set up the filter condition

Figure 3-5.

Next, to add more criteria to the filter, click the Or tab in the bottom of the window and enter a new condition, as shown in Figure 3-6. If you wanted all records in which the model was TB or a model year of 52, you would enter TB in the first row and then, after selecting a new Or tab, enter 52 in the new row.

Once you have finished entering conditions, select Filter | Apply Filter/Sort, or choose the Apply Filter toolbar button to apply the filter to the datasheet. You'll see the results of the filter in the datasheet, and the record number bar

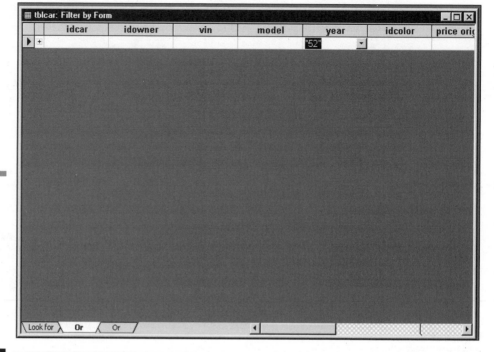

Additional
rows are
added to the
Filter by Form
criteria by
selecting new
Or tabs at the
bottom of the
dialog box
Figure 3-6.

at the bottom of the datasheet will reflect the results, including a legend that
indicates the datasheet has been filtered (see Figure 3-7).

To remove a filter, select Records | Remove Filter/Sort, or click the Remove
Filter toolbar button.

Changing the Order of Displayed Data

When you open a table, Access displays the data in primary key order—the
order in which the records were entered. This is often not the way you want
to see them. Using the MG application as an example, perhaps you've set a
filter to limit the records to a single model; but, within that model, you want
to see the records sorted by year and within year, by VIN, or by color.

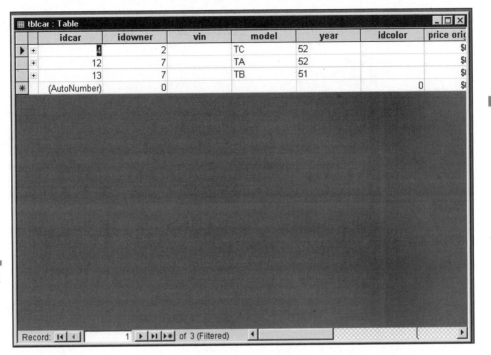

The results of a
Filter by Form
with two
criteria

Figure 3-7.

You can sort the datasheet based on values in a single column by simply
selecting the column and then clicking the Sort A-Z or Sort Z-A toolbar
button. Alternatively, you could select Records I Sort. For many purposes, this
functionality, combined with an appropriate filter, is all you'll need.

If you need to sort on more than one column, you must use Records I Filter I
Advanced Filter/Sort. Doing so will open the Filter dialog box and add a Filter
menu bar to the main menu.

You'll see a window in the top half of the dialog box and a grid in the
bottom half. You can use the grid to enter each field to be sorted on, with the
most important field in the leftmost column of the grid, and each succeeding
sort field in subsequent columns in the grid. For example, if you want to sort
by Model, and then by Year within Model, the grid columns would have

Model in the leftmost column, Year in the second column, and VIN in the third column, as shown in Figure 3-8.

TIP: There are several ways to enter the name of the field in the first row of the grid. Obviously, you can type it in. Or you can click the drop-down list and select the field name from the list. But you can also click the field name from the table window in the top half of the Filter window, and drag it to an empty column in the grid. While you're dragging the field, the mouse pointer will turn into a circle with a slash through it. Once the mouse pointer lands on an appropriate location in the grid, it turns into a rectangular bar (I think it's supposed to look like a text box or a field). At this point, you can release the mouse button.

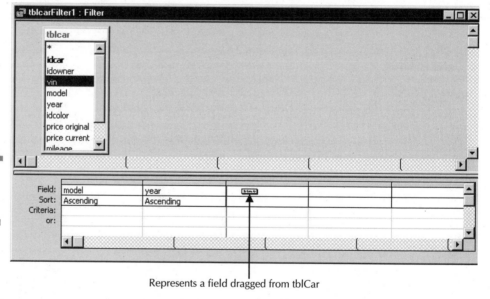

With the Advanced Filter/Sort command, you can create a sort based on multiple fields

Figure 3-8.

Represents a field dragged from tblCar

Using More Than One Sort Field

People new to database programming are often confused about how to use multiple fields for sorting. It's easiest to think of additional fields as tie-breakers for the previous field. For example, if you've got Al Smith, Bob Smith, Carl Rogers, and Zander Smith, you'll first sort on Last Name, so that Carl Rogers shows up before any of the Smiths. The second sort column, however, will be First Name, so that, within the Smiths, Al comes before Bob, and Bob comes before Zander. You wouldn't simply sort on First Name, because then Al and Bob Smith would show up before Carl Rogers. If you use Model as the first sort column, then the Year acts as a tie-breaker for cars of the same Model, as shown here:

3

	idcar	idowner	vin	model	year
▶ +	10	6		TA	49
+	1	1		TA	50
+	11	7		TA	50
+	12	7		TA	52
+	13	7		TB	51
+	9	6		TC	49
+	2	1		TC	51
+	3	1		TC	51
+	5	3		TC	51
+	7	5		TC	51
+	4	2		TC	52
+	15	7		TD	51
+	14	7		TD	53
+	8	5		TF	50
+	6	4		TF	53
*	(AutoNumber)	0			

tblcar : Table

Adding, Editing, and Deleting Data

As you have likely already discovered, a datasheet is an excellent tool to quickly enter, edit, and delete data.

Adding Records

You can add a record in Datasheet view simply by moving to the last row of data in the datasheet and moving the cursor down one more row. When the cursor is in the last row of data, you'll see an empty row with an asterisk (*) in the row selector, indicating that this is a blank record, ready for entering data. Note that this blank record isn't actually saved with the table—it's simply a convenience for you to add records to the datasheet.

You can move to the blank row by pressing CTRL-+, by selecting Edit | Go To | New Record, or by selecting the New Record button in the toolbar. Once you start entering data into the blank record, the icon in the record selector changes to a pencil, and another blank record is added, as shown in Figure 3-9.

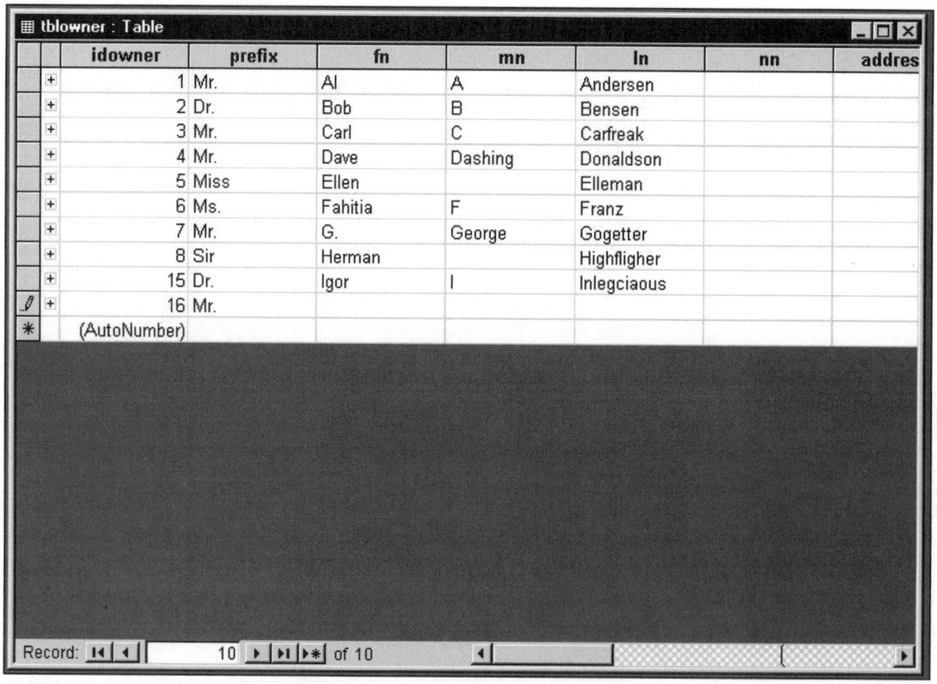

	idowner	prefix	fn	mn	ln	nn	addres
+	1	Mr.	Al	A	Andersen		
+	2	Dr.	Bob	B	Bensen		
+	3	Mr.	Carl	C	Carfreak		
+	4	Mr.	Dave	Dashing	Donaldson		
+	5	Miss	Ellen		Elleman		
+	6	Ms.	Fahitia	F	Franz		
+	7	Mr.	G.	George	Gogetter		
+	8	Sir	Herman		Highfligher		
+	15	Dr.	Igor	I	Inlegciaous		
+	16	Mr.					
*	(AutoNumber)						

Record: I◄ ◄ 10 ► ►I ►* of 10

Adding a record causes the Record Selector icon for the new record to change to a pencil and a new, blank record (with an asterisk in the record selector box) to appear below it

Figure 3-9.

Adding and Editing Data

Once you've got a new record, you're going to want to add data to it—and more than likely you're eventually going to want to change data in an existing record. Just type the new value over the old one, and tab out of the field. Unless the validation rule for that field or record is violated, you're done. If the validation rule is violated, you will receive a warning message, and you have to correct the entry or choose Undo before you can leave the field (or record).

However, Access does give you a number of keyboard shortcuts to help you enter repetitive data quickly, as listed in Table 3-2.

3

Deleting Records

To delete a record in a table, highlight the row (or rows) by selecting the record selector on the left side of the datasheet, and either press DEL or select Edit I Delete Record. Naturally, you can also perform this action with the toolbar—click the Delete Record button. Access' behavior is a bit disconcerting: the rows disappear, the rows below those deleted move up, and then—only then—are you asked to confirm your intent to delete. If you cancel your deletion, the records will reappear.

CAUTION: You can't Undo a deletion once you've answered yes to the delete confirmation dialog box.

Keyboard
Shortcuts for
Entering
Repetitive
Data

Table 3-2.

Keypress	Action
CTRL-;	Enters today's date
CTRL-SHIFT-:	Enters the current time to the second
CTRL-ENTER	Enters a carriage return in a memo or text field (like many word processors and text editors)
CTRL-' CTRL-"	Enters the value from the same field in the previous record (saves you from having to Edit I Copy and then Edit I Paste over and over again)
CTRL-ALT-SPACEBAR	Recovers the original default value defined for a field

Saving Data

I haven't discussed how to save a record. That's mainly because it's usually done for you automatically—as soon as you move off a row, any changes made to that row are saved to the table on disk. If you don't want to or can't move off the record, you can press SHIFT-ENTER or select Records | Save Record to explicitly save the data in the record. That's all there is to it.

Well, not exactly all. What if someone else is editing that same record at the same time? Time for the last section in this chapter—multiuser issues.

Multiuser Issues

Multiuser access is a new concept for Access users who are familiar with other Office applications such as Word and Excel, but it is a fundamental issue for database programmers.

By their very nature, documents and spreadsheets are designed to be used by a single person at a time, just like their paper counterparts. Recent advances in technology, of course, have provided workgroup capabilities so that multiple users can "share" a document. Fundamentally, however, only a single user can be actively editing a document at one time. The other users are still limited to either making a copy of the document or to viewing it in a read-only manner.

A database, on the other hand, can be thought of as having many documents, each of which may be accessed by a different user. These "documents," of course, are the individual records in a table. Only a single user at a time can edit each record, although multiple users can view the same record.

The first thing you have to know about multiuser database handling is how to allow multiple users to get into a database. When you open a database, you can choose to open it with Exclusive Use by checking the Exclusive Use check box in the File | Open dialog box. Once you do so, you are the only user who can modify data. Other users can view, query, and report on the data in the database, but they can't make changes to it.

You don't have to have two computers to experiment with multiuser issues. All you have to do is have a powerful enough computer to run two sessions of Access and, optionally, be a little schizophrenic, because you'll be pretending to be two persons using the same monitor and keyboard on a single computer. Here's how you do it:

1. If you have any sessions of Access open, close them, so that you're starting from scratch.

2. Open two instances of Access, and resize the windows so that one takes the top half of your screen and the other takes the bottom half.

3. Select the top instance, and open a database with File | Open. Be sure to check the Exclusive Use check box.

4. Open a table in the database in Datasheet view.

5. Select the other instance, and try to open the same database and table. Whether or not you check the Exclusive Use check box, you'll be warned and prohibited from opening the database.

6. Close all windows in both sessions of Access and start over again.

7. This time select the top instance, and open a database with File | Open, being sure to keep the Exclusive Use check box unselected.

8. Open the same database in the bottom session. If you try to open it with the Exclusive Use check box selected, you'll be warned that you can't, but Access will open the database for shared access.

9. Now that you've got the same database open twice (remember, you're simulating two users), open the same table in both sessions, and place your cursor in the same field in the same record in both sessions.

10. Make a change to the field in the top instance. Before you save the change, notice that there is a pencil image in the row selector at the left of the datasheet, as shown in Figure 3-10. Once you save, by pressing SHIFT-ENTER or by selecting Records | Save Record, the pencil image will go away. Select the same field, and you'll not see the change reflected in Datasheet view. If you move off the record and then back on, however, the change will be visible, because you have reread the value from the disk, and the datasheet will reflect new data.

11. Position the cursor on the same record, in the same field, in both instances of Access. Make a change in the top session, but don't save your change.

12. Select the bottom instance, make a different change, and save the change. Select the top instance, and attempt to save the change. Remember, the "other user" has already made a change and successfully saved it—what would you expect to happen?

    Well, you could just try to force your change on top of the first change without regard for what it was. Or you could just throw up your hands and say, "Forget about it!" Or, perhaps you'd like to know what the first

Running two sessions of Access on the same computer allows you to experiment with multiuser issues without a lot of overhead. Notice that the entry of Jay Jorgenson's record in the top window has not yet been reflected in the instance of Access in the lower window

Figure 3-10.

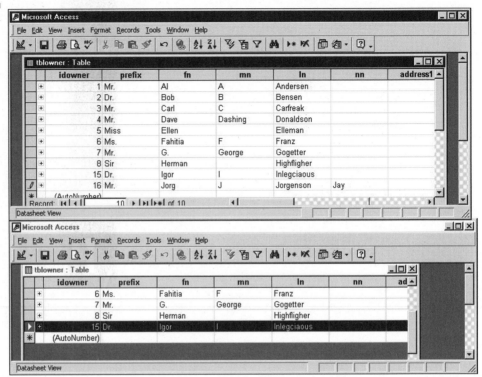

change was, and then decide if you want to keep that change, or let your change still override the first one.

This is what Access does. A Write Conflict warning dialog box displays informing you that another user changed the record since you started editing it. You then have three choices: you can either Save Record, in which case your data will be saved on top of the other change, or Drop Changes, in which case your changes will be ignored, and you will see the changes made by the other user. The third choice is to Copy To Clipboard, whose purpose isn't immediately obvious. It will save the changes you made to the Clipboard, and then show you the changes made by the other user. You can then decide which changes you want to keep—either by doing nothing (in which case you'll keep the other user's changes), or by pasting your changes from the Clipboard to the record after all (in which case you'll have overwritten the first set of changes).

PART II

Access Tools

CHAPTER 4

Getting at Your Data: Queries

Most applications require the ability to select a subset of data from one or more tables on a regular basis. After reading the previous chapter, you know you could do this manually—at least in one table—by setting up a Find condition and executing it. But there's a better way to selectively retrieve data. This mechanism is called a *query* and is a separate object in your database. There are actually two types of queries: *select queries*, which simply retrieve data, and *action queries*, which make changes to it. In this chapter, I'll discuss select queries.

Using a Query

Queries are objects stored in a database just as tables, forms, reports, and other things are. To run an existing query:

1. Open a database and select the Queries item in the left pane to display all the queries in the database.

2. Choose the Open button in the window's toolbar. A window that looks like a datasheet will display with the results of the query. Alternatively, you can highlight the query and press ENTER, or right-click the desired query and select Open from the context menu (see Figure 4-1).

fn	ln	holyoctagon	model	year
Al	Andersen	☑	TA	50
Al	Andersen	☑	TC	51
Al	Andersen	☑	TC	51
Bob	Bensen	☐	TC	52
Carl	Carfreak	☑	TC	51
Dave	Donaldson	☐	TF	53
Ellen	Elleman	☑	TC	51
Ellen	Elleman	☑	TF	50
Fahitia	Franz	☑	TC	49
Fahitia	Franz	☑	TA	49
G.	Gogetter	☐	TA	50
G.	Gogetter	☐	TA	52
G.	Gogetter	☐	TB	51
G.	Gogetter	☐	TD	53
G.	Gogetter	☐	TD	51

qry owners and their cars : Select Query

Record: 1 of 15

Running a query creates a recordset that is presented in a datasheet window

Figure 4-1.

CAUTION: The data in a query's result datasheet is *live*—that is, modifying the results will modify the tables from which the query was constructed. Many other database programs send the results of a query to a temporary table or cursor. Thus, edits to that table (if possible) aren't of consequence—they are made temporarily for the sake of convenience. Don't fall into the trap of assuming this is true with Access queries.

Query Quick Start

4

Running someone else's queries only takes you so far. The real power is being able to create your own queries. In fact, that's how Access was named—its primary intent was to provide access to data that resided on a variety of platforms. Once the connection to the data source was created, the important part was to provide easy access to that data.

First, let's walk through the steps of a simple, single-table query:

1. Create a new query by clicking the New toolbar button, by selecting Create A New Query in the Detail list in the left pane, or by selecting New in the context menu.

2. Select Design View, and the Show Table dialog box, which allows you to immediately add a table to the query, appears, as shown here:

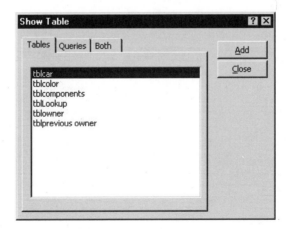

3. Select the desired table and click the Add button. The Query Design View window displays. Similar to a Find Filter window, it consists of two

panes. The top pane contains field lists for each table that's part of a query. The bottom pane contains a design grid that allows you to specify conditions that will produce just the data you want to see in the query results (see Figure 4-2).

You can think of a query as slicing your table into strips in two ways—vertically and horizontally. You might wish to only have certain fields from the table show up in your query—these would be the vertical strips you slice out of your original table. You might wish to have just certain records from the table show up in your query as well—these would be the horizontal strips you slice. Together, the result looks much like a mutilated checkerboard, with just certain squares ending up in the query result.

To restrict the query to certain fields, place those fields in the columns of the design grid in the bottom half of the Query Design View window. You can do this the hard way, by clicking in the Field row of an empty column in the grid and selecting the desired field. Or you can do this the easy way, by just dragging the field from the Field list in the top pane to an empty column in the grid. As you do so, the mouse pointer changes to a small rectangular Field icon that's supposed to look like a text field on a form—pretty cool. See Figure 4-3.

Even better—if you need to rearrange the order of fields once you put them in the grid, you can just drag them to a new position. Click the field, then

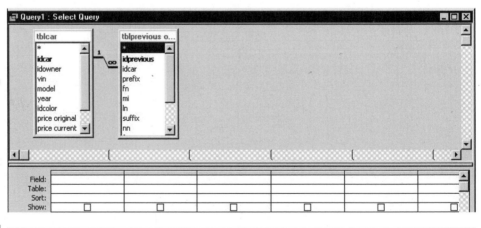

The top pane of the Query Design View window shows all the Field list windows in the query

Figure 4-2.

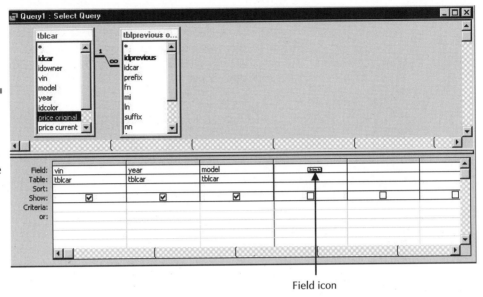

Dragging a field from a Field list window in the top pane to the design grid in the bottom pane changes the mouse pointer to a Field icon

Figure 4-3.

Field icon

click a second time to change the mouse pointer to a rectangle, the field section tool, which lets you drag the field (or fields) to the new location, as shown here:

NOTE: If you want to include all the fields in a table in the query, you don't have to drag all of them, one by one, into columns. Instead, drag the asterisk that's in the table window in the top pane to an empty field in the design grid. You'll see one entry show up with the name of the table, a period, and the asterisk. This is universal query shorthand for "all the fields in the table."

When you have finished selecting the fields in a query, run the query by clicking the Run toolbar button (the button with the red exclamation mark), or right-click the title bar of the window and choose Datasheet View. To get back to the query's Design view, click the View toolbar button and select the Design icon. You can also right-click the title bar of the resulting recordset window and choose Design View.

Remember that a query is an object in a database—so if you want to save the query for later use, you'll need to save it by using the Save toolbar button. If you attempt to close the query window without saving, you'll be prompted to save your query.

Setting Up Query Criteria

Once you've finished choosing which fields you want to display, you're halfway to slicing and dicing. To control which records show up in the result, create one or more criteria. To create a criterion based on a single field, enter the criterion's expression in the Criteria row for that field. For example, to show all automobiles with less than 10,000 miles on them, you would enter the expression < 10000 in the Criteria row for the Mileage field. For a text field, you can enter the value that you want matched. For example, to find all the TCs, you would just enter "TC" in the Criteria row in the Model field. You actually don't have to enter the quotes—Access will add them for you. However, if you are looking for a text expression that has spaces, you'll need to enclose the string in quotes. To find an owner named Mc Intosh, you would enter "Mc Intosh" as the expression.

If you want to look for more than one value, such as either TAs or TBs, you would enter each value on a separate row for that field. "TA" would be in one row, and "TB" would be in the row below it, as shown here:

Field:	vin	model	year	fn	ln	
Table:	tblcar	tblcar	tblcar	tblprevious owner	tblprevious owner	
Sort:						
Show:	☑	☑	☑	☑	☑	☐
Criteria:		"TA"				
or:		"TB"				

You can include criteria for more than one column in the same query. For example, suppose you wanted to find all the TAs with low mileage. You would enter "TA" in the Criteria row under the Model column and < 10000 in the Criteria row under the Mileage column. This would return just those TAs with less than 10,000 miles—in other words, both conditions would have to be true.

What if you want all the TA cars—regardless of what year they were made—and all the '52 vehicles? In other words, you want Owners that satisfy one condition, the other, or both. This can be a tricky concept at first, because the English language does us a disservice. You might phrase the query to yourself (or to another human) as "Show me all the TAs and all the '52s" when you meant "Show me all the Cars that are either a TA or were built in 1952." A computer will interpret these two requests quite differently.

4

Access interprets all the conditions on the same row as an AND, meaning that all the conditions have to be true in order for a record to be returned. So when Model = "TA" and Year = "52" were on the same row, only those TAs built in 1952 made it into the result. If you were to put the conditions on separate rows—"TA" under Model on the first Criteria row, and "52" on a second row under the Year column, as shown next—Access would interpret these conditions as "one or the other or both."

Field:	fn	ln	holyoctagon	model	year	
Table:	tblowner	tblowner	tblowner	tblcar	tblcar	
Sort:						
Show:	☑	☑	☑	☑	☑	
Criteria:				"TA"		
or:					"52"	

This becomes slightly trickier if you want to create multiple multifield conditions. For example, suppose you wanted all the TAs and TBs that were built in 1952. You would enter "TA" in the Model column and "52" in the Year column—both in the first Criteria row—and then enter "TB" in the Model column and "52" in the Year column (yes, again)—both in the second Criteria row. You need to duplicate the "52" in each row under the Year column.

Matching Multiple Values

It can be a nuisance to enter multiple conditions to match against a range of values—particularly when the values are fairly discrete. For example, if you wanted all the Cars built in the '40s but not in the '50s, you could enter ten separate Criteria rows: 1940, 1941, and so on. But that would be drag. You can use the BETWEEN operator to save yourself a lot of work, with an expression like BETWEEN(40,49) in the Year column. If the values do not fit a range as neatly—such as every other year—you can use the IN operator: IN(41, 43, 45, 47, 49).

You can even do pattern matching with wildcards. Just as with Find, an asterisk in an expression stands for zero or more missing characters, and a question mark stands for a single character. In addition, you can use a string like [a-c] to stand for the characters a, b, or c, or a string like [45-48] to stand for the numbers 45, 46, 47, and 48. Finally, you can use the exclamation mark to negate an expression. The string [!44-45] accepts any character except the numbers 44 and 45.

Handling date and time expressions can be confusing as well. Surround a date or time with pound signs (#) to indicate that the string is not just text. For example, #1/1/1980# represents January 1, 1980, and #23:59# represents a minute before midnight. Your text strings must match the Regional Settings formats in Windows (click the Regional Settings icon in the Control Panel).

Sorting a Query

Once you've added a field to the query, you can choose to sort the query on the contents of that field, either by ascending, descending, or not sorted (if you selected the field by mistake). If you don't, the query will return the records in the same order that they are in the underlying tables. *Ascending* means alphabetically from A to Z, numerically from 0 to 9, and chronologically from the earliest to the most recent date; *descending* means in the reverse order. Most often you'll want to use Descending order for numeric fields in which you want to see the largest values at the top, or for date fields in which you want to see the most recent date at the top.

If you want to sort on more than one field (such as by Last Name, and then by First Name within Last Name), you'll need to place the more important field to sort to the left of the less important field that will also be sorted on. You don't have to have the fields upon which you want to sort be the leftmost fields in the design grid, however. Access will simply read from left to right when determining which fields to sort on. For example, suppose the first column in your query is Owner First Name; the second column is Owner Last Name; the third column is the Holy Octagon Yes/No field; the last two are, in order, the Model and Year; and both Model and Year are sorted on Ascending, as shown here:

4

Field:	fn	ln	holyoctagon	model	year
Table:	tblowner	tblowner	tblowner	tblcar	tblcar
Sort:				Ascending	Ascending
Show:	☑	☑	☑	☑	☑
Criteria:				"TA"	
or:					"52"

When run, the multicolumn query would display the Owner Names but in order by Model, and then within Model by Year, like this:

qry owners and their cars : Select Query

fn	ln	holyoctagon	model	year
Fahitia	Franz	☑	TA	49
G.	Gogetter	☐	TA	50
Al	Andersen	☑	TA	50
G.	Gogetter	☐	TA	52
Bob	Bensen	☐	TC	52

Creating Calculated Fields

You'll often want to display a field in a query that is actually the combination of more than one field. For instance, instead of showing three fields (First Name, Middle Initial, and Last Name), you can concatenate all three fields into a single field that is easier to use. Similarly, you can do arithmetic on numeric and date fields—such as adding several Amount fields together, or showing the difference between two dates. For example, to determine how much a car has appreciated, you would take the original sales price and divide it into the current asking price. Another example would be to show the average number of miles driven per year; you would take the mileage and divide it by the difference of the Mileage As Of field and the year of the car. There's no need to store this information in the table because it can be easily calculated. You can use the standard arithmetic operators: + (addition), – (subtraction), * (multiplication), / (division), and ^ (exponentiation), as well as & (concatenation) to combine fields.

TIP: Access automatically converts numeric values to text strings if you concatenate text and numeric values.

You can also use Access' built-in functions by themselves or in concert with fields in order to create calculated fields. Sometimes it's difficult to remember all the functions that come with Access. You can use the Expression Builder, a tool used to build tricky or complex expressions, for functions that you don't use frequently.

To use the Expression Builder, place your cursor in the Criteria row under the field for which you want to build an expression, right-click, and select Build from the context menu.

The Expression Builder dialog box, shown in Figure 4-4, displays. In the leftmost window, you'll see a list of items from which you can either select or drill down (using an Explorer interface). Selecting an item in the left window will display a list of items in the middle window, such as fields. When you

After you select a field from a table in the Expression Builder, you can use the arithmetic operator buttons to build an expression with the field

Figure 4-4.

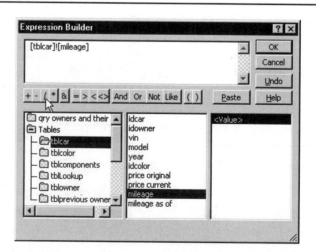

select functions, you'll see types of functions in the middle window, and specific function names in the right window.

Double-clicking on a field or function will display it in the text box window at the top of the Expression Builder dialog box. You can also select operators and enter values as desired to create virtually any expression you can imagine.

Hiding Fields

You may need to include a field in the query because it's used for sorting or as part of a criterion, but you may not want it to be displayed in the resulting recordset. You can uncheck the check box in the Show row of the design grid.

4

Controlling the Appearance of Fields

Fields in a query that come directly from a table inherit the properties of that field as they were set in the table definition. Access will automatically use those properties, but you can override them (and define them for fields in your query that don't come straight from a single field).

To do so, right-click a field and select Properties from the context menu. The Field Properties dialog box appears (see Figure 4-5). It allows you to set the same properties as you could with a field in a table, including Description, Format, Decimal Places, Input Mask, and Caption. You can also define a Lookup just as you could with a table.

The Field
Properties
dialog box
can be used
to override
default
properties from
the table
definition

Figure 4-5.

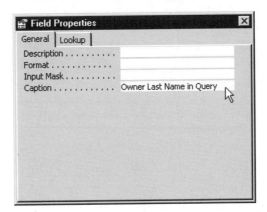

CAUTION: ··· If you right-click a field that is not included in the query (Show is unchecked), you'll get the Query Properties dialog box instead of the Field Properties dialog box.

The default properties from the table definition will not show up in the query's field definition. To see how this works, open a table in Design view, and enter a caption for a field, as shown here:

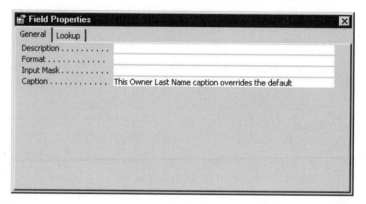

Change to Datasheet view, and your caption shows up as the column heading for that field. Save your table definition, and then open a query that uses that field. Run the query. The column heading is also the caption from the table. Finally, set the caption for that field in the query to a different value than that of the table definition and run the query again. The new caption displays as the column heading.

Summary Queries

Sometimes you just want to summarize data—showing totals instead of the details that were used to calculate those totals. For example, if you wanted to count how many cars were in each state, you wouldn't need to list every car, but just totals. This type of query is called a *Total query,* and requires an additional row—the Total row—to be added to the design grid. To add the Total row to the design grid, click the Totals toolbar button.

You'll see an expression, Group By, display in the Total row for every column in the query, as shown next. If you've added a Total row to an existing query, you may be confused; so it's worthwhile to discuss what types of fields are appropriate in a Total query.

Field:	fn	ln	holyoctagon	model	year	mileage		
Table:	tblowner	tblowner	tblowner	tblcar	tblcar	tblcar		
Total:	Group By	Group By	Group By	Group By	Group By	Group By		
Sort:				Ascending	Ascending			
Show:	☑	☑	☑	☑	☑	☑	☐	
Criteria:								
or:								

Unlike a regular select query, where you'll display many fields for the detail values they display, in a Total query you'll only need to include the field (or fields) upon which you want to summarize, and a field that will act as the description for the buckets into which you'll gather values. For example, if you're summarizing cars by model, you'll need two columns—one to indicate that you're going to group by Model, and the other to act as the actual counter of cars. See Figure 4-6. If you're summing number of cars per Model and average dollar value per Model, you'll need three columns—Model, a counter for cars, and an average of current price.

Access will create a single record for each distinct value in the Group By field; so, by identifying Model as a Group By field, the query result will contain one row for each model. To produce calculated values for each of the other

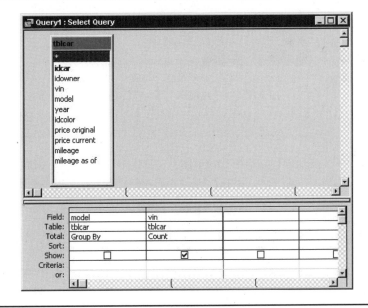

A summary query needs to have a column for the field that summarizing will be done on, as well as for each statistical field

Figure 4-6.

fields, change the Group By expression to a calculated expression. As shown in the following illustration, you have a number of choices, including COUNT, SUM, AVG, MIN, MAX, STDEV, and VAR. COUNT will simply return the number of records that contain the value in the Group By field. SUM and AVG will total or average the amounts in the selected column for each value in the Group By field. MIN and MAX return the smallest or largest values, STDEV returns the standard deviation, and VAR returns the variance.

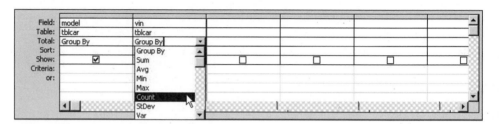

You may not always want every record in a query to be included in a Total query. You can create Criteria to include just certain records, just as you did for regular queries. The only difference is that you need to specify the "where" keyword in the Total row in the design grid. For example, suppose you only want to count the number of cars per Model but do not want to include cars for which there isn't a mileage figure. You would need three

How Functions Handle NULLs

As discussed in Chapter 2, a field in an Access table can be defined to allow NULL values. Since a NULL value means "I don't know what the value is," it doesn't make sense to include a row with a NULL in statistical functions like SUM, AVERAGE, or MIN. Each of these functions takes NULLs into account in a special way:

◆ **AVG, MIN, MAX**   Access ignores rows with NULLs.

◆ **COUNT**   Access ignores rows with NULLs. Specify COUNT(*) to include rows with NULLs.

◆ **STDEV, VAR**   Access ignores rows with NULLs and returns a NULL if the group has zero or one row.

columns. The first column would be Model, and the value in the Total row would be Group By. The second column would be VIN, and the Total row expression would be Count, because you want to count how many cars. The third column would be Mileage, and you would change the Total row expression from Group By to Where, and then enter the expression > 0 to select just cars that have a nonzero value in the field, as shown here:

Field:	model	vin	mileage			
Table:	tblcar	tblcar	tblcar			
Total:	Group By	Count	Where			
Sort:						
Show:	☑	☑	☐	☐	☐	
Criteria:			>0			
or:						

4

If you have to perform a statistical operation on the same column that you want to build a criteria expression on, simply add the column a second time. Put the statistical function in the Total row in the first instance of the column, and then change the Total row expression to Where and enter the expression in the Criteria row in the second column. Note that you would uncheck the Show check box in the column in which Total is set to Where, since you're going to want to display the column with the statistical values. For example, suppose you want to determine what the average mileage is per car, but you want to exclude show cars. (Some cars aren't normally driven except at shows, so their mileage is considerably lower than cars that are driven regularly by hobbyists. Including those cars would skew the figures.) You would add the Mileage column twice. The first Mileage column would have a Total row expression of Avg, and the second Mileage column would have a Total row expression of Where and a Criteria row expression of > 10000 (and the Show check box would be unchecked).

Field:	model	vin	mileage	mileage		
Table:	tblcar	tblcar	tblcar	tblcar		
Total:	Group By	Count	Avg	Where		
Sort:						
Show:	☑	☑	☑	☐	☐	
Criteria:				> 10000		
or:						

Queries with Multiple Tables

Remember that long diatribe about normalization back in Chapter 2? Breaking a single, monolithic table into lots of smaller pieces that were more granular? There were plenty of good reasons to do so, but it presents a problem—how do you get information from a database if it's spread all over the place? Initial misunderstanding of how to join information from more than one table is a primary reason that people ignore normalization and keep all their information in one table.

However, it's really not that hard. It may seem tough just because you don't know the techniques. But one of the features of normalization—placing foreign keys in tables that identify how they are mapped to other tables—is specifically there to make multitable joins easier.

Let's take a second to think about what's happening behind the scenes when you join two tables. First of all, what are you trying to accomplish? There are three kinds of joins possible. The first is when one table has zero, one, or more related records in a second table. For example, an Owner may have a single car or may have multiple cars. An individual in the Owner table may even have no cars, having sold his or her last one. This type of relationship is known as a *parent-child relationship*. The Owner is the *parent* table, and the Car table is the *child* table. Just as their terms indicate, a parent can have zero, one, or more children—and the same with our example. An Owner can have zero, one, or more Cars. This join between these two tables is known as a *one-to-many join*. One Owner has (in the real world) many Cars.

The second type of relationship is between two tables of *equals*—where each parent table has exactly one record in the child table. Suppose you have a table with Cars, and a second table that contains detailed information about the components that make up the car—such as chassis type and serial number, engine data, manufacturers of different items, and so on. You might not want to store all these details in the same table because the components are seldom used, and including all that additional information makes using the original Car table cumbersome. Thus, the component information is stored in a separate Components table. Each Car record has a foreign key that ties that car to a single Component record. This type of join—between two tables like Car and Component—is known as a *one-to-one join*.

IN DEPTH

Handle Multiple Relationships Between Tables

The third type of relationship is between two tables in which each parent might have zero, one, or more children, but a child record might have zero, one, or more parents. This type of relationship is commonly found throughout database applications and is even rife in the MG car club application. For example, if I had enough detailed information on ownership, I might restructure the Previous Owner table differently. Currently, each previous owner is tied to a single car. What if someone used to own more than one car? In this structure, that person's name would need to be entered into the Previous Owner table multiple times, each time with a foreign key that points to a single car.

A better solution is to have an intermediary table to record multiple ownership. Each person would be entered into the Previous Owner table only once. A separate record would be entered into the intermediary table for each Car-Owner relationship. Actually, to adhere strictly to Codd & Date, I should have defined two tables—one for Owners and another for Cars. Both previous and current owners would be entered into the Owner table—because the same person could be a current owner of one vehicle and a former owner of a different car. In fact, a person could be both a former owner and a current owner of the same car. Oh, the incestuous nature of owning vintage automobiles!

Obviously, with this more complex structure, the simple one-to-many relationships aren't enough. Each owner would have to be related to the car one or more times, and additional data would have to be stored according to when the ownership occurred.

This type of relationship in which a single Owner can be related to multiple Car records, but a single Car record can also be related to multiple Owners, requires a *many-to-many join*. The puzzle is determining how to handle the keys. If an Owner has many Cars, you can't put foreign keys for each Car in the Owner record, because you don't know how many Cars there might be. And obviously you can't create multiple fields, one for each key—that would violate the first rule of normalization. It seems that with vintage automobiles, like potato chips, it's difficult to have just one. Similarly, you can't put foreign keys for each Owner in the Car record, because, again, you don't know how many Owners a Car has had—perhaps one, perhaps two, perhaps more. In fact, you may have gaps of time where you don't know who the owner was, and there might have been more than one Owner during that time. So again, you can't create multiple Owner keys for a Car.

The solution is to use an intermediate table that can contain an unlimited number of keys from both tables. This table would contain a record for each combination of Owner and Car. For example, take a typical collector, Carl, who owns three cars—a TA, a TB, and a TF. The TA has had six previous owners, the TB has had two previous owners, and the collector has owned the TF since the day he spotted it in the showroom. (For simplicity's sake, we'll assume that each owner of each car was a different person, and that those individuals didn't own any other Cars.)

The Owner table would have nine records (the current owner, the six former owners of the TA, and the two former owners of the TB). The Car table would have three records—one each for the TA, the TB, and the TF. The join table would have 11 records:

Car	Owner
Key	Key
TA	First Owner
TA	Second Owner
TA	Third Owner
TA	Fourth Owner
TA	Fifth Owner
TA	Sixth Owner

TA	Current Owner (Carl)
TB	First Owner (Bob)
TB	Second Owner
TB	Current Owner (Carl)
TC	Current Owner (Carl)

4

If the original Owner of the TB, Bob, buys the TA from Carl, another record is added to the join table: a new current owner for the TA. The record for Carl's ownership of the TA is simply updated to include a sold date, which had been empty. Note that the Owner table doesn't have to be updated, since Bob was already in the Owner table (although, as a matter of practicality, his address and other personal data might need to be updated, since it's likely that he's not kept up to date since he sold the TB).

Key	Key
TA	First Owner
TA	Second Owner
TA	Third Owner
TA	Fourth Owner
TA	Fifth Owner
TA	Sixth Owner
TA	Seventh Owner (Carl)
TA	Current Owner (Bob)
TB	First Owner (Bob)
TB	Second Owner
TB	Current Owner (Carl)
TC	Current Owner (Carl)

IN DEPTH

CONTINUED

You can see that while this expanded structure is more flexible, it's also more complex—and producing queries and reports is going to be much more difficult. Thus, here is an example of where I decided to break the rules of normalization, and to create an entity of Previous Owners that consisted of just the name and address of the previous Owners. It's not worth the extra work of maintaining that information, since once someone has sold a car, that person will no longer stay in touch and that information will become outdated. While not strictly normalized, this denormalized structure makes for a much easier relationship and—while not obvious in a table of 500 or a thousand records—improved performance.

Creating a Multitable Query

To create a query between multiple tables, you need to perform two tasks before placing fields in the design grid. First, you need to add all the tables that will be involved in the query to the top of the Query Design View window. Second, you need to tell Access how to relate the tables. For example, suppose you placed a query on the Owner and Car tables. The Owner's primary key is in the Car table as a foreign key, so you would need to link the two tables using the Owner table's primary key field and the Car table's Owner foreign key field. Once you're finished, you can add fields from either table to the design grid, just as you did with a single table.

To add more tables to Query Design view, right-click in the top pane, and select Show Table. Highlight the name of the table, and click the Add button. Access will attempt to create the link between the tables automatically, matching fields with the same name and data type in both tables. Thus, if you name your foreign keys with the same name as the primary key in the other table, your relations will automatically be created. Clever idea, eh?

If the relation created was incorrect, highlight the line (so that it becomes bold), and press DEL. Then, to create a relation, highlight the field in one table, and drag it onto the matching field in the other table. As you drag the field, the mouse pointer will turn into a rectangular bar, the Field icon, just as it did when you dragged fields to the design grid. See Figure 4-7.

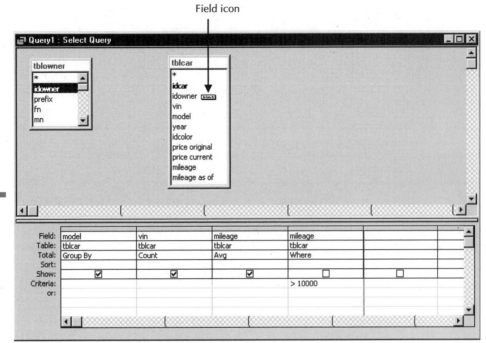

Dragging a
field from one
Field list
window to
another turns
the pointer
into a Field
icon

Figure 4-7.

Once you have placed the desired fields in the design grid, run the query as
usual. You'll see the results in a Datasheet window, with the appropriate
fields taken from each table.

Summary Queries Across Multiple Tables

Suppose you want to perform statistical calculations across multiple tables.
For example, perhaps you want to determine the total value of automobiles
per state. Since the State is in the Owner table but the current price is in the
Car table, the query will need to join the tables. There's really nothing special
about this type of query—the only difference is that you're putting fields in
the design grid from more than one table. This query would contain just two
columns: one for the State, and a second column for the Current Price. The
State column's Total row contains an expression of Group By, and the
Current Price's Total row contains the Sum function.

Suppose you want to calculate average mileage for show cars and, again, summarize by State. This is another summary query across multiple tables, but the difference is that the statistical function is being performed on the same field that the criteria are being applied to. Just as with a single table, add that column to the design grid twice. The Total row in the first instance of the Mileage column would contain the Avg function, while the Total row of the second instance would contain a Where expression. The Criteria row for the second instance would contain < 1000 as the expression.

Outer Joins

Within a multitable query, some interesting and unexpected situations can occur. For example, picture that poor Owner who has to sell his car, but hasn't had the good fortune to pick up a new one. Or what if an automobile has been found in a warehouse and the ownership is in question? By default, queries automatically join just those records that exist in both tables. Thus, in the query created earlier, only those Owners who currently own cars and Cars who have Owners were included in the resulting recordset.

What if you want to compile a list of Owners without Cars (for example, to match them up with cars for sale), or to list Cars without Owners (again, perhaps to offer for sale)? These types of joins are called *outer joins* and there are two kinds. A *right outer join* includes all records on the right side with records on the left, regardless if there are matches on the left. A *left outer join* does the opposite. You can change the way that a join is defined by changing the properties of the join, much as you changed the properties of a field in a table. Fortunately, Access actually hides the details of whether a join is a left or right outer join, so you don't have to determine, for example, whether the list of Owners without Cars is a right or left outer join. Instead, Access will interpret your desires and ask you how you want to handle a join using plain English terminology.

To change a join's properties, select the relation line and right-click to display the context menu. Choose Join Properties to display the Join Properties dialog box. Alternatively, you can double-click the relation line to display the Join Properties dialog box. You'll have three choices—to keep the join the way it is, or to redefine the join as either a left or right outer join—in plain English, of course. See Figure 4-8.

The second and third choices essentially ask the same question, but reverse the names of the tables. The second choice will offer to set up the join so that all the records in the table on the left side of the relation will show up in the

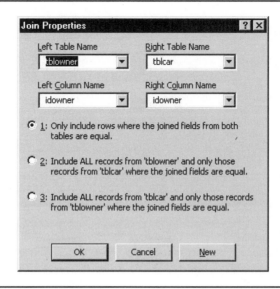

You can control the way an outer join is handled with choices in the Join Properties dialog box

Figure 4-8.

query result, regardless of whether there are matches with records in the right table. The third choice will offer to set up the join so that all the records in the table on the right side of the relation show up in the query result, regardless of whether there are matches with records in the left table. Suppose you remove one of the tables from the query, add it back, and set up the relation so that the relative position of the tables has been reversed. You'll see the wording in the Join Properties dialog box also reversed.

For example, suppose you want to see all the Owners, regardless of whether they currently own a car; but, if they do own a car, you want to know the Model and Year. Add the Owner and the Car tables to the query, and put the First Name and Last Name from the Owner table into the design grid. Then add the Model and Year fields from the Car table to the design grid. When you run the query, you'll get just those records in which an Owner has at least one Car (and the Car has an Owner). To display those Owners without Cars, double-click the relation line in the upper pane of Query Design view, and select the second option button: "Include ALL records from 'tblowner' and only those records from 'tblcar' where the joined fields are equal." Run the query again, and you'll see additional owners show up. See Figure 4-9.

What if you just want to see those poor unfortunate Owners without Cars? What you're really asking is to see just those records from the previous query

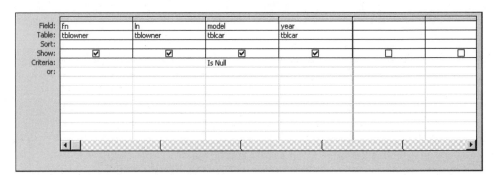

The left outer join query displays all owners—and their cars

Figure 4-9.

in which there is no car. You can do this by setting a criterion on the Model or Year—to show those records in which the Model value "Is Null," as shown here:

Field:	fn	ln	model	year		
Table:	tblowner	tblowner	tblcar	tblcar		
Sort:						
Show:	☑	☑	☑	☑	☐	☐
Criteria:			Is Null			
or:						

Queries Using Queries

You are not limited to using tables in queries, as you might have guessed when you added tables to Query Design view. Since a query is an object in a database just like a table is, you can use the results of a query to feed into a second query. You may find, in fact, that instead of attempting to build a complex query with multiple tables, criteria, and join conditions, it's easier to build several queries, each of which builds on the results of the previous query. I think that the KISS principle—Keep It Simple, Stupid—is one of the most important principles in developing software. Sure, there's an intellectual challenge in getting a complex query to work just perfectly. But more often than not, clever programming tricks, while fun to perform, also tend to produce support calls at 3 in the morning. If I'm going to be up at 3 in the morning, I want it to be because it was my choice, not because some slick bit of programming sleight-of-hand ended up being not quite slick enough.

4

As a result, not only can it be easier to build the final answer by using more than one query, but it also can be more reliable, and easier to debug and modify in the future. For example, what if you want to find out how many Owners who currently don't have Cars used to be Owners? This is pretty easy to do if you first create a query that contains a list of Owners who don't have Cars—using a query—and join it with the list of Previous Owners to see commonality. See Figure 4-10.

Use the Both
tab in the
Show Table
dialog box to
add both
queries and
tables to a
new query

Figure 4-10.

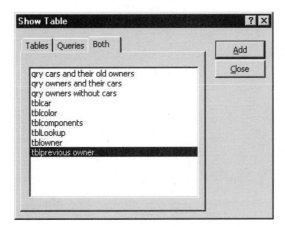

First, create a new query and add the Owners Without Cars query to it. Second, add the Previous Owner table to the query. Since there are no common fields, Access won't try to create a relation automatically—you'll have to do it manually. But if there are no common fields, how are you going to create a relation? How are the tables related? Actually, there are common fields—such as the First and Last Name fields. Access just didn't see them as such. We're going to assume that if someone has the same first name and the same last name in both tables, he or she is the same person. (You could make this mapping more explicit by adding more fields, such as Middle Initial, Address, and so on.) Draw a relation line between the First Name fields and the Last Name fields in both windows—you'll have two relation lines. See Figure 4-11.

Next, drag the First and Last Name fields from the Owners Without Cars query to the design grid, and then drag the From and To fields from the Previous Owner table to the design grid as well. Run the query, and you'll find those individuals in the Owners table who don't have Cars but used to. You could probably do this in a single query with all sorts of complex conditions—but why? This is a lot easier to create and understand, and it will be a lot easier to modify a year from now when you think of an additional criterion you need to include in the query.

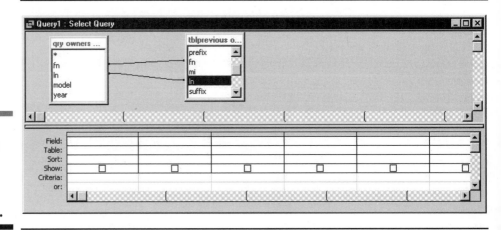

Using two relation lines to relate a query with a table

Figure 4-11.

Controlling How Queries Run

Just as fields and joins have properties, so do queries. These properties control various aspects of how a query runs, such as whether duplicate records will be displayed in the result, and how many rows to return.

You can display the Query Properties dialog box by right-clicking in the top pane of Query Design view and selecting Properties (see Figure 4-12). The Output All Fields option is normally set to No, but you might want to set it to Yes if you're going to use the output of a query in a form or a report in which you want to pick and choose fields from the query.

The Order By and Filter properties may be confusing at first. After all, you can specify a sort order and a filter right inside the query—why bother to set properties as well? And if you just try to play around with them, you may get unexpected results as well. These properties are stored with the query and can be applied to the query just as you do with a table, by selecting Records | Apply Filter/Sort. For example, if you were to enter a filter expression of mileage > 20000 and then run the query, all the cars, regardless of mileage, would be displayed. You need to apply the Filter/Sort command to see the subset in the query. Select the Remove Filter/Sort menu command to see the results of the entire query again.

4

The Query
Properties
dialog box

Figure 4-12.

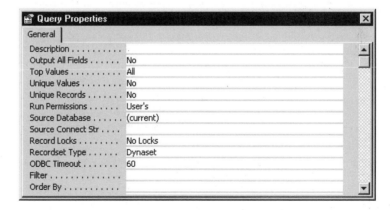

If you're working with large tables, you may find that the entire query takes a while to process, with the term "a while" being a relative term. If the type of query you're running produces the interesting results at the top of the result set, you may not want to wait for the rest of the uninteresting records to be queried. In this case, you can tell Access to show you results as soon as a certain number of records or a certain percentage of the result set has been calculated. Use the Top Values property to do so. You can select either an existing expression, such as top 5, top 25, top 100, top 5%, or top 25%, or enter your own value. If you enter an integer greater than 1, Access will display the result set when that number of rows is returned. If you enter a number between 0 and 1, Access will convert that number to a percentage and will display the result set when that percentage of rows has been returned.

Two very useful properties are the Unique Values and Unique Records properties. Unique Values allows you to winnow out duplicate values in the result set. For example, if you wanted to see how many different Models and years were represented in the Car table, you could create a query that contained two columns: Model and Year. However, upon running the query, you'd find duplicate values—you'd see every instance of a '51 TC, when all you want is just one record indicating that there's a '51 TC somewhere in the table. If you set the Unique Values property to Yes, however, duplicate values will be filtered out, and only one copy of a '51 TC will appear.

The Unique Records property is initially a little tougher to figure out. It is used in a multitable query to filter out duplicate records from the result set when the display fields are contained in one table and the criteria used to filter the query are contained in the other table. That's a mouthful, so here's an example. Suppose you want to find all the owners—their names and phone numbers—who have a '51 TC. Create a query with the Owner and Car tables, related on the primary key. Add the Model and Year fields from the Car table and the First Name, Last Name, and Voice Day fields from the Owner table. Set the Criteria row expression for the Model column to "TC" and for the Year column to "51." Then uncheck the Show row for both fields, so that the result set will only display the First Name, Last Name, and Voice Day fields. See Figure 4-13.

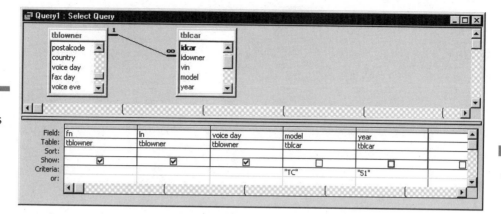

A query that
displays fields
from one
table but has
criteria from
another table
Figure 4-13.

4

When you run the query, you'll get one record for each '51 TC in the Car
table. If an Owner owns more than one '51 TC, that Owner will be listed
multiple times—once for each '51 TC he or she owns.

	fn	Owner Last Name	voice day
▶	Al	Andersen	.
	Al	Andersen	
	Carl	Carfreak	
	Ellen	Elleman	
*			

What a nuisance. Open the Query Properties dialog box (shown earlier in
Figure 4-12), and set the Unique Records property to Yes. Rerun the query
and you'll see each Owner show up only once, regardless of how many of
that type of car he or she owns. Note that if you include fields from the Car
table, the setting of Unique Records will be ignored. Try adding the Serial
Number field from the Car table to the query, and you'll see that the Owner
with more than one '51 TC will again show up multiple times.

CHAPTER 5

Building Data-Entry Forms

While quick-and-dirty data entry into datasheets may be acceptable to you, it may not be optimal. Wouldn't you like to have nice data-entry screens to add records to your tables, perhaps seeing fields from multiple tables on the same form, and having lots of user-friendly features like lookups and validation all at your fingertips? And even if you can deal with the raw look of a datasheet, other users of your database application might not be able to. In this chapter, you will learn how to build *forms*—windows that contain objects that provide the ability to view and edit data. Forms allow you to present information and control data entry with significantly more powerful and flexible features and capabilities than are available through a datasheet.

Form Terminology

There are a lot of new things to use when building forms, so let's define the terms for these items. As I said earlier, a form is a window that contains objects in which data is displayed and edited. These objects are called *controls* and can be roughly divided into three types. *Simple* controls, such as rectangles, lines, and images, serve to display an unchanging something on the form. *Data-aware* controls, such as text boxes and check boxes, are used to present table data to the user for viewing and/or editing. *Action* controls, like command buttons and page frames, are used to perform actions.

Types of Form Usage

Forms are a primary means to perform many types of tasks—not just the viewing and editing functions already described. For example, they can also be used to control the sequence in which an application is supposed to be used. You're used to a menu of choices in drop-down lists. But if you've ever looked over the shoulder of a server in a restaurant, you've seen him or her poke at a computer screen to reserve tables and enter orders. No menus on that screen at all—a third input device such as a mouse would be inconvenient and take up space. You could do the same thing as the restaurant—provide launching points for different parts of an application—by providing forms with buttons that act in place of menu bars.

You can also use forms to provide heads-down data entry, or to accept input to choose which part of an application is to be run next or how it's to behave. And, of course, forms can be used to provide feedback to the user—either during long processes, instructions for subsequent steps, or warnings and error messages.

Types of Forms

A typical form can be thought of as having just a single area where the data-entry controls are located, but even the simplest data entry actually has three parts: the header, the detail area, and the footer. See Figure 5-1. The *header* and *footer* can be thought of as static areas to present information that won't change. The *detail area* is used to present information from the table that will change as you move from record to record. At the bottom of a form is the navigation control similar to the one that you've already used in a datasheet.

Usually when you're designing user interfaces for others, they'll eventually come up with a request (or a requirement) to jam more data onto a form than is humanly (or technically) possible. You can design a multiple-page form that allows the user to page through a window and see more information than is visible in a single screen. See Figure 5-2.

An alternative to a multiple-page form is a continuous form, in which the detail area scrolls to show all the information for one record after another. Unlike a multiple-page form, which just shows a lot of information for a

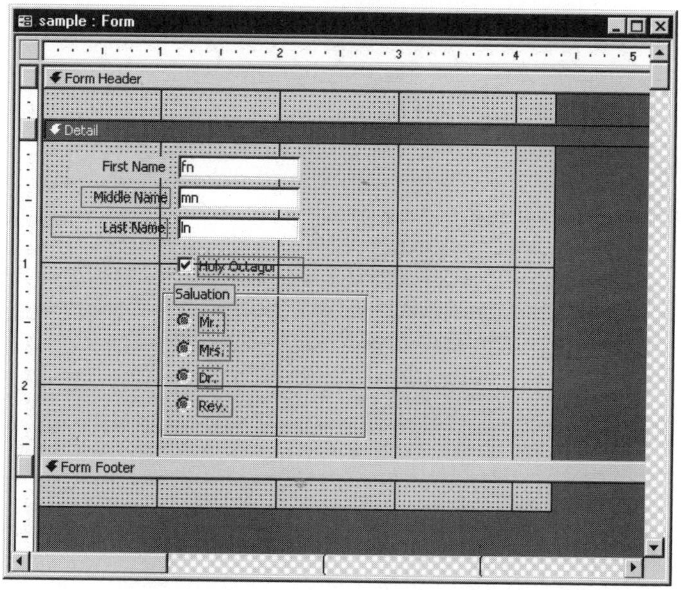

5

A typical
Access form
has three parts:
a header, a
footer, and
the detail area
in between

Figure 5-1.

A multiple-page form allows you to pack more information on a form than would normally fit. Press TAB to move from one page to the other

Figure 5-2.

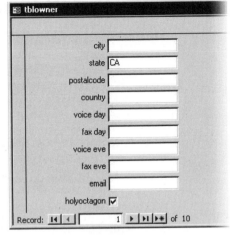

Page 1   Page 2

single record, the continuous form shows all the information for one or more records. Subsequent records can be viewed by scrolling the form, instead of needing to use the navigation controls. You can still use the navigation control to move through the table as well. See Figure 5-3.

A common requirement is to display both data from a parent record and data from one or more child records at the same time. The classic example is that of an invoice header that contains the customer name, ship-to address, and so on, and the line items details—each specific part or item that the customer purchased. You can use two types of forms to do so. A *sub form* is a child window in which child records are displayed placed right on the form. In our sample application, you might want to display information about the Owner on the form, and then show a list of Cars that the Owner currently possesses below the owner information. See Figure 5-4.

On the other hand, you might use a pop-up form when there's too much information to display in a sub form, or when you need to be able to manipulate the window that the child record information appears in. A *pop-up form* is a separate window that is launched from the form, perhaps via a command button, and that floats, independently, above the form. The pop-up window always stays in front of other windows—even when the other window has focus—much like the Help Assistant windows that stay visible while you work through a task in another window. Pop-ups are not to

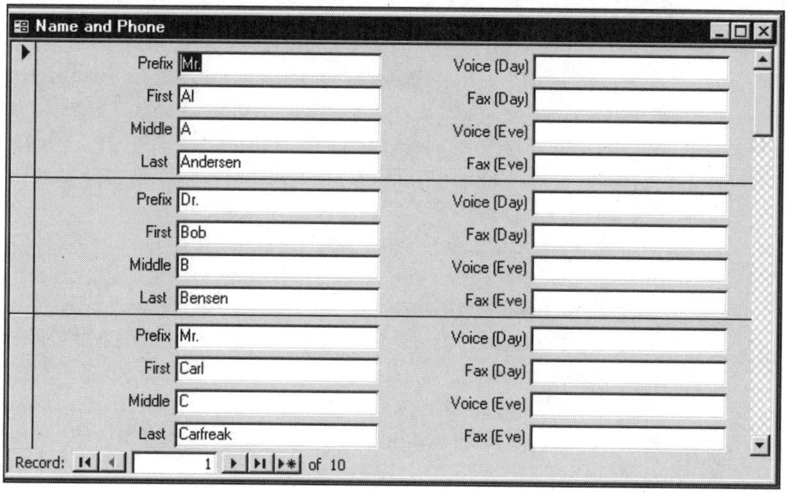

A continuous
form shows
information
for more than
one record
at a time
Figure 5-3.

be confused with *modal* windows, which appear on top of the calling window
and must be closed before you can return to the calling window. For
example, the Print window in Windows applications is modal, since you
must close it before you can perform another task with that application.

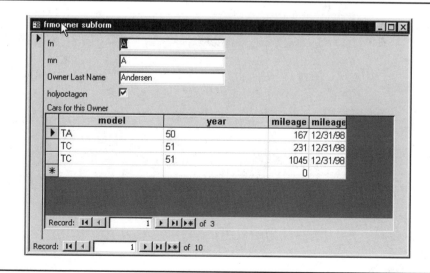

A sub form
can be used
to display
child records
for a single
parent record
Figure 5-4.

5

Form Controls

Access comes with about a dozen native controls that can be placed on a form. In addition, you can obtain more controls, called ActiveX controls, which provide additional or customized capabilities beyond the native Access set, from third-party vendors or from other applications.

Simple Controls

Simple controls are those that sit on a form to present a particular appearance for users. These include labels, lines, rectangles, and images. Labels place static text on a form—such as the caption for a control that will contain data. Lines and rectangles are often used to break a form into multiple areas such as logical groups of controls, or to provide clues for users on how to follow along—much like ruled paper lets users' eyes track better. Images, of course, are used to display images, such as logos or other visual aids. See Figure 5-5.

Data-Aware Controls

Data-aware controls are those that can be bound to fields in your table. Thus, they are used to display and allow editing of data from the database. See Figure 5-6.

Text Box   The most common data-aware control is a *text box*—and you're already familiar with these. It's used to display and edit data of a fixed length.

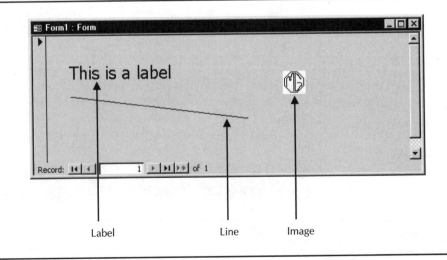

A form with label, line, rectangle, and image controls

Figure 5-5.

Label   Line   Image

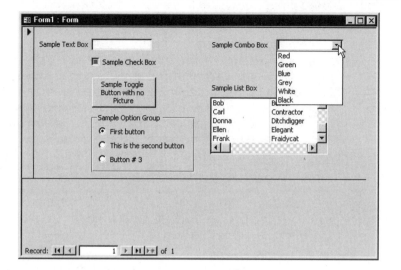

A form with text box, check box, toggle button, option group, combo box, and list box controls

Figure 5-6.

5

It's usually tied to a Text or Numeric field in a table, but can also be used to enter data that is used elsewhere, such as the user name or the heading of a report. You can make a text box several lines high to allow long strings to be entered.

Check Box   A *check box* has two purposes. The first is to present the contents of a Yes/No data field. The caption of the check box should reflect explicitly what a checked value indicates. The other purpose is to set a flag that is used later, but such that the value that the flag represents isn't stored in a table. For example, suppose your application imports a data file from another application on a regular basis. You may want a warning to be displayed for some users if invalid data is imported, so they can take an appropriate action. However, other users may be experienced enough that they won't want to or need to see the warning. You could place a check box entitled "Display Warning for Invalid Data" on the data import form, and make the default checked, so that experienced users could simply uncheck the box.

Option Button Group   An *option button group* is a collection of two or more option buttons and is used to present a small, fixed number of choices to the user, only one of which can be selected at a time. Formerly known as "radio buttons" because they worked like the old-style car-radio buttons where pushing in one button would automatically force out another button, option button groups have a practical limit in terms of the maximum number of allowable choices.

You obviously wouldn't use a single option button—since most users wouldn't know how to deselect it, and because a check box would be a more appropriate choice. When using an option group, be sure to provide enough choices for all possible situations. For example, suppose you were tracking which season a certain road rally was held. You'd need four option buttons in your option group, right? What if an event's date were going to be changed, but you didn't know the new date? You couldn't simply decide not to check an option button, since one might have already been selected for the original date. You'd need a fifth option button for "Unknown."

Toggle Button   You can think of a *toggle button* as a check box that uses a picture instead of a box with a check in it. For example, in the Owner table, the Holy Octagon field contains a Yes/No value that indicates whether the Owner has received the Holy Octagon, a lifetime achievement award that was invented for the purpose of having a logical field in this table. Either an Owner has received this honor or he or she hasn't, and once it's received it's never lost. Sort of like being President of the United States—you get Secret Service protection for the rest of your life. It would be *so* boring to simply have a check box indicating whether this great honor has been conferred upon an Owner—instead, let's use a picture on top of a button. By binding the button to the Yes/No field, you make the button appear to be "pressed in" when the field contains a Yes and not depressed when the field contains a No value.

Combo Box   A *combo box* is a rectangular control with an arrow on the right side that, when clicked, opens to display a series of choices. Once it's open, you can use the mouse or the scroll bar to locate the desired choice. Alternatively, you can simply type the first few characters, because a combo has incremental search behavior. Thus, if you wanted to search for Smyth but didn't want to let your hands leave the keyboard, press the SPACEBAR to pop open the combo box, and then type S, M, and Y. The highlight will jump down to the first S entry, then to the first SM entry, and then to the first SMY entry. Similar in purpose to an option group, a combo box allows you to select one of a group of choices. However, since the list of choices drops down, you can economically include more choices than by use of an option group, which takes up a lot of real estate on the form.

A combo box has an additional feature: it not only allows the selection of an existing entry in the list, but also allows entry of a new choice, just as would be done with a text box.

List Box   A *list box* is used to present a predetermined set of choices for the user to select from, or to display a set of multiple values that are all allowable values. A combo box is a good choice to display the value of a field when there's a single choice. For example, if you wanted to display which month of the year an automobile's license needs to be renewed, you could use a combo box and let the user pick one of the 12 months. What if the automobile's license needs to be renewed more than once a year? An obnoxious requirement, but that's what the licensing bureau is for, isn't it? You would want the user to be able to display more than one choice. A list box comes into play here rather nicely. You could show all the allowable choices in a list box.

A second example would be to allow the user to select a value from a large list—like using a combo box, but with more functionality. A combo box is somewhat limited in terms of size and usability—a list box can display a range of choices, making it easier for users to zero in on the desired choice. A list box is often used on a separate form—a pop-up form—for quick selection from a large number of values.

5

Object Frame   There are two types of object frames—*bound* and *unbound*. These are used to display OLE objects that are (bound) or are not (unbound) stored in an Access database.

Action Controls

Action controls have nothing to do with data—they are used to manipulate the form or to provide the user with some sort of mechanism to perform an action. See Figure 5-7.

Command button

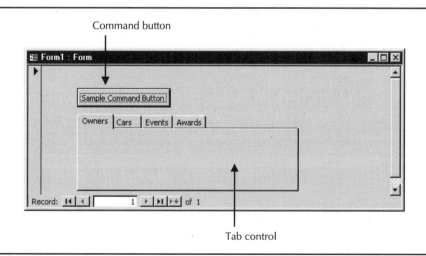

A form with command button and tab control (page frame) controls

Figure 5-7.

Tab control

Command Button A *command button* is used to allow the user to initiate an action. This action could be as simple as calling another form or letting the user close the form, or it could execute a process such as an end-of-month posting routine or printing a report.

Page Break Remember those multiple-page forms? How do you determine where one page ends and another begins? You do it by inserting a *page break control* at the desired location. Again, there's no data tied in to this control; it just manipulates the behavior of the form.

Tab Control One of the first things I said about Access is that there's rarely just a single way to do something. When you are faced with more data than will fit on a single form, you have the option of using a multiple-page form or a pop-up form. But your options don't end there. A *tab control* (also known as a *page frame*) provides another way to do so. It provides multiple sets of controls on a single form instead of creating multiple forms. Each set of controls is placed on a separate page with a tab (like a file folder) sticking up on the top, and the pages are placed on top of one another, much like a stack of folders with offset tabs. Selecting a tab displays that page.

Sub Form The *sub form control,* like the page break control, is used to delineate a separate area on the form. In this case, it's used to create a sub form on the form.

There isn't a hard line between these categories. For example, while a check box can be bound to a Yes/No field, it can also be used to indicate a status or used as a flag for later processing. When printing a report, you may choose to view the report on the screen before sending it to the printer. In this case, a check box could be used as an optional "View Before Print" control on the report setup form. However, it should not be used for directly initiating an action—that, again, is the domain of the command button.

Using a Form

Before getting into the design and creation of a form, it's a good idea to learn how to use an existing form. You wouldn't expect to take driving lessons if you'd never been in an automobile, right?

Select the Forms item in the left pane of the Database window to display the existing forms in the database. Highlight a form in the right pane, and double-click the name, press ENTER, or select the Open toolbar button.

Navigating in a Form

The *navigation bar* in the bottom of the form operates like it does in a datasheet. The buttons, from left to right, allow you to move to the first record in the table, to the previous record, to the next record, and to the last record in the table. The last button on the right, with the asterisk, still acts as an "add" button; it adds a record to the table and displays that record in the form—with empty values in all fields (except for fields that have default values). You can also use the record number box in the navigation bar to move from one record to another.

Moving around inside a record in the form works as expected—TAB and SHIFT-TAB move from field to field, and the cursor keys move the cursor within a field. The CTRL-TAB and CTRL-SHIFT-TAB key combinations move from the main form to a sub form, and the arrow keys you use in a datasheet are used in the same way in a continuous form. Note that you can have a second navigation bar in the sub form, but that can get pretty confusing, so avoid it unless really necessary.

5

Deleting Records

Deleting records isn't quite as instantaneously obvious as editing or adding a record:

1. Select the record you want to delete so that it's visible in the form and so the row selector (the gray bar on the left side of the form) is selected. If you don't select the row selector before pressing DEL, you may end up just deleting the contents of the control that the cursor is currently in.

2. Delete it either by pressing DEL or by selecting Edit | Delete. You will be asked to confirm your deletion in either case. Once the record is deleted, the form will display the next record in the table, unless you were on the last record, in which case the form will display the previous record (which is, naturally, now the last record).

Keyboard Shortcuts

In the olden days, data entry was easy. A clerk would plunk his or her fingers on the keyboard and not pick them up except for turning to the next page to enter. Now, with mouse-enabled, windowing GUIs that have all sorts of fancy graphical controls, it may seem impossible to provide a data-entry form that conforms to the Windows User Interface Guidelines, makes best use of each control, and still allows for rapid data entry. You can use keyboard shortcuts to move around on a form and to enter data quickly. With just a few minutes of practice, most of these can become second nature to even a moderately skilled typist. See Tables 5-1 and 5-2.

Keypress	Action
TAB	Moves to the next field
SHIFT-TAB	Moves to the previous field
HOME	Moves to the first control
END	Moves to the last control
UP ARROW	Moves to the current control of the previous record
DOWN ARROW	Moves to the current control of the next record
CTRL-UP ARROW	Moves to the current control of the first record
CTRL-DOWN ARROW	Moves to the current control of the last record
CTRL-HOME	Moves to the first control of the first record
CTRL-END	Moves to the last control of the last record
CTRL-TAB	Moves to the next field if no sub form is on the form; moves to the next field in the main form if you're on a sub form and a field is selected; moves to the first field in the next main record if you're on a sub form and the sub form is the last control on the form; cycles among tabs on a sub form's tab control
CTRL-SHIFT-TAB	Essentially the opposite behavior of CTRL-TAB; moves to the previous field if no sub form is on the form; moves to the previous field in the main form if you're on a sub form and a field is selected; moves to the last field in the previous main record if you're on a sub form and the sub form is the first control on the form; cycles among tabs on a sub form's tab control
CTRL-SHIFT-HOME	Moves to the first control in the main form
F5	Moves to the record number box in the navigation control

Basic Form
Keyboard
Shortcuts

Table 5-1.

Keypress	Action
F4 (and ALT-DOWN ARROW)	Opens a combo or list box
DOWN ARROW	Moves down one line
UP ARROW	Moves up one line
PGDN	Moves down to the next page of lines, with the last line in the previous page now becoming the first line in the current page
PGUP	Moves up to the previous page of lines, with the first line in the previous page now becoming the last line in the current page
TAB	Moves focus to the next control on the page

Combo and
List Box
Keyboard
Shortcuts
Table 5-2.

5

User Interface Design Fundamentals

Designing forms often seems to be the pinnacle of creative endeavor in software development. It's both an intellectual exercise and a visual puzzle, and the results are immediately apparent and rewarding. However, nowhere else in the application is there as great a risk of messing it up. You can hide a mistake in designing your data structures through additional programming or other chicanery. But a poor user-interface design will create problems both for the programmer, who has to figure out how to tie the data structures to the visual implementation, and for the users, who now have to go through agony every time they use the form. In fact, stories of poor user-interface design are so widespread that my most popular conference session is titled "User Hostile Interfaces," and contains dozens of real-life examples of forms and messages that immediately prompt the question, "What *were* the programmers thinking when they put that one together?"

As a result, it's a good idea to review some basic user interface design practices that you should follow as you design the interface for your application.

Make It Obvious

In the bad old days and even today, computers and software enjoy a well-deserved reputation for being hard to use. Interfaces were hard to program, so the "less is better" adage took hold and resulted in screens that were downright hostile.

Imagine a screen that simply said, "Enter sales code" and nothing more. If you entered an invalid code, you'd likely be greeted with a response about "invalid entry" and be asked to correct your entry. With today's advanced user interface capabilities, you can easily put together an interface that is obvious about how to use it. The same sales code request could be presented with a drop-down list of allowable codes, or at least a validation that provided a pick list of valid codes should the entered code be bad.

To some extent, the old style of software was reasonably good at preventing users from making obvious mistakes. Systems were procedural—they only allowed users to take one action, and then another, and then a third. These days, it's actually easier to design a screen that is hard to use because there's so much to choose from. It's not clear what to do first, or what effect one action will have compared with another action.

Make sure that your interface indicates which actions are good ideas or which are allowable. For example, suppose you have Save and Undo buttons on the form. These should be dimmed until a change is made to the data. Then the two buttons should be enabled. More strictly, the Add and Delete buttons should be disabled until either the current record has been saved or the changes have been abandoned.

Alternatively, you could allow users to choose the Add button, but then warn them that the current record has unsaved changes—and ask them if they want to save their changes before adding another record.

These ideas are known as *visual clues,* and it's important to be aware of them and to employ them appropriately. The rule of thumb I follow when designing application interfaces is that a new user to the system should be able to operate it without reading the documentation. By "operate" I mean that they should be able to perform the tasks without doing something out of order or initiating an incorrect or dangerous action. They may perform a task that is inappropriate for the business—such as entering a zero price for an item or specifying Surface Delivery overseas for perishable goods; but these aren't the fault of the interface—they're the fault of the business rules (programming code) used in the application. Users shouldn't be able to post an order that's incomplete, or to look at the detail screen if there are no details yet.

Warn the User in Advance

Many users still think that there is a particular button or sequence of keystrokes on their PCs that will launch nuclear missiles and shut down the power grid. So they're often timid about performing unknown actions. And when they hear of a coworker who accidentally deleted the entire year's worth of invoices because the system didn't warn them, you can understand their fear. You can do your part by telling users in advance what's going to happen before they initiate an action. Imagine a menu option that says "Delete" but with no explanation. By picking that option, the user suddenly sees a progress meter display on the screen as every customer in the system is removed. Better to provide a message: "About to delete the entire customer file. Do you wish to continue? Press Yes to Delete or No to abandon the delete operation."

Dangerous actions are not the only ones meriting a warning. What about those that are going to take a long time? Don't let users choose Print only to find that it's a 40-minute calculation and a 20-minute print job. Give them a dialog box that indicates that this is a time-consuming operation. Users may have expected to be able to print simply the current page, instead of the entire five-year history.

5

Let the User Escape

There are two parts to this rule. First, always allow a way out if the users were to pick a choice mistakenly. In the earlier examples, let them click "No, don't delete" so they can reconsider their intent. Let them abort the printing request before starting it. The only message with a lone OK button that a user should see is one of information—and the OK button indicates that they have finished reading the message.

Second, allow users to abort a process and to easily restart it. For example, they're in the middle of a print job, and someone else needs the printer for an emergency. Or the posting process is partway done, and then someone realizes that they forgot to enter all the credits for the month. Or the quarterly import of new data from the mailing house is being run, and the phone rings—a new data-entry clerk at the mailing house submitted this quarter's data in the wrong format, and the names and addresses were interchanged. If at all possible, processes should be able to be stopped, and then either restarted from the place they were stopped (you don't want to print the first 760 pages again) or rerun from scratch (the quarterly import needs to be run from record 1).

Protect the User when Appropriate

Don't let the user do something stupid if you can prevent it. This is kind of the pessimistic version of the first rule about making actions obvious. At the same time that you're making obvious that an action is the next choice, or one of the next choices, make sure users can't do things they shouldn't, and warn them if they can take actions that could be dangerous. But remember, there's a point of diminishing returns—we've all heard the line "make something idiot proof and only an idiot will use it."

Don't Use Jargon

Finally, as you become more comfortable with the internals of a system, you will slip into the trap of using terminology that to you seems basic, but that really isn't obvious to others. I'm referring to both technical jargon and business jargon. It's good to keep in mind that terminology that's comfortable to you may not be for your users.

Use Controls as Designed

One of my pet peeves is a control that is abused in an application. As I described earlier, each control has a purpose for which it was intended. Use it for that purpose, but not for others. One of the more glaring errors I remember was when a series of check boxes actually launched other forms.

Think about this for a second. The check box had a caption of "Fields." When you selected the check box, the Field Picker dialog box appeared, from which you were to pick certain fields (for placement on a report or a screen). Suppose you select this check box, and the Field Picker dialog box appears. You select a few fields, and then click OK. What happens next? Is the check box now checked? What if you clicked Cancel instead of OK? Would the check box be checked then? And what if, after the check box had been checked (whatever you had to do to make that happen), you clicked the check box again? What are you expecting to see in the Field Picker dialog box now? And just like before, what would happen if you clicked OK or Cancel? It's completely unclear what conditions will cause the check box to stay checked and which will uncheck it. A better solution would have been to have a command button that displayed the Field Picker dialog box, and to have the check box be read-only and indicate whether fields had been custom picked in the Field Picker dialog box.

Another example is a simple label control. Many programming tools have a "click" event for a label control, so that you can write code that will cause something to occur when you click the label. Excuse me? I thought that command buttons were invented to fill this need. It's a completely inappropriate use of the label control.

Be Considerate of Users with Limited Capabilities

Just because your vision is 20/20, you have terrific eye-hand coordination, and you have the latest screamer of a machine, doesn't mean your users enjoy the same circumstances. You may have users who are color blind or otherwise visually impaired (have you noticed that the displays from Microsoft are getting bigger as their programmers are getting older?). Users may not have full use of both hands, which would make the use of a keyboard (or the mouse) difficult. And you may have users with slow reflexes—who can't react to an action as quickly as the program requires. When you boot Windows NT, you have 30 seconds to choose a different display. You don't want to give a user too little time to perform an action.

We're often spoiled by the rich use of colors in day-to-day life. Old-timers may remember when color monitors were a luxury that not every PC user had. Now that color is standard, video cards provide a dazzling array of choices, and you have minute control over the color of every object on your form, why do most commercial packages you use come in three colors: white, gray, and black? This is because of increased awareness of those whose vision doesn't handle a complete spectrum of colors. Something like 10 to 20 percent of the population is color blind in at least some spectrum (and to see some programmers dress, you may think you know which profession the majority of that 10 to 20 percent has chosen).

5

Thus, use color sparingly, or at least judiciously. It should be included as an aid to the use of a form—not as the only distinguishing characteristic. For example, telling the user to pick the red button doesn't help the user who can't tell which button is red and which is green. Better to tell the user to click the red button labeled "Cancel." Furthermore, provide keyboard equivalents for mouse actions—both for those who find the use of a mouse difficult, and for those unfortunate souls whose mouse has gone bad 10 minutes before an important meeting or presentation.

Creating a Form

Start a new form as follows:

1. Select the Forms item in the left pane of the Database window.

2. Choose the Create Form In Design View item in the right pane. An empty Form Design window will appear, as well as a couple of new toolbars—the

Toolbox and the Form Design toolbar, as shown in Figure 5-8. The basic process involves placing controls on the form, and then setting properties of the form and those controls so that the form and controls behave as you want.

The Toolbox contains buttons for each of the controls discussed earlier; if you forget which is which, you can float your mouse pointer over the button until the ToolTip displays. To place a control on the form:

1. Click the control of interest (say, the text box control) in the Toolbox, and then move the mouse to the Form Design window.

2. Click the mouse where you want the upper-left corner of the text box to appear.

You'll note that more came along for the ride than you might have originally expected: a matching label control has been placed on the form to the left of the text box. You'll also note the phrase "Unbound" in the text box, indicating that this text box isn't tied to a field in a table. If you run this form right now (you can select the View button from the Form Design toolbar), you'll see a spectacularly uninteresting form—one with a label and an empty text box. At the bottom of the form, the navigation bar will

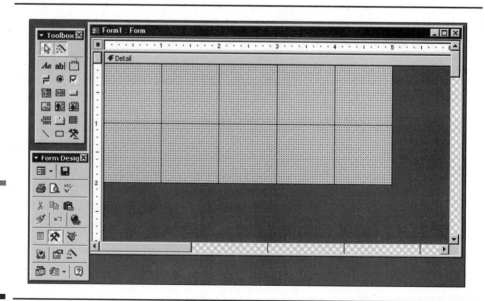

The Access
Form Design
window and
toolbar, and
Toolbox

Figure 5-8.

indicate you're on record 1 of 1. Furthermore, the navigation buttons are disabled—you can't add a new record—because you're not tied to a table.

NOTE: To run a form, you have several options. One that's often overlooked is the Form Design window's context menu. Right-click in the Form Design window but outside the form area itself, and then select Form View from the context menu. The form will run. To change back to Design view, right-click anywhere in the form and select Form Design from the context menu.

To bind the control to the table, right-click the control and select Properties from the context menu. If you drop down the control source property, you'll see that there are no available options. You can use the ellipses button next to the control source property drop-down list to open the Expression Builder. Eventually, you'll be able to get at the list of tables and the fields in the table you want, but that's a lot of work.

5

Better to tell this form that you want to work with a particular table, and then the fields in that table will be available in the drop-down lists for all the controls you place on the form. To do so,

1. Right-click in the Form Design window (again, outside the design surface itself) and select Properties. The Form dialog box will appear.
2. Select the Data tab, and you'll see the first property in the list is Record Source. This tells the form where to get data—and you'll be able to choose from tables and queries that are contained in the database. If you open the Record Source drop-down list, you'll see a list of tables and queries, as shown next. Select tblOwner and close the dialog box.

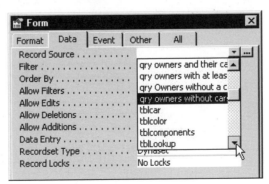

Now when you modify the properties of the text box in the form, the Control Source property drop-down list will be populated from the tblOwner table. Select, say, FN (the First Name field), and close the text box Properties dialog box. You'll notice, however, that the caption that was created along with the text box has not changed. You'll need to modify the properties of the label control separately. To do so, right-click the label, select the Properties menu command, and change the Caption property to "First Name."

IN DEPTH

Changing the Appearance and Other Attributes of Controls

After you create a few controls on a form, you're probably going to be unhappy with the way the form looks. You might want to change the size, alignment, or other control attributes.

First, to select a control so that you can manipulate it, click it so that the eight sizing handles appear at each corner and in the center of each side. If some controls are already selected, you can deselect all of them by clicking in an empty area of the form. Once these sizing handles appear, you can move the entire control to a new position on the form by moving the mouse over the control so that a hand with a thumb and four fingers appears, as shown here, and then clicking.

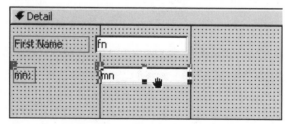

You'll notice that moving a control also brings the label along for the ride. If you want to move the control independently of its label, notice that the upper-left sizing handle of the control is larger than the other sizing handles. Moving the mouse pointer over that sizing handle will turn the mouse pointer into a hand with a thumb and forefinger sticking out (the other three fingers are tucked into the palm), as shown here:

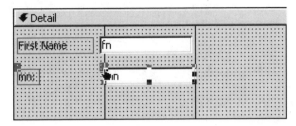

Click and drag using that sizing button, and the control will move independently of the label. If you simply want to resize a control, position the mouse pointer over one of the sizing handles so that the pointer turns into a double-headed arrow, as shown next. Click, and drag in the desired direction of resizing. You'll want to resize controls to accommodate differing lengths.

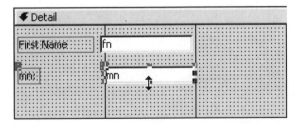

You can also delete a label control from its associated control by selecting it and pressing DEL. If you accidentally delete a label control, you can add another one to the form with the Label Control button in the Toolbox.

5

After you change the record source of a form, you'll see that a field list window will display. (If it doesn't, you can open it by selecting View | Field or by selecting the Field List button on the Form Design toolbar.) If you're familiar with other Form Design tools (or if you read ahead in the book), you're probably thinking that dragging a field name from the field list window to the form will automatically create a text box control that is bound to that field—and you'd be right. Furthermore, the label control that comes with the text box has as its caption the caption property of the field in that table, just as the caption shows up as the column heading in a datasheet. As you drag the field name, the mouse pointer icon changes to a rectangular shape, shown in the following illustration, as in other operations in which you drag a field name to a design surface.

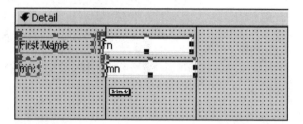

Now that you have a control bound to data, it's time to run your form again. As the form changes to Form view, notice the navigation buttons at the bottom of the form make sense—you can move back and forth through the table, add records, and perform other operations as discussed earlier in this chapter.

IN DEPTH

Arranging Controls on a Form

Being able to move and resize is only half the battle. One of the biggest hassles is the alignment of controls so they are properly arranged on a form. Different people have different tastes; I prefer to have the data-aware controls aligned on the left edge, and then have their corresponding labels aligned on the right edge. This way, labels are close to their data, regardless of how long the label is. If you right-align the label, you can end up with a very long label on one row keeping a very short label away from its control.

Access gives you several types of tools to make alignment easier. The first is the Snap To Grid setting that can be toggled on and off through Format | Snap To Grid. By selecting Snap To Grid, you can have Access

5

align each control with the grid shown on the screen. (If the grid isn't shown on the form, select View | Grid.) As you move controls on a form, they will jerk toward one of the gridlines—so you don't have to make minute adjustments manually.

The second tool consists of the Align commands in the Format menu. You can align the edges of multiple controls by selecting multiple controls and then executing Format | Align. You can choose to align the top, bottom, left, or right edge of a series of controls. The menu bars each come with icons so you can tell quickly what the end result will be. (I've created my own toolbar that contains menu options for each of these commands so I don't have to navigate through several menus to reach them.)

The third tool is to align text inside a label. While you can right-align a series of label controls, you'll see that the text in the labels may still not be aligned as desired. For example, if the caption is noticeably narrower than the label control itself, the caption will still not appear to be aligned to the right. To align the text within the label control, select the control (or multiple label controls if you like), and open the Properties dialog box (by right-clicking and selecting Properties from the context menu). The caption for the Properties dialog box will be Multiple Selection—meaning that the value for the property you're about to set will apply to multiple controls. Select the Format tab, find the Text Align property near the bottom of the list, and change it to Right (or whatever you want). Close the dialog box and you'll see that the text is aligned inside the label controls as you specified.

Form Appearance and Properties

Now that you've got a basic comfort level with building a form, it's time to dig into properties of the form that you can use to control behavior and operation. First, while in Design view, you'll see a Detail bar across the top of the form's design area. If you want to add information that doesn't change as you move from one record to the next on the form, you can add a header or footer. To do so, select View | Page Header/Footer or View | Form

Header/Footer. (You're probably going to want to use Form Header/Footer unless you're creating multipage forms.) Once you've selected the command, you'll see two more bars across the form. If you only want one or the other, you can close the other area by placing your cursor at the bottom edge of the area and dragging up so the area disappears. See Figure 5-9.

Once you have created a header or footer, you can place static text, images, or even controls in the area. You may want to add command buttons or other action controls to help the user.

If you right-click in the Form Design window (but not in the form itself) to display the context menu and then select Properties, you'll see billions and billions of properties (well, about 80) in the resulting Properties window. See Figure 5-10. By the way, you can resize the Properties window—I usually drag the bottom edge to the bottom of the screen so that I can see as many properties as possible. The term "properties" is actually a misleading term, since both properties and events are displayed in this window. You can choose to see just certain groups of properties by selecting the appropriate tab, or to see everything available to you by selecting the All tab.

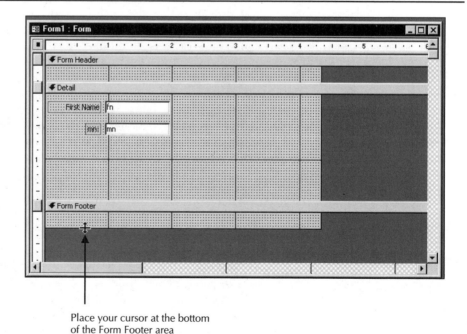

After you drag the mouse up, the Form Footer area disappears and no footer will appear on the form during run time

Figure 5-9.

Place your cursor at the bottom of the Form Footer area

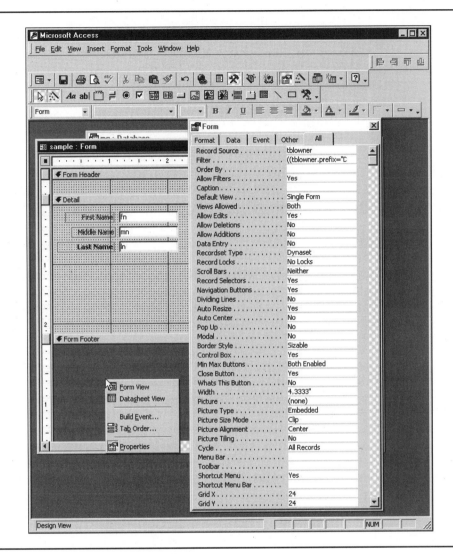

Right-click in the Form Design window but not in the form in order to display the Form Properties window
Figure 5-10.

A lot of these properties and events are irrelevant for now, but you can get a rough idea of them by selecting them and seeing their descriptions in the status bar. There are a few that you might find useful right away.

The Caption property is the string of text that displays in the title window of the form—you're going to want to specify a caption that describes what the

5

form does. You can control whether the user can add, edit, or delete records by setting those flags on or off. For instance, if you set Allow Additions to No, you'll see the New Record button in the navigation control dimmed when you run the form.

In fact, you can control the way the form looks to a remarkably granular degree. You can turn Scroll Bars, the Record Selectors, Navigation Buttons, the Control Box (the icon to the left of the caption in the title bar), the Min Max Buttons, and the Close Button in the title bar all on or off. You know what's really cool? You can even do all this while running the form! This is a great feature to see how your form is going to look—change a property while it's running and see the results immediately.

You can also add a picture to act as the form background, and control how the picture is used in the form. You can add a custom Menu Bar or a Toolbar and specify whether the form has a Shortcut Menu Bar, and what it is. As you scroll through the list of properties, you'll see a list of events. These are used for attaching macros or programs to a particular event. For example, you can automatically run a program whenever a record is added or changed; the form is resized, closed, or receives focus; or any number of other form-wide events. As you look through this list, you'll see that you have a very fine level of control over the form's appearance and behavior.

Controls: Up Close

Now that you've got the basic idea behind creating a form, popping controls onto it, and running it, it's time for an in-depth look at some of the controls.

Labels

You can change the appearance of labels in a variety of ways. For example, you can use your own choice for font—including which font (Font Name), what size (Font Size), and whether to italicize (Font Italic) or how bold (Font Weight) to make the label. You can also draw a line around the caption with the Border Style property, choose how thick the line should be with the Border Width property, and even raise or lower the box that the caption is contained in through the Special Effect property. Of course, you can also change the color of the label and the border with the Color properties. Back Color is the background color of the box in which the label sits, and the Fore Color is the color of the text itself.

I tend to make few changes to my forms except for situations that require a special look. While it's pretty cool to doctor up a form or two and make them look just absolutely beautiful, the process becomes old after a dozen forms. And it's difficult to remember each setting you changed so that new forms you create six months later for the same application have a uniform look—and an application in which the appearance varies from form to form is simply sloppy.

Text Box

Just as with labels, you can change the general appearance of a text box—both in terms of the font's name, size, weight, and color, and in the way the text box is displayed—its border style, any special effects, and color.

However, since there's real live data showing up inside the text box, there's a whole raft of other properties. For example, you can control the Input Mask (a pattern that is used when entering data into the field), the Format (how text, numbers, dates, and times are displayed in the field), and Decimal Places (if applicable). The ControlTip Text property allows you to provide your own custom ScreenTip (or ToolTip) that displays when the mouse is positioned over the control.

5

Another group of properties controls how the cursor moves with respect to the text box. The Status Bar Text property determines what text shows up in the status bar when the cursor is in the field. The Enter Key Behavior property determines whether pressing ENTER inserts a new line in the field or performs the default behavior (defined in the Tools | Options | Keyboard screen). The Auto Tab property determines whether the cursor is moved to the next control on the form once the field is full or the last character in the Input Mask field was entered. The Tab Stop and Tab Index properties determine whether the user is allowed to tab into the control and, if so, the sequence in which the TAB key moves the cursor.

Since this control handles data, you can also control what data gets into the system. The Default Value property is the initial value that is automatically entered into the field when a new record is added. The Validation Rule and Validation Text properties control what data can be entered into the field, and what message is displayed when that rule is violated.

You can also attach code—single lines to complete programs—to a variety of events that occur during the users' interaction with the text box. For example, you can control what happens when users click the text box, when they double-click, when they press the mouse button, when they release the mouse button, or when users perform the same type of action with the keyboard. You can also attach code that runs when the text box gets focus (such as when the users tab into the text box or when they click the mouse in the text box) or when the text box loses focus.

Check Box

When you add a check box to a form, you actually get two controls for the price of one. You get the check box itself and a label, similar to the one added with a text box. The label's properties are the same as elsewhere, but the check box has several new properties. First of all, since it can be bound to data, it's got a Control Source, a Default Value, a Validation Rule, and Validation Text.

Although a check box doesn't have a font associated with it, you can still define a Special Effect and various properties that have to do with the border. You also have the same properties that have to do with cursor control, including Status Bar Text, Tab Stop and Tab Index, and Control Tip Text.

One particularly interesting capability is the Triple State property. Normally, a check box either is checked or unchecked—two values. If you set the Triple State property to Yes, however, you can cycle the value of a check box among Yes, No, and Null. As you press the SPACEBAR to toggle the check box value, it will change from enabled and checked, to enabled and unchecked, to disabled and unchecked, and then to enabled and checked again.

Option Group

An option group is much like a check box in that it can be bound to a field in a table, but can also be used to influence an action. For example, when printing a report, you may want the output to go to a preview window on the screen, go directly to the printer, or be converted to a file on disk. These three choices would ideally be presented to the user through the use of an option group that contains three buttons. But the choice that the user makes wouldn't normally be saved as data in a table (unless, of course, you were saving print choices of the user for later recall).

To add an option group to a form, the easiest way is to use the Option Group Wizard:

1. Click the Option Group button on the Toolbox toolbar and then click the form. The wizard asks you a series of questions. The first dialog box asks you to identify the captions for each option button label. See Figure 5-11.

2. Choose which option button will be the selected default, and the drop-down list is automatically populated with the choices you entered in step 1. Consider carefully the choice you make, since many users will

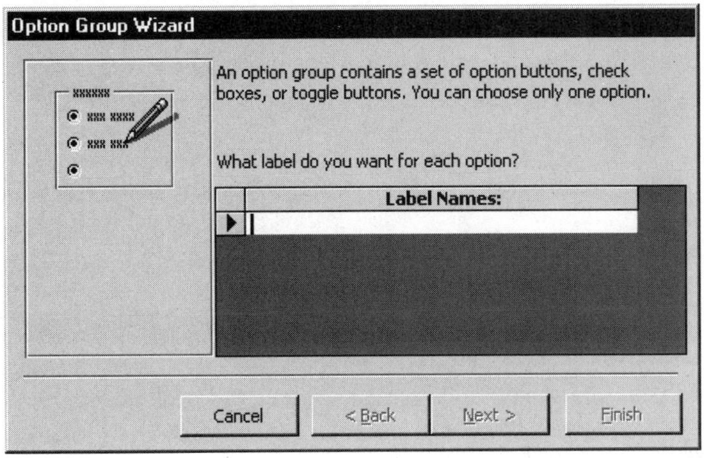

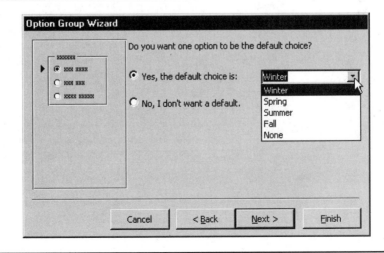

The first step in
the Option
Group Wizard
is to identify
the captions
for each
option button
Figure 5-11.

5

often want to accept the default choice rather than go to the trouble of
making a change. See Figure 5-12.

3. Match the option buttons with data values that will be placed in the
table for that field. Notice that Access provides default numeric values.
See Figure 5-13.

Select as the
default the
option button
that will be the
most popular
choice
Figure 5-12.

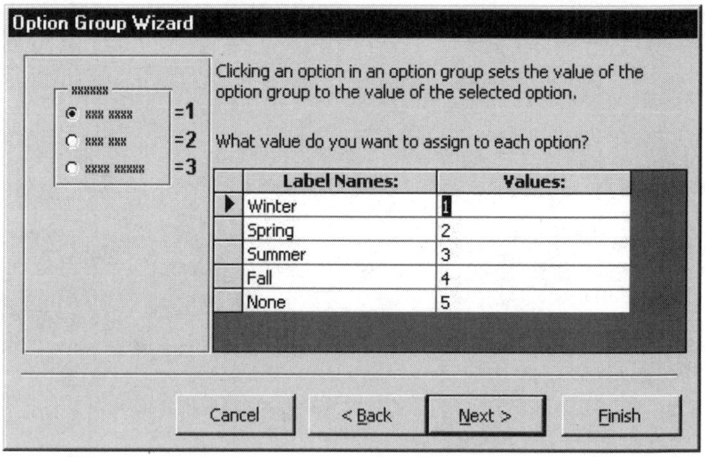

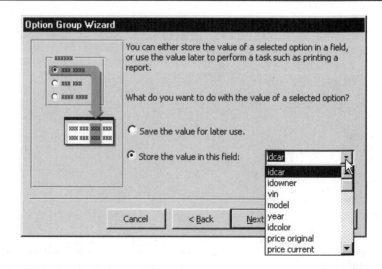

Match the
option button
captions with
data values
that will be
inserted into
the table

Figure 5-13.

4. Decide which field in the table you are going to stuff those values from step 3 into. If you designed your tables properly and named your fields appropriately, you'll easily spot the foreign key or ID field that you want to use. See Figure 5-14.

5. Set visual properties of the control. You can choose whether you want option buttons, check boxes, or toggle buttons, and what type of Special Effect you'd like the control to have.

Choose the
field into
which
the option
button data
values will
be inserted

Figure 5-14.

An option group is made up of a number of controls—the option buttons themselves, the labels next to the option buttons (like the label next to a check box), and the labeled box around the group of buttons. Each of these, of course, has its unique set of properties. The label next to an option button is much like other labels—nothing new here. Even though the option button acts much like a check box to the user, it behaves more like a display control in terms of available properties. This is because an individual option button is not bound directly to data—rather, the option group as a whole is the object that has to do with data. However, a single option button does have a Status Bar Text property, all the events related to focus, mouse clicks, and keypresses.

The option group can be selected by clicking the frame around the option group. Right-clicking then displays the Option Group: Frame Properties window (you'll know you have the right one if you have a Control Source property in the list). The Control Source property is the field that the value selected in the option group. As with other data-aware controls, you can set a Default Value (notice that the choice you made in the wizard is reflected in the Properties window), a Validation Rule, and Validation Text. An option group also has the Status Bar Text, Tab Stop, Tab Index, and Control Tip Text properties.

5

Naturally, you can also set visual properties that have to do with the Border, and add code to the Mouse and Keyboard events. However, since an option group doesn't get focus—only individual buttons do—you have to place code in each button's On Got Focus and On Lost Focus events.

Toggle Button

A toggle button is very similar to a check box, but has a few extra properties. The Caption and Picture properties allow you to specify what shows up on the button, and the Picture Type property allows you to determine whether an image file should be embedded or simply linked to externally.

Combo Box

The combo box can be an intimidating control if you start by trying to add it to a form yourself. Use the Combo Box Wizard that comes with Access to help you build the first couple of combo boxes so that you can get an idea of which properties are doing what. However, even stepping through the wizard can be confusing if you don't understand what is happening, so I'll first explain that.

A combo box is useful for displaying values from a lookup table on a form when there is always only one value in the lookup table that corresponds to a single record in the table you're working on. In other words, a combo box isn't appropriate for displaying multiple child records.

For example, in the Car table, there's a foreign key for color that links to a lookup table, Color. Each car can only have one color (for simplicity's sake—if a two-tone car comes along, that combination will be defined as a brand-new color), so each car's color foreign key points to one and only one record in the color table. This is a perfect candidate for a combo box. In contrast, you wouldn't use a combo box to display previous owners—since there may well be more than one. In this case, you'd use a list box or a sub form to display one or more child records.

The confusion with a combo box comes because the value that is displayed on the form—in the color combo box—isn't the value stored in the Car table. A combo box has properties that allow you to define which column or columns from the lookup table display in the combo box, and which column in the lookup table contains the values that are actually stored in the foreign key field of the table in question.

Launch the Combo Box Wizard by selecting the Combo Box button in the Toolbox and placing it on the form. You'll be asked what you want the combo box to do—in the case of a lookup table, you want the combo box to find its values by looking them up in a table or a query. Then you'll tell the wizard which table you want the combo box to get its values from—in this case, the Color table. The third step is to specify which columns in the lookup table you identified are to be displayed in the combo box. Be sure not to select either the primary key for the lookup table or any other extraneous

---

IN DEPTH

The Reasoning Behind Lookup Tables

You might be asking, "Why not just store the name of the color in the Car table and be done with it?" First of all, you might decide to change the name of a color—this fall the name is "Autumn Gold," but next spring the same shade might be called "Burnt Orange." Second, more than one table might use the same lookup values—by forcing users to pick from a list, you can ensure that the same spelling and values are being chosen uniformly across users and screens.

fields that won't make sense to users when they open the combo box. See Figure 5-15.

The next step is to define how the column or columns will be displayed in the combo box. You can resize columns as you have in other areas of Access. See Figure 5-16. Note that while you didn't select the primary key in the lookup table, it's still available if you uncheck the Hide check box.

Select the field in the main table in which the lookup table's primary key will be saved. This is the main table's foreign key—in the case of the Car table, the Color table's primary key, idcolor, will be saved in the idcolor field of the Car table. See Figure 5-17.

I think the wording in the wizard is confusing—it sounds like the displayed value will be saved, when it's actually the primary key value that will be saved. Finally, enter the caption for the combo box and choose Finish. I've found it useful to create a matching, if redundant, option group that also is bound to the values for the lookup table so that I can check my work with the combo box. See Figure 5-18.

5

If you open the Properties window for the combo box, you'll see many of the same properties that you've used with other controls. The new ones for a combo box are the Control Source, Row Source Type, Row Source, Column Count, Column Widths, and Bound Column properties. The Control Source

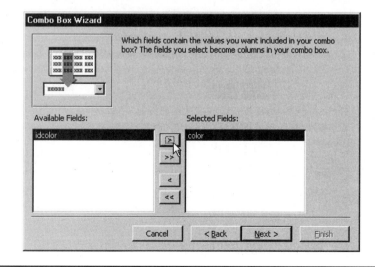

Use the mover buttons to select which fields in the lookup table are to be displayed in the combo box

Figure 5-15.

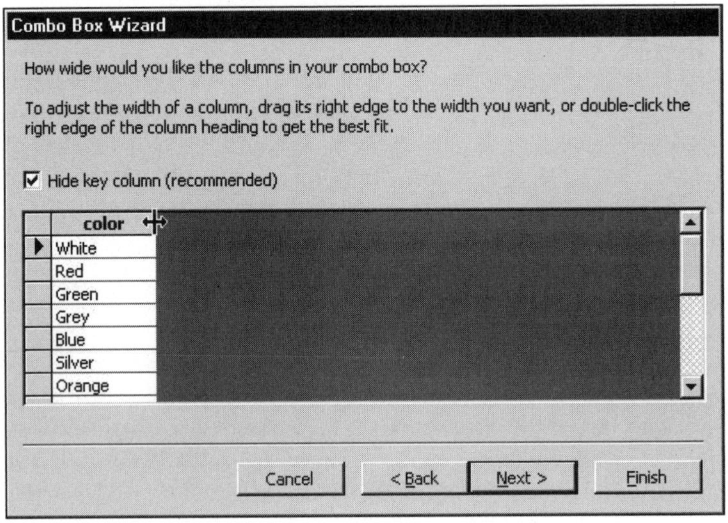

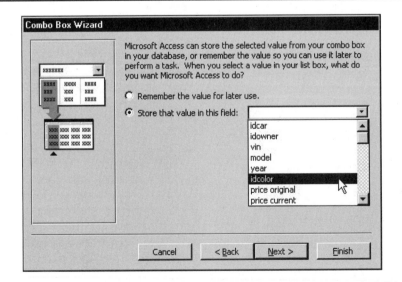

Drag the
column header
to resize a
column when
determining
how the
combo box
will display
columns

Figure 5-16.

The fields in
the main table
will be
displayed so
that you can
choose which
field will hold
the key from
the combo box

Figure 5-17.

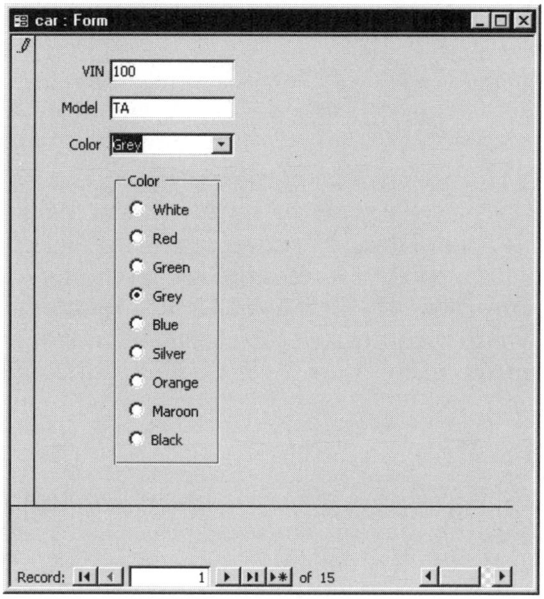

You can use a combo box and an option group that are both bound to the same field to verify how the controls are working

Figure 5-18.

is the foreign key field—the column in the main table that will hold the primary key from the lookup table. Combo boxes can be populated through several mechanisms; the mechanism selected in the wizard resulting in the choice of Table/Query. You can also fill a combo box with a set of fixed values (similar to the values you entered manually in the option group) or a list of fields from a table.

If you select Table/Query as the Row Source Type, you need to specify the Row Source—the list of columns that will populate the combo box. In the case of the wizard, it was automatically generated—the two columns, idcolor and color, were pulled using a SQL SELECT command—in essence, a programmatic version of a query.

The Column Count property describes the number of columns to display, but it's really sort of misleading. The next property, Column Widths, can act to override that—since you can specify the width of a column to be zero. In the case of the Color combo box, the width of the first column—the Color ID—is set to zero so it, in effect, doesn't display. The second column's width was set when you dragged the column header border to change the column width (in Figure 5-16).

The most critical of all these properties is the last—the Bound Column. First of all, remember that the form the combo box is residing on is reflecting data from a table, such as Cars. Also, recall that the combo box has two columns: the first is the ID and the second is the name of the color. The combo box is set up so that the first column doesn't display; only the second one does. But why is the first column even in there? Because its data is getting stuffed into the foreign key field of the Car table. The Combo Box Wizard sets several properties that bind the combo box to the underlying table, including the Row Source Type, the Row Source, the Column Widths, and the Bound Column. The strict terminology is that the first column is "bound" to the control source—the color ID field. You don't have to bind the first column— if your Row Source were to create a four-column result and the ID were the fourth column, your Bound Column would be 4, not 1.

List Box

A list box control is properly used for one of two purposes. The first is to display child records in a form (see Figure 5-19). However, an Access sub form can also display child records—but with additional functionality; so lists are not often used for this reason anymore. The second purpose is to provide the ability to select one or more items from a list for future processing. For

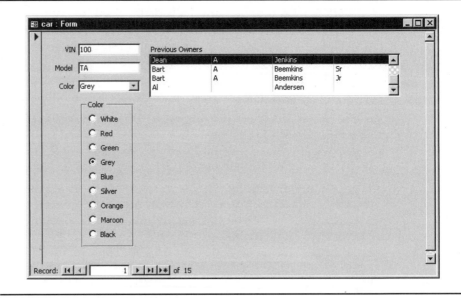

A list box can be used for displaying child records in a form, albeit with more limited functionality than a sub form

Figure 5-19.

example, suppose you want to give users the ability to search on all past and present owners of cars. You could allow them to enter part or all of a name in a text box and then choose a command button to look for that name.

However, what if the user doesn't know how the name is spelled? What if there were more than one person with the same last name, so a second field—or even a third—would need to be entered to locate the person? And what if the user wasn't sure what the first name was—"I know it's something like Ed, or Edgar, or Ervin, or maybe, oh, heck, I just know it's not Bob." By displaying a list of names, you make it easier for users to determine which name they're looking for. A list box is an excellent tool for this purpose. Furthermore, a list box can be designed so that the user can select one or more items in the list. Clicking on an entry selects it, of course. Holding down SHIFT and then selecting a second entry will select all the items in the list between the first item highlighted and the second. Furthermore, CTRL can be used to extend the selection even more. Once a range of items has been selected, press CTRL and then click a highlighted item—that item will be unselected while the rest in the range will stay highlighted. Conversely, while pressing CTRL, click another item outside the range, and that item will be selected as well. The SHIFT and CTRL keys give users precise control over which items are to be selected.

5

There are a couple of key properties to set when you create a list box for this purpose. The first that you'll probably want to use is the Column Heads property—so that the columns in the list box are each identified. Of course, if you haven't set the Caption property of a field to an English value, you'll get the field names in the header for the list box. The second property is the Multi Select property. If it's set to None, the user can only select a single item in the list box at any one time. If it's set to Simple, the user can select one or more items; but selecting a range through the use of SHIFT isn't available. If the Multi Select property is set to Extended, users can perform any type of selection.

You may be wondering how to use the results of a multiselected list box—I'll cover that in Chapter 17, when I discuss building applications.

Building Forms

I've already covered the basics of creating a form, plopping controls on it, binding those controls to data, and providing the essential navigation and maintenance functionality you'd expect in a data-entry form. Now it's time to discuss two specific types of forms: *multiple-page* forms and *continuous* forms.

Multiple-Page Forms

A multiple-page form is pretty straightforward, but requires some attention to detail. Figure 5-2 showed a multiple-page form, with the name and salutation on the first page, and the rest of the address fields and the phone number information on the second page. To create this "multiple-page" effect, all the fields were placed on a single form, and then a page break control was placed on the form where the start of the second page should occur. See Figure 5-20. While the form is running and PGDN is pressed, the controls below the page break will display on what appears to be their own page. Of course, if you were to resize the form, you could view controls on both pages if you had enough room on your monitor.

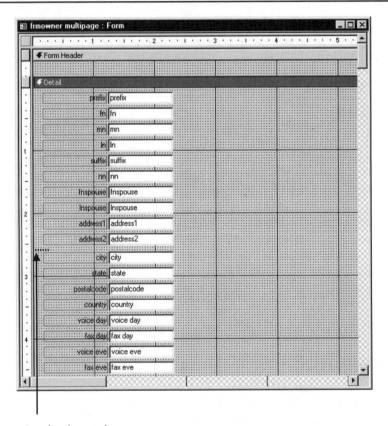

The page break control looks like a series of dots. It tells Access to place all the controls below it on a second page during run time

Figure 5-20.

Page break control

The trick to multiple-page forms is to size both pages (or, in the event of multiple-page forms with more than two pages, all pages) to be the same. For example, if the form in Design view is 6 inches tall, you'll want to place the page break at 3 inches. If you placed it at 4 inches, paging down would cause the form to appear to "jerk" as a 4-inch page displayed, and then a 2-inch page displayed, and then another 4-inch page, and so on. You probably wouldn't create pages with such a disparity in sizes, but that's even more of a reason to make sure that the pages are the same size. Having the first page be 3.06 inches tall and the second page be 2.94 inches tall will be noticeable enough to users to appear sloppy.

Continuous Forms

Creating a continuous form is actually easier than creating a multiple-page form. Just remember that the goal of a continuous form is to display more than one record on a page—almost like having a datasheet on which a single record could span more than one row. First, create a form with the fields you want to display for a record. You'll want to organize the fields (and other controls, if you're going to put combo boxes, check boxes, or whatever, on the form) so that they fit neatly within the form. Next, set the Default View property of the form to Continuous Forms.

There are a couple of other properties that you might find useful. The Cycle property can be set to All Records, Current Record, or Current Page. This property provides you with the ability to control where users can tab. Current Record means that users can tab from one field to the next only in the current record; once the focus has landed on the last control in a specific record, pressing TAB again will move focus to the first field in that record. At the other end of the spectrum is All Records, where pressing TAB will move focus from one field to the next. When the focus reaches the last field in a record, focus moves to the first field in the next record, and so on, throughout the table.

Sub Forms

Sub forms are one of the coolest mechanisms I've talked about so far. I've worked with a number of different database tools, and using Access' sub forms is by far the easiest way that I've seen to create a parent-child screen.

To put one together yourself:

1. Sketch out (either in your mind, or preferably, on paper), what you want to have display both in terms of a parent record and in terms of which

elements of that parent's child records. For example, suppose you want to see all the Cars that each Owner has. The parent table is the Owner table, and the child table is the Car table.

2. Create a form as you do normally, selecting the parent table as the Record Source, and place your parent fields on it, leaving a fair amount of space on the bottom half of the form.

3. Click the Sub Form button on the Toolbox, and position it on the form. Remember that you need to draw a box that will hold the entire sub form, as shown here:

4. Once you've placed the sub form control on your form, the Sub Form Wizard will automatically start. You can choose to use an existing form, or populate the sub form with a table or query. If you choose a table or query, you'll be asked to choose which fields you want to be on the sub form by use of mover buttons (see Figure 5-21).

5. The next step in the wizard is the most critical step—it's when you define how the records in the sub form are related to the table used as the record source in the form. In this example, the Owner table is the record source for the form, and this step in the wizard defines how the Cars in the sub form are related to the Owners table. The Sub Form Wizard will attempt to guess—and if you've named your primary and foreign key fields consistently, the guess will likely be correct. See Figure 5-22.

6. Finally, you'll be asked to name the sub form. Once you've finished with the wizard, the sub form control will be placed on the form. You'll likely want to resize the form more precisely, and perhaps modify a couple of properties before you end up with results similar to those in Figure 5-3. You may not like the results of the wizard—you can use the Link Child Fields and Link Master Fields properties to define how the sub form table

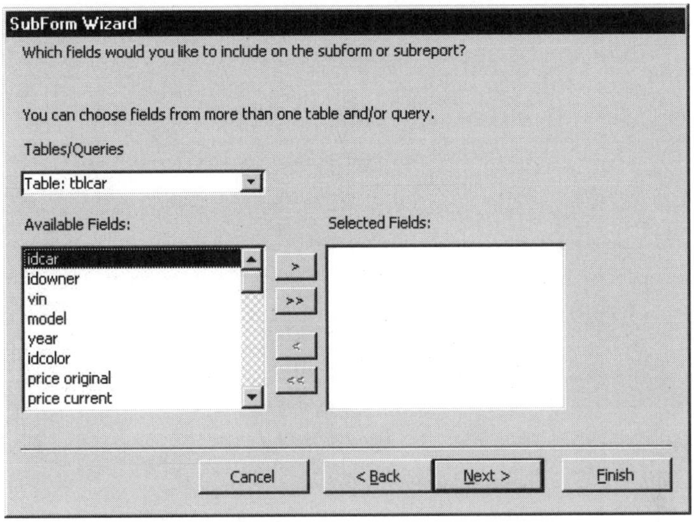

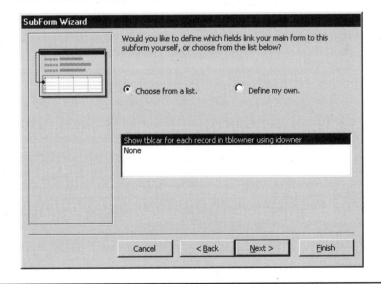

The mover buttons allow you to choose which fields will be displayed in the sub form

Figure 5-21.

is related to the form. The Link Child Fields property defines the field in the child table that is used to link to the parent table. The Link Master Fields property is the corresponding property in the parent table.

Access attempts to guess at the relation to be used to link the sub form data to the main form

Figure 5-22.

Naturally, there are a host of other properties for the sub form, such as Status Bar Text, Tab Stop and Tab Index, and Border and Special Effects, that have already been discussed. Remember also that the sub form hosts its own controls—and you can modify those controls or add new ones as you desire, just as you did with the main form.

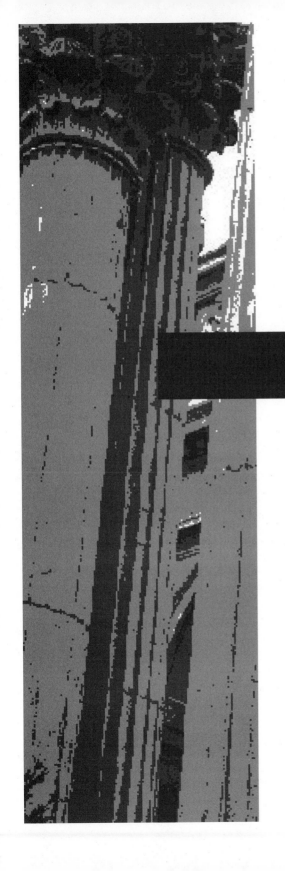

CHAPTER 6

Reports

Reports are probably the least rewarding part of an application to design and program but they are the most important part to the user. Few people are interested in jamming data into a system and never retrieving it—data-entry screens are a necessary evil in their quest for output. I've found it useful to maximize the robustness and flexibility of an application while minimizing the amount of custom design needed.

Access 2000 users are fortunate when it comes to reports, because the Access Report Writer is the most wonderful of all the database tools I've used.

Of course, the Report Writer allows you to produce simple columnar listings—hardcopy references of tables. But it also enables you to create more complex parent-child reports, similar to the form-subform forms discussed in Chapter 5, and even sophisticated multilevel reports with complex calculations and a variety of images and fonts.

You can use forms to print data, but the options available are limited. Much more worthwhile to concentrate on is the Report Writer. It's easy to use and contains a rich feature set. If you've fooled around with printing from forms, you may be wondering what advantages reports have. Here are three significant differences:

◆ Reports can display, organize, and summarize large amounts of information.

◆ Reports can display information in multiple levels—up to ten deep—and perform calculations within and across groups in a variety of ways.

◆ Reports can contain headers and footers—both for the entire report and for each level.

Before jumping into the creation of reports, let's take a look at what I mean by "reports." Traditionally, a report has been printed output—most people are familiar with those 5-inch stacks of greenbar that came from a mainframe computer. Recently, people have begun using the term "reports" and "output" interchangeably. In this sense, *output* means a report that can be directed to a variety of places: the screen, a printer or plotter, a text file, a file format for another type of program (like .XLS for Excel or .DBF for Xbase programs), or even to an HTML file formatted specifically for publishing on the Web.

Access' reports follow the traditional definition—output to the printer—and include a print preview option. Access data can be output to other file formats by use of File | Export.

Running an Existing Report

You can run an existing report "out of the box," not changing anything, or choose to tweak the various page settings before printing.

Print Preview

Running a report is as straightforward as running a query or a form:

1. Select the Report object in the left pane of the Database window.
2. Select the desired report.
3. Choose the Preview toolbar button, or right-click in the right pane and select Preview. The Print Preview window and toolbar will display. See Figure 6-1.

Print Preview is a very flexible tool. First, if you look carefully, you'll see a magnifying glass with a plus sign in it in Figure 6-1. You can toggle between a magnified view or a bird's-eye view. Clicking in the Print Preview window will enlarge the object in the window and result in the plus sign turning to a minus sign (which means that clicking again will reduce the size of the object in the window).

When the object in the window is enlarged, scroll bars appear on the sides of the Print Preview window, and you can use these to maneuver in the window. You can use the navigation bar control at the bottom of the window to move from page to page in the report, just as you would move from record to record in a form.

6

The Print Preview toolbar has a number of useful features. The first icon combines a triangle, pencil, and straightedge; clicking on it will switch the report to Design view. The second button, with the Printer icon, will send the report to print. See the next section, "Page Setup," for more information about sending a report to the printer.

The three buttons to the right of the magnifying glass will display, respectively, one, two, or multiple pages of the report in the Print Preview window. The Multiple Pages button is a little tricky—clicking on it opens a small window below the toolbar in which you can select a variety of views. Move your cursor over the various icons, and the number and arrangement of pages to be displayed will appear in the text box below the page icons, as shown here:

You can further control what shows up in the Print Preview window by selecting a Zoom factor from the combo box next to the Multiple Pages button. The Close button closes the Print Preview window. The Office Links

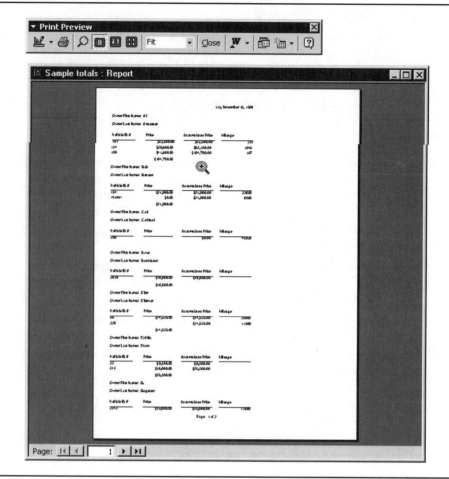

The Print
Preview
window shows
you what a
report will
look like
before printing
Figure 6-1.

button allows you to connect to Word or Excel. The Database button displays
the Database window. The last button before the Help button opens a
drop-down list you can use to create new objects.

Page Setup

Before you actually fire off a report to the printer, you may want to configure
some settings through the use of the Page Setup dialog box. Found by means
of the File menu, the Page Setup dialog box's Margins tab allows you to set
margins for the report. You can also inhibit the display of column headings
and just print the data objects by selecting the Print Data Only check box.

On the Page tab, you can choose either portrait or landscape orientation, change the size and source of paper, and even choose a different printer. The controls on the Columns tab will be discussed in "Multiple-Column Reports," later in this chapter.

Creating a Simple Report

There are a lot of similarities between creating a report and creating a form. In fact, you may occasionally find yourself mistaking the Form Design window for the Report Writer, and vice versa.

To create a brand-new report, open a database and select the Reports object in the left pane of the Database window. You'll have two options: Create Report In Design View and Create Report Using Wizard. You can walk through the Report Wizard if you like; it's straightforward and useful for creating simple types of preformatted reports—but it doesn't require any explanation in this book. Select the Create Report In Design View option, and the Report Design View window will display, as shown in Figure 6-2.

6

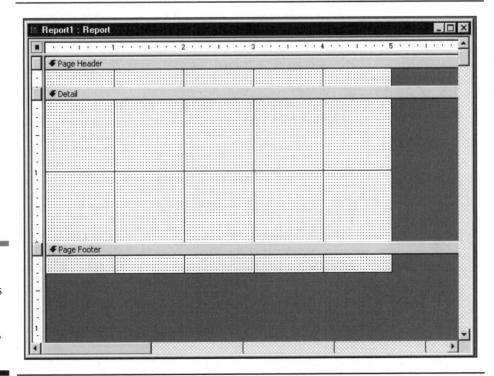

The Report Design View window looks a lot like the Form Design View window

Figure 6-2.

You'll notice the three bands, similar to the Form Design View window, and they work in a similar fashion.

Objects in the *detail band* (the area below the gray bar that is labeled "Detail") will appear once for every record in the record source of the report. This is important to remember—you can use this behavior to easily produce some fairly sophisticated reports. Objects in the *page header band* are printed once at the top of the page—this is often an ideal place for the title of the report, column headings, the date and time of the report, and the page number. Objects in the *page footer band* are also printed once for each page—at the bottom of the page. You may want to place the date, time, and the page number at the bottom of each page instead of at the top.

It's really important to understand *when* data is printed in various bands. Earlier, I said that the detail band would print the values from the current record of a table or query for each record in that table or query. This means that you could construct a query that contains the same value for a range of records, and display that same value for each record or use that value to group the records. For example, you could produce a roster of members that contains different values for each member number, but similar values for the city and state that they live in. You could even insert a value that varies according to certain conditions, and then display that varying value in the detail band.

This concept also holds true for the page header and page footer bands. If you put a field from the table or query in the page header, for example, the value will be evaluated according to which record the detail band is processing at the beginning of the page. This could be handy if you wanted to display a header that indicated where the range of records started, somewhat like the headers in a phone book.

Typically, a report draws its data from a table or query, so the first thing you'll do is set the report's record source to the table or query of interest. To do so, right-click in the Report Design View window but outside the report form itself, and select Properties from the context menu that displays.

When you open the Record Source combo box, all the tables and queries will be available to choose from, as shown next. After you select a record source, the field list window will display as well. If it doesn't, you can open the field list window from the View menu pad. Now you can drag fields from the Field list to the report form.

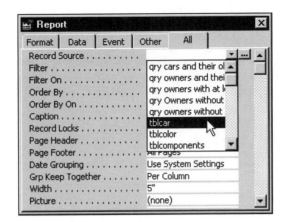

T IP: You may find that when you give tables and queries long names, you can't distinguish between them in the Record Source combo box, since only the first 15 or 20 characters are shown. You can widen the properties window simply by dragging the edge of the window (much as you would resize any other window). The property values and associated combo boxes will be resized proportionally. When you pop open the combo box, you'll be able to see the entire name.

6

Since a report isn't an interactive tool like a form is, you don't have the same variety of controls you can place on a report. Essentially, the only things available to you are labels, text boxes, and images.

When you drag a field from the Field list to a report form, the label for that field comes along for the ride, just as it does when you drag a field onto a form. It's just one more reason you'll want to make sure that the Caption property for the field in the database is set to an understandable expression. All the same mechanisms for manipulating a field—resizing, moving with and without its accompanying label, and setting display properties—work the same way as with forms.

However, given that you'll want to perform certain types of tasks over and over, you may find that some toolbar options and context menu choices will come in handier even than in the Form Design view. Normally, the Formatting toolbar will appear when you're modifying a report (it's the same one that appears with forms), as shown in Figure 6-3.

Object combo box

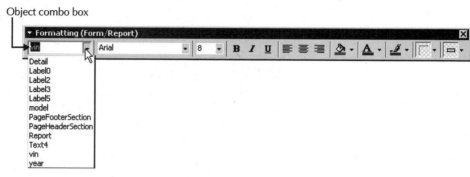

The Formatting
toolbar allows
you to set a
variety of
formatting
properties with
the click of
a button

Figure 6-3.

The Object combo box allows you to select an object in the report, and then to set formatting properties for that object. The formatting properties include Font, Font Size, Bold, Italic, Underline, Alignment (left-, center-, or right-aligned within the box), Back Color, Fore Color, Border Color, Width Of The Border Line, and Special Effect (such as Sunken, Raised, and so on).

Just as with a form, you can set properties of a field on a report, although not all the same ones are available. A couple of new ones are available only for reports. For example, report controls don't have events.

The Hide Duplicates property will inhibit the display of the control if the value is the same as the value in the previous record. This is extremely useful when you're printing a long list in which values may be repeated. For example, if you're printing a long list of cars sorted by year, you may not want to see the same year printed row after row. Instead, set the field's Hide Duplicates property to Yes, and notice that the report will only display the first instance of that field. See Figure 6-4 for an example of this effect. Remember that the report has to be ordered on that field to achieve the results you want—if you didn't sort on the year, only those records in which the year was the same as the previous record would have the year hidden.

Another great property is the Running Sum property (found on the Data tab of the Text Box properties window). When set to Yes for a numeric field, it will tally the running total from record to record. See Figure 6-5 for an example of the car price being accumulated from car to car. With other report writer tools, you have to go to some lengths to make this happen. You can choose to accumulate throughout the life of the report, or to start summing again at the start of a new group.

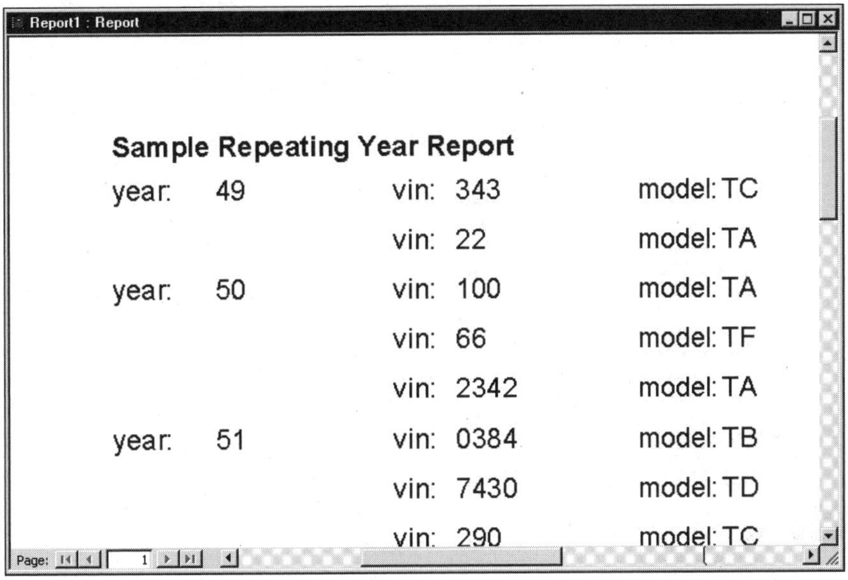

6

Setting the Hide Duplicates property to Yes for a field will cause only the first instance of that value to be displayed

Figure 6-4.

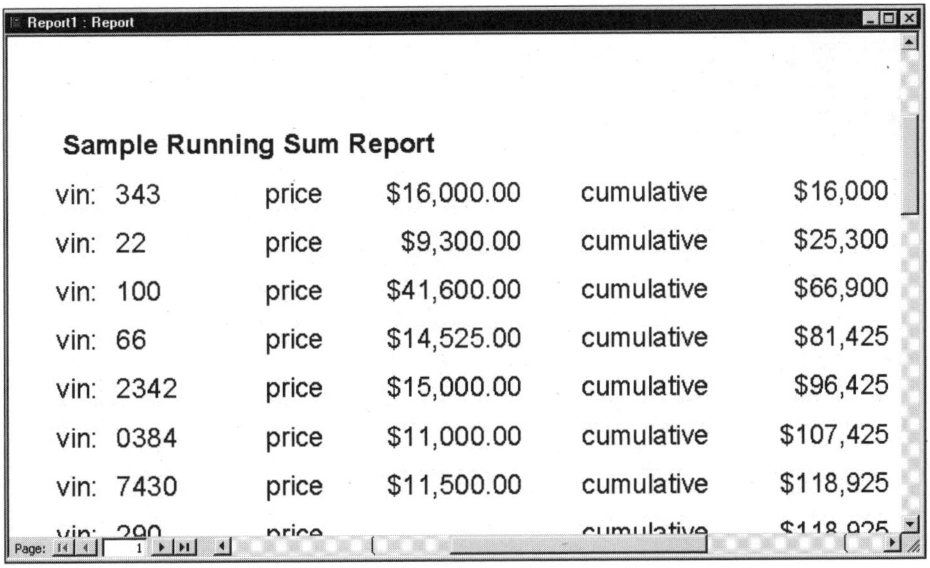

```
┌─ Report1 : Report ──────────────────────────────── _ □ X ┐
│                                                       ▲ │
│                                                         │
│       Sample Repeating Year Report                      │
│       year:    49         vin:  343       model: TC     │
│                           vin:  22        model: TA     │
│       year:    50         vin:  100       model: TA     │
│                           vin:  66        model: TF     │
│                           vin:  2342      model: TA     │
│       year:    51         vin:  0384      model: TB     │
│                           vin:  7430      model: TD     │
│                           vin:  290       model: TC   ▼ │
│ Page: |◄ ◄ |    1  ► ►| ◄                          ►    │
└─────────────────────────────────────────────────────────┘
```

The Running Sum property allows you to accumulate the sum of a numeric field from record to record

Figure 6-5.

```
┌─ Report1 : Report ──────────────────────────────── _ □ X ┐
│                                                       ▲ │
│                                                         │
│     Sample Running Sum Report                           │
│     vin:  343      price     $16,000.00   cumulative    $16,000  │
│     vin:  22       price      $9,300.00   cumulative    $25,300  │
│     vin:  100      price     $41,600.00   cumulative    $66,900  │
│     vin:  66       price     $14,525.00   cumulative    $81,425  │
│     vin:  2342     price     $15,000.00   cumulative    $96,425  │
│     vin:  0384     price     $11,000.00   cumulative   $107,425  │
│     vin:  7430     price     $11,500.00   cumulative   $118,925  │
│     vin:  290      price                  cumulative   $118,925 ▼│
│ Page: |◄ ◄ |   1  ► ►| ◄                          ►    │
└─────────────────────────────────────────────────────────┘
```

A third property that may at first seem to be a quirky ability is the Vertical property (found on the Other tab in the Text Box properties window). Setting this property to Yes will turn the values in the text box on their right side (well, OK, your right side, as you're looking at the screen or report). See Figure 6-6 for an example. This capability is handy when you have a report with many columns, each of which is very narrow. For example, suppose your report tallies make and model by state and country. Each make and model of automobile is printed across the top—but those descriptions would probably be too long to print horizontally. Vertical column heads here would enable you to fit more data onto a single page.

Labels aren't quite as interesting as text boxes—but they do have a Vertical property that isn't found in labels on forms. Images are even less interesting—the same properties from forms apply to reports.

Don't forget the Layout toolbar, either—once you've selected at least two controls on a report, the buttons become enabled and you can use them to align the controls along the left, right, top, or bottom edges of the controls.

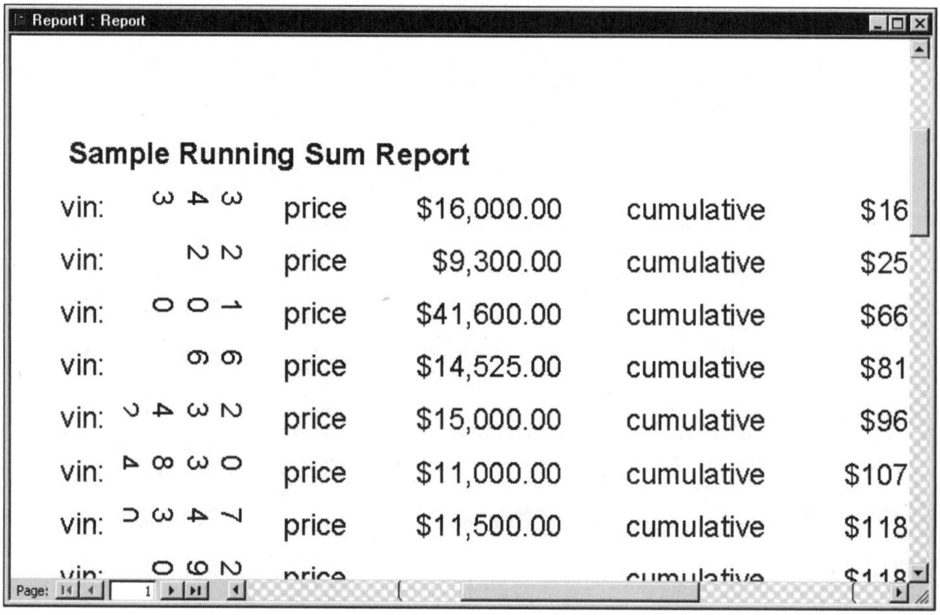

The Vertical property of text boxes and labels allows you to flip the contents of the control on its right side

Figure 6-6.

Adding a Page Header or Footer

When you create a new report, the report form automatically displays a page header and a page footer band. All you need to do is add controls (labels, text boxes, or images) to the band, and that band will print. However, what happens if the band accidentally disappears? Take heart—it's not really gone—it's just been minimized beyond recognition. Just position the mouse on the bottom of the gray Page Header/Footer separator bar so that the double-headed arrow appears, as shown here, and then drag down until the band reappears.

If they've both disappeared, you can also get them to display by opening the Report context menu (right-click in the detail band), and selecting Page Header/Footer.

6

Adding a Report Header or Footer

A report header or footer is only printed once—at the beginning or end of the report. You can think of a *report header* as a title page (kind of like the one you did for your 50-page history report in your high-school civics class), and a *report footer* as the summary for the report that would contain report totals and other ancillary information. To add one, the other, or both, right-click in the detail band of the report, and select Report Header/Footer.

Controlling the Sort Order

You can control the order in which records are displayed in a report by using the Sorting And Grouping Expression Builder. Right-click anywhere in the report form, and select Sorting And Grouping. The Sorting And Grouping dialog box will display. You can then select a field whose values will be used to order the report, as shown in Figure 6-7.

To sort on multiple fields, select additional fields in subsequent rows in the Sorting And Grouping dialog box, as shown in Figure 6-8. You can add up to ten levels of sorting, although more than four or five levels would be fairly rare. Remember that each subsequent sort field is a tiebreaker for the previous field. In the example shown in Figure 6-8, the FN (First Name) field is used to sort owners who have the same last name. Within records in which the first and last names are the same, the records will be sorted by car model, and, finally, by year.

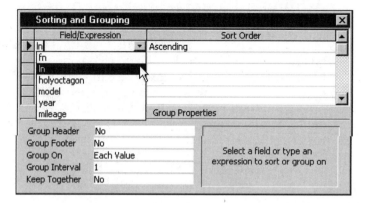

The LN field in the Field/ Expression combo box will be used to sort the report on Last Name

Figure 6-7.

Dividing a Report into Groups

As you saw in the previous example, when sorting a report, it is common to have the same information repeated on multiple lines. You can prevent the repetitive display of this information by setting the Hide Duplicates property on a specific field to Yes, but that doesn't always do the trick. For example, you might have so much information that it won't fit on a single line anyway. Suppose you wanted to show not only all the cars for each owner, but also a great deal of information about each owner. There wouldn't be enough room on a single line to display it all.

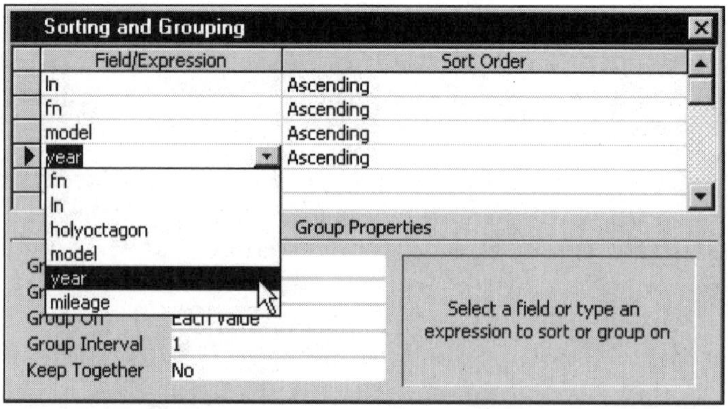

Multiple rows in the Sorting and Grouping dialog box are used to create multiple levels of sorting

Figure 6-8.

You could create a bigger detail band and arrange controls so that there were two or three rows of controls for the same record, much as some people do with a spreadsheet. But this is often unsatisfactory—since there isn't a single row of data, the columns don't line up and the result looks messy.

A better way to handle this would be to display the owner information in a separate band that would be printed just once for the list of the cars. In essence, the only data in the detail band would be the data for each car; the owner information would be printed selectively, much like a page header or footer is printed selectively—once per page.

To create a *group band,* you set additional properties in the Sorting And Grouping dialog box. Select the row in the Field/Expression combo box that contains the field that will be grouped on. In this example, that field would be the LN field (Last Name). Then set the Group Header (and, if desired, Group Footer) property to Yes, and select what expression you want to Group On. The Group On property can be set to various values, depending on what type of data populates the expression. For a text expression, you can Group On the entire expression, or just the n first characters (by selecting Prefix Characters). If you select Prefix Characters, set the Group Interval to the value n desired.

Once you've created the group band, you'll want to move the associated fields to the group band. You might also want to adjust the fields that remain in the detail band, and perhaps add new labels for those fields. (See Figure 6-9 for an example.) When you do so, those fields will only print when the value in the group expression changes. In other words, the detail band will continue to print once for every record in the record source, but the group band will only print when the Last Name changes. Obviously, that's why you would want the report sorted on the same value. Otherwise, you'd end up with a group band being printed for nearly every detail record.

6

Report Properties

As with forms and controls, various parts of a report have properties (and, in some cases, events) associated with them. I've already covered the properties for individual report controls. Let's take a look at the properties for the various bands.

Detail Band Properties

There are several useful properties that are part of the detail band. Remember that the contents of the detail band are printed once for every record, and

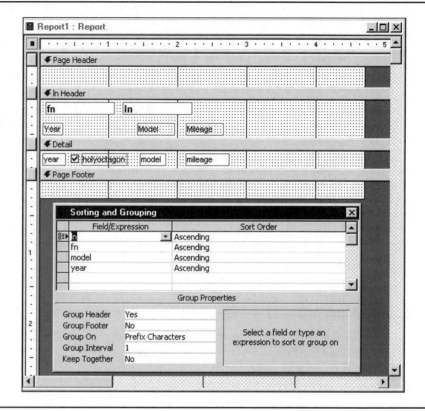

Figure 6-9.

normally the contents consist of labels and text boxes. To open the detail band properties, right-click in the detail band area (but not on top of a control). You can control when page breaks occur with respect to the contents of a detail band—by using the Force New Page property. You have four choices:

◆ To have no page breaks and let the report run from one page to the next as each page is filled with data

◆ To start a new page before a new section is started

◆ To start a new page after a section has ended

◆ To force a new page before and after a section

The second interesting detail band property is New Row Or Col, and it identifies where the section starts printing in a multiple-row or -column report. As with Force New Page, the same four choices are available.

The third new property is Keep Together. The purpose of this property is to keep the entire section on one page. You would use this to prevent the first few records of a section from printing on the bottom of one page and the last couple of records on the next page. It's most useful when just the first bit of the section would squeeze onto the bottom of the page.

These properties aren't the only cool thing about the detail band—it also has three events to which you can attach a macro or a function. The *On Format* event fires just before the section is formatted. The *On Print* event, obviously, fires just before the section is executed—printed, previewed, or sent to a file. The *On Retreat* event executes when you move to a previous page in a report.

Page Header and Page Footer Properties

6

It's easy to miss the properties window for the page header and page footer bands, because right-clicking in one of the bands when there isn't an object in it will display the Report Properties window (covered next). This makes sense—the band isn't going to print if there's nothing in it, so why would you want to set properties?

T IP: If you need to set a property or run a macro or function when an event fires in a band that contains no objects, you can place a label control in the band and set its Visible property to No.

There isn't anything particularly new or fascinating in these two bands (the properties are the same for both). Each band does have an On Format and an On Print event, so you have additional flexibility to hook into your own code throughout the report.

Report Properties

You can open the Report Properties window by right-clicking in a band that doesn't contain any objects, or by right-clicking in the area outside the report form but still in the Design View window. There are quite a few properties (including about a half-dozen events) available to the entire report.

You've already used a couple of the properties—the Record Source property drives the population of the report, for example. Others should be quite familiar by now. The value in the Caption property will display in the title bar of the report; Filter and Order By, respectively, allow you to control which records from the Record Source show up in the report and in which order they are displayed. Note that the Filter On and Order By On properties don't do exactly what they sound like. They both indicate whether the related property is on or off. Many people mistake the property name "Filter On" to mean "the value on which to filter," and the same for Order By On.

The Page Header and Page Footer properties allow you to determine when those bands are printed. For example, you may not want to print the page header on the same page that a report header is being printed. You have complete control as to which pages—All, Not With Report Header, Not With Report Footer, or Not With Report Header Or Footer—the Page band will print on.

IN DEPTH

Grouping Records by Date Spans

The Date Grouping property allows you to specify how to group date fields on a report. You can set a Date/Time field to "Group On" a number of values, including Each Value, Minute, Hour, Day, Week, and so on. If you set the Group On property (discussed in the next section) to Week, the report will group dates in a seven-day span. Which seven-day span is used depends on this Date Grouping property. If you select US Defaults, the first day of the week will be Sunday, so the span will run from Sunday to Saturday. If you select Use System Settings, the settings based on the geographic region selected in the Window Control Panel, the Regional Settings Properties dialog box will be used. This property setting applies to the entire report—not just to one group in the report.

Sorting and Grouping Properties

The properties associated with a sort expression are pretty straightforward—Ascending or Descending. However, I should mention a couple of the interface features in the Sorting And Grouping dialog box. You can rearrange the order of the rows by clicking and then clicking again to get the Row Selection tool (much like when you were rearranging columns in a table's Datasheet view). You can also get rid of a row by selecting it—clicking in the gray row selector box to the left of the row—and then pressing DEL.

The group properties are a bit more involved. I've already discussed the Group Header and Footer properties—note that you don't have to have both—you might only have a group footer if you just want to display totals, for example. (That might be a rare occurrence, but it would work.) The Group On property has already been discussed as well for text and date/time fields. You can also Group On fields with AutoNumber, Currency, and Number data types. In each of these cases, you can Group On each value, or on interval values within an interval range you specify. The Interval Values choice means that you can group records by price, within intervals of, say, $100. Set the Group Interval property to the range desired.

6

The Keep Together property is used to keep some or all parts of a group on the same page if possible. To print the group header, detail, and footer for the group on the same page, set the Keep Together property to Whole Group. To print the group header on a page only if the first detail record can also fit on that page, set the Keep Together property to With First Detail. Note that if there is too much information to fit on one page, the Keep Together property setting is ignored.

Group Header and Footer Properties

A group can have a header band for obvious reasons—you need to be able to place repetitive information in a separate band so that it's only printed once. You might also want to print column headings for the fields in the detail band in the group header—putting those fields in the page header may remove them too far from the detail rows if there end up being multiple group headers on a single page.

A group footer's purpose may not be as evident, but it's commonly used for placing subtotals that relate to that group. Right-clicking on a group header or footer displays the properties dialog box. You can set the Force New Page, New Row Or Column, and Keep Together properties for a group, and they behave much the same way as their counterparts in the Page Header And Footer Properties dialog box. You can also choose to display the group header or footer at the top of every page. This feature acts much like a page header or footer that changes from group to group. I don't even want to think about the hundreds or thousands of lines of programming code that used to be required to make these types of effects happen in older database tools!

Report Expressions

Dragging fields from a Field list only goes so far when you're creating a report. It is possible, and quite common, to create expressions that are displayed on a report—in the detail band, in group headers and footers, and even in page and report headers and footers.

An *expression* is a combination of fields, constants, functions, and operators, and there are virtually limitless ways to put expressions together. An expression starts with an equal sign (=) and then is followed by one or more of the arguments just mentioned.

```
= [field] [operator] [value]
= [field] [operator] [field]
= function(field)
```

Examples of the first would be the multiplication of a field times a number, or division of a field by a number—in this case, the conversion of the mileage to kilometers (is that called kilometerage?)—or a rough calculation of how many months something has sat on the shelf.

```
= [mileage] * 1.62
= [days unsold] / 30
```

You'll notice that the field name is enclosed in square brackets. In most computer languages, a space is interpreted as a character that marks the end of an expression. Since Access field names can consist of more than one word, it needs a way to determine when a multiword expression refers to a single field—and the brackets, known as *delimiters*, do that.

T IP: You don't have to enclose single-word field names in brackets, but it's good practice to do so. Then you'll not be confused about whether a single-word expression is a field name, an Access expression, or some other type of value. Furthermore, Access inserts the brackets in expressions in the Expression Builder and other places, so it's good to get used to it and to be consistent.

Examples of the second expression type, = *field operator field,* would be the concatenation of two strings or the addition of two numbers:

```
= [sales price] + [discount]
= [first name] & [last name]
```

In the first example, the discount is being added to the Sales Price field. In the second example, the field names are First Name and Last Name, and the operator is the ampersand. In this situation, the ampersand "adds" the two fields together, performing a concatenation of the two string expressions. When you add two numbers, you use the plus (+) sign. You use the ampersand (&) instead of a plus sign to add two strings together. When used this way, the addition is called *concatenation* (and the ampersand is often referred to as the *concatenation operator).*

6

Examples of the third expression type, = *function(field)*, would be the conversion of a string to uppercase, or returning the integer part of a value:

```
= ucase( [fn] )
= int([mileage])
```

The first example converts the First Name field to all uppercase, and the second truncates any decimals from the display of the mileage value. You'll notice that a function name is followed by an open parenthesis, then an argument, and then a closing parenthesis. You can get a complete list of functions available in Access through the Expression Builder (the Expression Builder button is the ellipsis next to the Control Source combo box in any properties window).

To create an expression, drag a text box control from the Toolbox onto the report form. Then enter the expression in the Control Source property of the text box.

Building Complex Report Expressions

If you enter an invalid expression (for example, with a misspelled field name, or one that's missing a bracket), Access will display an error message. If it can, Access will give you an idea of what might be wrong and what to do to fix it. One of the most annoying things, however, is when Access runs the report but displays "#Error" in place of a field. While it's impossible to cover every possible error-causing situation, there's one that comes up often enough and that can be almost impossible to figure out without someone looking over your shoulder.

I've briefly discussed the Name property in Chapter 5, but haven't really addressed what you'd use it for. You can ignore the Name property if you aren't going to write functions or programs that will refer to that object. But if you do need to refer to the object, you'll need some way of identifying it and—voilà!—the Name property lets you do so. I'll address this idea in more depth in future chapters when we build more sophisticated forms, but for now we can get our feet plenty wet by dealing with expressions.

When you build an expression with field names, the field name is just that, a name that refers to a field in a table. You can assign a name to an expression—a text box control on a report form—and use that expression in other expressions. I'm not saying you'd necessarily want to do that, but it works. For instance, you could create an expression like so:

```
=[fn] & " " & [mn] & " " & [ln] & IIf(([suffix]>"!"),", ","") & [suffix]
```

If you needed to display this expression somewhere else on the report, you might not want to go through the hassle of building it again. Then if you discovered a change you wanted to make in one, you'd have to remember to make the change in the copy as well. Instead, you could set the Name property of this expression to something like "full name" and then refer to "full name" everywhere else on the report. If you wanted to display the full name in a group footer when showing a total, you could append a text string to the full name by using the expression

```
=[full name] & "'s total balance is "
```

You can run into trouble, however, if you refer to an expression's name in that expression—and this is easy to do. Let's take an example of how you might innocently cause this to happen.

First, create a new report and set the report's record source to the name of a table or query. Next, drag the First Name and Last Name fields from the Field list to the report. The first text box created should have the name "first name," and the second text box should be named "last name." Third, decide that you want both First and Last Name in the same expression, so you edit the control source of the First Name text box to be

```
=[first name] & " " & [last name]
```

When you run the report, however, you'll get "#Error" in place of the concatenated first and last name as you may have expected. You've created a self-referential expression—the text box of the combined First Name and Last Name fields has the name of "first name" since you dragged it from the Field list (and assuming you didn't rename anything).

To fix this problem, change the name of the text box from "first name" to "full name" or something else. When you run the report again, you'll get the results you expected.

6

You can use multiple fields, constants, functions, and operators in an expression—and they are evaluated left to right, unless you control the order operation using parentheses (just like you learned in grade-school math class). I never trust a program to evaluate correctly, because it seems every application does it slightly differently. Therefore, I always use parentheses to explicitly control the order of operation whenever I have more than two arguments.

TIP: It can be very frustrating to build a great big expression, run it, and then find out Access won't accept it or that the result it generates produces an incorrect result. In these cases, start small and build on what you know. For example, start with just two fields or arguments, and get that expression to work. Then add a third argument, and the fourth, until you finish the expression. If you run into a situation in which the expression with five of the arguments works, but doesn't with the sixth, try building a second expression with, say, just the fifth and sixth arguments. Figure out what's going wrong when you add the sixth argument to the original expression. The worst thing you can do is to randomly try to change things, hoping to magically fix something. Good programming practice requires that you not only get something to work, but that you also understand *why* it works, and that you're able to *repeat* that success.

Calculations and Totals

Now that you're comfortable building expressions in a report, let's move on to another highly useful feature—the ability to put calculated fields, subtotals, and totals in nondetail bands (for example, header, footer, and group) in order to summarize values in the table.

Before we do that, though, let me remind you about the Running Sum property that allows you to create an accumulated total for records in a detail band. Just make a copy of the field that you want to accumulate. Set the Running Sum property of the duplicate field to Over Group (if you want to restart the accumulator at the beginning of each group) or Over All (if you want to accumulate through the life of the report).

Now, on to calculated values in group, page, and report header and footer bands. Typically these will go in the footer band, and the group and report footers are the most common locations—a calculated total in a page footer might be used for cross footing or just to double-check for counting in a long report.

Before I get into how to create a calculated field, I should discuss what options you have available. Calculated expressions use an *aggregate* function that acts on a range of values, and Access has nine of these aggregate functions. These are listed in the following table:

Sum	Sums all values in the range
Min	Returns the minimum value in the range
Max	Returns the maximum value in the range
Avg	Calculates the average of all the values in the range
Count	Counts how many values are in the range
First	Returns the first value in the range
Last	Returns the last value in the range
StDev	Returns the standard deviation of the values in the range
Var	Returns the variance of the values in the range

The range of values depends on where you put the expression that contains the function. If it's in a group band, the range is all the values in that group; if the expression is in the report footer, the range is all the values in the report.

The easiest way to create a calculated expression is to make a copy of a field that contains the value that you want to aggregate, and then to edit the control source to include the aggregate function. For example, if you want to sum the current price for all cars per owner, you could just copy the current price field from the detail band to the group (by last name) band, and then edit the control source to read

```
=sum([price current])
```

The cool thing about this technique is that you can repeat it, placing a copy in the report footer, and thus getting a grand total of the same field with just a couple of extra keystrokes or mouse clicks. See Figure 6-10.

Access comes with a number of built-in functions that you would commonly use in certain areas of a report. For example, you'll probably want to number

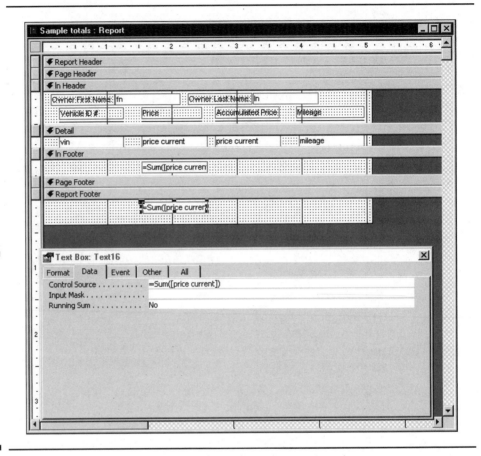

Copying a field
to another
band and
changing the
control source
is an easy way
to create a
calculated
expression in
a report

Figure 6-10.

pages, put the date the report was printed on, and so on. The Date( ) function
returns the current system date; the Page function returns the current page;
and, very handily, the Pages function returns the total number of pages in
the report. Thus, you could put an expression like

```
=date()
```

in a text box control, and the value would be evaluated when the report is
run. You'll want to change the Format property of the text box. When you
open the Format combo box, you'll see some useful choices for displaying the
date. See Figure 6-11.

If you want more granular control, the Now( ) function returns the system
date and time. Be careful if you use this for reports that other people will

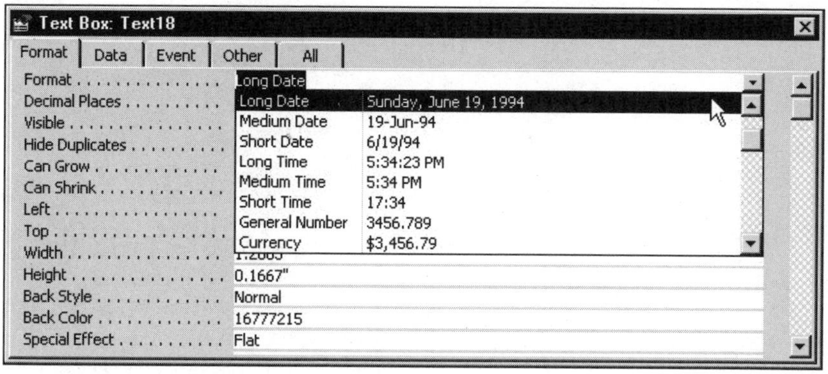

Use the Format property of the Date text box to control how the date is displayed on the report

Figure 6-11.

generate; sometimes people are a bit sensitive as to exactly when the report was printed. Telling your boss in a 4 P.M. meeting that you had the report done first thing this morning might be unwise when the report you hand her has a time stamp of 3:56.

6

You can create one of those fancy "Page 14 of 22" report footers quite easily by using the Page and Pages functions. You can create four controls—two labels and two text boxes—to do so, but it's actually easier in the long run to create a single expression with everything in it, like so:

```
="Page   " & [Page] & " of " & [Pages]
```

and place it in the page footer band of the report.

Multiple-Column Reports

It's easy to create multiple-column reports in Access. Open the Page Setup dialog box (found under the File menu) and select the Columns tab. Set the number of columns, how much room between rows, and how much room between columns. The Column Width and Height will automatically be calculated, but you can change them if you wish. Finally, select whether you want columns to run Down And Then Across or Across And Then Down.

The only trick is to produce a layout that will fit nicely into however many columns you want to show up on your report. For example, if your report layout is 6 inches wide, three columns aren't going to fit on a standard 8½"×11" page. However, if your report layout is 3¼" wide and you select a landscape orientation, you won't have any trouble fitting three columns on the report (as long as the space between columns is small enough).

CHAPTER 7

Macros

There are two mechanisms in Access 2000 to automate a group of tasks: macros, the focus of this chapter, and Visual Basic for Applications, the subject of Chapter 8. A *macro* is an object in an Access database that contains one or more actions that you would otherwise execute with the keyboard or mouse. It can be run on its own or called from within another Access object.

You've already seen that forms and reports contain events, but I haven't discussed what those events are used for. You can place a call to a macro in one of those events, so that when the event occurs, the macro is also executed. For example, a button on a form has an On Click event—you can call a macro from that event to run a macro when the user clicks the button.

Thus, macros are a basic form of programming—creating an automated series of steps that would otherwise be performed manually. Macros can be made more complex than that. They can include logic structures that enable them to make decisions based on conditions in the database at the time the macro is run, and then selectively run one part of the macro or another. They can even make calls to other macros. Remember, virtually any action you can do yourself can be performed with a macro.

Given all this power, you may be wondering, why bother with that other mechanism, Visual Basic for Applications? Macros are good for three types of tasks:

◆ Automating a series of steps

◆ Building small applications that will be used by a few persons occasionally

◆ Developing prototypes of larger applications that will routinely be used by more than one person

When you need to create programs that range beyond the casual use of one person, you'll need to make them more robust—both in terms of providing sophisticated functionality and in having the ability to recover gracefully from errors. You'll need a richer programming language, Visual Basic for Applications, to provide these features.

Specifically, these actions include the following:

◆ Opening in any available view or closing any table, query, form, or report

◆ Opening a report in Print Preview or sending it directly to a printer or to an .RTF (Rich Text Format), Excel, or Notepad file

◆ Manipulating a table, including sorting, filtering, or navigating to a record

◆ Executing another macro, either directly or based on a condition that depends on values found in a table, form, or report, or a VBA procedure

◆ Querying or setting the value of any form or report control, and then taking action based on that value

◆ Creating new toolbars or menus, manipulating (opening, closing, or resizing) windows, and changing focus from one object to another

◆ Displaying feedback to users, including message boxes and beeps, and disabling regular Access feedback

Creating and Running a Macro

A macro, just like a table or a form, is an object in a database. Thus, the first step is to select the Macros object in the left pane of the Database window. You'll see, however, that, unlike Tables, Queries, Forms, or Reports objects, there aren't the same options available to you in the toolbar or the list in the right pane of the Database window. The Run and Design View buttons stay dimmed until you select a macro in the list.

7

Creating a Macro

To create a macro, either select the New button in the Database toolbar or choose Insert | Macro. A blank Macro window and the Macro Design toolbar will be displayed. See Figure 7-1.

The Macro Window

The Macro window has two sections. The top part is a grid where you enter the steps that the macro will execute. Ordinarily, only the Action and Comment columns are displayed; the Macro Name and Condition columns can be displayed by selecting the corresponding buttons on the Macro Design toolbar. The *Macro Name* identifies a set of steps in the macro—you can have several procedures in a macro, and selectively run them according to various conditions. The *Condition* is a logical expression that determines whether steps in the macro are run. The *Action* column contains the steps that will be executed when the macro runs.

Finally, the *Comment* column contains your own description of what is happening. Most people don't enter comments in their macros (just like most programmers don't write comments in their programs) and that's a big

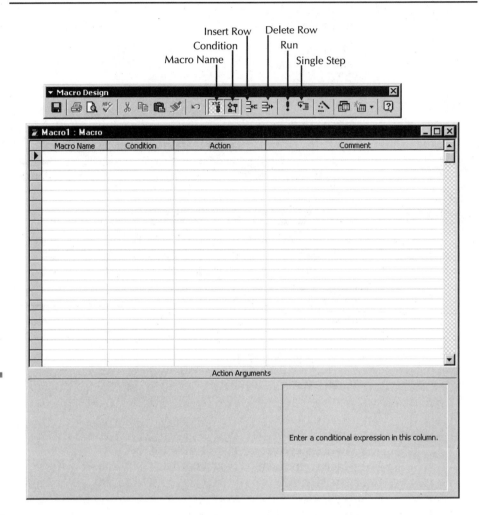

Insert Row   Delete Row
Condition   Run
Macro Name   Single Step

The Macro
window and
accompanying
toolbar enable
you to create
and edit
Access macros

Figure 7-1.

mistake. The purpose of a macro is obvious when you create it, but that
stark clarity may have disappeared later when you have to change the macro
or work with someone else's macro. In the 20 years I've been programming,
I've become increasingly detailed in my comments because I've been burned
too many times, looking at code that I've written and wondering, "Why
did I do *that?*"

TIP: When writing comments for macros or in VBA programs, don't document what you did—that should be obvious from the actions or commands in the program. Instead, focus on *why*. All too often that's the logic that escapes you when you go back to look at something later.

The bottom part of the Macro window will display a list of text boxes in which you can enter arguments for various pieces of a macro, much like you set properties of fields in the Design view of a table. I'll go in depth into this once we start creating some macros.

The Macro Design Toolbar

The Macro Design toolbar has some familiar buttons, and a few new ones as well. Starting from the left, the first four allow you to save, print, print-preview, and spell-check your macro. The next five are also common—Cut, Copy, Paste, the Format Painter, and Undo.

The next two buttons on the Macro Design toolbar are toggles—the first displays or hides the Macro Name column in the Macro window, and the other displays or hides the Condition column in the Macro window.

7

The next two buttons are used to edit a macro. You can insert a row by selecting the Insert Row button. It inserts a row where the current row is highlighted and moves the currently highlighted row (and all subsequent rows) down one row. The Delete Row button does just what it says—deletes the highlighted row. If you highlight more than one row, selecting the Delete Row button will delete all the rows, so be careful. You can also move a row in a macro just like you move rows in other grids in Access. Click the row selector (the right-pointing arrow in the gray column at the far left of the grid), and then click again so the cursor turns to the Move icon (a box with a shaded border). Drag the cursor up or down so the highlight lands between the two rows where you want to move the row, and release the mouse button.

The Run button (with a red exclamation mark, known to programmers as a "bang") will execute the macro; and the next button, Single Step, allows you to execute a macro line by line for testing and debugging purposes. The last four buttons, Build, Database Window, New, and Help, are found on other toolbars as well and have already been discussed earlier in this book.

Steps to Create a Macro

Once you've got an open Macro window, you'll want to enter a name and choose an action from the combo box. I'll discuss conditions in "Referencing Objects from Macros," later in this chapter. You'll see there are dozens of possible actions. I'll list each of them, together with what you might want to use them for, in "Macro Actions," later in this chapter. See the top part of the Macro window in Figure 7-2 to see the combo box in action. Once you've selected an action, the text boxes in the bottom part of the window change to provide possible attributes for that action. In this example, the MsgBox (message box) action will display a message box on the screen and it has four attributes.

The Message is the text that will display inside the message box, and the Beep property controls whether the computer will beep when the message box is displayed. The Type property isn't that intuitive—it controls what type of icon displays in the message box alongside the message. Different versions of Windows display slightly different icons. Finally, the value of the Title property will display in the Title bar of the message box window. See the bottom part of the Macro window in Figure 7-2.

Once you've created a macro, you will need to save it before you can run it. Selecting the Save button from the toolbar or choosing File | Save will perform that task. The Save As dialog box will appear, in which you'll type the macro name.

Running a Macro

If you have a macro in the Macro window, you can run it simply by selecting the Run button in the Macro Design toolbar. See Figure 7-3. You can also run a macro by choosing Run | Run. (Yes, that sounds redundant; but when you have a Macro window open, a new menu pad displays on the menu bar and the first menu option under this pad is Run.)

NOTE: You can store more than one macro in a Macro window, and give them each different names, but you can only execute the first one with the Run button. The others need to be explicitly called from another mechanism, such as from the On Click event in a button on a form.

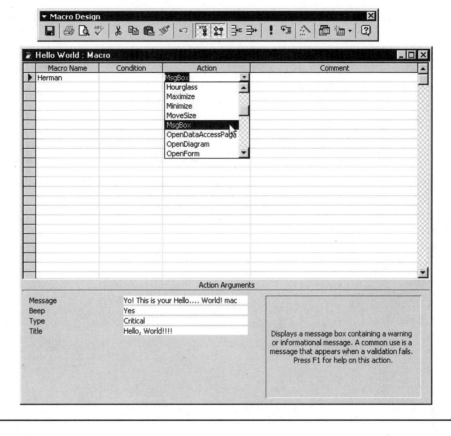

The combo box allows you to choose one of many actions for a macro step; specific attributes for the action can be entered in the bottom part of the Macro window

Figure 7-2.

7

Debugging a Macro

So far, so good. But what happens when you run into a problem? You've put together a macro with a few actions and it works fine. Then you add another one and it still works. Then a few more, and a couple more, and suddenly, something's blowing up. Either an error message is displaying, or worse, everything is running, but you're not getting the results you expected. How do you handle these situations?

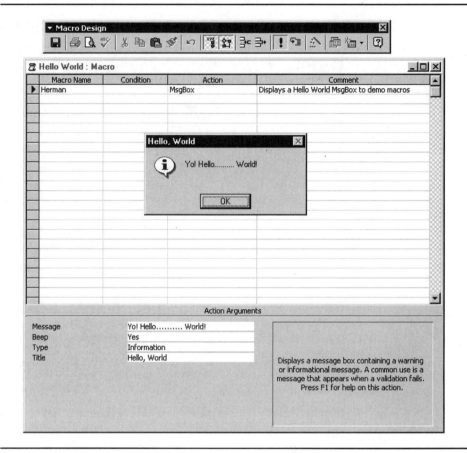

Running the
Hello World
message box
macro by
choosing the
Run button in
the Macro
Design toolbar

Figure 7-3.

Remember that the Access macros functionality isn't a full-fledged programming environment, so you're not going to have a complete debugging toolkit. However, you can step through a macro one action at a time, and get feedback from Access at each step. Feedback consists of either a confirming message box or a dialog box that explains more about the error just encountered.

To step through a macro before running it, choose the Single Step button in the Macro Design toolbar, or choose Run I Single Step. Then execute the macro. Before each action, a dialog box displaying information about the action will be displayed, as shown in Figure 7-4.

Selecting the
Single Step
mode while
running a
macro
causes an
informational
dialog box to
display before
each action is
executed

Figure 7-4.

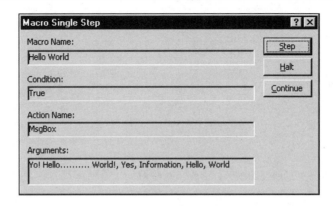

Once you've had a chance to review the information in the dialog box, you
have three choices. First, you can choose the Step button, in which case the
action will be executed and then another dialog box will be displayed before
the next action is executed. Second, you can terminate the macro by
choosing the Halt button. Third, you can execute the rest of the macro
without further informational dialog boxes displaying by choosing the
Continue button.

If you choose Continue, the Single Step toolbar button will be toggled, and
you'll be released from Single Step mode. Step and Halt will keep the Single
Step button pushed in.

Macros with Multiple Actions

You've already seen a hint of a multiple-step macro in the previous example,
in which I had three consecutive MsgBox actions. It was rather contrived,
to show how the Single Step function works; so let's look at a couple of
real examples.

Opening a form and navigating through the table to the last record entered
could be a fairly common task:

1. Turn the cursor to an hourglass so that, depending on the speed of
   the machine, the user is alerted that processing is going on.

2. Set the Echo action to No, so the screen doesn't flash from one step
   to another.

7

3. Open the form. You'll see in Figure 7-5 that the View attribute is set to Form (as opposed to Design or Datasheet), and the Data Mode is set to Read Only. Finally, the last action is a GoToRecord, and the Record attribute is set to Last, so the last record in the table is displayed automatically.

4. Save the macro and execute it. You'll see the form open and the last record will display in the form. Edits can't be made to the data in the form, and you'll notice that the Add button in the record navigation bar at the bottom of the screen is dimmed. See Figure 7-6.

Macros That Run Automatically

You can make a macro automatically run when you open a database by naming it "Autoexec" and saving it in the database. For example, you could create a macro to display a "welcome" message when the database is opened.

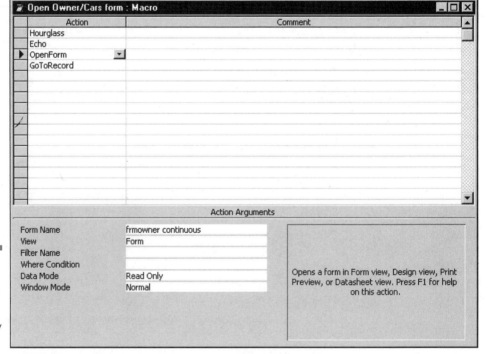

A multistep macro is simply a list of actions in a Macro window

Figure 7-5.

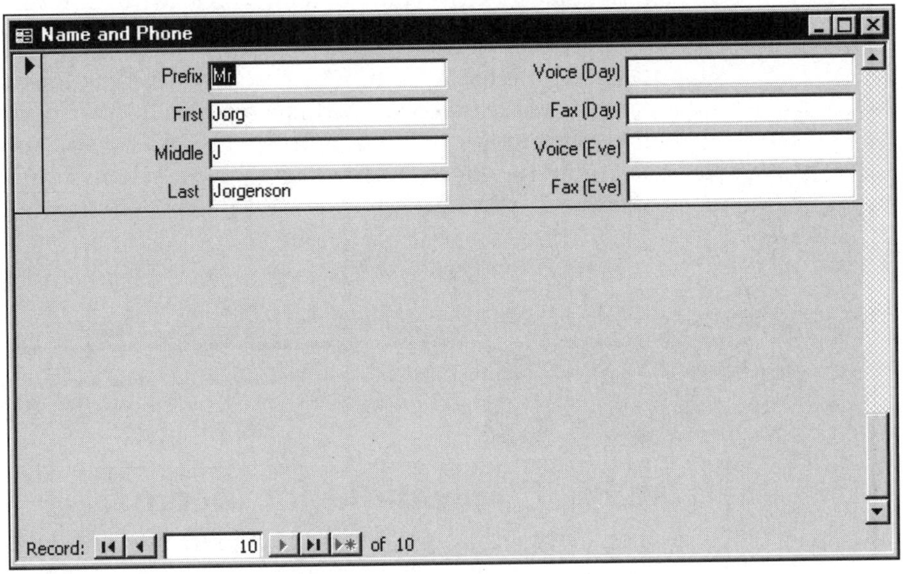

The results of
the multistep
macro that
navigates to
the last record
in the table

Figure 7-6.

Running Macros from Forms

You've learned how to automate a sequence of steps, but there's more to a
macro than just dumbly repeating a single set of actions. Here's where the
fun starts. However, you need to know more about macros than what I've
covered so far.

First, how do you call a macro from an event in a control, form, or report? To
do so, I need to refine the terminology I've been using. So far, I've used the
term "macro" to refer to the object in the database that, when opened,
displayed the Macro window. I've also used it to refer to the actual collection
of actions inside the Macro window. But, as you've seen, you can have
several collections of macro actions in a single Macro window.

Strictly speaking, each of the macro action collections is a separate macro,
while the object that contains one or more macros is a *macro group*. Why the
distinction? Why does Access provide the ability to store several macros in a
macro group? You could create a separate macro group for each individual
macro in your database—but you might end up with dozens or hundreds of
macros, many of them just a few lines long. It would be a nightmare trying to

find a particular macro—you'd end up duplicating some and forgetting about others, until your macro list became unmanageable.

Suppose a form had four buttons, each of which ran a macro, and several other controls that also controlled macros. Wouldn't it make sense to have a single macro group for the entire form? Or perhaps you would want to group your macros by function—print macros in one macro group, form-handling macros in another, and so on.

IN DEPTH

Naming Conventions for Macros

To call a macro from, say, a form or a control, you need to know how to refer to the specific macro. Suppose your macro group is called macGeneral, and within it you had macros called OpenCarsForm, OpenOwnersForm, and RunLabels. (You'll see that, as with forms and queries, the generally accepted naming convention for macro groups is to start them with a "mac" prefix.) Within a form, you might have three buttons, each of which performed one of these actions. The On Click event in the Open Cars Form button would refer to its macro like so:

```
macGeneral.OpenCarsForm
```

while the On Click event in the Run Labels button would refer to its macro like this:

```
macGeneral.RunLabels
```

Given this bit of background, you can construct a form that acts as a launching pad for other forms and reports in the database. First, you'll need the launching pad form (the *launcher)*. Second, you'll need the forms (and reports) that the launcher is going to call. Third, you'll need a macro group that contains all the macros called from the launcher.

Create a new form and place three buttons on it. Change the properties of each button like so:

Button 1

Name	cmdOpenCarsForm
Caption	Open Cars Form

Button 2

Name	cmdOpenOwnersForm
Caption	Open Owners Form

Button 3

Name	cmdRunLabels
Caption	Run Labels

Figure 7-7 shows how your form should look with the properties of one of the buttons already set.

Next, create two forms—one for Cars, one for Owners—and a label report based on, of course, tblOwner. To do this quickly, you might try the Form and Label Wizards for practice. Name these objects as follows: frmCars, frmOwners, and lblOwners.

Now it's time to start work on your macros. Create a new macro group called macGeneral, and start a macro on the first line named OpenCarsForm. Set the action to OpenForm, and in the bottom part of the Macro window, set the Form Name property to frmCars (to match the object of the same name

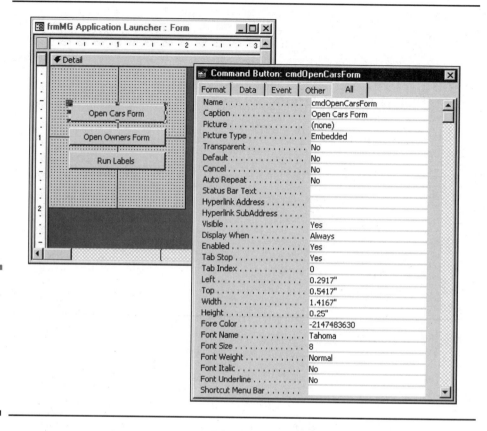

The launcher form with the three buttons and the properties set for the first button

Figure 7-7.

in the Forms collection). Do the same for the other two macros, as shown in Figure 7-8.

Notice that when you select a Form Name property, the available forms and queries are displayed in the combo box, and the reports are available in the Report Name property for the third macro.

All that remains is to have the On Click event of each button on the launcher run its own macros. This is remarkably easy to do, since when you select the On Click event in a button, all the available macros, organized by macro group, are displayed in the combo box. Pretty good idea to keep all the macros for a single form organized in one group, eh? See Figure 7-9.

After you do the same for the other two buttons, save the forms, reports, macros, and anything else that you haven't saved yet. Then run the launcher form (select the Forms object in the left pane, and double-click the

Create three macros in the macGeneral macro group, and set their actions and properties to match the actions of the buttons in the launcher form

Figure 7-8.

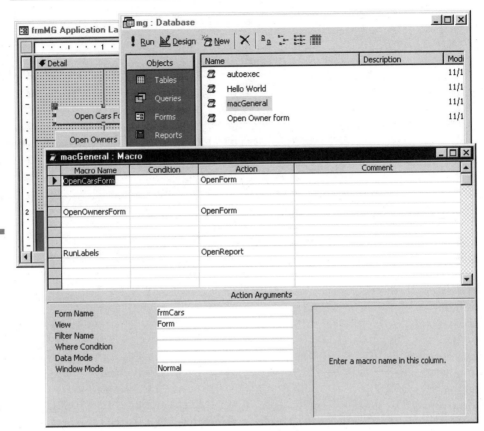

Application Launch item to open the form). An example of your finished launcher might look like the following:

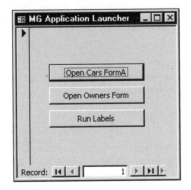

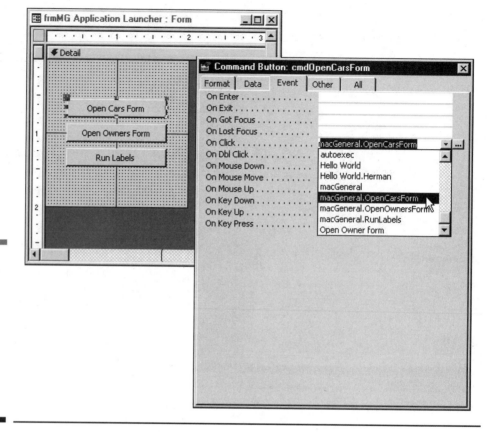

Select the
macro group
and macro
from the
combo box
when
attaching a
macro to
an event

Figure 7-9.

You could, of course, polish up the launcher by removing the navigation bar and the controls in the title bar, adding a Quit button, and so on. When you click a button, you should see the form or report run as expected. If it doesn't, try using the Single Step button in the Macro Design toolbar.

Referencing Objects from Macros

This heading sounds sort of daunting, but all it means is that you can dynamically make changes to forms—reading and setting values of properties of controls, forms, and reports—from within macros. For example, you might have a macro automatically calculate values based on user entries, or enable and disable certain controls based on user choices. This type of control is what makes programming in Windows—and, specifically, designing user interfaces—so much fun.

Suppose we're going to design a form that will handle data entry for a variety of road rally events. There isn't yet a table in the MG database for events—can you hardly wait for the words "This is left as an exercise for the reader"? These events can be held throughout the year, but there are different features according to which time of year the event is held. For example, a summer event can be held in the morning, afternoon, or evening, while a winter event can only be held in the afternoon—when it's likely to be relatively warm.

Another interesting set of conditions has to do with venue. Again, the summer and winter require indoor facilities, due to weather extremes, while the spring and fall do not. Furthermore, the size of the event—number of expected cars—while not determining absolutely how the hungry mob is going to be fed, will have an impact. For 20 or fewer, the event can be held potluck, while with more than 30, a caterer must be brought in. In between, it's up to the user. However, obviously, if a caterer is chosen, the caterer's name and phone number must be entered.

To make data entry easier and less susceptible to error, you can set up a form that enables and disables certain options based on these conditions. See Figure 7-10 for an example of how one event set in the spring for 28 cars would look—disabling the Venue Name and Phone Number, suggesting that the event be catered, and enabling the Caterer text boxes once the Catered option button was selected.

Set Up the Form with Named Controls

The first thing to do when creating a form is to place the controls on them. From now on, we're going to name controls properly, instead of just leaving the default Access names attached to the controls. For example, option groups will have the prefix "opg," followed by the label on the option group frame. A check box will have the prefix "chk," followed by the caption of the associated label. Text boxes will have the prefix "txt," followed by the caption of the associated label.

Thus, the form in Figure 7-10 will have the following named controls:

◆ opgSeason
◆ opgSpring, opgSummer, opgAutumn, opgWinter
◆ chkMorning, chkAfternoon, chkEvening

You can create macros that selectively enable and disable controls on a form, depending on the state and value of other controls

Figure 7-10.

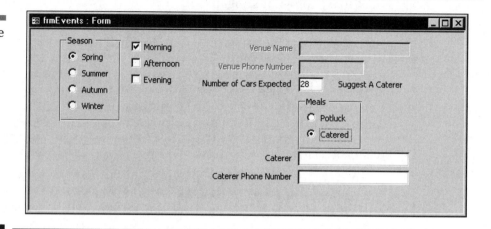

◆ txtVenueName, txtVenuePhoneNumber

◆ txtNumberOfCarsExpected, lblHowToFeed

◆ opgMeals (this covers both Potluck and Catered in the opg)

◆ txtCaterer, txtCatererPhoneNumber

Note that the rest of the name has been typed in mixed case, with the first letter of each new word capitalized. Access doesn't require this style, but it's a lot easier to read (and avoid misspellings) than if you use all uppercase or all lowercase.

Identify Macros, Set Up Actions, and Set Properties

Now that each control that's going to be manipulated has a name, it's time to set up the macros needed and decide what actions each macro will need to perform. The Season option group is easy. The HandleTimeOfDay macro will be executed when the user clicks any of the four seasons in the option group. The first thing to do when this happens is to set the value in each check box to No. Since the user has made a change in the season, we don't want the choices from the previous season to linger. This action will take place regardless of which choice the user made.

For example, to turn the Morning check box to unchecked, the following macro properties are used:

Action	SetValue
Item	[Forms]![frmEvents]![chkMorning]
Expression	No

Once the values for all three check boxes are set, the macro that will handle the enabling and disabling of the Winter check box, as well as the venues, is run. The following macro properties are used:

Action	RunMacro
Macro Name	macEvents.HandleTimeOfDay2

In the HandleTimeOfDay2 macro, the actual choice in the option group will be examined. In each case, the Winter check box will be either enabled or disabled, and then the Venue Name and Phone Number will be enabled or disabled. Since the handling of the venue text boxes is the same in two cases, it doesn't make sense to repeat the actions both times. The text boxes will both be disabled for Spring and for Autumn, while they both will be enabled for the other two seasons. Thus, instead of repeating a pair of SetValue actions for both seasons, a single RunMacro action will be used. The Spring and Autumn RunMacro actions will both point to the DisableVenue macro, and the Summer and Winter RunMacro actions will both point to the EnableVenue macro. Both macros handle the enabling or disabling of the text boxes. See Figure 7-11 to see the structure of the HandleTimeOfDay2 macro.

7

There are a couple of nonintuitive aspects to this new macro. First of all, the line

```
1 = [Forms]![frmEvents].[opgSeason]
```

tests whether the value of the Season option group is set to the first button. In the Action column, the SetValue action has the following properties:

Item	[Forms]![frmEvents]![chkEvening].[Enabled]
Expression	Yes

The first line identifies the value that is being set—in this case, the Enabled property of the Evening check box on the form frmEvents. Makes sense,

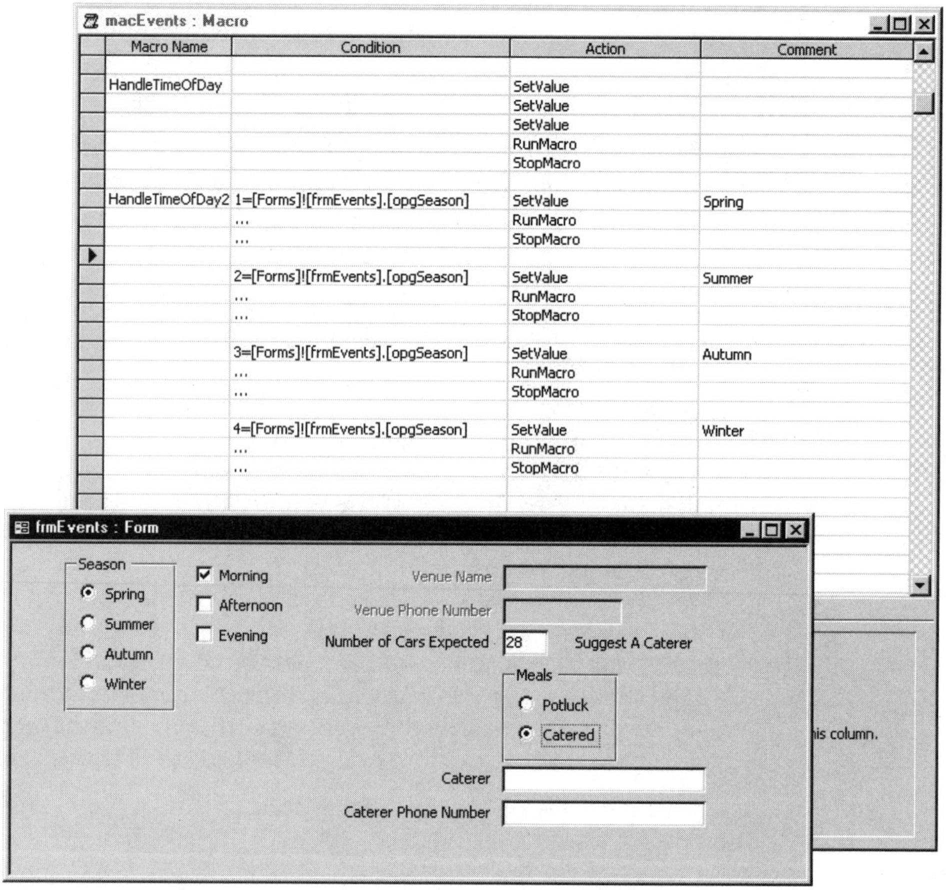

Macro Name	Condition	Action	Comment
HandleTimeOfDay		SetValue	
		SetValue	
		SetValue	
		RunMacro	
		StopMacro	
HandleTimeOfDay2	1=[Forms]![frmEvents].[opgSeason]	SetValue	Spring
	...	RunMacro	
	...	StopMacro	
	2=[Forms]![frmEvents].[opgSeason]	SetValue	Summer
	...	RunMacro	
	...	StopMacro	
	3=[Forms]![frmEvents].[opgSeason]	SetValue	Autumn
	...	RunMacro	
	...	StopMacro	
	4=[Forms]![frmEvents].[opgSeason]	SetValue	Winter
	...	RunMacro	
	...	StopMacro	

The HandleTime-OfDay2 macro has four conditions, each of which has several actions associated with it

Figure 7-11.

doesn't it? The hardest part is remembering all the names and periods and stuff, and I'll get to that in a minute.

The second line identifies the value that the Enabled property is being set to. You've done this a dozen times—only manually—when building a form and setting properties. Now you can do the same thing programmatically, or even better, have Access do it for you, depending on conditions at the time.

The second line in the HandleTimeofDay2 macro has a series of three dots under Condition and a RunMacro action as the action. The three-dot expression means to continue processing additional rows under a condition. The RunMacro action calls the macEvents.DisableVenue macro and the code in this macro is as follows:

Action	SetValue
Item	[Forms].[FrmEvents].[txtVenueName].[Enabled]
Expression	No
Action	SetValue
Item	[Forms].[frmEvents].[txtVenuePhoneNumber].[Enabled]
Expression	No

This same code—in the DisableVenue macro—is also run if condition 3 is met, in which the Autumn option button in the Season option group is chosen. This makes future modifications easier, since if other things have to happen when a venue is disabled, code has to be changed in only one place.

7

The macro executed in response to a user entry in the Number Of Cars Expected text box is a little different. The macro is executed when the user enters a value in the text box, with the result being a suggestion of whether to host a Potluck supper or have it Catered. Figure 7-12 shows the form being run and the two conditions in the HandleNumberOfCars macro. Notice that this condition is structured a bit differently. The same hierarchy—form and control description—is followed, but the value of the control that the user has entered is compared to a hard-coded value in the macro. If the first condition evaluates to True, the following SetValue action is executed:

Condition	[Forms]![frmEvents].[txtNumberOfCarsExpected]<= 20
Action	SetValue
Item	[Forms].[frmEvents].[lblHowToFeed].[Caption]
Expression	"Suggest Potluck:"

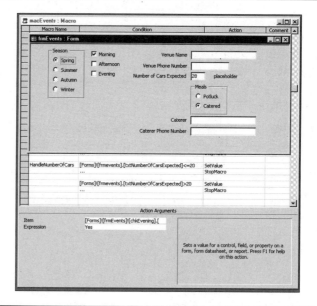

The condition
for evaluating
the contents of
a text box
control

Figure 7-12.

Thus, if the value is less than or equal to 20, the label next to the text box is turned to "Suggest Potluck." If it's larger than 20, the label is set to "Suggest a Caterer."

The last macro used in this form handles the enabling and disabling of the Caterer text boxes, depending on whether the user selected the Potluck or Catered buttons in the Meals option group. This operates just like the Venue text boxes, so it's not necessary to repeat the same explanation here.

The last item in the Macro window that I haven't covered yet is the Stop Macro action—this simply terminates the macro instead of letting it continue on down from one action to the next. It's a safe programming practice to explicitly terminate a program.

Attach Macros to Form Events

The last step is to call macros from the appropriate events. As seen earlier, the call to the HandleTimeOfDay macro is made by the following call in the On Click event of the Season option group:

```
macEvents.HandleTimeOfDay
```

For the Number Of Cars Expected text box, instead of putting a call to a macro in the On Click event, it's placed in the On Lost Focus event, which is fired when the text box loses focus. This way, users can enter a value, and when they leave the text box, either by tabbing out or by selecting another control (since that control will gain focus, the previous control will automatically lose focus), the macro will be executed. The macro call in the On Lost Focus event is as follows:

```
macEvents.HandleNumberOfCars
```

IN DEPTH

Building Macro Expressions

The syntax for all these expressions can be confusing, but it doesn't have to be. Most of the time you can build an expression for an item by using the Ellipsis button, to the right of the text box, to bring forward the Expression Builder, instead of typing in the expression by hand. After doing a couple of dozen that way, you'll become very familiar with the way these expressions are built, and find yourself typing in more and more of them.

Second, if you're a fast typist, you may find yourself wanting to type in expressions as soon as possible. You can skip the open and close square brackets; when you leave the text box, Access will ordinarily update the expression to reflect the complete syntax.

You may also be wondering when to use an exclamation mark and when to use a period to delimit the various parts of a reference to an object. The syntaxes

```
Forms!<form name>.<control name>
```

and

```
Forms!<form name>.<control name>.<property name>
```

are all you need to remember. Again, if you're confused, let the Expression Builder create the first few for you until you get the hang of it.

When selecting the name of a macro, it's common to simply enter the name of the macro in the Macro Name text box—that's a mistake, because you have to include the name of the macro group that the macro is in. I've found it easier to select it by using the combo box drop-down list, thus ensuring that I've included the correct macro group.

7

Macro Actions

You've now tasted the power and flexibility of what an Access macro can do—but you may be wondering how you're supposed to know whether to use a SetValue action or a RunMacro action. Was I born with some special macro knowledge? Heck, no. The most common way to learn a programming language, which is really what Access macros are, is to go through the list of available commands or functions, eyeballing the purpose of each one, and keeping them in the back of your mind. If you do this several times, then, when you're trying to accomplish a task, a little voice will whisper "I think there's a macro action that does that," and you can look back for that action.

As with most things in life, you'll probably find that you use about 20 percent of the actions, 80 percent of the time. In fact, when you look at the 50 or so lines of macro code used in this simple form, only three different actions were needed. With that in mind, let's take a look at the rich variety of macro actions available to you. Each of the remaining sections in this chapter groups macros by purpose and briefly describes each macro and its arguments.

Opening and Closing Objects

The following macros and their arguments (shown in italics) deal with opening and closing objects:

Macros and Arguments	Description
OpenDataAccessPage	Opens a data access page in Browse or Design view
Data Access Page Name	Name of data access page to open (required)
OpenDiagram	Opens a schema in Design or Print Preview view
Diagram Name	Name of the schema to open (required)
OpenForm	Opens a Form in Form, Datasheet, or Design view
Form Name	Name of the form to open (required)
View	Form, Design, Print Preview, or Datasheet
Filter Name	Query or filter saved as a query to apply on the form
Where Condition	SQL WHERE clause to apply on the form
Data Mode	Add, Edit, or Read Only

Macros and Arguments	Description
Window Mode	Normal, Hidden, Icon, or Dialog
OpenModule	Opens a module in Design view
Module Name	Name of the module to open (required if Procedure Name is not provided)
Procedure Name	Name of the procedure in the module (required if Module Name is not provided)
OpenQuery	Opens a query in Datasheet, Design, or Print Preview view
Query Name	Name of query to open (required)
View	Datasheet, Design, or Print Preview
Data Mode	Add, Edit, or Read Only
OpenReport	Opens a report in Print Preview or Design view, or prints it
Report Name	Name of Report to open (required)
View	Print, Design, or Print Preview
Filter Name	Query or filter saved as a query to apply on the form
Where Condition	SQL WHERE clause to apply on the report form
OpenStoredProcedure	Opens a stored procedure in Datasheet, Design, or Print Preview view
Procedure Name	Name of stored procedure to open (required)
View	Datasheet, Design, or Print Preview
Data Mode	Add, Edit, or Read Only
OpenTable	Opens a table in Datasheet, Design, or Print Preview view
Table Name	Name of table to open (required)
View	Datasheet, Design, or Print Preview
Data Mode	Add, Edit, or Read Only
OpenView	Opens a view in Datasheet, Design, or Print Preview view

7

Macros and Arguments	Description
View Name	Name of view to open (required)
View	Datasheet, Design, or Print Preview
Data Mode	Add, Edit, or Read Only
Close	Closes the active window for a table, query, form, or report, or a specified window
Object Type	Type of object to close
Object Name	Name of object to close
Save	Whether to automatically save during close

Printing and Output

The following macros and their arguments deal with printing and output:

Macros and Arguments	Description
PrintOut	Prints the active datasheet, form, module, or report
Print Range	All, Selection, or Pages
Page From/To	Page numbers
Copies	Number of copies to print
OutputTo	Outputs the named object to an external file format
Object Type	Type of object to output
Object Name	Name of object to output
Output Format	Type of format to output to
Output File	Full path of file to output the object to
Auto Start	Automatically outputs the object when the macro command runs
Template File	Full path of file to use as a template (HTML only)
SendObject	Includes the specified database object in an electronic mail message

Macros and Arguments	Description
Object Type	Type of object to output
Object Name	Name of object to output
Output Format	Type of format to output to
To/CC/BCC	Recipients of the e-mail message
Subject	Subject of the e-mail message
Message Text	Text of the e-mail message
Edit Message	Allow editing of e-mail message before it's sent
TransferDatabase	Imports data from and exports data to an external database file format
Transfer Type	Import, Export, or Link
Database Type	Type of database file format
Database Name	Name of database to transfer (required)
Object Type	Object in database to transfer
Source/Destination	Location of object (required)
TransferSpreadsheet	Imports data from and exports data to an external spreadsheet
Transfer Type	Import, Export, or Link
Spreadsheet Type	Type of spreadsheet file format
Table Name	Name of table to transfer (required)
File Name	Full path of spreadsheet to transfer (required)
Has Field Names	Use first row of spreadsheet as field names
Range	Area in spreadsheet to transfer
TransferText	Imports data from and exports data to an external text file
Transfer Type	Multiple types of Import, Export, or Link
Specification Name	Specifications for the type of transfer
Table Name	Name of table to transfer (required)
File Name	Full path of text file to transfer
Has Field Names	Use first row of text file as field names

7

Logic Structures

The following macros and their arguments deal with logic structures:

Macros and Arguments	Description
CancelEvent	Aborts the event that executed the macro
Quit	Closes Access
Options	Prompt, Save All, Exit
RunCode	Executes a VBA procedure
Function Name	Name of function to execute (required)
RunCommand	Executes an Access command
Command	Name of command to execute (required)
RunMacro	Executes an Access macro
Macro Name	Name of macro (required)
Repeat Count	Number of times the macro will run
Repeat Expression	Expression that will stop the macro when the expression evaluates to False
StopAllMacros	Aborts all macros in the call stack
StopMacro	Aborts the current macro

Setting Values

The following macros and their arguments deal with setting values:

Macros and Arguments	Description
Requery	Refreshes the data in the current control if it is bound to a query
Control Name	Name of control to requery
SendKeys	Stores keystrokes in the keyboard buffer for later replay
Keystrokes	Sequence of keys
Wait	Yes to pause macro until keys are pressed
SetValue	Sets the value of a control or property

Macros and Arguments	Description
Item	Control or property that will be assigned a value
Expression	Value to set

Searching for Data

The following macros and their arguments deal with data searches:

Macros and Arguments	Description
ApplyFilter	Limits the information displayed in a table, form, or report
Filter Name	Name of filter saved as query
Where Condition	SQL WHERE clause that restricts the records
FindRecord	Locates a record that meets the given criteria
Find What	Data to find (required)
Match	Whole Field, Start of Field, Any Part of Field
Match Case	Makes the Find case-sensitive
Search	Both Ways, Up, Down
Search As Formatted	Searches either as formatted or as stored in database
Only Current Field	Only current field or all fields in each record
Find First	Starts from first record in database or from current record
FindNext	Locates the next record that meets the criteria previously set by a FindRecord action
GoToRecord	Moves to a different record
Object Type	Type of object that contains the record to make current
Object Name	Name of object
Record	Next, Previous, First, Last, New
Offset	Number or expression

7

Menu and Toolbar Operations

The following macros and their arguments deal with menu and toolbar operations:

Macros and Arguments	Description
AddMenu	Adds a menu to a custom menu bar
Menu Name	Name of this menu (required)
Menu Macro Name	Name of macro group (required)
Status Bar Text	Text to display in status bar when this menu is selected
SetMenuItem	Sets the state (enabled, disabled, checked, unchecked) of a menu option
Menu/Command/ Subcommand Index	Relative position of menu item
ShowToolbar	Controls the display of a standard or custom toolbar
Toolbar Name	Name of toolbar to display (required)
Show	Yes or No

Controlling Display and Focus

The following macros and their arguments deal with display and focus:

Macros and Arguments	Description
GoToControl	Sets focus to a control
Control Name	Name of field or control to receive focus (required)
GoToPage	Sets focus to a form's page
Page Number	Number of page on which to set focus
Maximize	Maximizes a window
Minimize	Minimizes a window

Macros and Arguments	Description
MoveSize	Manipulates a window
Right/Down/Width/ Height	Attributes of location
RepaintObject	Updates the display of a window
Object Type	Type of object to repaint
Object Name	Name of specific object to repaint
Restore	Restores a window to its normal size
SelectObject	Selects an object
Object Type	Type of object to select (required unless in Database window)
Object Name	Name of specific object to select (required)
In Database Window	No if object is already open
ShowAllRecords	Removes filters

7

User Feedback

The following macros and their arguments deal with user feedback:

Macros and Arguments	Description
Beep	Signals the user through the computer loudspeaker
Echo	Controls the display of actions during the execution of a macro
Echo On	Yes shows results of macro while it runs
Status Bar Text	Text to display in status bar when Echo is Off
Hourglass	Changes the display of the cursor to an hourglass
Hourglass On	Changes pointer to an hourglass until macro terminates
MsgBox	Displays an informational dialog box
Message	Text of message to display in message box
Beep	Beep when message box is displayed

Macros and Arguments	Description
Type	Type of icon in message box dialog box: None, Critical, Warning?, Warning!, and Information
Title	Contents of title bar of message box dialog box
SetWarnings	Automatically processes all warning dialog boxes (but not error dialog boxes)
Warnings On	No will turn off all system messages

Manipulating Objects

The following macros and their arguments deal with manipulating objects:

Macros and Arguments	Description
CopyObject	Copies an object in a database using a new name
Destination Database	Database object will be copied to
New Name	Name of copy of object
Source Object Type	Type of object to be copied
Source Object Name	Name of object to be copied
DeleteObject	Removes an object from a database
Object Type	Type of object to be deleted
Object Name	Name of object to be deleted
Rename	Changes the name of an object in a database
New Name	New name of object (required)
Object Type	Type of object to be renamed
Old Name	Original name of object
Save	Saves an object in a database
Object Type	Type of object to be saved
Object Name	Name of object to be saved

CHAPTER 8

Including Visual Basic for Applications in Your Access 2000 Database

Working with Access 2000 macros is kind of like riding a motor scooter—it can take you a lot of places in your day-to-day journeys—to the post office, to the pet store, to the library. But you wouldn't use it to go to work every day, nor on vacation, nor to bring all the in-laws home from the airport. You would need a more powerful vehicle, like an automobile or a van. With Access 2000, that vehicle is a version of Microsoft's Visual Basic programming language, called Visual Basic for Applications (VBA).

One of the design goals for Access has been to enable users to do most of their work without having to learn how to program, so you may be approaching this topic with a bit of trepidation. However, you've already been "programming" when you were using macros. VBA simply fills in the gaps when you run into things that macros can't do. I'm not belittling VBA, though—it's a full-fledged programming language that can be used to develop full-fledged multiuser applications for business on a day-to-day basis.

Uses of VBA

What would you use VBA for? Here are a number of typical uses for VBA:

◆ Creating complex functions that, while possible to build natively inside Access, would be really onerous.

◆ Creating complex functions that simply aren't possible to create in Access.

◆ Handling complex user input, such as multiple fields and data types. Macros only allow a single string as user input.

◆ Creating decision structures that involve loops of various sorts. While macros can handle simple decision structures that involve the processing of a choice, VBA allows repeated processing of a section of code until a condition is satisfied or a value is found.

◆ Providing error trapping and handling of those errors, so that bugs in programs or the logic behind the programs don't crash the application or otherwise confuse the user.

◆ Providing access to the Windows API—a set of functions that allows you to "talk to" Windows, just as Access "talks to" your data.

Again, some of these things are possible from within Access, but they're more difficult or more prone to error, and VBA is a better solution.

What VBA Looks Like

When you use VBA, you create programs that are stored in *modules*—objects that are part of an Access database just as tables, queries, and macros are. Either you can create a module in the database and from within that module open a Code window to create your program there, or you can have Access open a Code window for you. You may want to let Access do the work for you, and watch what it produces until you're comfortable poking around yourself.

VBA programs come in two flavors: *functions* and *subprocedures* (subs). Subs are simply combinations of VBA commands and keywords, and are typically used to perform processing that can't be done in a macro. For example, you could use a sub to iterate through a collection of items until it found one that met a certain criterion, and then stopped processing. Subs are called from events in forms, controls, and reports.

Functions you write in VBA work just like native Access functions—you can use them in expressions, including control sources, and they return values. In addition, you have complete access to the VBA programming language, so you can do complex processing inside the function, as well as straightforward calculations. Functions can be called as part of an expression in a control source or from an event in a form, control, or report.

Some programmers prefer to use functions for work that would normally be done with a sub, and use the return value as a flag to indicate success or failure within the process. I'm in this group, preferring to have as much control over what's happening in my application as possible, including feedback about what's going on.

8

How to Create and Use a Subprocedure

To demonstrate where all the pieces of a sub are, I'll walk through the creation of a button on a form that calls a sub:

1. Create the form and put a command button on it. Remember that when the Command Button Wizard starts, you can choose the Cancel button in the first page so that you can attach your own custom code to it.

2. Open the properties window of the command button and select the Event tab.

3. Select the On Click event and open the combo box. You'll see all the macro names available from the database, but the first line will be the phrase "Event Procedure" enclosed in square brackets. Select it, so your properties window looks like Figure 8-1.

4. Select the Ellipsis button to the right of the combo box to open a VBA editing window.

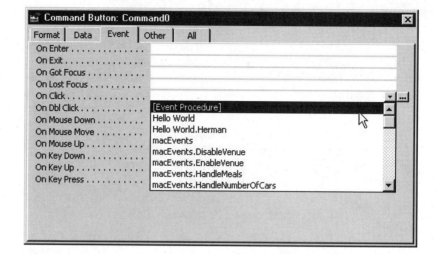

Select the
Event
Procedure item
from the On
Click combo
box in the
Properties
window

Figure 8-1.

A number of things automatically happen here; I'll direct your attention to the most important. First, this VBA editing window has two combo boxes at the top: one identifies the control to which this subprocedure is being attached, and the other identifies which event the code is being attached to. If you have code in more than one event, you can use these combo boxes to easily move from one piece of code to another.

The third part of the window is the actual editing window. The phrase "Option Compare Database" is automatically entered as a delimiter for the window, and the beginning and end of the subprocedure are already set up for you with the "Private Sub" and "End Sub" lines. You'll place your code in between these two lines. See Figure 8-2.

Notice that the name of the sub has already been entered for you. The name, Command0_Click( ), is easily discernable—it's the code that is attached to the Click event of the Command0 control. This is yet another reason why you'll want to provide easily understandable names to your controls. In this example, we know what "Command0" does, since it's the only button on the form. However, on a real form with a couple of dozen objects, it's nearly impossible to remember what "text1," "text2," and "text3" are without devoting a lot of brainpower to it. I've found that, as I get older, I want to devote that brainpower to something more important, like remembering to put socks on before shoes.

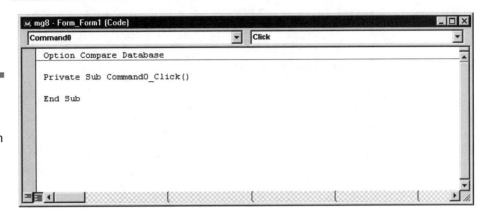

The Code
window is
already
populated with
some helpful
code as soon
as you open it
Figure 8-2.

Because I want to demonstrate where all the pieces go, I'm not going to
write oodles of code in this sub—just a single call to a message box
function. The resulting code will look like this:

```
Private Sub Command0_Click()
 MsgBox ("This message is courtesy of a SUB!")
End Sub
```

8

5. Change back to Access and run the form. Upon clicking the button,
   you'll get a message box as shown in Figure 8-3.

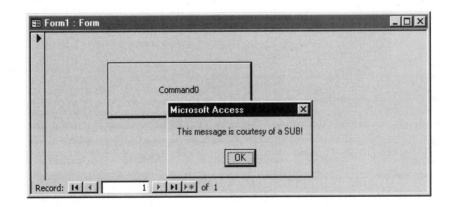

Clicking the
button runs the
sub, resulting
in a message
box appearing
Figure 8-3.

How to Create and Use a Function

By way of contrast, I'm going to add a second button to the same form to show how to build a function, and how it differs from a subprocedure. Taking the same form from the last example:

1. Add a second a button to the form. Next, we're going to build the function in a module, and then attach that module's function to the On Click event of the button.

2. Select the Modules object from the Database window.

3. Select the New toolbar button and a new Code window will be opened for you, as shown in Figure 8-4. You'll need to identify the name of the function, unlike a sub.

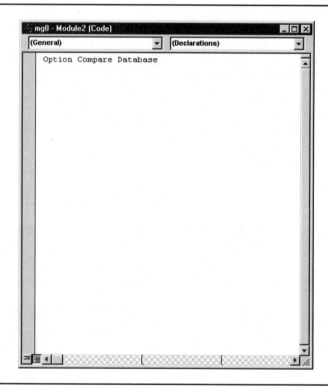

A Code window created for a function isn't automatically populated with the function name

Figure 8-4.

4. Enter the phrase

   function DisplayMyMessage( )

   in the Code window, and press ENTER. An "End Function" line will be entered for you, and you can see that the combo box on the right side now identifies the function's name. You enter code in between the Function and End Function lines, just as with a sub, as shown here:

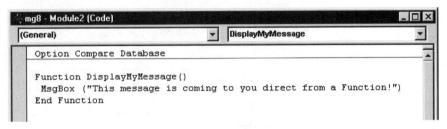

```
mg8 - Module2 [Code]                                    _ □ X
(General)                          ▼   DisplayMyMessage              ▼
  Option Compare Database

  Function DisplayMyMessage()
    MsgBox ("This message is coming to you direct from a Function!")
  End Function
```

5. The final step is to connect this function call to the button's On Click event. Switch back to Access and select the button if necessary.

6. Open the properties window and go to the On Click property in the Event tab. Instead of selecting the Event Procedure property, however, enter the following

   =DisplayMyMessage( )

   in the line, as shown here:

8

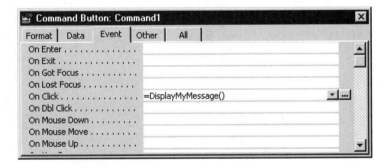

```
Command Button: Command1                                 X
Format │ Data │ Event │ Other │ All │
  On Enter . . . . . . . . . . . . . .
  On Exit . . . . . . . . . . . . . . .
  On Got Focus . . . . . . . . . .
  On Lost Focus . . . . . . . . . .
  On Click . . . . . . . . . . . . . .  =DisplayMyMessage()
  On Dbl Click . . . . . . . . . . .
  On Mouse Down . . . . . . . . .
  On Mouse Move . . . . . . . . .
  On Mouse Up . . . . . . . . . . .
```

Running the form and pressing the second button will result in the message box displaying as shown in Figure 8-5.

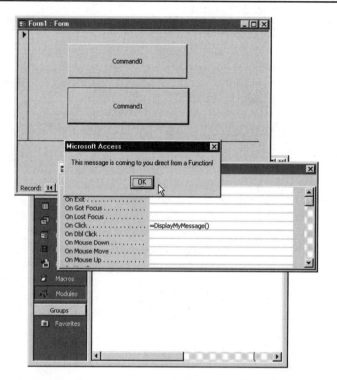

The message box that results from clicking on the second command button

Figure 8-5.

Connecting Functions to Form Controls

Now that you've got the basic steps down for creating functions and subprocedures, it's time to make them useful. From here on, I'm going to build functions, but you can use subprocedures (when appropriate) if you like. As I go through these, it's important for you to remember that I'm showing you how to use the tools—not specific techniques that you should take as gospel. There are a zillion ways to accomplish the same goal; I'm demonstrating how to create functions, not how to calculate prices.

The goal of this first example is to calculate a shipping price for some car parts, based on what country the purchaser lives in, and then to tally the total price, based on the price of the parts and the shipping amount. The form will use two different functions to calculate these amounts, to show off different logic structures inside VBA. The end result of the form looks like Figure 8-6.

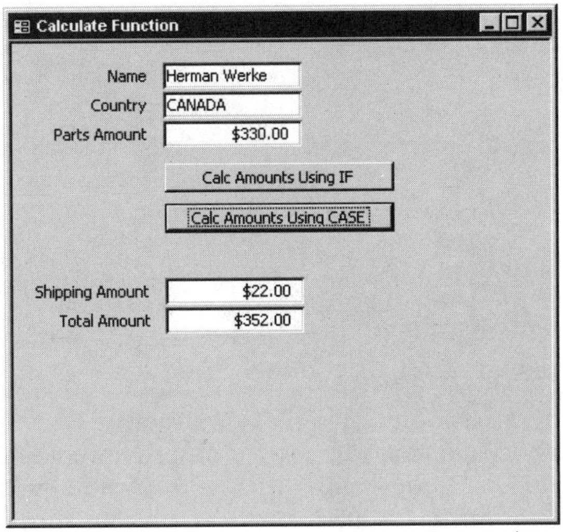

The Calculate Function form uses a function to determine the shipping and total amounts

Figure 8-6.

1. Create a new form and add five text boxes to the form. The text boxes are named, in order

   txtName
   txtCountry
   txtPartsAmount
   txtShippingAmount
   txtTotalAmount

   The Format property for the last three controls was also set to Currency.

2. Add the Calc Amounts Using IF button, changing the caption in the process. Now it's time to create the function that will be called by the On Click event of the button.

3. Select the Modules object in the Database window and create a new one (you'll call it "modCalculate Function" shortly).

4. Add the following code to the open Code window:

```
Function CalcAmounts()
If [Forms]![frmCalculate Function]![txtCountry].Value = "USA" Then
  [Forms]![frmCalculate Function]![txtShippingAmount].Value = 10
```

```
Else
  [Forms]![frmCalculate Function]![txtShippingAmount].Value = 25
End If
[Forms]![frmCalculate Function]![txtTotalAmount].Value = _
    [Forms]![frmCalculate (this line is continued from previous)
Function]![txtPartsAmount].Value + [Forms]![frmCalculate
Function]![txtShippingAmount].Value
End Function
```

Before getting back to Access, I should walk through this block of code and explain a few things. First, as you probably figured out, this function is called CalcAmounts (it's the name you'll put in the On Click event of the Calc Amounts Using IF command button).

This function uses an IF logic structure that will evaluate a condition and then calculate a value based on the results of that evaluation. Specifically, the shipping amount will be assigned a value of $10 if the user enters "USA" in the Country text box; else, the shipping amount will be set to $25. This means that if the purchaser is in Canada, England, or Kenya, his or her shipping cost will be $25. But, it also means that if the user doesn't enter any country, the shipping cost will also be $25. The programmer is probably intending for this behavior to happen—he or she probably expects that the users will always enter a country—after all, why else would the field be there? Of course, the users are probably expecting that they can skip the country field if they want, assuming that "USA" will be inferred.

I mention this to bring up a point—when you are creating programs that have logic contained in them, you can't assume that the program is going to do what you intended to do—it's going to do what you told it to do. This error will be corrected shortly.

Note the syntax of the IF logic structure—the line containing the condition starts with an IF keyword, followed by the condition, and terminates with a THEN keyword. If the condition is true, the code following will be executed, until either an ELSE or an END keyword is encountered. The ELSE keyword is used to provide a place for code that will be executed if the condition is false.

The last thing to mention is the specific syntax of the references to controls on the form. For example, the statement

```
[Forms]![frmCalculate Function]![txtShippingAmount].Value = 10
```

assigns an amount to the Shipping Amount text box.

You may be expecting a simple expression like

```
TxtShippingAmount = 25
```

but that won't work for several reasons. First, the value that the control contains is a property just like the size, color, and font used. Thus, you have to reference the .Value property just as you would reference the .Enabled property. Second, remember that this function is not contained in the form—it's stored in a completely separate object in the database. Thus, conceivably, it could be called from anywhere—not just from this specific Calculate Function form. As a result, you have to explicitly tell the function what control is being referenced, including where that control is found. The first part of this expression, [Forms], tells the function to look in the forms collection of the database (as opposed to, say, the reports). Next, the [frmCalculate Function] string identifies which form. The last part, [txtShippingAmount], identifies the control itself. As you saw earlier, the square brackets define each part (so that it's clear that "txtCalculate Function" references a single form, instead of two objects), and the exclamation mark separates each part of the expression.

5. Call the CalcAmounts( ) function from the command button by entering the string

    =CalcAmounts( )

    in the On Click event of the command button's properties window.

Running the form, entering a name, country, and parts amount, and then clicking on the command button will generate a shipping amount, based on whether you entered "USA" into the Country field, and a total amount.

8

Multivalued Logic in Functions

What if the shipping amount varies according to which country was entered? In a macro, you saw how you could present several decision points and branch off according to which of several choices the user selected. You can do the same thing in VBA, but with more power. The code in the function, CalcAmt2( ), is as follows:

```
Function CalcAmt2()
Select Case [Forms]![frmCalculate Function]![txtCountry].Value
Case "USA"
 [Forms]![frmCalculate Function]![txtShippingAmount].Value = 10
```

```
Case "CANADA"
 [Forms]![frmCalculate Function]![txtShippingAmount].Value = 22
Case "MEXICO"
 [Forms]![frmCalculate Function]![txtShippingAmount].Value = 29
Case Else
 [Forms]![frmCalculate Function]![txtShippingAmount].Value = 50
End Select
[Forms]![frmCalculate Function]![txtTotalAmount].Value = _
    [Forms]![frmCalculate (this line was continued from previous)
Function]![txtPartsAmount].Value + [Forms]![frmCalculate
Function]![txtShippingAmount].Value
End Function
```

As you can see, the SELECT CASE logic construct allows you to build, essentially, a multivalued IF construct. The first line identifies the expression that will be evaluated. In this example, it's the name of the control that contains the name of the country. Subsequent lines simply provide a variety of expressions against which the expression's evaluation will be compared. In each CASE, the code below it will be executed if the comparison is true.

An important keyword is CASE ELSE. The segment of code following this will be executed if none of the other conditions are met. While not necessary, it's good programming practice to include one of these to handle that unexpected condition—such as if the user didn't enter a country at all. I've found that the one time that it's obvious that the CASE ELSE condition could never happen also becomes the one time it's most urgently needed. As a result, I always include one and put a call to a message box function, like so (should be all on one line):

```
MsgBox("Unexpected condition: <description> Please call your
developer.")
```

One final note: where does this second function go? You can put it in its own module, or add it to the existing module. See Figure 8-7. The function call in the second command button is the same:

```
=CalcAmt2()
```

In either case, give it a unique name so that there isn't any confusion about which function is being referenced.

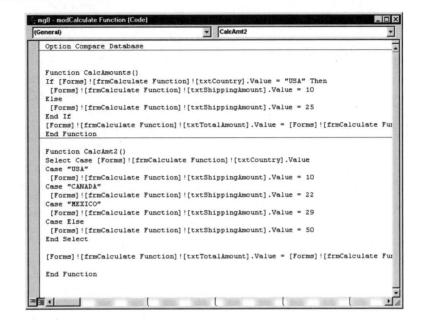

```
mg8 - modCalculate Function (Code)                        _ □ ×
(General)                    ▼    CalcAmt2                           ▼
    Option Compare Database                                          ▲


    Function CalcAmounts()
    If [Forms]![frmCalculate Function]![txtCountry].Value = "USA" Then
      [Forms]![frmCalculate Function]![txtShippingAmount].Value = 10
    Else
      [Forms]![frmCalculate Function]![txtShippingAmount].Value = 25
    End If
    [Forms]![frmCalculate Function]![txtTotalAmount].Value = [Forms]![frmCalculate Fur
    End Function

    Function CalcAmt2()
    Select Case [Forms]![frmCalculate Function]![txtCountry].Value
    Case "USA"
      [Forms]![frmCalculate Function]![txtShippingAmount].Value = 10
    Case "CANADA"
      [Forms]![frmCalculate Function]![txtShippingAmount].Value = 22
    Case "MEXICO"
      [Forms]![frmCalculate Function]![txtShippingAmount].Value = 29
    Case Else
      [Forms]![frmCalculate Function]![txtShippingAmount].Value = 50
    End Select

    [Forms]![frmCalculate Function]![txtTotalAmount].Value = [Forms]![frmCalculate Fur

    End Function                                                     ▼
```

You can put multiple functions in the same module

Figure 8-7.

8

Passing Arguments to a Function

There is one problem with the previous function samples—they all rely on hard-coded references to objects. For a specialized function, that might be fine; but in other cases, when the function might be applicable across a variety of forms, troubles quickly arise. For example, suppose you needed to calculate the shipping and total amount on another form. Your only option would be to make a copy of the function and change the names of the references to the various controls. This is a bad idea for three reasons. First, you risk creating bugs every time you write more code—as the saying goes, "there's never a bug in code that's not there." Second, it's more work. Creating copies of the function takes time and is unrewarding work (and boredom again leads to a greater likelihood of creating bugs). Third, if the formula you were using ends up having an error or the formula changes, you now have to change it in multiple places.

A better solution is to create a generic function that can be called from a variety of places. You do this by passing arguments to the function, and then having the function operate on those arguments, instead of operating on hard-coded references to objects.

In this example, the user will enter the name, country, and parts amount. Two functions will then calculate the shipping amount and the total amount automatically, based on the country and parts amount. The formulas are already fairly obvious, so start by creating the form, as shown next. Add five text boxes, and set the Name and Format properties as in the Calculate Functions form.

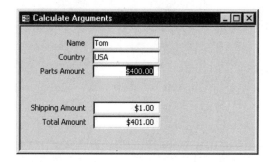

Next, create a new module, called "modCalcAmtByArguments," and enter the functions as listed next. (Due to the design specficiations for this book, the text for each line that begins with "Function" wraps to a second line; each should be entered on one line in the program.)

```
Option Compare Database
Option Explicit

Function CalcShippingAmtArg(strCountry As String, curPartsAmount As
Currency) As Currency

Dim curShippingAmount As Currency

Select Case strCountry
Case "USA"
 curShippingAmount = 1
Case "CANADA"
 curShippingAmount = 2
Case "MEXICO"
 curShippingAmount = 2
Case Else
 curShippingAmount = 5
```

```
End Select

CalcShippingAmtArg = curShippingAmount

End Function


Function CalcTotalAmtArg(curPartsAmount As Currency,
curShippingAmount As Currency) As Currency
CalcTotalAmtArg = curPartsAmount + curShippingAmount
End Function
```

See Figure 8-8 for what it should look like in the Code window.

Finally, switch back to Access and call these functions by entering the following lines in their respective Control Source properties (see Figure 8-9).

For Shipping Amount Text Box Control Source, enter

=CalcShippingAmtArg([txtCountry],[txtPartsAmount])

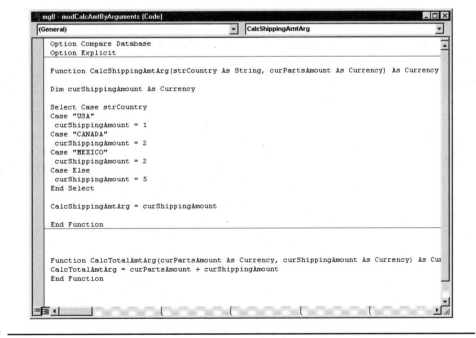

Two functions that are passed arguments instead of using hard-coded references to objects

Figure 8-8.

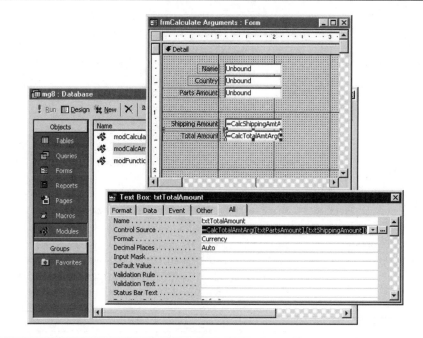

The call to a
function with
arguments
goes in the
Control Source
property
Figure 8-9.

For Total Amount Text Box Control Source, enter

=CalcTotalAmtArg([txtPartsAmount],[txtShippingAmount])

When the form runs, the Control Sources for both the Shipping Amount and
Total Amount text boxes are evaluated. Each evaluation makes a call to the
respective function, passing the arguments inside the parens. The functions
receive the values from the form, do their thing, and then return the result of
the function as the value of the Control Source, just as if you had used a
built-in Access function on a field in a table, like so:

```
=upper(myfield)
```

Let's take a look at the contents of the function, because there are a couple of new pieces of syntax—the Option Explicit declaration at the top, and the "as <type>" keywords sprinkled throughout the code. I'll discuss these shortly, but first, implementing the function with arguments.

You'll notice that the line that declares the function doesn't end in an empty pair of parens. Instead, there are two expressions inside the parens. These are the arguments that are passed to the function. Inside the function, these arguments are used for the calculations instead of hard-coded references to external objects. Makes the code much more readable, doesn't it? The other advantage is that this function can be called from anywhere in the database—it doesn't just refer to one specific form.

Now look at the function itself. The first new line, "Option Explicit," opens a whole new discussion—the topic of explicit declarations.

In the olden days, programmers had to do a lot of grunt work to craft even a simple program. One of those tasks was to reserve an area of memory that would hold the contents of a variable. Other programs wouldn't be able to use that same space. Another similar task was that of having to define a variable ahead of time—the type of data to be stored in it and, thus, how much memory would be required for that data. While safe, this was also a lot of work. Newer languages started doing this work for the programmer. Now some languages, such as VBA, allow the programmer to use variables "on the fly" without any previous definition. The programming language then creates the variable as it needs.

8

While less work for the programmer, this is not as safe a practice. Suppose your program assigns a value to a variable named "intAmount" on the fly. Later, that variable is updated with a line of code like this:

```
intAmont = intAmount + intMoreData
```

Look carefully—there's a typographic error on the left side of the equal sign. So what has happened? The variable intAmount has not been changed—instead, a new variable, intAmont, has been created—on the fly.

You can prevent this from happening by setting a flag in VBA to force all variables to be declared at the beginning of the program. Then, when a variable that hasn't been declared is used, such as intAmont, an error will be generated. This technique is called *explicitly declaring* variables, and it is done by including the Option Explicit statement in the program, as was done in this example.

T IP: Instead of typing "Option Explicit" in every program, you can set an option to have it happen automatically. While in the Code window, select Tools | Options, select the Editor tab, and check Require Variable Declaration.

However, once you do so, you need to be rigorous about your use of variables. You can't use any variables without first declaring them and defining what type they are. Stand-alone variables are declared through the DIM statement, like so:

```
Dim curShippingAmount As Currency
```

Arguments are declared slightly differently (the code below should be entered on one line, but had to be broken here for the book):

```
Function CalcTotalAmtArg(curPartsAmount As Currency,
 curShippingAmount As Currency) As Currency
```

Here you see that the argument uses a similar syntax—the name of the variable as the type of variable. However, don't forget to also declare the variable that the function will return. In this case, the name of the variable is the name of the function: CalcTotalAmtArg, and its type is Currency, as well.

You'll notice a very handy feature pop up as you start typing variable declarations. For example, if you enter the following statement,

```
Dim intMyVar as i
```

you'll see a combo box pop open as soon as you type the space after "as," and the highlight will skip down to the first item in the combo box that begins with "I" as soon as you type the "i." See Figure 8-10. This is called "AutoComplete" and can be turned on (or off) in the Tools | Options dialog box.

A reminder about naming functions that receive arguments: the name of the function is also the name of the variable that is returned to the calling source, so be sure to assign the result of the function to the name of the function just before the End Function statement.

The AutoComplete feature allows you to select common keywords from a list instead of typing the entire expression yourself

Figure 8-10.

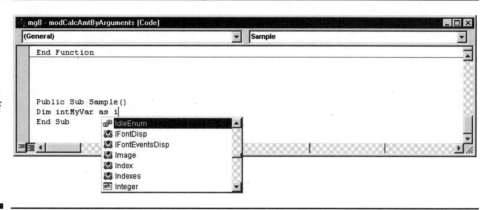

How Do I Learn All These Programming Statements?

You may be feeling overwhelmed by the number of VBA keywords on top of last chapter's list of macro expressions. You may be wondering how you are ever going to learn them all. As with macros, though, the 80-20 rule applies. You'll find yourself using a handful of statements a great deal, and their use will quickly become second nature. You've already seen several in this chapter, including the IF/THEN/END IF and SELECT CASE logic structures, and the FUNCTION, SUB, DIM, and END statements. Next, open up Help | Reference | Language Reference, and look through the Statements and Keywords sections. There aren't that many, and a few will jump out at you immediately as being useful.

8

CHAPTER 9

Application Control Elements: Adding Menus and Toolbars to Your Database

You've had a pretty thorough tour through the tools that you can use to build applications—forms, queries, reports, macros, and even a smattering of programming. But you're probably going to want one more thing in your applications—customized menus and toolbars. When you load a form, you're likely to need to substitute your own menu and toolbar set for the standard Access ones. Perhaps you'll use some of the commands and buttons from Access' standard components but use more of your own. In this chapter, I'll discuss how to build your own custom menu bars, shortcut (context) menus, and toolbars, and where they fit in with the rest of your database.

By the way, make sure you've had a good night's sleep before heading into this task. While intellectually not difficult, there are a lot of tricky little keyboard and mouse tricks required to get things just right—so you'll want to be fully attentive.

Custom Menu Bars

You can attach a custom menu bar to each form in your database—and that's a very important relationship to understand. You don't create a stand-alone menu for the application and then run forms from it; you create a menu and attach it to a form. You can, however, designate a menu to be used during startup, and I'll get into that in "Setting Up an Application to Use Custom Menus," later in this chapter. You might attach the same menu to every form, of course, or you could customize each form's menu as you wanted. I like to spend my time working the interesting parts of the application—the forms—so I try to make the menus as generic as possible.

Creating a Custom Menu

Here's how to create a custom menu:

1. Open a form in your database so that all the form-related menu commands are available as you're creating your new menu.

2. Right-click any menu bar or toolbar, or choose Tools | Customize, to display the Customize dialog box.

3. This step is nonintuitive, so watch closely. Select the Toolbars tab of the Customize dialog box, and choose the New button (you'll be working in the Commands tab shortly, but you start out in the Toolbars tab). The New Toolbar dialog box displays.

4. Enter a name for your menu. You'll be using this name when attaching it to forms, so make it fairly descriptive, such as "Car and Owner Maintenance Menu" (as opposed to something like "New Menu," which is probably not going to be very helpful in short order).

5. Choose OK and you'll get a new window (about the width of a single toolbar button or menu pad name) with the text you entered in the New Toolbar dialog box as the caption of the title bar. You'll also see the new name show up at the bottom of the list of menus and toolbars on the Toolbars tab.

6. This step is important. In the Customize dialog box, select the Properties button, and change the Type (the first combo box in the Toolbar Properties area of the dialog box) from Toolbar to Menu Bar. See Figure 9-1.

   You can change other properties at the same time. You can navigate from one toolbar or menu bar to another using the Selected Toolbar combo box; change its name with the Toolbar Name text box; change the way the user can manipulate it with regard to docking capability; and either allow or disallow other properties as well, including customizing, resizing, moving, and showing/hiding.

7. Move your empty menu to a free area in the Access desktop. Your next step will be to copy menu pads from the existing menu to your new menu. You'll be dragging copies of the menu pads from the Access menu to your empty menu, but there's a trick here. It's easiest to do this if you undock the Access menu, as shown in Figure 9-2.

8. Drag a copy of a menu pad to your new menu. To drag it, hold down CTRL, click the desired standard Access menu pad, and drag it to your menu. If you don't hold down CTRL, you will be moving, not copying, the menu pad, and your standard Access menu will be short a pad.

9

Be sure to change the Type property of your new menu bar from Toolbar to Menu Bar

Figure 9-1.

TIP: If you do accidentally blow away pads from your standard Access menu bar, you can get them back by selecting the Toolbars tab in the Customize dialog box, checking the Menu Bar item in the list box, and then choosing the Reset button.

As the mouse hovers over the new menu bar, an I-beam icon will appear on the menu bar indicating the left side of the location of the menu pad, as shown here:

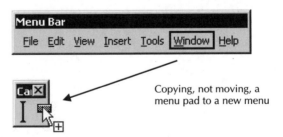

Copying, not moving, a menu pad to a new menu

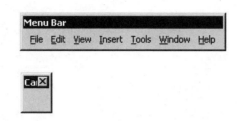

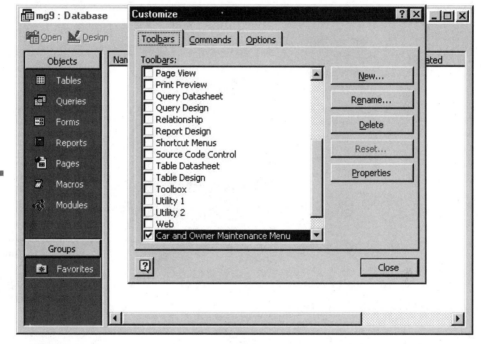

In preparation
for copying
menu pads
from the
standard
Access menu,
undock it and
place it near
your new
menu

Figure 9-2.

9

his may not seem terribly important when you drag your first menu pad
over; but as the number of pads on the toolbar grows, you'll need this
capability to place the pad exactly where you want it in relation to the other

pads. Once you release the mouse button, the menu pad will be displayed on the new menu bar.

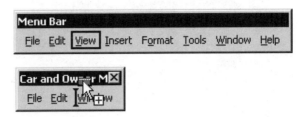

Finally, it's time to move to the Commands tab:

1. There are two list boxes on the Commands tab: Categories and Commands. Scroll down the Categories list until you get to the last item, New Menu. Select it to display the New Menu command as shown in Figure 9-3.

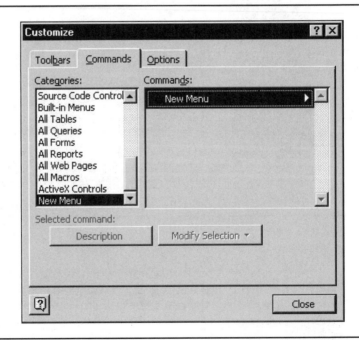

The only command associated with the New Menu category is New Menu

Figure 9-3.

2. To create your own menu pads (suppose you wanted to have a pad that said "Cars"), you'll drag the New Menu command (not category) to your new menu bar, using the I-beam to place it as desired, as shown here:

Of course, you're not home free just because you've got a New Menu pad on your menu bar. First, you'll want to change the name.

3. Right-click the menu pad and use the Name menu command to change the name of the pad.

4. To establish a hot key for a menu pad, precede the letter to be used as the hot key with an ampersand (&), as shown here:

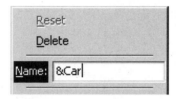

Next, you're probably going to want to add commands to your menu pad:

5. Click (don't right-click) one of your menu pads to display an empty drop-down list, as shown here:

9

6. Locate the command you want to place on your new menu pad drop-down list in the Customize dialog box. Then drag the command from the Customize dialog box to the empty drop-down list, just as you dragged the New Menu command to the menu bar itself.

You may not always want to put existing menu commands in your new menu. Instead, you'll want your own custom menu commands that do things like open forms, run queries, run reports, and so on. You can do this by dragging the Custom menu command and setting properties. The Custom menu command is the first item in the Commands list box for the File category. Once you've got a Custom menu command on a drop-down list, you'll want to set properties so that when users select the menu command, they will get the results they expect.

For example, suppose you want to run a query and then open a form based on that query. You could set up a macro that runs those steps, and attach that macro to the new menu command. Alternatively, you could create a VBA function that would perform the same tasks. The first step would be to change the name of the new menu command from "Custom" to something more descriptive, such as Run Query/Form. Be sure to click the menu pad (Cars) to open the drop-down list, and then right-click the menu command to display the context menu.

Once you have changed the name of the menu command, you'll want to select the Properties menu command (the last item on the menu command's context menu) and either select an already created macro, or enter the name of a VBA function, as shown in Figure 9-4.

You'll notice the Begin A Group check box at the bottom of the Custom Popup And Control Properties dialog box. You can use this to place a separate

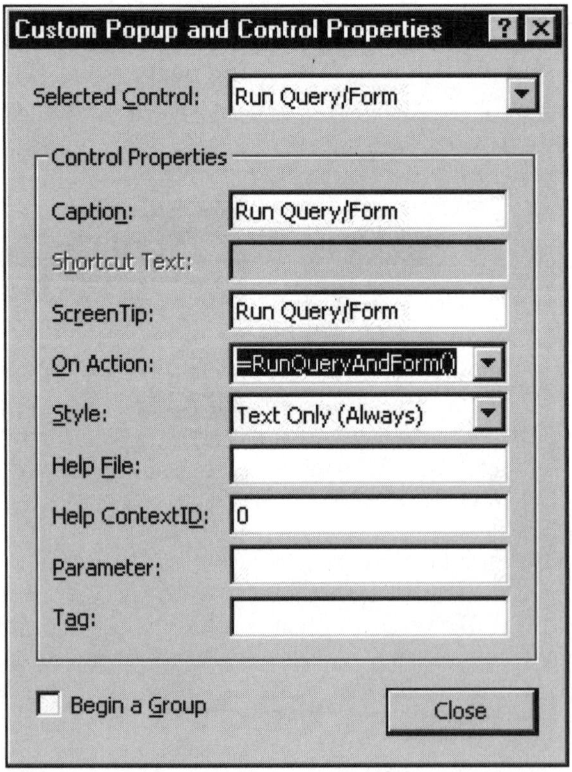

Select the name of a macro or enter the name of a VBA function in the On Action combo box to control what happens when the menu command is selected

Figure 9-4.

bar above the current menu command in the drop-down list. If you don't, all the menu commands in the drop-down list will be placed one after another without any visual clue about what types or groups of functions they perform.

If you want a menu pad to initiate an action directly, you can do so by creating a macro or VBA function, and selecting the macro or entering the VBA function in the On Action combo box in the Properties dialog box (available by issuing the Properties menu command from the menu pad context menu).

Once you've finished setting the names and properties of each menu pad and menu command, close the Customize dialog box, and you can use your custom menu just like any other menu.

Connecting a Custom Menu to a Form

Unlike the rigorous, exacting steps you had to go through to create a menu, attaching a custom menu to a form is as straightforward as can be:

1. Open the form in Design view, and open the properties window.
2. Set the Menu Bar property to the name of the menu (you can use the drop-down list instead of trying to remember the name of the menu) and save your form. The next time you run that form, the menu will change to display your custom menu. See Figure 9-5.

9

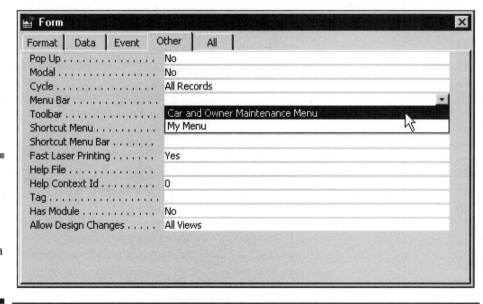

Use the Form properties window to choose which menu should display when a form is run

Figure 9-5.

Custom Shortcut Menus

A *shortcut menu*—also known as a *context menu*—is the menu that appears when you right-click in various places in Access. You can create your own shortcut menus and attach them to forms.

First, create a new menu as you did a new menu bar:

1. Open the Customize dialog box, select the Toolbars tab, and choose the New button. Enter a descriptive name in the New Toolbar dialog box, and choose OK.

2. Next—and this is, again, *very important*—in the Toolbar Properties dialog box (shown in Figure 9-1), change the Type property from Toolbar to Popup. (You say "Shortcut," I say "Context"—but then Microsoft says "Popup." Go figure!) You'll be given a long, fairly arcane warning about your shortcut menu being added to the Shortcut toolbar. Choose OK in response to the message.

3. Close the Toolbar Properties dialog box. This is confusing, because your shortcut menu seems to have disappeared. To get to it again, select the Shortcut Menus item in the Toolbars list box. The Shortcut Menus toolbar will display. Click the Custom menu pad, and you'll see the shortcut menu that you just named in the drop-down list:

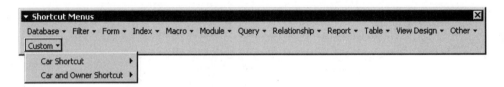

Adding menu commands to a shortcut menu is pretty straightforward. It's essentially the same operation as you performed when adding menu commands to a menu bar drop-down list:

1. Open the Shortcut Menus toolbar, and then select the Command tab of the Customize window.

2. Click the shortcut menu to which you want to add a command in order to open the empty drop-down list.

3. Drag a standard Access menu command or the Custom command from the Commands list box.

After you've finished adding menu commands to the shortcut menu, adding a shortcut menu to a form is almost anticlimactic:

1. Close the Customize dialog box, and then open the properties window for the form to which you want to add your shortcut menu.

2. Change the Shortcut Menu property to Yes if necessary, and then select the shortcut menu you want to attach to this form from the Shortcut Menu Bar property combo box. See Figure 9-6.

Custom Toolbars

Creating a custom toolbar is going to seem pretty old hat by now, but I'll still run through each step, because they're not identical to the steps for menu bars:

1. Open the Customize dialog box, select the Toolbars tab, and choose New.

2. Enter a name for your new toolbar and choose OK. A new, empty toolbar will appear, bearing the title of the toolbar you just entered in the New Toolbar dialog box.

3. Select the Commands tab of the Customize dialog box, and start dragging the desired commands over to the toolbar. You'll see the command icons appear in the toolbar. So far, so good.

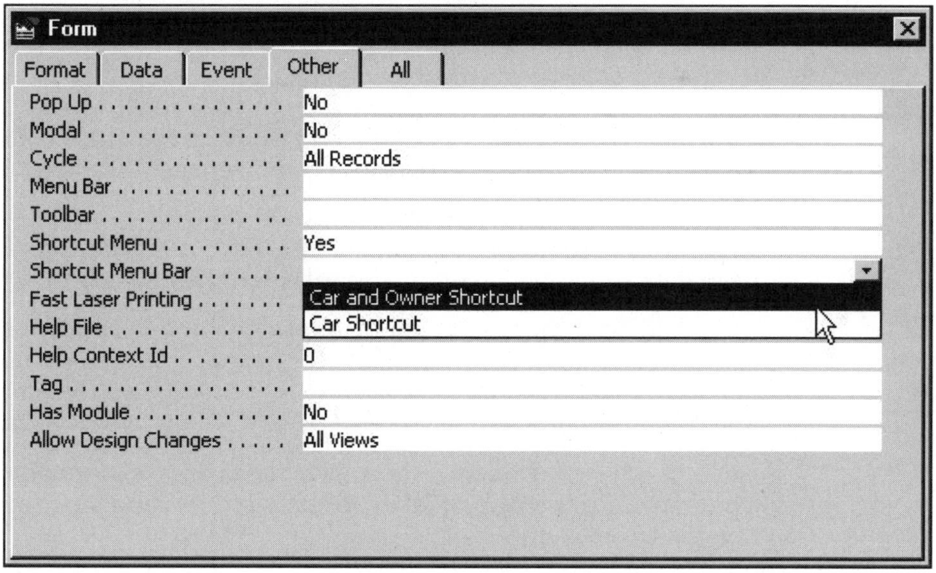

9

Add a shortcut menu to a form by setting two form properties— Shortcut Menu and Shortcut Menu Bar

Figure 9-6.

Form					⊠
Format	Data	Event	Other	All	
Pop Up		No			
Modal		No			
Cycle		All Records			
Menu Bar					
Toolbar					
Shortcut Menu		Yes			
Shortcut Menu Bar					▼
Fast Laser Printing		Car and Owner Shortcut			
Help File		Car Shortcut			
Help Context Id		0			
Tag					
Has Module		No			
Allow Design Changes		All Views			

However, just as with menu bars and shortcut menus, you'll probably want to add your own toolbar buttons to the toolbar:

1. Drag the Custom command from the Customize dialog box over to the toolbar. You'll end up with a big button that has no icon but does have the word "Custom" on the toolbar.

Of course, you're probably not going to want the "Custom" label on your toolbar.

2. Right-click the button and select the Change Button Image menu command to select an existing icon, as shown here:

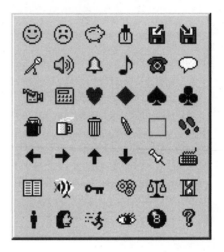

Alternatively, you can select the Edit Button Image menu command to create your own icon. As you can see in Figure 9-7, I should stick to developing software.

You can choose whether to display just the icon, the icon and text, or just text, with other menu commands in the context menu.

However, even the fanciest toolbar button won't do you much good if selecting it doesn't do anything. You can attach, just as with menu bars and menu commands, a macro or a VBA function call to a toolbar button through the On Action property in the toolbar button properties window.

Finally, add the toolbar to a form just like you have for menu bars and menu commands: open the properties window for the form, and select the name of the toolbar from the Toolbar combo box. See Figure 9-8.

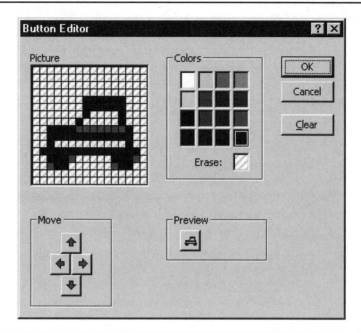

You can create your own icon to attach to a custom toolbar button

Figure 9-7.

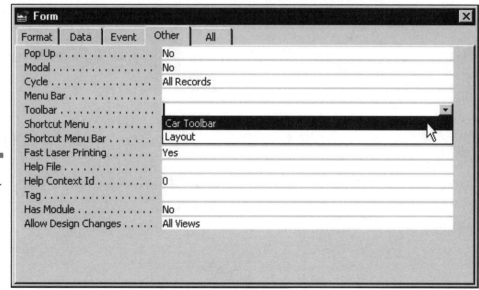

Select the desired toolbar for the form from the Toolbar property combo box

Figure 9-8.

9

Setting Up an Application to Use Custom Menus

You can have an Access database customized to use a specific menu bar and shortcut menu bar, and to display a specific form when the database is initially opened—without having to resort to a long Autoexec macro. Choose Tools | Startup to display the Startup dialog box, as shown in Figure 9-9.

As you open each of the combo boxes, you'll see each of the available menus, shortcut menus, and forms (data access pages haven't been discussed to this point). If you have created an Application Launch form, you can set it to be opened automatically. You can customize the environment your users see, and prevent them from getting into places, such as special menu commands or other functions, that you don't want them to, by customizing the menus and toolbars they have access to.

Note that since these options are all database specific, the Tools | Startup menu option is not available unless you have a database open.

The Startup dialog box allows you to set a number of properties that affect what happens when a database is opened

Figure 9-9.

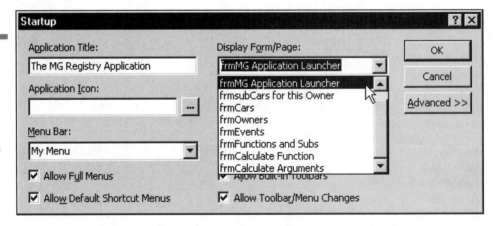

CHAPTER 10

Database Maintenance and Security

You spend a lot of time constructing your database application, and your users spend a lot of time putting data into it. It sure would be nice to have it there the next time you open your application, wouldn't it? There are three things that can happen to an Access database that would cause you grief in this department:

◆ Data becomes corrupted through "natural" causes.

◆ The database becomes slow and unmanageable because it's gotten bloated.

◆ Data or the application itself has been modified by an unauthorized user.

It's important, then, to consider what types of insurance you might be able to take out to protect yourself from the inevitable. These tasks, collectively, are known as *database maintenance* and consist of three operations:

◆ Repairing a corrupted database

◆ Compacting a database that has become bloated

◆ Providing security from access or edits by unauthorized users

Repairing a Corrupted Database

There's an old saying among software developers:

> *There are two kinds of computer users—those who have lost data, and those who are going to.*

As solid as the data you see on the screen may seem, remember that your data is just a bunch of high and low voltages temporarily stored on a piece of Mylar by means of a miniscule electrical charge. This Mylar may be spinning at several thousand revolutions per second, with a piece of sharp metal hovering just millimeters away. When you factor in that the position of an electron is actually never known—it's just guessed at through the means of complex statistics—you're faced with a stark reminder of how fragile your data really is.

Access expects a database to have a certain structure, with certain types of data in certain positions. If it encounters data in the wrong positions, or finds that data is missing, the database is said to be *corrupted*. How can this happen?

First, as I said earlier, your data is simply electronic voltages—which, obviously, are subject to all sorts of interference ranging from some dope with a kitchen magnet to sunspots. I ran into a situation once in which an application's data was getting corrupted on a regular, but infrequent, basis.

The application was used throughout the company, but corruption was only occurring on one workstation, and only once in a while. It took months to hunt down the culprit—the workstation was against a wall in an office that backed up to a secondary freight elevator; and when the elevator was in use, the magnets in the elevator drive caused enough interference to corrupt the database.

Another reason for corrupt data is incomplete writes to the file that holds the data. Incomplete writes could be caused by a user accidentally kicking the cord out of the wall or power fluctuations overloading circuits in the machine.

A third reason for corrupt data is a crash in the actual database application, in a related piece of software running at the same time that interfered with your data, or even in hardware.

Yet another reason a database could be corrupted is that it was attacked by a virus. This could be an Access-specific virus, or a general-purpose virus that hit your database when it got in the way.

At any rate, "corruption happens"—so what do you do?

Access 2000 is somewhat more prone to corruption causing a meltdown of the application because everything is contained in a single file. However, Access also comes with a utility that allows a user to repair a corrupted .MDB file. While extremely good, it's not going to save your bacon every time. So before I get into the details of using the repair utility, let me caution you that the best way to keep yourself safe is to make backups early and often. I make backups of important applications just about the time I think "I would be really unhappy if I lost all the changes I've made since my last backup."

When you open, or should I say, attempt to open, a corrupted Access database, you'll be warned that the database is corrupt and that you should run the repair utility. Select Tools | Database Utilities | Repair And Compact Database. If you have managed to open the database, the command will simply run. If you can't open the database, you'll be presented with a File Selection dialog box that allows you to select the database to repair.

10

T IP: Before attempting to repair a database, make a backup copy. If the repair process doesn't work, you'll still have a copy of the original to work with. There are third-party utilities and other services that can, in some cases, repair an Access database that the Access repair utility can't handle.

You'll be asked for a name under which to save the new database (the one without the corruption). Enter a name and choose Save. The status bar will display informational messages as the repair process is running. Once the repair is done, the message will say "Ready," and the mouse cursor will return to its normal state. Any data in the database that can't be repaired will be removed. That might sting at first, but it's data of no use to you anymore, so why not get rid of it?

Compacting a Bloated Database

Over time, operations with an Access database will cause it to "bloat." For example, deleting data or structures (such as tables or forms) will leave empty spaces in the database. Thus, after a while, a 10MB database may only contain 9MB of information—the other megabyte is empty—wasted. While a single megabyte isn't much, imagine a 200MB database with 40MB of unused space. I've got one application that grew to over 300MB before I cleaned it up.

Getting rid of empty space in a database is called *compacting;* and in Access 2000, it's done at the same time that repairing is done. This is a good idea both ways. A repaired database often has empty space in it (since data that can't be recovered is removed), so it should be compacted as part of the repair process. On the other hand, a database may have corruption that isn't immediately detected—if the repair process is run even on a database without symptoms of corruption, it will fix any problems it finds. Why not do it when a database is being compacted?

Thus, to compact a database, select Tools | Database Utilities | Repair And Compact Database. If you have managed to open the database, the command will simply run. If you can't open the database, you'll be presented with a File Selection dialog box that allows you to select the database to repair.

TIP: If your database is being used by more than one person at a time, they all must close the database before you can repair and compact the database.

Securing a Database

Database security is significantly more complicated than simply compacting and repairing a database, because there are several levels of security. First, you can simply provide a password to the file, so that no one can open the database without knowing the password. The second level of security is to add user-level security, so that an individual has to log in before accessing selected functions of the database. The third level is to convert the database to an .MDE file, which prevents users from using Design view to modify objects in the database, or from viewing or changing the application's Visual Basic source code.

NOTE: There are third-party utilities that purport to be able to open a password-protected database file. For this reason, consider password protection to be the same as a fancy security system for your house—deterrence for all but the most determined thieves. If someone truly wants to get at your data, they'll be able to. These security techniques are simply countermeasures you can employ to dissuade the casual snoop.

Adding Password-Level Security to Your Database

The easiest way to protect your database is to add a password to it. This will prevent all but the most determined snoops from even opening the database.

To set a database password, open the database in Exclusive mode. If you don't, you'll get the warning shown here:

10

In earlier versions of Access, there was an Exclusive Use check box on the File | Open dialog box that gave you an immediate hint on how to open a database exclusively. In Access 2000, the interface isn't nearly as obvious. The Open button in the File | Open dialog box has an arrow on it indicating that the button acts as a drop-down list as well. Click the arrow part of the button, and you'll see you have four choices: Open (the default), Open Exclusive, and the same two choices with Read-Only mode.

NOTE: I think this is a ridiculous change to the interface. What used to take three controls—an Exclusive check box, a Read-Only check box, and an Open button—has now been replaced by four options on one control. The problem comes when someone decides there needs to be another option, such as "Open As HTML." This could have been handled easily by the addition of another check box; but now that all the controls have been added to one button, there need to be four more options added to the existing four—each of the options with "As HTML" added.

Once you have opened the database exclusively, choose Tools | Security | Set Database Password. The Set Database Password dialog box will display as shown here:

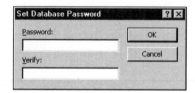

After you have attached a password to a database, you will need to enter it in the Password Required dialog box, shown next, whenever the database is opened, whether you select it from the most recently used file list in the File menu or simply select it in the File | Open dialog box.

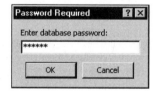

Once you have added a password to the database, the Tools | Security | Set Database Password menu command changes to Tools | Security | Unset Database Password. In other words, if you want to change the database password, you will have to remove it with the Unset Database Password menu command, and then create a new one. You will have to enter the database password when you attempt to unset it—this prevents another user from sneaking up to your computer when you're taking a break while the database is open and changing it without your knowledge.

While useful, this may not provide the desired level of protection. Once users have opened the database, they're in, and they have complete freedom to run around in your database. The next level of security is user-level security.

Enabling User-Level Security for Your Database

The best way to restrict access to your database is to enable user-level security for the database. This is done in two stages—first, the user must enter a user name, and then he or she must enter a password.

However, the underlying structure is actually more complex than that. User-level security is provided through the use of workgroups. Access comes with two workgroups, Admin and Users, and you can create more of your own if you like. Workgroups have permission to access various objects of a database and you determine these permissions. Users belong to workgroups and you will assign a new user to a specific workgroup. Users' permissions are inherited by the workgroup they belong to, but can be overridden in special cases.

This can quickly get ethereal, so let me use an example to describe what is happening behind the scenes. Suppose you have ten users, User A through User J. You need three groups of users: one for administrative and programming personnel, another for the data-entry folk who will do the day-to-day data entry, and a third for a few managerial types who, frankly, should never have been let within ten feet of a keyboard in the first place.

T IP: You will often want to restrict managerial types to a fairly limited type of access, but you can't very easily assign these "high ego" individuals to a group called "Read-Only Access." Instead, I create a special workgroup called "Manager Access," and then restrict the living daylights out of the group. They're happy, since "Manager Access" appears to confer a high level of access, but it still allows the administrator to control the level of access those individuals actually have. If they protest that they can't change anything, gently explain that "only data-entry clerks" have editing permissions, since, after all, they're the ones with all the supporting paperwork.

10

The first step is to create three workgroups—Admin, Users, and Managers. The second is to create ten users, and to assign those users to the appropriate workgroups. The next (but not last) step is to tie access to specific objects or functions in the database to workgroups. This will ensure that data-entry folk can access all the regular maintenance and data-entry screens, while the managers can only run queries and reports. The last step is to provide user-specific permissions, so that you can either restrict or enlarge permissions for a specific user as needed, without having to create a brand-new workgroup just for one specific case.

Create a Workgroup

Workgroup and user accounts are both created in the same dialog box. Select Tools | Security | User And Group Accounts to display the dialog box shown in Figure 10-1.

To create a new workgroup, click the New button, and enter a Name and Personal ID. Note that you can't create a workgroup using the same name as an existing user name. Once you have created the workgroups you want, you'll need to create users to add to those workgroups.

Create a User

The next step is to create a user. Select the Users tab of the User And Group Accounts dialog box, as shown in Figure 10-2. First, add a new user by selecting the New button and entering a name and password in the New

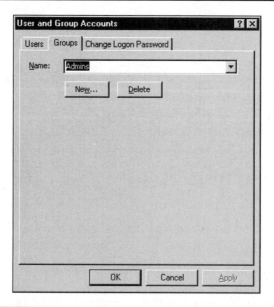

The Groups tab of the User and Group Accounts database is used to create new workgroups

Figure 10-1.

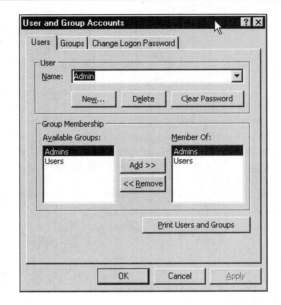

The Users tab
of the User
and Group
Accounts
dialog box is
used to add
new users

Figure 10-2.

User/Group dialog box. Choose OK and the name you entered will be
displayed in the User Name combo box.

Once the new user is displayed in the User Name combo box, you'll see the
workgroups that the user has been assigned to. The available groups are listed
on the left, and the groups of which the current user is a member are listed
on the right. Use the Add and Remove buttons to add and delete items from
the Member Of list.

Assign Permissions to Objects

Once you have defined workgroups and user names, you can assign
permission to access specific objects to those workgroups and user names.
Display the User And Group Permissions dialog box by selecting Tools |
Security | User And Group Permissions. See Figure 10-3. First, in the List
option group, choose whether you want to see Groups or Users in the
User/Group Name list box on the left side of the dialog box. Next, select a
specific group or user in the User/Group Name list box.

You'll see all the available objects—forms, reports, queries, and so on—appear
in the Object Name list box on the right side of the dialog box. You can filter

10

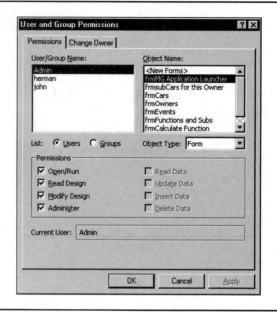

Use the User and Group Permissions dialog box to define access permissions to specific objects for each workgroup and user

Figure 10-3.

the objects that appear by selecting the type of object with the Object Type drop-down list under the Object Name combo box.

Once you've selected a user or workgroup and a specific object name, you can set permissions for that object that are applied to the user or group by checking and unchecking the check boxes in the Permissions box in the lower half of the screen. Note that the check boxes available will depend on what type of object type you've selected.

The Open/Run permission check box allows the user or group to open or run the object, but not to view or make changes to the design.

The Read Design check box allows the user or group to view the object in Design view, but not to make any changes.

The Modify Design check box is actually a superset of the Read Design check box. It allows the user not only to open the object in Design view, but also to make changes.

The Administer object allows the user to have complete control over the object. (The name of the currently logged-in user is displayed in the read-only box at the bottom of the screen.)

NOTE: If you want to enable a user to execute more than one type of task, you will have to check more than one check box. For example, if you want a user to be able to Open/Run an object and also to see the object in Design view, you'll have to check both the Open/Run and Read Design check boxes.

Change Owner for an Object

You can also change the owner for a specific object in the database. Select the Change Owner tab of the User And Group Permissions dialog box, select the object of interest, and then make the change using the New Owner combo box. You can filter the objects shown in the list box by making a selection in the Object Type combo box, and filter the available owners (Users or Groups) by use of the List option group.

Change Logon Password for a User

You can also use the User And Group Accounts dialog box to change the log-in password for a specific user. First, display the dialog box as described in the "Assign Permissions to Objects" section earlier in the chapter. Second, select the user for whom you want to change the password. Next, select the Change Logon Password tab, as shown in Figure 10-4.

Enter the old password (which, of course, means that you'll need to know the password), and then the new password. Reenter the password in the Verify text box to ensure that you entered the first version of the new password correctly.

Protecting Your Database from Changes Using an .MDE File

10

You can prevent users from changing the underlying application in your database by converting it to an .MDE file. Doing so will prevent users from viewing or modifying forms, reports, queries, and other modules using Design view; from creating, importing, or exporting those same objects; and even from viewing or changing your Visual Basic for Applications source code.

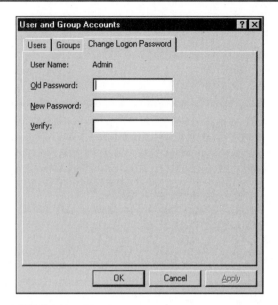

Use the
Change Logon
Password tab
of the User
and Group
Accounts
dialog box to
change an
individual
user's pass

Figure 10-4.

NOTE: This feature is much like compiling an application written in
Visual Basic and then distributing the executable (.EXE) file without the
source code. You'll distribute the .MDE file to your users, and keep the
original .MDB yourself. You'll want to keep the original database so that you
can modify it when desired. You won't want to distribute the .MDB file,
because users could get into it and make changes—the very thing you don't
want to happen.

Before you do so, however, there are a couple of things you should know. If
you have security features (database passwords, and workgroup and user
accounts and permissions) built into your database, they will be included
with the new .MDE file as well. If you don't want them in the .MDE file,
you'll have to remove them from the original database.

If you have several databases that refer to each other and you want to save
any (or all) of them as .MDE files, you'll have to start at the lowest point in
the chain, and convert the files "backward." For example, suppose that you
have two databases—A and B—and that A references B. You would first
convert B to an .MDE file. Then, open A, and change it so that it references

the new .MDE version of B. Finally, convert A to an .MDE file. If you convert A first, it will always point to the original version of B, no matter what you do to B later.

Also, if you have a replicated database, you will have to remove all replication features before saving it as an .MDE file.

To create an .MDE file, open the database for exclusive use. Next, select Tools | Database Utilities | Make MDE File. You'll be presented with a dialog box that asks for the name of the MDE file—it will default to the same database name but with an MDE extension. Choose Save. The progress bar at the bottom of the screen will blip along until finished.

To use an .MDE file, simply distribute the .MDE file to your users (they'll need a copy of Access 2000, of course), and have them open it just as they would open a regular Access database. When they do, they'll find that all the menu options, toolbars, and command buttons that allow modifications to be made to the database have been disabled.

10

CHAPTER 11

Collections and the Access Object Model

There is one last topic to cover before I get into the meat of building an application for real. The topic is "collections"—something important to understand, in a conceptual way, before you tackle the construction of a complete application. You don't need to know about them to "get by" in Access for a while, but you will need this information for some tasks, and it will help make more sense of other tasks.

A *collection* is a generic term that refers to a group of objects, such as a group of forms, a group of reports, or a group of controls on a form. Collections refer to how the various objects are related and talk to each other. You've already seen collections in action in Chapter 8 on VBA—you may recall how we used the syntax

```
If [Forms]![frmCalculate Function]![txtCountry].Value = "USA" Then
```

to refer to a specific control. The [Forms] expression refers to one of the collections in Access; there are several others, and they can be used to manipulate virtually any element in an application or database.

Most of the chapters in this section provide you with skills that are useful by themselves—you don't need to build forms before you can build reports. This chapter, however, is different. Collections, while perhaps interesting, aren't very useful in and of themselves. If you've been skipping around, you will find that Chapters 7 and 8 are helpful prerequisites before tackling this one.

Access 2000: An Object-Based Tool

Before diving in head first, it would be a good idea to discuss a couple of terms you're going to hear about more and more over the next few years. With the popularly of Visual C++ and Visual FoxPro as components of Microsoft's Visual Studio development toolkit, object-oriented programming (OOP) has become very popular. As a result, the OOP label is being applied to everything—whether or not it really fits—and, unfortunately, Access 2000 is one of those targets.

In the olden days (about five years ago), programming involved a hierarchy of programs that called one another in a chain. Each program contained both variables that were used internally within a program and variables that could be passed from one program to another and back. Some of these programs drew characters on the computer screen and occasionally took input from the user. Other than the explicit passing of variables from one program to a subroutine, programs didn't know about each other, and certainly didn't know about the hand-painted user interface on the computer monitor.

Access 2000 is object based, which means entities have properties and methods, and that they belong to collections of other entities. These entities are called objects. An object's counterpart in the olden days (the term brings to mind women in hoop skirts and men in bowlers, all hunched over Apple iMacs and IBM Thinkpads, doesn't it?) is a program. Object properties used to be variables, and subroutines are now methods. But life is so much easier now. For example, if Program R7 needed to reference a variable in Program H12, an explicit call had to take place. With object-based programming, a reference like

```
R7.MyProperty = ProgramH12.AnotherProperty
```

is all you need. Furthermore, objects can reference their own properties in the same manner. And even better, a screen is also an object, and thus other objects can reference specific controls or other properties of a screen—a feat that was impossible to do with the old procedural programming techniques.

Methods of an object can be run both from within the object and from other objects. Additionally, methods can be attached to events and automatically run when that event is fired—thus, a program (method) can automatically be run when a user performs an action, such as leaving a text box or changing the value in a combo box.

An object-based tool is much easier to work with than non-object-based tools for a variety of reasons. For example, object-based tools encourage a much more structured programming approach.

IN DEPTH

11

A Strict Definition of Object-Oriented Programming (OOP)

You may run into people who apply the term "object-oriented programming" (OOP) to anything that is remotely connected to an object. It's good to be strict about the proper usage of a term. As Abraham Lincoln said, "If you call a tail a leg, how many legs does a dog have? Five? No—it still has four—calling a tail a leg doesn't make it a leg."

You will hear others talking about how Visual Basic is OOP, but it's really object based, not object oriented. Access, too, is object based, but not OOP. That doesn't mean it's bad—but simply calling a vehicle a SUV doesn't mean you can go off-roading with it.

Strictly speaking, OOP has three primary features—and a language must have all three to truly qualify as an OOP tool.

The first is inheritance, and this is where object-based tools most commonly fall short. In an object-oriented language, you can create a definition of an object, and this definition is called a *class*. Then, you can create variations of that class, called *subclasses*, that inherit the properties and methods of the class. For example, if you were going to create a password maintenance form, you might create a password maintenance form class first. This password maintenance form would have a text box for entering an original password, and then a second text box for entering the new password, and a third text box for repeating the new password. This class would also have a method that would perform some sort of rules check for the new password—verifying that, perhaps, it wasn't the same as the original password, that the new password was at least a certain length, and that it wasn't on a list of passwords that had already been used. When you use this password maintenance form class, you actually create an instance of the class that you use as the data-entry form in your application.

What if, however, you had to incorporate a different type of rule, such as requiring that the password be changed every so often. Instead of putting together a whole new password maintenance form, you would simply subclass the password maintenance class, add a new rule, and then create an instance of the subclass to use as your data entry from within your application.

The subclassed form would inherit all the other behaviors of the class—the three text boxes, the existing rules, and so on. But you would also be able to add, modify, or override behaviors and properties as desired.

Finally, changes to the class will automatically be inherited by all the classes' subclasses.

In object-based tools, inheritance is usually implemented as "cut and paste inheritance." The code is copied to the subclasses, which means (1) that you'd be just as well off simply making a copy of the original form, and (2) changes to the class (original form) aren't reflected in the subclasses.

The second feature of OOP is encapsulation. I've discussed the idea of how properties and methods are tied to an object, instead of buried in layers of program hierarchies. This is the basis of encapsulation—each object knows about its own properties and methods, and hides everything except those properties and methods that are supposed to be exposed to the outside world (other objects.)

The third feature is polymorphism—the use of a single noun that is implemented differently or the use of a verb to perform multiple tasks depending on its environment. For example, a report object and a label object may both have a "print" method; but the actual task performed—sending an 8 1/2 × 11-inch page to a portrait printer or a 2 × 4-inch shipping label to a dot matrix printer—varies. Similarly, many objects have a "caption" property—a form's caption appears in the title bar while a label's caption is all you see of the label and a check box's caption appears to the right of the actual check box itself. The object takes responsibility for knowing how to actually perform the verb or use the noun.

Nonetheless, the object-based techniques you learn will stand you in good stead should you move to a fully object-oriented tool in the future.

11

The Object Model Concept

A *collection* is a group of objects, such as a group of forms, a group of reports, or a group of controls on a form. Some collections just contain a single group of objects, and so the hierarchy—or containership—only goes one level deep. For example, both forms and reports can contain controls. Other collections, however, can go several levels deep—databases have table definitions, which then have fields.

When you open an Access application, Access sets up two objects—a top-level application object and a database engine object. The application object contains three collections and two open objects. The application object itself contains properties that you can reference to determine various attributes of the application, such as which forms, controls, and menu commands have focus. The collections are the Forms collection (all the open forms), the Reports collection (all the open reports), and the Modules collection (all the open modules). The open objects are the DoCmd and Screen objects. These allow you to determine the current control, form, and report, as well as the control, form, and report that most recently had focus—without knowing the specific names. In addition, the DoCmd object allows you to execute most macros from within VBA.

The database engine object allows you to access the entire database hierarchy through a series of collections and objects. The engine first establishes a workspace, which can point to Access' native data engine—the Jet database engine—or another, such as SQL Server 7.0, in its place. Once the workspace has been established, all the objects in a database—tabledefs; querydefs; relations; recordsets; and, if necessary, ODBC connections (for non-Jet databases)—are available as subsequent collections. The tabledefs collection can be used to add, edit, and delete tables programmatically; the querydefs collection is used for the same purpose on queries.

Referencing Parts of the Object Model

There are three ways to address objects in the object model. You got a quick look at one way in Chapter 8 and now it's time to examine the technique, as well as discuss the other ways, more thoroughly.

The first method involves explicitly naming the object within the collection, like so:

CollectionName![Object Name]

For example, to reference the Cars form, you could use the expression

Forms![frmCars]

The second method uses a string constant in place of the object name reference, like so:

CollectionName("Object Name")

The previous example would look like this:

Forms("frmCars")

The third method, potentially the most confusing, but also the most useful in terms of playing tricks and working around limits in the product, is to indirectly reference an object through its relative object number. Each object in a collection has a number. The .Count property tells you how many objects are in a collection, and so you can iterate through all the objects in a collection by incrementing a counter from 0 to .Count–1. Suppose you wanted to change the caption of every form in the application. You could do so with a piece of generic code like so:

```
for i = 0 to collection.count-1
   Forms(i).caption = "New Caption"
next
```

You've undoubtedly noticed that long object expressions that contain many pieces may use a combination of exclamation marks and periods to separate the various arguments in the expression and, often but not always, use brackets as well. You're most likely confused about when to use each of these special characters.

First, use a set of brackets to enclose a name that contains embedded blanks or special characters such as underscores. It's best to always use brackets— Access will insert them automatically in property sheets and action arguments, so why not be consistent and use them throughout?

A period is used before an argument that is a name of a collection, a property, or a method that can be executed. One common rule of thumb is to use a period when the name "belongs to" the preceding argument. The Update method belongs to the grid object, or the Caption property belongs to the form. For example, the expression

```
DBEngine.Workspaces(0).Databases.Count
```

11

returns the number of databases in the current workspace.

Use an exclamation mark before an argument if the object is a member of the collection, such as a form or report that you created. As an example, you could use the expression

```
Forms![frmNew Members].Caption
```

to return the value of the caption of your form, frmNew Members. The form name is a member of the Forms collection, while the Caption property belongs to the frmNew Members form.

Safely Referencing Workspaces and Databases

You'll notice that I used an argument of 0 in the previous Workspaces argument. This is just another example of the third method of object referencing—the 0 indicates I want to use the first workspace in the DBEngine collection.

This isn't always the safest method to reference a workspace or database. A better method is to use the native Access CurrentDB( ) function. In fact, when referencing a database in a VBA procedure, you can create a variable that you can use in place of a long object reference. You do this by declaring a variable (using a Dim, Public, or Static statement) and then use the Set statement to actually create the variable assignment. For example,

```
Dim dbMyDatabase as Database
Set dbMyDatabase = CurrentDB()
```

declares a variable named dbMyDatabase as type Database (similar to declaring a variable as int or variant), and then uses it to create an object reference to the current database. You can then use dbMyDatabase as shorthand instead of the long DBEngine.Workspace(0).Database type of expression. For example,

```
dim tblCWO as TableDef
set tblCWO as dbMyDatabase![tlbCars Without Owners]
```

One more note: Several objects have a default collection, and you can concoct expressions that infer that default collection instead of explicitly naming it. For example, the following two statements

```
dbMyDatabase.TableDefs![tblCars]
dbMyDatabase![tblCars]
```

are identical since TableDefs is the default collection in a database object. I recommend that you don't depend on this, since it doesn't buy you much and it's easy to make mistakes if you've read the expression incorrectly.

PART III

Building an Access Application

CHAPTER 12

Structuring an Access Application

It's time to build an application! In this chapter, I'm going to provide a road map for designing an Access application. Up to this point, I've shown you the tools you need to use Access 2000 in your own day-to-day work and to begin building applications that you can turn over to others. However, just as having lessons on using a hammer, saw, screwdriver, and router doesn't prepare you for building a house (or even a doghouse), there's more to learn before you can build complete Access applications.

I'll use this analogy of building a house frequently throughout this section, because there are a lot of parallels. I've built perhaps 50 applications over the 15-plus years that I've been in this business, and I've learned a lot about what to do (and what not to do) during that span. (Fifty applications may not seem like that many until you consider that several of these took more than 2,000 hours each.)

People get into building applications on a PC platform because they *can*—all that's required is a thousand-dollar computer and a copy of Access or Visual Basic. Unlike with mainframe programming, for which you needed access to a multimillion-dollar mainframe computer and sufficient knowledge and intelligence to work with that type of computer, PC programming has no artificial barriers to access. However, with this immediate access to programming comes another problem: Software development isn't subject to the same legal restrictions as other professions—but that doesn't mean that it shouldn't be. Businesses nowadays depend on their computer systems, and problems with those computer systems can cause significant other problems as well.

Thus, software should be developed with the same rigor that accounting systems are managed, factories are built, and products are engineered. But as I just said, there are no requirements nor is there enforcement of any professional standards or regulations. This lack of rigor can lead to three problems. First, a lack of rigor means no prior planning may be used during the process of development, which means applications can end up looking like they were slapped together—because, indeed, they were. Would you want your surgeon to make things up as he operates, with each operation being performed haphazardly? Second, poor practices may be used, because the developer doesn't know any better. Would you want your house wired by someone who didn't understand electricity, and whose primary measure of quality was whether or not he got electrocuted by the end of the job? And the third problem is simple sloppy work because at some point, the pressure of having to get something to work leads to shortcuts being taken.

If I was going to build a dog house or a lean-to for the garage, or convert the basement to a family room, I'd probably sketch out a few drawings on a piece of paper, go to the local hardware store, and come back with a station wagon full of wood, nails, and assorted hardware fixtures. Then I'd just start sawing and hammering until the project was done.

And it would look like that's what I'd done—plunged head first into building before laying out some plans. The walls wouldn't be straight, I'd be missing a piece here or there because I ran out of materials, there'd be nails here and screws there, and a hole where there shouldn't be one, and so on.

Of course, the end result would be acceptable if it was for my own family. But if I was doing this for someone else—even a friend—it most likely wouldn't be good enough.

The same holds true for building applications. If you're going to be the only one using it, you can be considerably more relaxed about how it's built and what lies under the hood. And this is particularly true if the application is a "casual" one—say, for maintaining the mailing list for the church choir or tracking your holiday season list.

But as soon as you're going to have someone else use the application, even casually, you're going to have to be more rigorous about how it's put together. In the previous chapters, I didn't spend a lot of time discussing these topics—I wanted you to become comfortable with the tools you were learning to use. The rigor comes now.

The ideas and concepts I'm going to introduce in this chapter are not the only way to structure an application, but it's one way. If you find a methodology that you prefer, go ahead and use it. The important message of this chapter is that a well-planned process for structuring and building an application is essential and will serve you well.

What Is the Pain?

12

Writing applications is hard. At the same time, it's a lot of fun. I guess this is like mountain climbing or surfing—it's difficult work, but it's also very enjoyable. These two attributes—difficulty and pleasure—lead to a couple of immediate issues.

◆ Since it's hard, you "gotta wanna." Application development is not for the faint of heart or the easily cowed.

◆ Since it's fun, you're very likely to get distracted unless you keep your eye on the ball.

For these two reasons, you must have a goal. When I go to see a potential customer, I always ask right off the bat, "What is the pain that you're experiencing?" It may be difficult to ask your users (or customers) this in so blunt a fashion, so another way to put it is "What is the 'big win' you're expecting for this app?" The "big win" is, ultimately, to remove the pain they are feeling. After all, why go through all this trouble if nothing significant is to be gained as a result?

This problem must be refined into one or two sentences. For example, each of these is a valid "pain" for the MG Car Club:

◆   "It takes far too long to produce labels, member lists, renewal notices, and other types of reports and forms for the membership; and the current manual process is also heavily prone to error."

◆   "We can't easily find out who has what type of car, or whether a certain type of car is owned by a club member, and it is very difficult to submit club rosters of members and cars to event organizers who want to list event attendees."

◆   "Members (and nonmembers) want to be able to buy and sell cars and parts through a centralized type of system, perhaps through the World Wide Web."

Whatever the pain is, it serves as a yardstick against which you can measure the success of the project when complete. Is the pain gone? If not, the project can't be considered successful even if the app is done and it runs.

Working with a computer and, specifically, programming, for a certain part of the population, is a lot of fun. It's a creative and yet intellectually stimulating task. The nature of what we do with visual tools like Access, furthermore, lends itself to iterative development, and thus to a series of discoveries. This discovery of the new capabilities of the tool you're working with, combined with increasing abilities of your own as you become more experienced and skilled, results in "more stuff" being added to the application than was originally planned. This is a common occurrence—and, in fact, it has a formal name: Scope Creep, or Feature Creep—when the scope of the project or the list of features gets bigger and bigger as the project development process goes on.

While not inherently bad in itself (after all, more functionality is often good), it's critical to keep in mind whether or not the new features being discussed or added are important to address the pain originally discussed.

The Goal of the Application

Once the pain has been defined, it's often easy to describe what is needed to fix it—at least in general terms. However, it's also easy to go down the wrong path, defining the purpose of the application incorrectly, without having defined what the pain was initially.

The goal describes what the computer system and application is going to do. For example, the different pains described in the previous section might have the following corresponding goals:

Pain: It takes far too long to produce labels, member lists, renewal notices, and other types of reports and forms for the membership, and the current manual process is also heavily prone to error.	**Goal:** The Access 2000 MG Car Club Member Tracking System will provide a centralized place for the entry and editing of member and car information and the ability to automatically produce a variety of reports, labels, and forms.
Pain: We can't easily find out who has what type of car, or whether a certain type of car is owned by a club member, and it is very difficult to submit club rosters of members and cars to event organizers who want to list event attendees.	**Goal:** The Access 2000 MG Car Club Vehicle Roster Application will allow members to locate a variety of demographic data regarding the makes and models of vehicles owned by members of the club.
Pain: Members (and nonmembers) want to be able to buy and sell cars and parts through a centralized type of system, perhaps through the World Wide Web.	**Goal:** The Access 2000 MG Car Club Auction System will enable members and nonmembers to submit items for sale, as well as view and purchase items that others have put up for sale through a web site.

Defining the Feature Set

12

Once you have decided what the application should do in a general way, it's time to be more explicit. A typical Access application may have anywhere from a half-dozen to a couple dozen key functions, including a variety of data-entry screens; perhaps some processing; and, of course, output, such as reports and labels.

It's easy to get roped into a lot of detail at this stage, as users get elbow-deep into specific issues that they've thought a lot about and want to share with you immediately. The technique I use to avoid getting bogged into details when we're still trying to look at the big picture is to identify the "big pieces" of the application. I position the description of these "big pieces" as the "bullet points" on the back of a box of shrink-wrapped software that you would buy in a retail store. Those descriptions don't list specific functions as much as they cover broad capabilities. For example, bullet points might read

◆ Add, edit, and delete information about members and the automobiles they currently own or used to own.

◆ Print labels of 28 different sizes containing user-defined data fields for user-selected categories.

◆ Share data with up to six users simultaneously over a local area Novell, Windows 98, or Windows NT network.

With the types of applications that Access is well suited for, these bullet points will lend themselves to the identification of specific forms, queries, processes, and reports needed in the system.

Identification of Forms, Processes, and Reports

The next step is to create a list of specific forms, processes, and reports that the application will contain. The key here is to identify what the user will be doing with each component. Will a form be used to enter and edit data, or will it be used to run a query and display the results? Will a report be run whenever a new member joins or at the end of every month, to be included with the next month's club newsletter? Applications don't just sit there—people *use* them, and so the challenge here is to define how a particular component will be used.

In an automobile club application like the one being described in this book, the list of components might look like this:

◆ Member Maintenance (add, edit, and delete members)

◆ Car Maintenance (add, edit, and delete cars)

◆ Owner Maintenance (add, edit, or delete an owner record)

◆ Ownership Maintenance (attach or detach a car to an owner for a particular period of time)

◆ Event Attendance (attach attendance at an event to a specific member)

◆ Event Maintenance (add, edit, and delete information about events)

◆ Membership Renewals (produce membership renewal notices)

◆ Mailing Lists (produce mailing lists to members based on a variety of criteria)

◆ Membership Reports (produce lists of members, including or not including cars and events, based on a variety of criteria for selecting which members to print and how)

There are obviously more functions that would be needed for a complete application, but my purpose here is to illustrate a range of functionality, not deliver a complete system.

Now that you've got a list, it's time to draw up the blueprints for these components. I could write a whole book on this specific phase alone (and, indeed, I have!), but the basics can be covered in short order.

I take out a blank piece of paper, and sketch out—by hand—what I want this form or report to look like, or, in the case of a process, what the steps are that it will perform. Once I am done with a sketch, I start the computer and create a "prototype" in Access—not putting any data or logic in the form, but just showing what the form is going to look like. Many people will argue with this seemingly "old-fashioned" method, claiming that you could skip the first step, and do this "prototyping" on the computer immediately. They're certainly correct.

If you like, you can do this on the computer, but I've found I do a better job if I have a first whack at it by hand. First of all, it's tempting to do "too much" if you're prototyping on the computer—before you know it, you've got a half-dozen macros and a bunch of VBA code written when all you wanted to do is figure out what the form is going to look like. Second, by transferring my hand-drawn prototype to the computer, I get a second pass at it, during which I normally discover better ways of doing things—or find mistakes in the initial pass. This two-pass prototyping process allows me to refine the component in a way I couldn't if I just used the computer.

12

It's important to be consistent when laying out your screens and reports. I've run into far too many applications in which each component of a system looks like it was created by a different person, and each person was inflicted with his or her own special case of dementia. To avoid ending up with an application that looks like it was designed by Picasso, group the components in terms of general functionality, and decide on a general "look and feel" for each of those.

For example, all your "quick data entry" forms should work in a similar fashion, all your "search" screens should function in the same way, and all your query functions should follow the same set of procedures. You'll save yourself time programming and testing, and you'll save your users time while they are trying to learn the application.

There are five parts to this process of "specification," as discussed in the following sections.

Purpose

Even before I draw a single line on that blank piece of paper, I write out exactly what this component is going to do. It may seem trivial or even silly, but that's because you're in the middle of the application right now. It may not be nearly as clear to you six months later, or to a new user to the system. I've seen far too many systems about which a customer will tell me "This screen was here when I joined the department. No one knows what it's for and we never use it."

Prototype and Screen Shot of Form or Report

This is the hand-drawn sketch and the corresponding prototype in Access. Having a picture to accompany the description of the component makes it easier to understand. Ever try to follow directions given in writing without a map? Much harder than if a map was provided as part of the directions. The screen shot of the prototype is the map.

Access

No, I'm not talking about the Access product, but about the access mechanism. How do users get to this component? They may run a menu command, or click a button on a startup form, or select a toolbar button. But many forms are not only called from one of these mechanisms, but also from another form. Here you should explain all the different ways that users will be able to get to this component.

Usage

At this stage, you must describe how the user will use the component, particularly in the context of processes outside of the component. For example, you might describe that the membership application form is received by the club secretary who uses this form to enter the data in the application. You would also want to describe operations that are not completely obvious. For example, the user may need to enter data elsewhere before using this form, such as adding colors to the lookup table before selecting a color for a car. Or perhaps he or she needs to run a "month-end" process before adding members in the following month.

Rules

Now you can describe, in detail, how the component works. The operation of each control, including default values, validation rules, and macros and VBA code attached to events, is outlined here. There are several types of operations to consider.

First, you must describe the data that belongs in the component—how it is initially populated (default values) and what values are allowed (validation rules).

Next, consider the effect that data entry has on other parts of the form. Entering a value in one text box may cause a calculation to be performed and a value entered in another text box. If a certain value changes the operation of the form, it's described here. For instance, an option group may allow the choice of one of the four seasons. You may choose to enable or disable other controls based on which season is chosen. Describe what is going to happen—and why.

The third type of rule to describe concerns the interaction of controls with respect to each other. A control may be disabled until another operation is performed, either through data entry (as just described) or through another action, such as selecting a check box, pressing a command button, or issuing a menu command.

Describing the rules for a process is both easier and harder than doing so for a user interface control. They're easier to describe in that you don't have to contend with a user interface. On the other hand, the process itself has to be defined—you're almost writing "pseudo-code" while describing the process. An important part of describing a process is defining what happens if something goes wrong—a file being imported isn't properly set up, for example.

12

Rules for reports are also fairly straightforward if you base a report on a predefined query. The majority of the description defines how the query is built, and the remainder is just frosting—describing how the report will be formatted and the special attributes for groups, totals, and so on.

Once you have described all the rules for the component, the programming you have to do will be considerably easier since these descriptions act as an outline for the code you will write.

Common Components

After you build a few Access applications, you'll find that there are several components that show up in every one of them. For example, you'll most likely have a menu option that calls data maintenance operations, but you'll probably provide a form from which those operations are launched. You may provide user and security maintenance options for selected permission levels. You may have an "About" screen or a User-Defined Help screen. Perhaps you always have a Lookup Maintenance screen. It's more efficient to identify those components and list them as "standard features" that just come along for the ride.

It's not only a more efficient practice to do this, but it also leads to fewer bugs, as components that have already been written and are proven to work are less likely to cause problems than components that are written from scratch.

You may even find yourself copying custom components from one application to another, either using them as is or modifying them slightly to fit the requirements of the new application. After all, how many variations on a customer data-entry form can there possibly be?

Describing Access to the Components

The components of the application have been defined in the previous section, but how does a user get to them? There are several ways that this can be accomplished. Probably the most commonly used technique is to have a startup form that provides a jumping-off point for each component. When the application loads, a form displays automatically. The form contains buttons for each component—whether it's a form, process, or report—and a custom menu and toolbar may or may not be displayed for each component.

My personal preference—a main menu whose menu commands launch components—runs a little counter to this technique, but it's simply my personal preference. You can offer both options to your users, and see what they prefer.

At any rate, you'll need to specify what your access mechanism—form, toolbar, menu, or combination thereof—is, and how it operates.

Listing Your Naming Conventions

In the first section of this book, I dabbled with naming conventions of various pieces of Access, including forms, tables, and so on. Now it's time to get more rigorous about these conventions.

Before I do so, however, I need to make it clear that these conventions are guidelines that ought to be followed except in special cases, not hard and fast rules that must be followed come hell or high water. Just as with normalization, it's OK to break the rules once you know (1) what rule you're breaking and (2) why you are breaking it. Second, there are a lot of naming conventions out there, and there isn't necessarily one that's better than another—a lot has to do with your personal preferences. What's important is to choose one and then to follow it. Any naming convention is better than randomness.

The first set of objects to name is the objects in a database. Each of these has a prefix as listed in the following table.

Object	Name	Example
Form	frm<name>	frmOwnerMaintenance
Subform	frmSub<name>	frmSubOwnerMaintenanceCars
Query	qry<name>	qryOldCars
Report	rpt<name>	rptEnginesForSale
Module	mod<name>	modPriceCalculations
Check box	chk<name>	chkIsMember
Combo box	cbo<name>	cboColor
Label	lbl<name>	lblCompany
List box	lst<name>	lstMembers
Option button	opt<name>	optWinter
Option group	opg<name>	opgSeason
Text box	txt<name>	txtCompany
Toggle button	tgl<name>	tglIsActive

12

However, having a list of common prefixes, while a good start, isn't really enough. The next part of a naming convention for objects is structuring the name that follows the prefix. For example, suppose you have a number of reports that are rosters of various entities, like Cars, Owners, and Components. You could name these reports like so:

```
rptCarRoster
rptOwnerRoster
rptComponentRoster
```

because that's how you would reference them in English: "The Owner Roster." But if you wanted to keep all the rosters together, you could name them like so:

```
rptRosterCar
rptRosterOwner
rptRosterComponent
```

Whichever way you choose, make a decision and then stick with it. My personal preference is to create a name that moves from the general to the specific. I start with the most general noun possible, and then add qualifiers to it. For example, an "Amount" field is often found in a table—in fact, there are often many amount fields. I would name them as follows:

```
txtAmtBase
txtAmtList
txtAmtAddOn
txtAmtTaxFederal
txtAmtTaxState
txtAmtTaxLocal
```

You'll see that all the Amount fields are grouped together, and then additional qualifiers are appended to the name as needed. And even these qualifiers are named in the same fashion—the generic "Tax" qualifier is then followed by what type of tax it is.

The second set of objects to name are data and variables, including tables, fields, and variables.

Object	Name	Example
Table	tbl<name>	tblCar
Field	One character identifying data type	Autonumber: aIDCar
		Text: tNameLast
		Memo: mDescription
		YesNo: yIsMember
		Numeric: nAmtTaxLocal
		DateTime: dBirth
		Currency: cInitiationFee
Library module variable	g_<name>	
Global variable	q_<name>	
Global constant	k_<name>	
Form variable	f_<name>	
Form/local constant	c_<name>	
Local variable	l_<name>	

You'll notice that the field names follow the same order of general noun first followed by increasingly descriptive adjectives. Thus, the fields for a person's name would be

    tNamePrefix
    tNameFirst
    tNameMiddle
    tNameLast
    tNameSuffix

12

You may be cringing at this, thinking it's awkward to refer to a field as "NameLast" instead of "LastName" but there's a very practical reason for doing so. When you need to pick a couple of name fields for a mailing label or report, do you want to scroll up and down the list looking for "FirstName," and then scroll through the list again looking for "LastName"? Or do you want to find them all grouped together, in alphabetical order? I find it's much easier to have "NameFirst," "NameLast," and "NameMiddle" grouped together.

I also don't have to worry about what I named a field—all I have to do is remember what the field represents. So instead of trying to remember if I called a list price field "ListPrice" or "BasePrice" or "CatalogPrice," I just look under "Price," knowing they're all grouped together.

Defining the Data Structures

You'll probably notice that the functions listed in the "Identification of Forms, Processes, and Reports" section earlier in this chapter don't match exactly with the description of the database back in Chapter 2. First of all, remember that the users describing how an application will best serve them don't think in terms of normalized structures. To them, "Members," "Owners," and "Previous Owners" may be completely separate entities, with no relationship or commonality between them except that they're all probably people. (An organization such as a company, museum, or car club might also own a car.)

Second, this happenstance is an example of one of the fundamental rules of computer applications: *Useful applications are dynamic.* This means that if a system is a useful one, the users will discover new functionality, or want changes in the functionality they already have, either because they've found a better way to do things or because the processes the system works under have changed.

For example, during the development of this book, a new requirement was discovered—the ability to track members' attendance at events. Why wasn't this brought up before? Because people are human. Perhaps they forget, or maybe those involved in the design of the system didn't think to ask the Event chairman what his requirements would be. It's even possible that this requirement came about as a new Event chairman, in the midst of corresponding with his peers in other car clubs around the world, came up with it as a brand new idea.

At any rate, I brought this situation up to draw your attention to the fact that this occurrence—a change to the system—is not an anomaly, it's not a screw-up on the part of the developer, it's not the fault of the user. It's part of the process; so instead of trying to resist it, accept the fact that it's going to happen and plan for it accordingly.

You may be wondering how to plan for something when you don't know what it is that's going to happen. Well, one of the easiest ways is to properly structure your data. In Chapter 2, I purposely created two tables that both contained people: Owners and Previous Owners. This, as you might have been suspecting, was a mistake, since the same entity—a person—is contained in both tables, and the distinction is fairly arbitrary—and can shift at any time. One day a person is an owner; the next, after the sale goes through, they're not. It would be pretty awkward to move someone from one table to another just because he or she sold (or bought) a car. But other things could happen as well. For example, suppose this new requirement— the tracking of attendance—is added. Since a previous owner could have attended an event just as easily as a current owner, links have to be created for both Owners and Previous Owners to the Event table. And several forms have to be changed as well—twice as many, in fact, as there should have been. If the table had been designed properly in the first place—having all people in one table, and then letting the current ownership of a car determine whether or not someone was an owner or a previous owner—tracking attendance at events would be made easier.

In fact, another subtle requirement would also be made easier—tracking membership in the club. An owner may be a member one year and then move out of the area and no longer be a member, but the club may want to still keep track of the owner. The owner may move back to the area, for instance, or may get involved in other activities, such as auctions, so that the club wants to maintain contact.

As a result, the data structures we'll use to build our application will vary from those used to demonstrate the various pieces of Access. You can open up the Chapter 11 MG database to see all the details; but so that you can follow along in the text without having to go to your computer, here's a summary of the data structures:

Owner	Contains one record for each person, couple, or organization who has at one time owned a car.
Dues	Contains one record for each payment of membership dues.
Event	Contains one record for each MG-related event, such as a membership meeting, a car rally, or a GOF (Gathering of the Faithful).
Car	Contains one record for each automobile.

12

Component	Contains one record for each major component of an automobile. A major component is one that has its own serial number, such as a chassis or engine block.
Lookup	Contains records for lookup values such as color.
Ownership join	Provides the many-to-many relationship between Owners and Cars. Contains one record for each instance of automobile ownership. For example, if an owner currently owns two cars and has in the past owned three others, there would be five records in this table for that owner, each identifying (1) the owner, (2) the car, and (3) the length of time of ownership.
Attendance join	Provides the many-to-many relationship between Owners and Events, so that one owner can attend many events and one event can be attended by many owners (what fun would it be if only one owner could attend an event?). Contains one record for each instance of event attendance by an owner. For example, if an owner has attended three events, there would be three records in this table for that owner, each identifying (1) the owner, and (2) the event. In this case, additional information is not needed, since the presence of an Attendance join record is all that is needed. Either the owner attended or didn't. The Event record would contain information such as date and time, cost, and location.

When you describe the structure of the data, there is a lot of ground to cover. First, obviously, you have to define each table, and an example of this is shown in the previous table. Next, each field in each table has to be described. The attributes for each field include several necessary properties, including the name, what data type, and how long. However, you can define additional attributes for each field as needed. For example, you may decide to define a format, an input mask, a caption, a default value, whether the field is required or null, and so on.

Developers attack this problem of field definitions in different ways. One way is to simply list each attribute that has to be changed, doing the very minimum necessary. While this requires a minimum amount of work, it's also more likely that you'll forget to define attributes. Another way is to create a worksheet that lists every possible attribute of a field, and then fill in every blank—even if it's to indicate that that particular attribute will be the default.

If you're developing an application with the assistance of a knowledgeable user, you can often give these worksheets to the user and have him or her fill in much of the information, such as field lengths, default values, and so on.

Finally, you'll want to define the relationships between the tables. If you've named your tables, fields, and indexes properly, this will be easy, since the foreign keys in each table will match easily with their primary counterparts in the tables that should be related.

Initial Structure Considerations

Up to this point, I've assumed that everything in the application will be contained in one MDB file, but that's not always going to be the case. First, if you build a large number of Access applications, you will eventually find yourself writing the same routines over and over. Instead of doing so, doesn't it make sense to create a separate MDB that contains all that common code? This is called a *library*, and all professional programs make use of this technique.

You may not want to jump into this type of structure immediately, instead preferring to get comfortable with building a complete application, and then getting more sophisticated as your experience grows. However, it's a good idea to be aware of this capability now, so you can be ready to start experimenting with it when you're comfortable.

Second, you may not include everything in your MDB if your Access application talks to non-Access data—which can be done in a variety of ways. For example, you may want to reference data in Excel spreadsheets or lists of files in a directory, or you may even connect to another data source, such as Microsoft SQL Server.

Third, you may not include everything in your MDB if you are going to distribute your application to other users. In this case, you may want to put the data in one MDB and the rest of the application—the forms, queries, reports, modules, etc.—in another. The reason for this is maintainability. Suppose you create an application and distribute it to your users (or customer). They work with the application for a few weeks or a couple of months, and what do you know, they develop a "wish list" of changes to the application. But they've already entered data into the application. If you take a copy of their populated MDB to work on, what are they going to do? Either you have to prohibit them from entering data into the application until you have finished with the changes, or you make them enter all their data in again once you deliver an updated version of the application. Either way is unpleasant at best. If, however, you can deliver a new version of the forms, reports, modules, and queries, and simply plug it into the database they've still been able to use, then everyone is happy.

12

CHAPTER 13

Building an Application Foundation

In the last chapter, I developed a road map for designing an Access application. In this chapter, I'm going to start building the application. You can think of the last chapter as the "training film" you watched to learn how to hit a tennis ball—the theory and classroom instruction are all well and good, but it's time to get on the tennis court. Of course, you wouldn't expect to grab a racket and start serving aces during your first 15 minutes. Similarly, you shouldn't expect to build a world-class application by the end of this chapter. Instead, we'll venture onto the court and walk through the first few swings together.

The MG Car Club Application Specification

In Chapter 12, I described some possible forms, reports, and other components that would be included in our MG Car Club application. It's time to be more detailed, but I'm not going to describe the entire spec. Instead, I'll go through it piece by piece, covering each part of the spec as appropriate.

It's essential to plan your application first, instead of clicking File | New | Form and starting to drag controls onto the design surface. The latter seems much easier—thinking is hard work, after all. Making changes to software doesn't seem drastic; the only thing you're wasting if you have to rework a form or end up duplicating a report is your time. But isn't your time a valuable asset? Just as you probably wouldn't spend all afternoon driving around town to save 40 cents on a cord of firewood, you shouldn't treat the time devoted to your programming effort as limitless or free.

For the purposes of this book, as well as to get my dad started on the automation of tasks for his MG car club, I'll define the application's Pain, Goal, and Bullet Points as follows.

Pain With the growth of the MG Car Club, the day-to-day administration has become an overwhelming burden for the volunteer officers of the club. In addition, the car club has a number of interesting and rare automobiles whose availability for shows and rallies should be more widely known.

Goal The goal is to automate the administration of the MG Car Club, and to provide a computerized registry of all members and their automobiles.

Bullet Points The key functions needed are to:

◆   Maintain (add, edit, delete, and search) contact information for all past and present members

◆   Maintain membership information, including dues paid

◆   Maintain information about MG-related events

◆   Maintain event attendance information

◆   Maintain information about automobiles owned by or of interest to members

◆   Produce mailing labels according to a variety of conditions

◆   Produce dues invoices for memberships about to expire

◆   Produce lists of members together with the events they've attended, awards they've won, and other information

◆   Produce lists of automobiles together with a component description and an ownership history

◆   Export a list of members for the National MG Owners Association

To make this book compact enough that you can finish it before the next version of Access is released, I won't build every component described here, but will build enough of them to show you how to do it yourself. You'll be able to build each of the forms here, as well as others of your own, after we've practiced with just a couple of them.

Startup Process

Now that we know what the application is supposed to do, how is the user going to use it? As I said earlier, I prefer a standard CUA (Common User Access) menu instead of the popular Access switchboard startup form.

The menu bar will contain the standard list of pads, with one exception. I use "Forms" instead of "Files" because users typically think in terms of forms rather than computer files. The menu pads are

Forms
Edit
Processes
Reports
Tools
Window
Help

The Forms menu pad drop-down list contains menu commands for

13

Owner Maintenance
Event Maintenance
Car Maintenance

Note that these three forms are not simply for data entry. The Owner Maintenance form will contain information on dues paid (and due), events attended, and automobile ownership. The Event Maintenance form will contain information on events that members have attended, are scheduled to attend, or may attend in the future. The Car Maintenance form will contain information on automobiles.

The Processes menu pad drop-down list contains a menu command for

Export Member Data to National

This pad may become more robust in the future as data from other sources may be imported into the application or other types of exporting become needed.

The Reports menu pad drop-down list contains pads for

Mailing Labels
Membership Renewal Notices
Member Scorecard
Automobile Scorecard

The first two menu commands are fairly obvious; the last two are less so. Both scorecards are a complete snapshot of the information related to the entity in question. In the case of a Member Scorecard, for example, the report will show all relevant information for a specific member, including dues history, automobile ownership, and event attendance. The Automobile Scorecard, on the other hand, will concentrate on a specific automobile, detailing its ownership as it changed hands over the years, as well as a description of the major components.

The Tools menu pad contains commands for supporting functions in the application, such as Database Maintenance, User Maintenance, and so on. The Window menu pad is automatically populated with the names of each open form so that the user can maneuver from one form to another as in all standard Windows applications.

Creating the Database and Application Menu or Switchboard

The MG Car Club database is contained in the online source code files for Chapter 13, so you can simply open the database and look at everything. However, I encourage you to create your own database as well, following along as I build it.

First, create a new directory in which you'll keep all your files. While an Access database is pretty much self-contained, there will be other files you'll want to include as well. Next, after starting Access, create a brand-new database with File | New, and select the Database icon from the General tab. Name the database (I've named mine MG13 for this chapter), and choose the Create button in the File | New Database dialog box.

You've now got a completely empty database, even though it's already taking up nearly 100K on your disk. Now that you've got the foundation— the database .MDB file—you'll build on it by creating the menu. If you prefer a switchboard form to be your startup user interface, now's the time to build that form.

Creating an Application Menu

You can create your menu even without having any data in the database, any forms, or other components. In effect, it will be the only thing in your database when you have finished.

First, select Tools | Customize to display the Customize dialog box. Make sure the Toolbars tab is selected, choose the New command button, and enter the name of the menu you are creating (even though the dialog box caption says "New Toolbar" and the text box prompt asks for a Toolbar Name). I gave my application menu the name "Application Menu" because I thought it was a pretty clever name.

Next, add blank menu pads to the menu. Select the Commands tab, scroll through the Categories list box until you get to the last item, and click the New Menu category. The New Menu command will display in the Commands list box on the right. Select the New Menu command and drag it to the toolbar. Repeat several times, because you'll need pads for Forms, Processes, and Reports.

13

Finally, add existing menu pads for Edit, Tools, Window, and Help. You'll want to duplicate the functionality of these menu pads from Access' menus instead of creating them from scratch. Undock the Menu Bar toolbar if necessary; position it near your application menu, and while holding CTRL down, drag the Edit, Tools, Window, and Help menu pads to your new menu, as shown in Figure 13-1. If you don't hold CTRL down, you'll be moving the menu pad from the Menu Bar instead of copying it.

Now that your menu application has all its placeholders, you'll notice that each of the pads has an arrow to the right of the text prompt. This is a visual clue that Access considers the object you are working with is still a Toolbar. Select the Properties button on the Toolbars tab, and change the Type drop-down list from Toolbar to Menu Bar. If you have particular preferences about properties for your main application menu (such as allowing the user to dock and undock the menu, and so on), here's the time and place to make those preferences known.

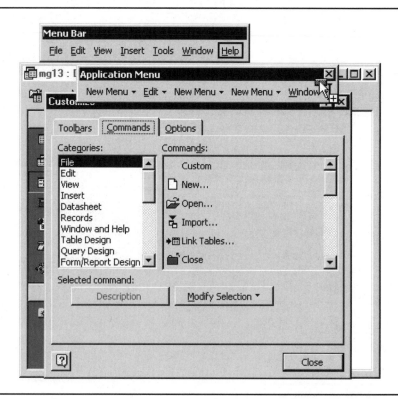

Hold CTRL down to copy menu pads from another menu, such as Help from the Menu Bar

Figure 13-1.

Now it's time to change the prompts from "New Menu" to something more appropriate. Right-click the menu pad to display the context menu, and change the Name property to **&Forms**. Remember that the "&" tells Access to make the "F" in the name a hot key, so that the user can select the menu by pressing ALT-F.

If you click one of the menu pads you've added and renamed, you'll see that there's nothing underneath. To add menu commands, follow these steps:

1. In the Commands tab of the Customize dialog box, select the File category. Make sure that the Custom command in the Commands list box is highlighted.

2. Click the menu pad so that the empty drop-down list is displayed.

3. Drag the Custom object from the Commands list box to the open drop-down list, as shown in Figure 13-2. You'll get a menu command with a prompt of "Custom."

4. Right-click the Custom menu command, and change the Name property to **&Owner Maintenance**.

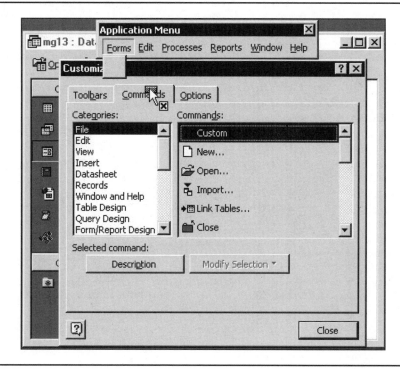

Dragging the Custom object from the Commands list box to the empty drop-down list under the Forms menu pad

Figure 13-2.

13

Continue adding menu commands to the Forms, Processes, and Reports menu pads to reflect the spec described earlier in this chapter.

You'll want to pay attention to a couple of special details at this point. First, when changing the Name property of a menu command, you can also select the Begin A Group menu command from the context menu (third from the bottom). Doing so will cause a separator bar to display above the menu command you are working with. Having separator bars between groups of similar menu commands makes the whole menu drop-down list easier for users to use, as shown here:

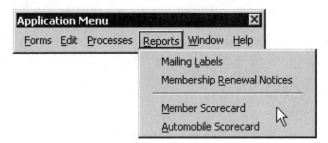

Second, make sure that you don't use the same letter as a hot key for more than one command. Choosing appropriate hot keys isn't always easy. In the Reports drop-down list, there are several menu commands that began with the letter "M." I chose the first letter for each scorecard menu command, instead of the "S" for one and the "A" for the other, because if the user were to associate the "S" as a mnemonic for "scorecard," it wouldn't be clear which scorecard was being referred to.

Finally, you'll want to customize the Forms menu drop-down list to include a way to close the application. You can do so by dragging the Exit command (found in the bottom of the Commands list box when the File category is selected in the Categories list box) to the bottom of the Forms drop-down list. Be sure to mark the Exit command to begin a new group, as it does in other Windows applications.

Now that your application menu is built, the next step will be to tell Access that it's to be used when loading this database. You'll note that there are no commands attached to any of the custom menu commands, but all the Edit, Window, and Help menu commands are already completely defined. We'll customize a couple of these menu commands a bit later.

Creating a Switchboard Form

Since it's such a popular mechanism, I would be remiss not to discuss the creation of a switchboard form to start your application. You can decide which mechanism you prefer. For the remainder of the book, I'll be using the application menu exclusively.

There are two steps to creating a switchboard form: creating the form itself and telling Access that it's to be used when loading the database, much as with an application menu.

Open your database and select the Create Form In Design View object in the Forms pane of the Database window. Next, create buttons for each component of your application. If you have a large number of components (say, more than a dozen or so), you may want to create a switchboard that is simply a launching pad for additional switchboards. Each main switchboard button would direct the user to one of these switchboards. For example, your main switchboard would have a button for "Data Entry Forms," and that button would open a switchboard that contained buttons for all the data-entry forms in the application. Another button would have a button for "Reports," a third for "Queries," and so on.

You may choose to put a picture on the buttons of the switchboard, or include both picture and text. Another common look is to place a series of empty buttons that look like large check boxes on the switchboard, and then to add text labels next to them with complete explanations of what the buttons do. In Figure 13-3, you see a sample switchboard form in Design view. I've not put all the components of the MG Car Club application on this form for simplicity's sake.

Once you've placed buttons on the form, you'll want to change some properties of the form so that it looks better. The properties and settings you most likely will want are

Name	Application Switchboard
Caption	The MG Car Club Application
Views Allowed	Form
Scroll Bars	Neither
Record Selector	No
Navigation Buttons	No
Auto Resize	Yes
Auto Center	Yes
Border Style	Dialog Box

13

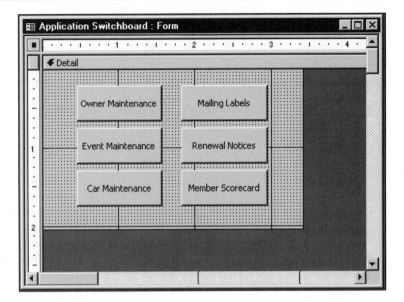

A sample
switchboard
form during
design
Figure 13-3.

Once these settings are in place, running the form as your application's
switchboard will result in a display like that shown here. The database
MG13SW.MDB has an example of the database with a switchboard form.

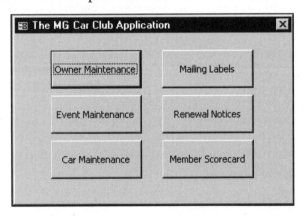

Note that, just as with the application menu, there's no code behind any of
the buttons—you can click all day and simply get tired. You would put code

in the On Click method of each button to call each form, much like each menu command in the application menu will call the forms.

Defining the Startup Options

You define startup options through options on the Startup dialog box, shown in Figure 13-4, that appears when you choose Tools | Startup.

The first important property is the name of the application that will display as the caption on the application's title bar. Here, I've set it to "The MG Car Club Application." You can also choose what application icon to display to the left of the caption in the title bar. See Figure 13-5 to see how the name and icon will display when the application runs.

You will use the Menu Bar drop-down list to define which menu bar, if any, will be used as the default menu bar when the application starts. If you elected to use a switchboard form instead, select it in the Display Form/Page drop-down list. Take special note of the Display Database Window check box. If you uncheck this control, the database will not be visible when you run the application. I'll discuss this option, and the dangers it presents, shortly.

I keep the four check boxes under Menu Bar and Shortcut Menu Bar unchecked, since they really don't provide much benefit and I like to control exactly what the user can or cannot do in the applications I develop.

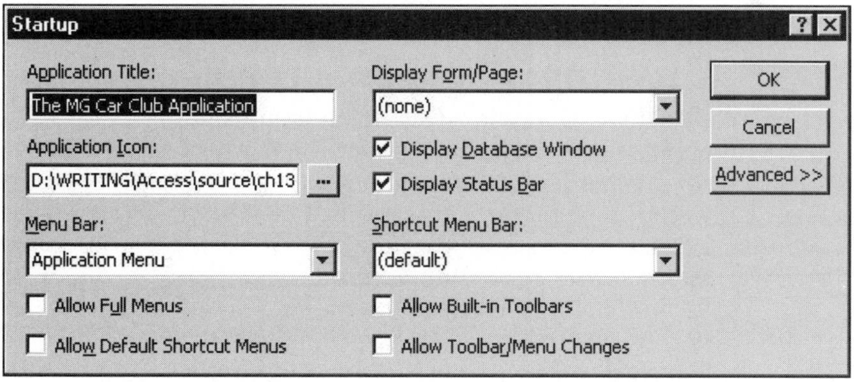

The Startup dialog box allows you to specify a number of options that control how your application loads

Figure 13-4.

13

The application icon and title display in the application's title bar when your application is executed

Figure 13-5.

Creating a Splash Screen

Remember that annoying screen that displays when you start nearly any application? It usually contains the name of the program, a copyright notice, some other legal-sounding jargon, and an image of some sort to give the screen some pizzazz. This is called a *splash screen,* and it serves two purposes. First, it informs users that they did, indeed, click the correct program icon, and that they're loading Access and not Tomb Raider or Flight Simulator. Second, it distracts the user for a few seconds while the program loads. If nothing were to happen, users might think they hadn't clicked hard enough, and try again and again, only to end up with multiple instances of the program running. A splash screen that appears immediately tells the user that the program is loading but that it might take a while.

You can create your own splash screen in two ways. You can create a splash screen made of a regular Access form and call it during startup—either during an Autoexec macro, or from the Open method of your startup form. I'll discuss this technique in Chapter 17.

The other, much quicker way is to simply create a bitmap file to act as your splash screen. Give it the same name as your database, and place it in the same directory as your database. When you load the database, the bitmap will automatically display for a few seconds until the program has finished loading.

While easier to use, this technique has a couple of downsides—you don't have as much control over when it's displayed or for how long. But to get something up and running quickly, this is a good way to start.

Running Your Application Foundation

Now that you've got a database, as empty as it may be, and a foundation menu, you probably want to execute the application to see what it looks like. Just close the database and open it again, either by selecting File | MG13 if you've still got Access open, or by double-clicking the MG13.MDB file in Windows Explorer.

If you've unchecked the Display Database Window check box in the Startup dialog box, you'll get the result shown in Figure 13-6. I opened the Forms menu just to make the image more interesting. You can experiment with opening the various menu drop-down lists, and even with selecting Forms | Exit to close the application. So far, so good.

Now it's time to get back to development. However, as you try to open your database, you'll find that you can't get back to the Database window. Access keeps opening the database with your custom application menu, and, of course, no database is visible—or available—anywhere. This is because you unchecked the Display Database Window check box. All the work you've done to this point appears to be gone—well, not gone, exactly, but you can't get to it. Kind of like forgetting the password.

Not to worry. Simply close the application, and then open it again while holding down SHIFT. The startup options will be ignored, and you'll be back in

13

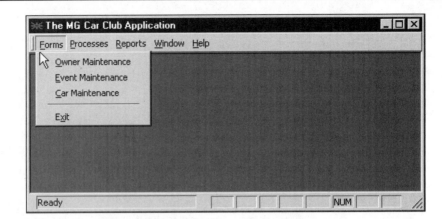

design mode for your application. I'll discuss additional options involved
with packaging and shipping your application in Chapter 20.

You can also execute your application in "run-time" mode through a special
"/runtime" command-line switch:

1. Make a copy of the Access icon on the desktop.

2. Right-click the icon and select the Properties menu command to display
   the Properties dialog box.

3. In the Shortcut tab, select the target text box and enter the following
   string (all on one line, but shown broken here because the of book's
   specifications), adjusting as appropriate if you've installed Access 2000 in
   a different folder:

   "C:\Program Files\Office 2000\Office\msaccess.exe"
      d:\writing\access\source\ch13\mg13.mdb" /runtime

Note that this shortcut will run Access and open the specified database in
run-time mode. It won't simply open Access by itself. See Figure 13-7.

Adding Tables to Your Database

Having a complete, if nonfunctioning, application menu in your database
might be fun, but it's not going to get you far. It's time to add tables to

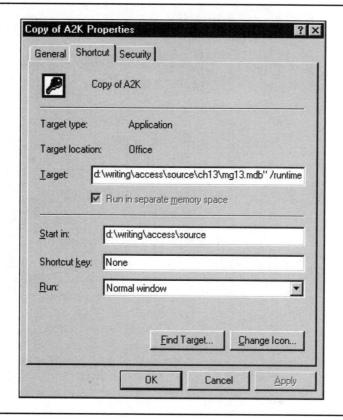

Using the
"/runtime"
command-line
switch to
execute an
application in
run-time mode
Figure 13-7.

your database. To refresh your memory, here is a list of the tables, together
with a description of each.

Table.	Description
Owner	Contains one record for each person, couple, or organization that has at one time owned a car.
Dues	Contains one record for each payment of membership dues.
Event	Contains one record for each MG-related event, such as a membership meeting, a car rally, or a GOF (Gathering of the Faithful).

13

Table	Description
Car	Contains one record for each automobile.
Component	Contains one record for each major component of an automobile. A major component is one that has its own serial number, such as a chassis or engine block.
Lookup	Contains records for lookup values such as color.
Ownership join	Provides the many-to-many relationship between Owners and Cars. Contains one record for each instance of automobile ownership. For example, if an owner currently owns two cars and has in the past owned three others, there would be five records in this table for that Owner, each identifying the owner, the car, and the length of time of ownership.
Attendance join	Provides the many-to-many relationship between Owners and Events, so that one Owner can attend many Events and many Owners can attend one Event. (What fun would it be if only one Owner could attend an Event?) Contains one record for each instance of Event attendance by an Owner. For example, if an Owner has attended three events, there would be three records in this table for that Owner, each identifying the owner and the event. In this case, additional information is not needed, since the presence of an Attendance join record is all that is needed. Either the Owner attended or didn't. The Event record would contain information such as date, time, cost, and location.

Initial Structure Considerations

You may remember that I closed the last chapter with some comments about structuring an application in Access with multiple database files instead of jamming everything into one file. Just because I haven't done that here doesn't mean that I'm going back on my word. Instead, I still recommend doing so. In fact, let me propose a structure to keep in mind for future applications.

First of all, you should plan to use multiple databases in every application:

◆ You'll keep your data in one database—or, more accurately, you'll keep test data in one database and production data in another.

◆ You'll keep your common library code, including VBA routines, generic forms, and other often-used tools, in another database.

◆ You'll build your application-specific components, including forms and reports, using a third database.

◆ You'll begin each application with a database skeleton, or foundation, that you've created and enhanced over time, instead of starting from nothing each time.

However, I'm purposely not structuring this application in that way. Why? Because, in the immortal words of a friend of mine, "It's too hard that way." I don't mean that it's too hard and that you should never consider it, simply that it's too hard to do during the development of your first application. Once you've got a firm grasp on the fundamentals and know them by heart, you can graduate to more complex architectures, including multiple databases, common libraries of code, and so on.

CHAPTER 14

Debugging: When Things Don't Go as Expected

Now that you've started to write VBA code, you're probably running into problems. It's not always easy to find what went wrong. The error information the computer provides may be incomplete or misleading, and most importantly, may not explain what you have to do to make it better.

Thus, when you're faced with unexpected results from Access 2000, you've got a challenge. This chapter provides information on how to use the tools you have to solve those problems. Even better, it provides a philosophy and techniques for using those tools properly.

Types of Misbehavior

I'm going to assume that you're running an application, and that your problems are occurring through the use of the various components in Access, including Visual Basic for Applications. I'll also assume you're not just trying to put a control on a form or set a property a certain way. There are five general types of errors you will run into: product defects, compile-time errors, run-time errors, logic errors, and user-generated errors.

Defects in the Product

Access is in its fifth major revision and has been used by millions of people around the world. Most of the defects have been found and remedied. It's highly unlikely that the problem that you're running into is a defect in the product. It's much more probable that the problem lies elsewhere. Nonetheless, it's good to be aware that when all else fails—really fails—the behavior you're experiencing is truly a bug in Access itself. But we'll leave that possibility for the very last.

Compile-Time Errors

In Access, a *compile-time* error is a programming error that is caught before you save your work. For example, if you include the Option Explicit statement in a VBA procedure and then reference a variable that has not been declared, Access will complain and not let you save the procedure. While initially annoying, this is actually helpful.

There's a truism in our industry that also applies to other businesses. The earlier a defect is caught, the easier and less costly it will be to fix. By catching errors almost as soon as you create them, Access greatly reduces your time and cost to fix them.

The only problem may occur when you can't figure out what the error is. In those cases, it can be quite a nuisance. All you want to do is save the darn form and be done with it, but Access keeps complaining and won't let you save until you correct the problem.

Run-Time Errors

A *run-time* error is one that occurs once you run the program. An example of this would be the following. Suppose you are tracking the dollar value of automobiles owned by individuals who are attending an event. To do so, you would sum the total value of the automobiles, and then divide by the number of people at the event. However, if your program did this calculation before anyone was registered for the event, the calculation performed would be zero divided by zero. When a computer divides by zero, an error is generated. However, the application didn't know it would be dividing by zero when the program was compiled, so the error passed through the compiler. The error was not caught until the program was run and those two statements were executed. Thus, it's called a "run-time" error.

Logic Errors

A *logic* error is one that violates the business rules the program uses to function properly. For example, suppose that you have a CASE structure that calculates dues based on what season the member joined the club. The CASE structure could look something like this:

```
Select Case txtSeason
Case "Winter"
   ' they get charged a full year of dues
   cDues = txtDuesAnnual
Case "Spring"
   ' they get charged for nine months of dues
   cDues = txtDuesAnnual * 0.75
Case "Summer"
   ' they get charged for six months of dues
   cDues = txtDuesAnnual * 0.5
Case "Fall"
   ' they get charged for three months of dues
   cDues = txtDuesAnnual * 0.25
End Select
' multiply dues by number of cars
cDues = cDues * txtNumberOfCars
```

14

What's the problem? First, if users could enter the season via a text box that allowed any type of data (admittedly, a bad choice of controls), they might end up entering a value like "Autumn" or misspelling a season, like "Witner." Or suppose you provided a four-button option group instead, and the users could only choose one of those four choices. What if they didn't make a choice? The value of txtSeason (it would probably be called opgSeason, actually) would be empty.

In any of these cases, there wouldn't be a value assigned to the variable cDues; and then the next line, in which the number of cars is factored into the dues, would fail. This is an example of a logic error that then generates a run-time error. There are two ways to correct this problem. The first is to initialize the value of cDues before the Select Case statement, like so:

```
cDues = 0.00
```

Then the statement in which the number of cars is factored into the dues wouldn't cause a run-time error. However, this still might not produce the correct answer. The second way, and the better alternative, is to include an Else statement in which you handle the possibility that none of your Case statements accounts for the actual value of txtSeason. For example, the following code placed before the End Select statement would work fine:

```
Else
  cDues = 10.00
```

Another example of a logic error is when you haven't analyzed the rules for the application correctly. You are performing the operation correctly, but it's the *wrong* operation. For example, suppose the club rule was that members were charged the minimum annual amount for dues—regardless of how many cars they owned, or even if they didn't own any—and then an additional amount was included for each automobile they owned. The code might look like this:

```
' multiply dues factor by number of cars
cDues = (cDues + cDuesFactor) * txtNumberOfCars
```

The parens mean that the Dues and the Dues Factor would be added together and the result multiplied by the number of cars. This would produce the wrong result for two reasons. First of all, the DuesFactor would be an additional value multiplied by the number of cars—and that result would be added to the Dues calculated in the Case structure. Second, the intent was to have a base amount that every member was charged, regardless of how many cars they owned. The preceding equation would result in a dues amount of $0.00 if they owned no cars. The statement wouldn't throw an error if txtNumberOfCars were equal to zero, but it would not calculate the correct amount, either. Again, it's a logic error.

Here is the correct code:

```
cDues = 0.00
Select Case txtSeason
Case "Winter"
  ' they get charged a full year of dues
  cDues = txtDuesAnnual
Case "Spring"
   ' they get charged for nine months of dues
   cDues = txtDuesAnnual * 0.75
Case "Summer"
   ' they get charged for six months of dues
   cDues = txtDuesAnnual * 0.5
Case "Fall"
   ' they get charged for three months of dues
   cDues = txtDuesAnnual * 0.25
Else
   cDues = 10.00
End Select
' multiply dues by number of cars
cDues = cDues + cDuesFactor * txtNumberOfCars
```

User-Generated Errors

The last type of error cannot be controlled by the developer—a *user-generated* error is an action by users outside the realm of the application. For example, suppose a user is printing a report and turns off the printer partway through, or the printer runs out of paper. Or what if your application is set up to use a separate "library" .MDB, but some unwitting user, trying to be helpful and clean up some disk space, has deleted that .MDB file? The application will fail as soon as a function from the library is called anywhere in the application. Or perhaps the user is exporting data from the application or importing from another source; and during the operation, another user on the network copies a big file onto the same drive, so that there is no more disk space.

You will have to consider the possibility that these types of errors could occur, as applicable to your application. (If you don't ever let your user print,

14

you won't worry about printer errors, for example.) You'll have to plan your application so that you can detect and react to user-generated errors and the application won't simply crash or stop operating.

Debugging Covers Developer-Generated Errors

This chapter will cover the middle three errors: compile-time, run-time, and logic errors. You are at the mercy of Microsoft when it comes to those rare defects in Access itself. And while it is incumbent upon you to handle user-generated errors as well, that topic is covered in Chapter 15.

The Debugging Mindset

Typical programmers—self-taught amateurs who lack discipline, rigor, and an interest in achieving those attributes—approach debugging as a series of random, uncoordinated attacks at various parts of the application. They base those attacks on wild guesses and perceived ease of implementation. If they succeed, it's simply because they're lucky. A great many of these programmers narrowly escape great danger as they get lucky one time after another. It's not uncommon because many problems—not all—can be solved through such a haphazard method of trial and error. However, when it doesn't work, the aforementioned programmers must resort to any number of tricks: simply accepting an error that doesn't occur often enough to fix; unnecessarily rewriting pieces of code that were 99 percent finished; and telling the customer, erroneously, that "it can't be done" or "there's a bug in Access that prevents me from making this work."

There is a better way, obviously, or I wouldn't be spending so much time berating the "wild, random guesses" methodology I just described. It is important to develop a "debugging mindset" in which you approach an issue of misbehavior in a logical, rational manner, much as you learned about the scientific method in 7th grade.

Make Observations

The first step is to describe the errant behavior. There are three parts to this description. Part 1 is a list of steps to reproduce the behavior. If you can't reproduce the behavior, you might as well put it down as "one of those things" and move on. This entire process depends on being able to duplicate the behavior so it can be analyzed. Furthermore, by writing down the steps, if it goes that far, you will often find that the behavior was caused by forgetting to perform a step, not by anything else.

Part 2 is a description of what happens as a result of following the steps described in Part 1. Sometimes this description gets intertwined in the steps because there are several related behaviors. Each generates an additional step on your part, which then causes the application to exhibit another behavior.

Part 3—and this is the key—is to describe what you expected to happen. By doing so, you make it very clear what the difference in expectations is. Part 2 describes reality and this part describes your intended result. The difference, then, is what needs to be investigated. Again, as in Part 2, actually thinking through (or even writing down) what you expected to happen will often generate the "Aha!" moment in which you realize that your expectation was misguided because it becomes obvious what behavior should really have occurred.

An additional part in this first step is to list any "other interesting facts" you think may have bearing on the problem.

Go Through the Scientific Method

Now that you have a description of what the problem is, it's time to figure out what is going wrong.

Generate Hypothesis

In this step, you'll create one or more hypotheses, and then test each hypothesis. Did a light bulb suddenly go on during this last sentence? If you're thinking that this process maps closely to the traditional scientific method, you're correct. Gather facts and observations, and then generate hypotheses about what might be the cause. You thought 7th-grade science would never be useful.

What could *possibly* be going wrong? There isn't, unfortunately, any magic methodology for creating these hypotheses, and that's why scientific geniuses aren't a dime a dozen. It's a special talent to be able to come up with "good" hypotheses. You can begin by tracing the code and seeing if you can generate possible problems based on what you see. Perhaps you aren't using a function properly. Perhaps it doesn't return the type of value you think it does. Perhaps you're assuming that a variable contains a certain value when, in fact, it contains a different one. And so on, and so forth.

Test Your Hypothesis

Now that you have a hypothesis, test it. For example, suppose you suspect that a function is returning a value other than the one you think it is. Don't wait until the end of the routine to find out the answer you're getting isn't correct—find out what that value is right away. Shortly, I'll show you several tools for snooping inside of programs that are running to determine what intermediate values are.

Repeat

This is the tough step. If your hypothesis is correct, you're basically done. Make the appropriate change to the code, or figure out what else you need to do to fix the problem, and then test it again. If, however, your hypothesis was not correct, you need to repeat the prior two steps—again and again until you find the answer.

I can't stress this enough—you must repeat these steps until you find the answer. Start at the very beginning and examine every assumption, including the ones you *know* to be true; check each fact, and check it again. Check your observations, and do everything step by step. Most problems occur at this stage for one of two reasons. Either you're rushing through and making an incorrect assumption, or you don't understand how the product actually works, which, really, is another case of making an incorrect assumption.

Know Why It Worked

Simply fixing a defect isn't enough, though. It's kind of like whacking your TV upside the tuner every time the picture goes fuzzy. It may seem like you've fixed it, when all you've done is shake a bad tube partway out of it's seating. In a few minutes, as the temperature in the case rises, the tube will fall back into place, and the picture will go fuzzy again. Wouldn't it be better to just get the tube replaced and fix the root of the problem?

Same thing here—only more so. If you perform an action that "*seems*" to fix a bug, you can pretty much count on it appearing somewhere else. You may have found a clever work-around for the particular situation, but you've not learned anything. Thus, you're bound to make the same mistake somewhere else, perhaps where it's not going to be as easy to work around.

And don't relax if you run into one of those bugs that "just went away on its own." As has been said many times, "Bugs that go away on their own tend to come back by themselves." Steve McConnell, in his landmark programming text, *Code Complete* (Microsoft Press, 1993), says, "If you aren't learning anything, then you're just goofing around."

Find One Thing at a Time

Finally, resist the temptation to fix a bunch of bugs at the same time and then run the application to see if you've fixed them all. This technique is tempting because it seems much more efficient. Fixing defects one at a time seems an awful lot like going to the car dealership to get the muffler fixed, picking it up and returning it later that day to get the window repaired, and then picking it up and returning it yet again to have the engine tuned. Why not have it all done at once?

Two reasons, folks. The first reason is that you're simply not going to remember everything to fix or, if you did, everything to test afterward. There are just too many other things that can intrude, and your concentration is much more apt to be interrupted if you try to juggle a chainsaw, a flaming torch, and a balloon full of sharp glass than if you handle one at a time. The other reason is that one fix might improperly affect the other. If you fix one defect and test it until the issue is resolved, you can put it to bed, knowing the "whats" and "whys." If you change two things at the same time, you don't necessarily know which change had the effect on which, or even possibly both, problems. As I've said before, "A man with a watch knows what time it is. A man with two is never quite sure."

A Final Word

Now that you've read through all this, it may seem that each bug you run into is going to take, if you approach it properly, the better part of an hour to squash. That's not necessarily so, although sometimes, sadly, it will. Often you can perform all these steps mentally, in seconds. You don't necessarily have to write out "Steps to Reproduce," "Expected Behavior," formally documented hypotheses, and such when you run into an "Invalid Value" error message on a statement that only has two variables.

However, just because many bugs can be detected and disposed of quickly doesn't mean that you can always do so. And when the bugs get tough, it's time to introduce more rigor and formality into your bug-stomping process. Now you have a guideline for doing so.

The Debugging Tools

Access comes with a nice pair of debugging tools. The first is, appropriately, the Debug window, and the other is the Message Box function.

The Debug Window

You're likely familiar with a heart monitor; it displays the current heartbeat and other vital signs of the patient. Wouldn't it be nice if you could attach a similar monitor to your code and examine various vital signs of your application while it was running? The Debug window in Access provides such a monitor. You can use the Debug window to see the values of variables and properties, to change them, and even to test VBA and user-defined functions.

I'm using the term "Debug window" a little loosely, as there are four related windows that have to do with debugging. Furthermore, none of them is actually inside Access, any more than the module editor is inside Access. To get to the Debug window, you can press CTRL-G or select View | Code from the Access menu.

You'll be presented with the Debug window (or environment) as shown in Figure 14-1. If you don't have the same window layout as shown in Figure 14-1, you can use the View menu (in VBA, not Access) to select which windows to display. The Immediate window allows you to enter and display the results of expressions—both those you create and those that are generated from your application by use of special commands. The Watches window allows you to display the ongoing value of an expression, and the Locals window allows you to evaluate the value of an expression at a specific time. I'll get into each of these shortly and will use the form shown in Figure 14-2 to demonstrate several techniques.

The Immediate Window

If it's not already visible, display the Immediate window by selecting View | Immediate. The Immediate window provides "immediate" feedback on a variety of expressions and commands. In Figure 14-3, you'll see four expressions (each begins with a question mark) and the results of the evaluation of each expression on the next line. The first expression is a simple addition problem, resulting in the answer below it. The next two evaluate the value of two different text boxes on the form named "Debugging"and the last one evaluates the value of the Caption property of one of the command buttons on the form.

You can also use the Immediate window to set values of expressions. If you wanted to change the caption of a button or the value of a text box, for

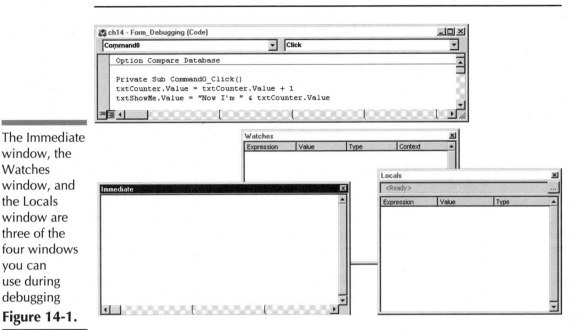

The Immediate window, the Watches window, and the Locals window are three of the four windows you can use during debugging
Figure 14-1.

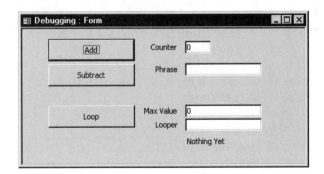

The sample form includes two buttons for incrementing and decrementing a value and a third button for processing a loop
Figure 14-2.

14

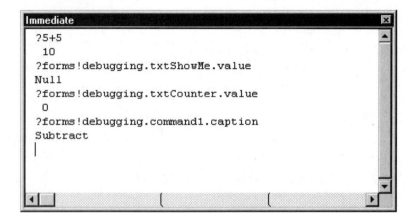

The Immediate
window is
used to
evaluate
expressions

Figure 14-3.

example, you could do so with the following expressions entered into the Immediate window:

```
forms!debugging.command1.caption = "Herman"
forms!debugging.txtCounter.value = 12345
```

as shown in Figure 14-4.

The Immediate window can also be used to echo the results from a special command that you place in your VBA modules. The following sub, placed in the click( ) method of the Loop command button, will generate the results in the Immediate window as shown in Figure 14-5.

```
Private Sub Command6_Click()
For i = 1 To txtMaxValue.Value
 txtLooper.Value = i
 lblLoopDisplay.Caption = "Loop value is " & txtLooper.Value
 Debug.Print "Loop value is " & txtLooper.Value
Next
End Sub
```

Using Break Points

A *break point* is a flag on a line of code or an expression that will cause execution of the program to be suspended when that line is executed or when a condition based on that expression is met. The easiest way to set a

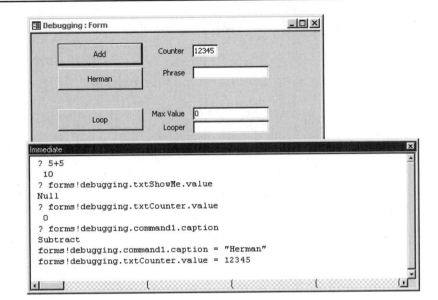

The Immediate window can also be used to set the values of variables or properties

Figure 14-4.

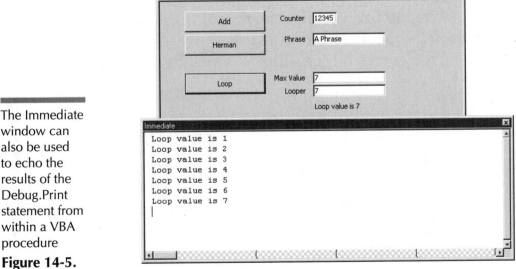

The Immediate window can also be used to echo the results of the Debug.Print statement from within a VBA procedure

Figure 14-5.

break point is to open the Code window and click the gray margin to the left of the line you want to break on. A fat red dot will display in the gray margin, and the line of code will be highlighted (in red, unless you've changed the Access defaults), as shown in Figure 14-6.

When you run the application, the break point will force the application to temporarily (until you do something to make it continue) stop execution. The fat red dot will be overlaid with a yellow arrow, and the line of code will be displayed in yellow highlight. In Figure 14-7, I've shown the results of the txtCounter text box in the Immediate window while execution was suspended.

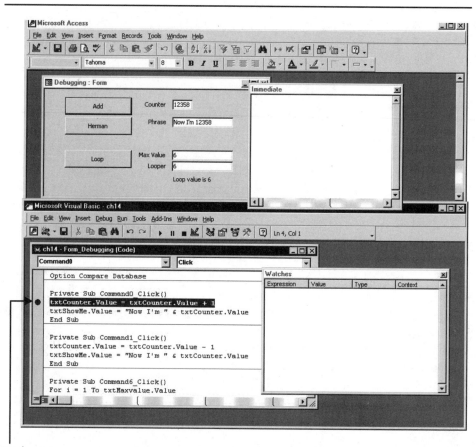

Setting a break point in the Code window marks the line with a fat red dot

Figure 14-6.   Break point

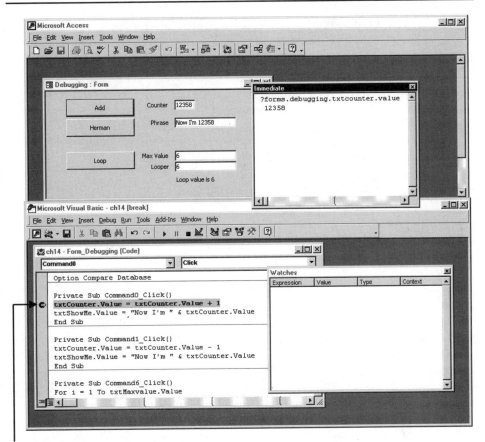

Once an application is suspended from a break point, you can see the line of code upon which the break point was set and use the Immediate window to examine variables and properties

Figure 14-7. Code suspended at a break point

Using the Immediate window can be inconvenient, and Figure 14-8 shows you a couple of nifty tricks. First, if you let your mouse cursor hover over an expression in the Code window, you'll see the evaluation of the expression display in a light yellow ToolTip window. The ToolTip shown here displays the value for the txtShowMe text box. However, while handy, this feature can be inconvenient if you wanted to see the values of several variables or properties at one time. You can thus set a *watch point,* and the value will display in the Watches window, also as shown in Figure 14-8.

The easiest way to set a watch point is to right-click over the line of code that contains the expression that you want to watch, and to select Add Watch

14

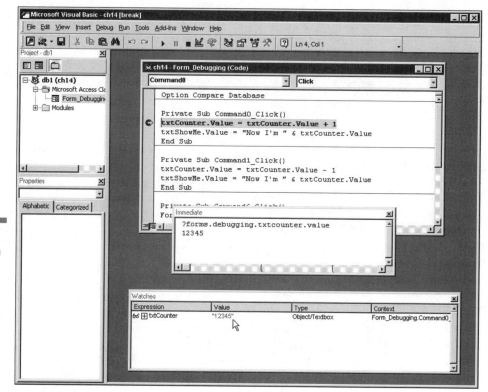

Hovering the cursor over an expression in the Code window will display the value of that expression in a ToolTip

Figure 14-8.

from the context menu. The dialog box shown in Figure 14-9 will be displayed. You'll notice that the expression is entered into the dialog box by default, but you could type in your own expression. You could just right-click anywhere and enter your own expression. Using the default value simply saves typing and probably will prevent a few typos.

There are three types of watches you can choose from: A Watch simply displays the value in the Watch window. You can also set a break point in this window (instead of using the fat red dot mechanisms in the Code window) by selecting the Procedure and Module in which the expression will be found, and then choosing to have the break occur either when the value is true or when it changes. Use each of these as your situation dictates.

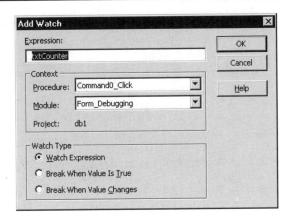

The Add
Watch dialog
box allows you
to add a watch
point based on
an expression

Figure 14-9.

When you run your application and the watch or break point is triggered, the value of the expression will be displayed in the Watches window, again as shown in Figure 14-8.

The Call Stack Window

When you run a nontrivial application, your code will undoubtedly have many subroutines, functions, and methods. It can be difficult to keep track of which module is being executed. You can open the *Call Stack* window to display both the currently executing module and the *call hierarchy*—a list of which routine called which.

The Locals Window

The *Locals* window can be used to watch the value of a variable or property (or, of course, many of them) in the currently executing module. You can use View | Locals to open the Locals window if it's not already open. There are three columns in the Locals window: Expression, Value, and Type. Single variables are displayed in the Locals window by themselves. Objects that have a collection, such as an array or a form with controls on it, appear with a plus sign to the left of the name. Clicking on the plus sign opens the collection and displays its' component pieces in an explorer-style view. See Figure 14-10.

14

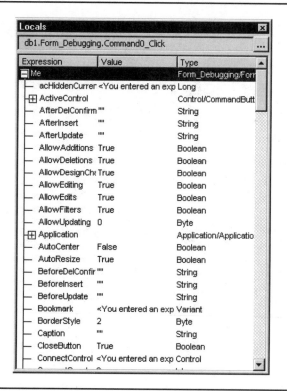

The Locals
window shows
collections
in an explorer-
style view

Figure 14-10.

Don't Forget the Message Box!

Another commonly used tool during debugging is, interestingly enough, the
Message Box. You can use the Message Box function to cause execution of a
routine to pause and, correspondingly, to display the values of one or more
variables as the message in the Message Box.

However, you can accomplish the same thing with the Debug window in
many cases. You can also use a series of Message Box functions to show the
order in which routines are being fired, which lines of code inside complex
logic structures are being executed, and what the values of certain variables
are at those times. Make generous use of the Message Box function to hunt
down those nefarious errors.

When you do so, take care in constructing the messages you display in the
Message Box. First of all, don't use messages that you wouldn't want the user

of your application to see if you accidentally left the Message Box in the routine. So, despite how aggravated you are while in the midst of the third hour of trying to hunt down one last bug, try to avoid messages like so (edited here because this *is* a family book!):

"Now display the *#$^#& counter variable you stupid old #($&@#("

Second, take the time to construct messages that will guide you through the process later as well as now. For example, here is one possible set of messages:

```
"Value is " & cAmt
"Value is now " & cAmt
"Value has now become " & cAmt
"Finally, the value is (ta dah!) " & cAmt
```

While these make sense as you're stuffing them into subsequent Message Box functions in your code, they won't seem nearly as obvious when you're running the application right after lunch. Here's a much better set:

```
"1. Sales Amt before adding tax is " & cAmt
"2. Sales Amt after adding tax but before discount is " & cAmt
"3. Sales Amt after discount is " & cAmt
"4. Sales Amt after user accepts transaction is " & cAmt
```

Notice that I've numbered each of the message box steps. When I have to remove them, I can be more sure that I've gotten every one of them, instead of accidentally leaving one in for my user to find. Also notice that I've been explicit about describing what value I'm displaying, and at what point in the routine I'm displaying it.

Debugging Techniques

Now that I've covered the tools you've got at your disposal, let's load you up with a couple more secret weapons. Just as there are "best practices" in other industries—techniques that have been proven to produce the best results for a given situation—there are "best practices" with respect to programming in Access and Visual Basic for Applications. Adhering to these techniques will help you, in some part, keep bugs out of your code. And that's an important subtlety—bugs don't get in there by themselves—you have to put them in there. So here are a few time-honored techniques that will help you avoid introducing bugs.

14

Option Explicit

As explained earlier, including the Option Explicit statement at the beginning of each of your procedures will require that every variable used in that procedure be declared before it's use. Doing so will help you avoid bugs in two ways.

First, the VBA compiler will automatically find typos in variables—if you've declared a variable cAmtDue but later assign a value to "cAtmDue," the compiler will flag this (unless you've also declared cAtmDue to be a variable).

Second, you won't be able to simply create variables on the fly, which is another practice that commonly causes logic errors in code. Your code may compile and run correctly, but the calculations performed may be incorrect. For example, suppose you use a variable to hold the amount due, cAmtDue. Later in the routine, you create another variable for the same purpose, forgetting that you've already got one. You can easily create hard-to-find bugs by flip-flopping between one value and the other when assigning, incrementing, or comparing subsequent values.

Naming Conventions

You can also help yourself by following a naming convention. It doesn't have to be the one described in this book; there are several popular standards used in the Access community. Prefixing your variables with a data type indicator helps you avoid assigning or concatenating incorrect values. Additional standard naming practices make your code easier to read and, thus, to maintain and debug.

Strong Typing

Strong typing refers to the additional declaration of type when declaring a variable. The Option Explicit keyword simply requires you to declare a variable; strong typing requires you to declare what type of data it's going to contain. The following two statements simply create a variable:

```
Option Explicit
Dim cAmtDue
```

cAmtDue, while it may look like a currency variable, is defined internally as a variant. Visual Basic for Applications doesn't relate the name of the variable to its type; the naming convention of a "c" prefix is simply an aid to you and me, fallible humans who need the crutch of a naming convention. On the other hand, these two statements

```
Option Explicit
Dim cAmtDue as Currency
```

will cause the VBA compiler to generate an error any time you attempt to assign a non-Currency value to the cAmtDue variable.

Variable Scoping

Restricting the scope of a variable to as small a range of procedures as possible is another "best practice." It reduces the chances of a variable in one routine stomping on a similarly named variable in another routine. A very common example of this is the use of a variable like "i" or "j" as a counter for a routine and then, within that routine, having a line of code that calls another routine that also uses—and changes the value of—"i" or "j" as well. Thus, the value that "i" or "j" contains when coming back from the second routine is different from the value it held going in.

```
' RoutineA
i = 0
for I = 1 to 10
   ' some processing goes here
   call RoutineB
next i

' RoutineB
for i = 1 to 5
   ' some processing code goes here
next i
```

If you haven't restricted the scope of the first "i" or "j" counter to that routine, its value will be changed once control passes to the subroutine. When control returns to the parent routine, the counter's value is something other than what you thought it would be. In the example shown, the value of "i" is 5 when control is returned to RoutineA, no matter what iteration you were on when you initially called RoutineB. Thus, the loops in RoutineA for i = 2 through 5 will be ignored, and RoutineA will be stuck in an endless loop, as it will never advance past 6. It's truly an aggravating bug to track down—and spending time doing so is completely unnecessary.

14

Modular Code

When you call a VBA function within one of your routines, you don't worry much or at all about the internals of the function. There's a bunch of code written in C that supports that function, but all you care about are the parameters you pass it, and the value it returns when finished. This is known as a *black box function*—you put something in and get something out—what happens in between is of no consequence.

You can extrapolate that same type of behavior into the routines you write, so that the interface between one routine and another is clearly defined and sparse. Furthermore, you want to make the routine simple, so that it performs only a single type of function or process, instead of throwing all sorts of disparate functionality into it. By doing so, you make it easy to define what the module will do, and what other routines need to do to work with it.

These types of routines exhibit an attribute known as *"modularity"*—much like prefab houses, which were built by dropping entire rooms onto a common foundation. Another example of modularity is the modern stereo, where each component has a single, specific purpose, and can be easily replaced with another component.

Constructing your code in the same manner provides many of the same benefits. Each small piece is easier to design, build, and test, and it can be replaced by a more modern piece, or one with different functionality, reasonably easily. Following this procedure will also reduce the number of bugs you generate, since complexity tends to increase geometrically the number of bugs associated with the piece.

Consistency

Do things the same way each time. Once you find a method that works, use that same method each time you need to use it—don't reinvent the wheel just to make things "interesting." Software development is "interesting" enough without you doing more work. You'll also find that you can perform common chores faster as you get more used to doing them, which leaves more time to spend on the challenging and truly interesting parts of your application.

This also has benefits in future maintainability. If you found the same basic chunk of code in two widely dispersed procedures, you would probably have an easier time determining what the purpose of the routines were, as well as changing or fixing those routines.

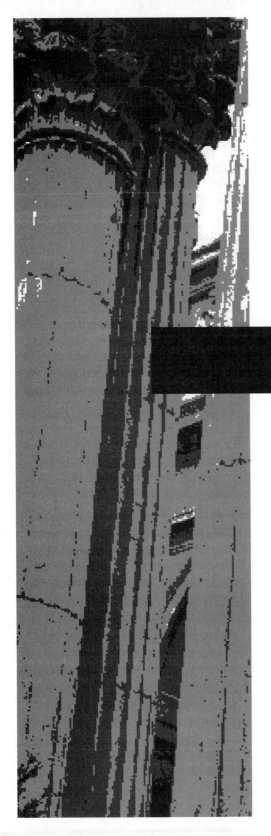

CHAPTER 15

When Things Don't Go as Expected: Setting Up an Error Handler

In the last chapter, I discussed what to do when the application you're working on doesn't perform as expected. That discussion was presented in the context that you, the developer, were the user, with Access 2000's debugging tools at your disposal.

In this chapter, I'm going to discuss how to handle errors that occur after your application has left the safety of your development environment. Now it is subject to the whims and weaknesses of the users. Errors need to be handled differently for users—though you may be comfortable dealing with cryptic and arcane error messages, your users certainly won't be.

Furthermore, once the error occurs, there are a number of decisions that can be made and actions that can be taken. With your detailed knowledge of computers and software, you can decide what to do with the error, but your users might be unable to. For example, suppose you're faced with an error that a variable has gone out of bounds after looping through an array. You may know that it's fine to ignore the error and continue with the program, but the users may be frightened off and simply want to shut down the application. On the other hand, a "disk full" error or an "internal consistency—cyclic redundancy check failed" error may make you decide to shut down immediately; some users might just blow by the message and get into deep trouble by letting the error cause incorrect results, data corruption, or worse.

It is up to you, the developer, to provide a mechanism to handle unexpected results in your application. This mechanism is called an *error handler*. It is a piece of code that lies dormant, waiting for an error to occur. When the error occurs, it intercepts it. Once intercepted, the error is hidden from the user's view. The error handler gathers information about the error, determines what kind of error it is (including how severe it is), and makes a decision about how to present it to the user.

In this chapter, I'll explain how to build an error handler and how you can incorporate one into your applications.

Types of Errors—Revisited

It's important to understand what types of errors an error handler can handle and what types it can't. As I explained in the last chapter, there are five types of errors. Defects in the product and compile-time errors are typically discovered by the developer during the programming and testing of the application; it's unlikely that a user will run into either of these.

More likely is a *run-time* error, in which the program executes code that creates an error, such as the division of a number by zero. The better the job of testing you've done, the less likely these errors are to occur. Still, run-time errors are probably going to cause a program crash unless you have set up an error handler that will detect and handle them properly.

Logic errors, while more likely to occur than run-time errors, are going to be caught by an error handler only some of the time. A logic error usually causes an incorrect result to occur, but Access has no way of knowing that the result is incorrect. Skipping a case in a CASE structure or calculating a value incorrectly because the supporting formula was put together wrong can only be detected if you've planned in advance to detect it. And if you've planned in advance to detect it, you could probably write the code in a different manner that wouldn't allow the incorrect result to be generated in the first place. Nonetheless, you can use an error handler to detect certain types of incorrect results and then handle them as needed.

Finally, *user-generated* errors, such as inputting bad data or performing actions that are detrimental to the system, can and should be caught by an error handler.

In the remainder of this chapter, I'll first demonstrate what happens when you encounter a run-time error. Then I'll construct a very simple error-handling mechanism that works in a single procedure. Next, we'll take a look at some of the options for recovering from an error. Finally, I'll build an error handler that is more flexible and can be used beyond a single procedure or form.

Constructing a Simple Error-Handling Mechanism

A classic example of a run-time error is dividing a number by a variable that's currently equal to zero. Another common example of a run-time error is referencing a control that doesn't exist. The sample form in Figure 15-1 will be used to demonstrate these errors. Clicking any of the buttons in the form will cause the value in the Numerator text box to be divided by the value in the Denominator text box, with the result displayed as part of the label to the right of the button. Rather, each of the buttons contains code that will attempt to perform this function—obviously, since this chapter is on error handling, those buttons will cause errors.

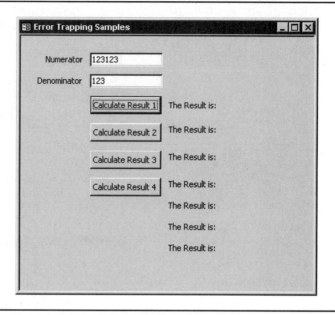

Figure 15-1.

The Numerator text box is named "Text1" and the Denominator text box is named "Text3." The labels next to the four buttons are named, from top to bottom, "Label6," "Label8," "Label10," and "Label12."

The code in the Click( ) event of the first command button is as follows:

```
Private Sub Command0_Click()
cResult = Text1.Value / Text2.Value
Label6.Caption = "The result is: " & cResult
End Sub
```

If you're following along carefully, you'll see that the first line in the sub references the Text2 text box—but there is no Text2 text box on the form. As a result, when you click the top button, you'll be presented with the error dialog box shown in Figure 15-2.

If you don't
include an
error handler
in an
application,
errors will
generate a
standard
Access or VBA
error dialog
box that
contains an
error number
and a
descriptive
message that
may or may
not be helpful

Figure 15-2.

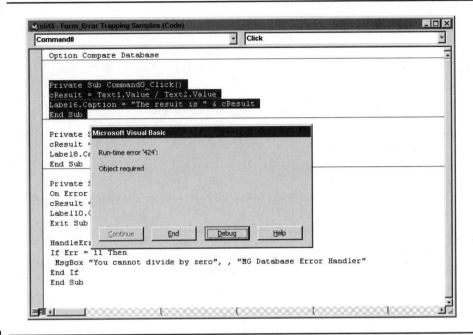

Your two choices are either to terminate the current procedure by selecting
the End button, or to get into the VBA debugger by selecting Debug. While
these two options make sense to you, you certainly wouldn't want to present
this dialog box to your users. Hopefully, your testing would uncover defects
like this; but we'll see that you can trap errors like this just in case you
haven't caught all of them.

The code in the click( ) event in the second button looks like this:

```
Private Sub Command7_Click()
cResult = Text1.Value / Text3.Value
Label8.Caption = "The result is: " & cResult
End Sub
```

Pressing this button results in the screen shown in Figure 15-3.

15

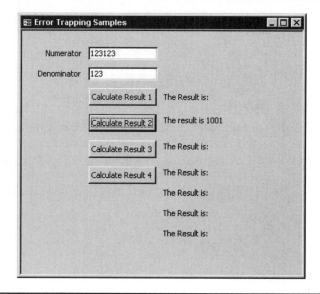

When values
are entered
into both the
Numerator and
Denominator
text boxes,
pressing the
second button
generates a
proper result
label

Figure 15-3.

However, if you change the value of the denominator to zero and then choose the second command button again, the code will attempt to divide by zero, resulting in the error message shown in Figure 15-4.

Now that we've got a segment of code that represents code we might find in an application, let's create an error handler to deal with it. The code in the click( ) event in the third button looks like this:

```
Private Sub Command9_Click()
On Error GoTo HandleError
cResult = Text1.Value / Text3.Value
Label10.Caption = "The result is: " & cResult
Exit Sub

HandleError:
If Err = 11 Then
 MsgBox "You cannot divide by zero", , "MG Database Error Handler"
End If
End Sub
```

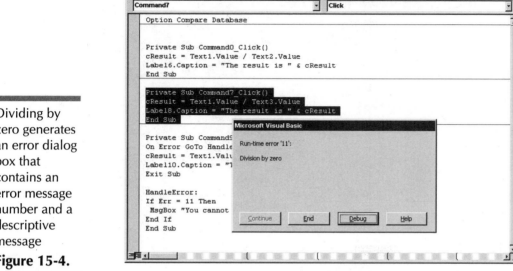

Dividing by zero generates an error dialog box that contains an error message number and a descriptive message

Figure 15-4.

When you enter a zero in the Denominator text box and then choose the third button, you'll be greeted with a custom, error-handler dialog box, as shown in Figure 15-5.

I used the contents of the click( ) method of the second button and just added some additional code to handle the specific "divide by zero" error for demonstration purposes. There are three pieces to this additional code.

First is the On Error statement at the beginning of the routine. This simply tells Access to transfer execution to a different segment of code when the application throws an error that would otherwise cause Access to display its standard error dialog box. The object of the GoTo command is a label, in this case named HandleError, that is found elsewhere in the procedure.

The second piece is the label that identifies the start of the segment to which control will be transferred when an error is caused. Notice that the label is simply a text string that is followed by a colon—if you don't include the colon, Access will generate yet another error.

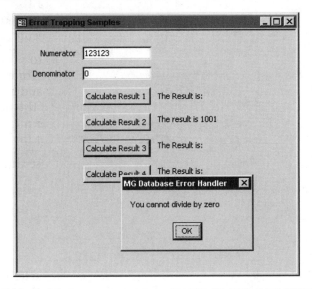

An error handler will trap an error and provide both a more useful description of the error and the appropriate actions to take

Figure 15-5.

The third piece is the actual code, following the label, that will be executed because of the error being executed. This code isn't particularly robust—it just traps for one type of error and, upon detection of that error, responds with a message box and then terminates the procedure. The error message in the dialog box isn't terribly sophisticated, but then a "divide by zero" error isn't terribly complex to figure out.

Controlling What Happens After an Error Occurs

In the previous example, in which a number was divided by zero, I simply displayed an error message and then terminated the procedure. In actuality, you would want to be able to perform several types of actions, and which type of action was executed may depend on internal conditions or on a choice made by the user.

There are two additional choices: to have the same line of code executed again, and to skip the offending line but have the program continue on the following line. You might want the same line of code executed again if the user can correct the situation that caused the error and then choose a button to try again. For example, he or she might be copying a file to a disk but have forgotten to put a disk in the disk drive, or the user might be printing a report but have failed to turn on the printer. In both cases, the user would want to correct the situation and then execute the function again.

In another scenario, the user might want to skip the line that generated the error, but continue executing the routine. For example, suppose your application had a process that created an audit file of events happening during the process, and during one run of the process, the hard disk filled up. After freeing up space on the disk, the user might simply want to continue—but without re-creating the text file a second time.

To have the same line of code executed, use the Resume statement, like so:

```
If Err = 11 Then
 MsgBox "You cannot divide by zero", , "MG Database Error Handler"
 Resume
End If
```

This is a great example of the danger of the Resume statement, because it will execute the same line of code that caused the error to be generated—the divide-by-zero statement. However, since the divide-by-zero statement is still invalid the second time through, the error will be thrown a second time, and the error handler will be called again. This scenario is known as an *endless loop* because you can't get out of it. Each time you click the OK button in the error handler dialog box, you execute the divide-by-zero line again, which displays the error handler dialog box again. Obviously, you'll only want to use the Resume statement when the user can change the situation so that the statement will be executed correctly.

In the case in which you want to skip the offending line and continue, use the Resume Next statement. The fourth button on this form performs four arithmetic calculations with the results of the calculations to be displayed in four labels. The second calculation is division, and, thus, when the denominator is zero, the program generates an error. In this case, we'd like the statement that divides by zero to be ignored, and the rest of the routine to continue to be executed. The Resume Next statement, placed after the detection of the divide-by-zero error as shown in the following code, will do so.

```
Private Sub Command11_Click()
On Error GoTo HandleError
cResult1 = Text1.Value * Text3.Value
cResult2 = Text1.Value / Text3.Value
cResult3 = Text1.Value + Text3.Value
```

15

```
cResult4 = Text1.Value - Text3.Value
Label12.Caption = "The result is " & cResult1
Label13.Caption = "The result is " & cResult2
Label14.Caption = "The result is " & cResult3
Label15.Caption = "The result is " & cResult4
Exit Sub

HandleError:
If Err = 11 Then
 MsgBox "You cannot divide by zero", , "MG Database Error Handler"
 Resume Next
End If

End Sub
```

When you choose the fourth button after entering zero as a denominator, the program will trip the error handler when the divide-by-zero statement is encountered. You will be presented with the error handler dialog box, and then the rest of the routine will be executed, resulting in the screen shown in Figure 15-6.

The Resume Next statement can be used to continue execution of a procedure so that the rest of the arithmetic calculations are performed

Figure 15-6.

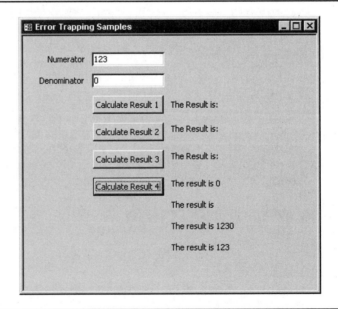

Creating a Generic Error Handler

While this capability to trap an error and handle it as you please—instead of being held hostage to the default error-handling behavior built in to Access and VBA—seems at first blush to be sophisticated and powerful, you'll quickly find a shortcoming. It can be laborious and subject to error to create error handlers for every routine in your application. If you try to do so anyway, you'll find yourself nearly falling asleep as you create virtually the same code over and over. Wouldn't it make sense to create a centralized error handler that could be called from throughout your application?

I've got good news and bad news for you. The good news is that you can create a generic error handler that can be called from every module, and you can make that generic handler quite robust so as to handle a wide variety of errors. This is good, because you can concentrate on putting all the horsepower of your error handler in one place, instead of having to write customized error handlers in every procedure in your application. The bad news is that you still have to manually call the error handler from each procedure—there isn't a "global error handler" variable you can set to identify your generic error handler to the entire application.

The first step is to create a VBA module that contains the error handler function. This module will have a set of declarations in the general section that will define variables that contain information about the most recent error generated, and a function that is called by every module's error-trapping routine.

To start, create a new module called basErrorHandler in your database. In the general declarations section, use the following code segment to define the error number, message, and other attributes of the error:

```
Type typErrors
intNumError As Integer
strMessage As String
strModule As String
strRoutine As String
datDateTime As Variant
End Type
Public ptypError As typErrors
```

Next, create a function called Error Handler. Each module that calls this function will pass a number of parameters, such as the number and description of the error that caused the error handler to kick in. The error handler function will then take over, perform whatever magic is appropriate, and then return control to the calling module. In this simple example, the error description and number and the name of the routine that caused the error are passed to the error handler. The handler then displays a generic error message.

```
Function ErrorHandler(strDescError As String, _
    intNumError As Integer, _
    strNameRoutine as String) _
    As Integer
ptypError.strMessage = strDescError
ptypError.intNumError = intNumError
ptypError.strRoutine = strNameRoutine
ptypError.datDateTime = Now

MsgBox ("Error #: " & ptypError.intNumError & Chr(13) & _
"Error Description: " & ptypError.strMessage & Chr(13) & _
"Routine Name: " & ptypError.strRoutine)

End Function
```

Now that you've got a generic error handler, how do you get to it?

In a procedure, you'll need as before the same three pieces that call the error handler. The only difference is that the third piece won't handle the error itself, but will call this generic error handler that is located in the basErrorHandler module. The Generic Error Trapping form in this chapter's source code is shown in Figure 15-7. Each of the buttons performs a different type of arithmetic on the two numbers in the text boxes above the buttons. However, the code in each button's click( ) event calls the same error handler.

In the click( ) event of the Add Numbers command button, the On Error statement sets up the transfer of control to a different segment of code when an error occurs. Next, a variable is declared and initialized that describes the name of the current routine. Then the regular business of the method—adding the numbers—is carried out.

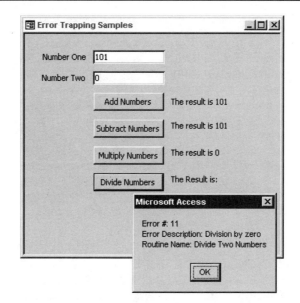

The code in
each button's
click( ) event
calls the same
generic error
handler

Figure 15-7.

After the HandleError label, the ErrorHandler function is called, with the error
description and number and the name of the current routine passed as
parameters. Finally, the return value of the ErrorHandler function is used to
determine what the next step is. In this example, the ErrorHandler function
doesn't actually do anything, but the structure is there for you to expand upon.

```
Private Sub CommandAdd_Click()
On Error GoTo HandleError
Dim strNameRoutine As String
strNameRoutine = "Add Numbers"
cResult = Val(Text1.Value) + Val(Text2.Value)
Label6.Caption = "The result is " & cResult
Exit Sub
HandleError:
Dim intToDo As Integer
```

15

```
intToDo = ErrorHandler(intNumError:=Err.Number, _
  strDescError:=Err.Description, _
  strNameRoutine:=strNameRoutine)
Select Case intToDo
Case ERR_RESUMENEXT
 Resume Next
Case ERR_RESUME
 Resume
Case ERR_EXIT
 Exit Sub
Case ERR_QUIT
 Quit
End Select
End Sub
```

You'll notice that the error-handling code for the Divide Numbers command
button is identical except for the initialization of the variable that holds the
name of the routine that is passed to the error handler. I still think it's a lot
of unnecessary work to enter the same error-handler–calling code in every
procedure, but it's still less work than having to investigate errors without
enough information.

```
Private Sub CommandDivide_Click()
On Error GoTo HandleError
Dim strNameRoutine As String
strNameRoutine = "Divide Two Numbers"
cResult = Text1.Value / Text2.Value
Label12.Caption = "The result is " & cResult
Exit Sub
HandleError:
Dim intToDo As Integer
intToDo = ErrorHandler(intNumError:=Err.Number, _
  strDescError:=Err.Description, strNameRoutine:=strNameRoutine)
Select Case intToDo
Case ERR_RESUMENEXT
 Resume Next
Case ERR_RESUME
 Resume
Case ERR_EXIT
 Exit Sub
Case ERR_QUIT
 Quit
End Select
End Sub
```

The advantage of centralizing your error-handling code in one function is that you can expand how you choose to deal with the errors and only have to change code in one place. For example, you may choose to

◆   Log the error that occurred to a table. You'll want to do so before any other error handling, so that you are assured of capturing the error. A user can't always be counted on to write down the error.

◆   Use a predefined table that contains Access error codes and a recommended action when that error occurs, look up those errors, and choose a return code that will then present the appropriate actions for the user. For example, when one error occurs, you may want to allow the user to retry, while when another error occurs, you may want to shut down the application immediately.

◆   Capture system and environment information, and log that to a table for future examination along with the error log described earlier.

You still have to make the call to the error handler in each procedure you write; but once designed properly, that code will be the same in every procedure, so you don't have to worry about propagating changes throughout your application because of a change in your error-handling mechanism.

Error handling is much like insurance—you hope you'll never need it, but it's always better to have it and not need it than vice versa. Robust error handling is one of those features that distinguish a professional application from the rest.

CHAPTER 16

Advanced Queries

Queries are the lifeblood of Access 2000—they are the key way you get data from the tables to your forms and reports. Chapter 4 showed you how to create and modify queries. In this chapter, I'll show you how to use queries to make changes to your data as well.

Action Queries

Up to this point, you've used queries only to get data from tables and other queries. However, other types of queries do much more than just grab existing data. These are collectively called *action queries* and add a considerable amount of power to Access. For example, *Update* queries allow you to make changes to data in a whole group of records in one or more tables—using them is considerably faster than having to write VBA code to accomplish the same task. *Delete* queries allow you to delete one or more records from a table based on conditions you specify, instead of you having to manually open the data source and delete each record yourself. *Append* queries append records to a table in a batch mode, instead of entering the data one record at a time. *Make Table* queries allow you to create a brand-new table, and *Crosstab* queries allow you to perform a cross-tabulation of data from multiple data sources. Each of these is explained in greater detail in the following sections.

Update Queries

Suppose you were going to send a copy of the Cars table to a friend in the United Kingdom, home of the original MG Motor Car Company. Most of the information would be readily useful, but not the mileage column. Folks on the east side of the Atlantic Ocean use kilometers instead. Wouldn't it be nice to convert the mileage figures to kilometers? (We'll keep the field name of "Mileage" because "Kilometerage" just sounds funny.) You can use an Update query to do so in one stroke, instead of having to update each record manually, or taking the time to write a VBA procedure to accomplish the same task.

First, you'll create a query like you normally do: select the Queries object in the Database window and choose the New button. Select Design View from the New Query dialog box and choose OK. You'll see the dialog box in which you select which tables and queries are to participate in the query. Do so and you'll end up with the query window as you would expect: The tables and queries you've selected are in the top half, and the field selection grid is in the bottom half of the window. The Query menu pad and the Query Type button, as shown next, will also appear.

By default, a new query is defined as a Select query—the kind you are used to. To change this query to an Update query, either select Query | Update Query, or click the Query Type button and select Update Query. Two things will change. First, the caption of the query builder window will change from "Select Query" to "Update Query." Second, the Sort and Show rows in the grid will be replaced by an "Update To" row.

Since the purpose of this particular Update query is to convert the mileage to kilometers, the field to select will be nMileage, and we'll update it using a conversion formula of 1.62 KM per mile:

```
[nMileage] * 1.62
```

as shown in Figure 16-1.

The Update To row contains the expression that you want to use for the new value

Figure 16-1.

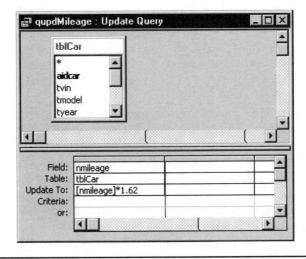

The last step is to execute the query by choosing the Run button (the red exclamation mark) or by selecting Query | Run.

Naturally, you can choose to update certain rows only. You would use the Criteria row to build the conditions as you desire, just like in ordinary Select queries. When you execute the Update query, Access will prompt you, warning you that you are about to permanently change data.

NOTE: Update queries are named with a "qupd" prefix.

Delete Queries

Delete queries are created much the same way as Update queries. First, you'll create a query like you normally do: select the Queries object in the Database window and choose the New button. Select Design View from the New Query dialog box, choose OK, select which tables and queries are to participate in the query, and you'll again end up with the query window as you would expect. The tables and queries you've selected will be in the top half, and the field selection grid will be in the bottom half of the window. Change this query to a Delete query, either by selecting Query | Delete Query, or by clicking on the Query Type button and selecting Delete Query. The caption of the query builder window will change from "Select Query" to "Delete Query," and the Sort and Show rows in the grid will be replaced by a "Delete" row.

In this case, we're going to get rid of any cars with low mileage—between 0 and 1,000 miles—with a condition as shown in Figure 16-2.

TIP: Executing a Delete query as soon as you've created a condition might not be such a great idea—particularly if you're still a little new to Access queries. What if you got the condition wrong? Those records will be history, and nothing will get them back for you. Instead of running the Delete query, select the View button on the toolbar (the one that allows you to switch between Design and Query views). You'll see the "results" of the Delete query display in a datasheet, so you can confirm that you got the condition right.

Use the Delete
row in the grid
to enter the
condition
you'll use to
choose which
rows will
be deleted

Figure 16-2.

If you've followed the preceding tip, you'll see that the condition in which
nMileage must be less than 1,000 isn't totally satisfactory. A few of the records
have NULL values in the nMileage field. Why doesn't "nMileage < 1000" pick
those up? Because a NULL value doesn't mean zero or less than zero. It means
we don't know what the mileage is. It may well be a bazillion miles—we simply
don't know—and thus we certainly can't delete those records.

To get rid of all low mileage cars as well as unknown mileage cars, change the
Delete condition as shown in Figure 16-3.

NOTE: Delete queries are named with a "qdel" prefix.

Append Queries

An Append query is used to add records to a table. You would do this, for
example, during a process in which you are moving records from one table to
another, such as in an end-of-period archival process. For example, you may

Include an
"Is Null"
condition in
order to
remove all
records with a
NULL value
in the field
of interest

Figure 16-3.

not want to keep all the event attendance records over the past 20 years in the current Event Attendance join table—why not move those to an Event Attendance History join table?

The first step in an Append query is to create a query as usual, selecting the table *from* which records will be coming; and changing the query to an Append query. Doing so will display the Append dialog box, as shown here, in which you can choose the table *to* which the records will be appended.

You'll notice that the Table Name drop down is populated with tables in the current database. You can also specify another database that contains the table you want to append records to by selecting the Another Database option button.

NOTE: Append queries are named with a "qapp" prefix.

16

Make Table Queries

You'll probably need to create a History table before performing an Append query that is intended to archive history data to it. You can use a Make Table query to do so. Just as before, create a query and change its type to Make Table. You'll see the same type of dialog box, shown next, as with an Append query, asking for the name of the table to create.

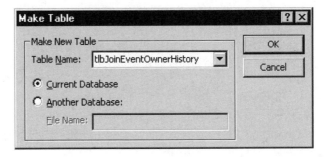

Once you've finished with the Make Table dialog box, select which fields (using the "*" identifier will select all the fields in the table) and which records to query, using standard Access conditions. Then run the Make Table query. The number of records that qualify will be displayed in the warning dialog box. If you've decided to copy records (that's *copy* records, not move them!), the appropriate records will be copied as well.

NOTE: Make Table queries are named with a "qmak" prefix. Tables created as a result of running a Make Table query can be named anything you want, although you'll probably want to use a consistent naming scheme so as not to get confused down the road. As you can see, I kept the name of the tblJoinEventOwner and tblJoinEventOwnerHistory tables similar.

Crosstab Queries

Crosstabs are wonderful tools for getting a big-picture view of data in a time-oriented way. For example, suppose you wanted to see when dues were paid by each member in a spreadsheet-like format, showing each member down the left side of the spreadsheet, and the amounts paid each month across the top. However, you don't actually want each individual owner. Rather, you want them categorized by whether they've received the Holy Octagon, so the left column will include just one field and the spreadsheet will contain two rows: one for Holy Octagon members and another for non–Holy Octagon members.

The intersection of each row and column—each *cell* in spreadsheet parlance—will contain the total dues paid for a certain month by either all the Holy Octagon members or all the non–Holy Octagon members. Creating such a query, however, isn't as straightforward as the other types of action queries I've already described. The easiest way to create a Crosstab query is to use the Crosstab Query Wizard, which I'll walk you through with this example.

First of all, since this crosstab will require data from two tables—the Owners table and the Dues table—we'll need to create a query that will be used as the data source for the crosstab. You've done this a hundred times before—select both the Owners table and the Dues table, pick the dPaid, cAmtPaid, tNameFirst, tNameMiddle, tNameLast, and yHasHolyOctagon fields, and run the query, naming the result qryDuesPaidPerHolyOctagonOwner.

Then create a new query by selecting the New button and choosing the Crosstab Query Wizard option in the New Query dialog box.

Next select the Queries option group button in the View box, and select the qryDuesPaidPerHolyOctagonOwner query, as shown in Figure 16-4.

Then select the field (or fields) that will populate the rows in the leftmost column. In this case, it's simply the yHasHolyOctagon field. You'll see the results in the sample screen shown in Figure 16-5.

Next select which field will be used to create multiple columns in the query. This field usually contains a date of some sort and can be parsed daily, weekly, monthly, quarterly, and so on. In our case, we'll use the dPaid field so that a variety of dates will appear as column headers across the top. See Figure 16-6.

Next you'll select how you want the date to be parsed out—if you wanted, you could tally up dues by Date or by Quarter. In this case, I'll select Monthly. You can see that the months of the year are automatically entered into the sample, as shown in Figure 16-7.

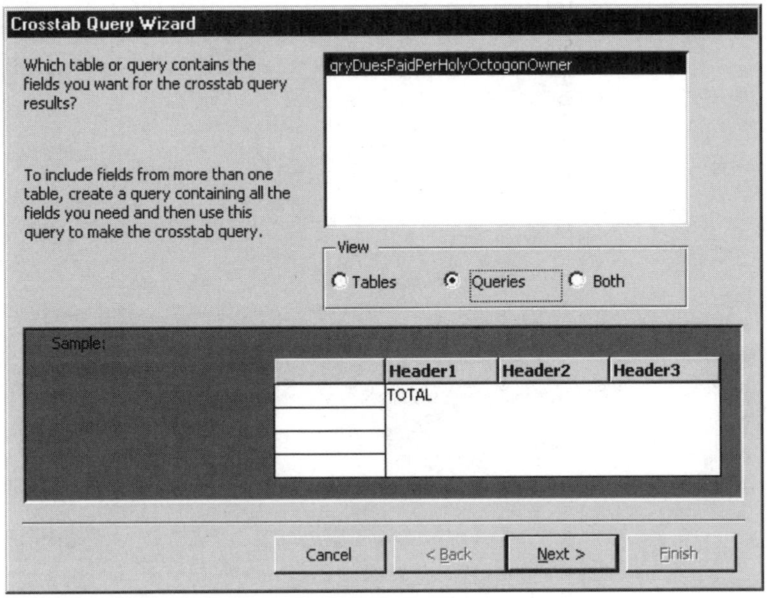

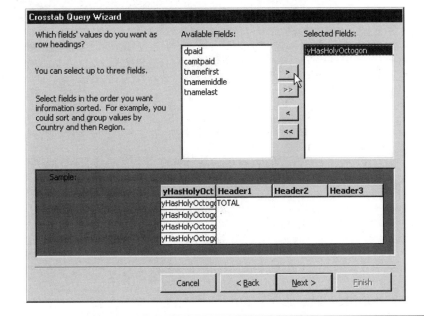

Select the table
or query to
be used as
the data source
for the
Crosstab query

Figure 16-4.

Select the
fields that
will populate
the rows of
the query

Figure 16-5.

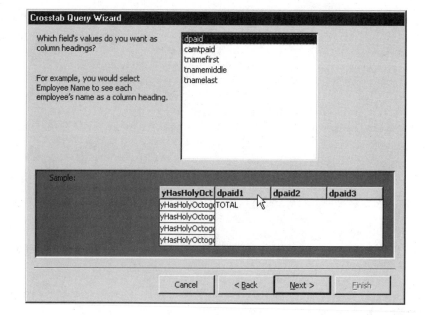

Select the field that will be used to create the columns of the query

Figure 16-6.

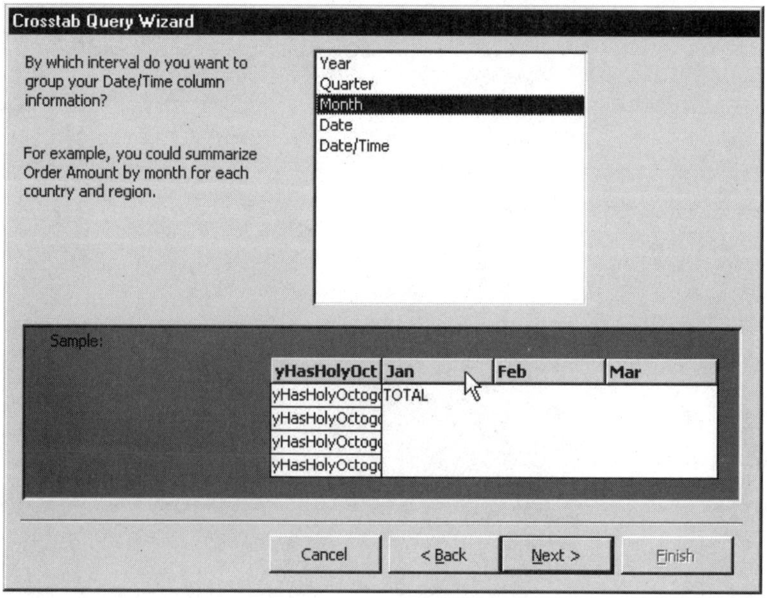

Select how the date will be parsed out

Figure 16-7.

The last major step is to define what value is going to be placed in each cell, and how it's going to be calculated. In this case, we'll just sum the amount of dues paid, as shown in Figure 16-8.

Finally, run the query and see the result, as shown here. You can quickly see that both members and nonmembers have contributed approximately equally over the years to the dues fund, and that January is by far the month in which the most dues have been collected.

yHasHolyOctog	Total Of camtp	Jan	Feb	Mar	Apr	May	Jun	Jul	Aug
☑	$398.00	$244.00	$44.00	$86.00	$24.00				
☐	$440.00	$68.00	$52.00	$28.00		$88.00	$44.00	$132.00	$28.00

qryDuesPaidPerHolyOctogonOwner_Crosstab : Crosstab Query

Record: 14 < 1 > >I >* of 2

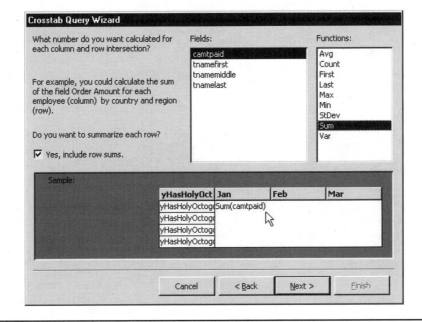

Determine which value is to be placed in each cell, and how it's to be calculated

Figure 16-8.

Special Query Properties

There are several special properties that can be attached to a query to produce certain kinds of results. These properties can be set in the Query Properties dialog box, shown in Figure 16-9, that appears when you right-click in the query window and select Query Properties.

Setting the *Unique Values* property, a logical value, to Yes will force the query output to contain unique instances for each record. In other words, the combination of all fields in the query result will be unique for each record. This is handy if you want to determine just the unique values for a series of records.

The *Top Values* property can be set to a numeric value or a percentage, so that the query can return just the largest *n* records. You can choose from one of the default values: top 5, 25, or 100, or top 5% or 25%, or you can enter your own absolute record count or percentage. Note that the result may not contain exactly the number of records you specified. If you asked for the top ten values, but records 9, 10, 11, 12, and 13 all contained the same value, your result set would contain 13 records.

The Query
Properties
dialog box
allows you to
set a number
of special
properties

Figure 16-9.

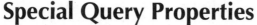

Query Properties	
General	
Description	
Output All Fields	No
Top Values	All
Unique Values	No
Unique Records	No
Run Permissions	User's
Source Database	(current)
Source Connect Str	
Record Locks	No Locks
Recordset Type	Dynaset
ODBC Timeout	60
Filter	
Order By	
Max Records	
Subdatasheet Name . . .	
Link Child Fields	
Link Master Fields	
Subdatasheet Height . . .	0"
Subdatasheet Expanded	No

16

Note that with the Top Values property, the field being used to determine the top values must be the leftmost column in the query, and that the sort order for the column will determine whether you get the top values or the bottom values.

You can also specify what the maximum number of records to be returned from a query is through the use of the Max Records property. This can be handy if you're just looking for a bunch of records but don't necessarily need every one that meets a qualification. For example, suppose you wanted to do a mailing to a group of owners, but you didn't want to mail to everyone in the database. You could specify that you only wanted a maximum of 50 records, assuming that randomness was either not important or that you had selection criteria of some sort that provided the necessary randomness.

SQL: The Language Behind Access Queries

Much as your forms are user-friendly data-entry forms that a user can take advantage of when entering data into one or more tables, the query window is a data-entry form for creating queries. The underlying query is contained in a long command built from a language known as *SQL* (pronounced "sequel") and there are times—when you run into a limitation of the query window—that you'll need to create your own SQL commands.

T **IP:**   If you're tempted to skip over this section, I'd advise not. Virtually every database tool in the world uses (or can use) some variation of SQL, so it's one of the most transportable skills you'll develop while reading this book. When you've finished with this chapter, you'll be able to walk up to a Sun SPARCstation running Oracle or an HP9000 running Informix, and, assuming proper permissions have been set up, run queries against databases on those machines without any additional training or knowledge. Pretty powerful stuff, indeed.

You can enter your own SQL commands in the query window's SQL View window, and use the SQL View window to see the SQL command generated by the work you do in the graphical query window. To get to the SQL View window, shown in Figure 16-10, right-click in a query window and select SQL View.

Once you have a SQL View window displayed, you can use the View button in the toolbar to get back to Design view or to see the results of the query in a datasheet. Now let's jump into the SQL language.

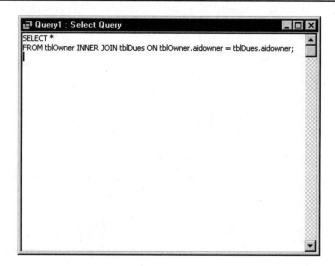

The SQL View window displays the SQL command behind the query you have built in the query window

Figure 16-10.

About 25 years ago, SQL was devised at IBM as a standard mechanism to access data. At the time, each type of computer had its own peculiar requirements for getting at data, and this was becoming both confusing and expensive. IBM's answer, Structured English Query Language (SEQUEL), provided a standard interface that gave access to data regardless of the platform it was used on—much like File | Save in Windows does the same thing whether you're in a spreadsheet, a word processor, or an e-mail program. SEQUEL evolved into "SQL," and the latest standard definition is SQL-92. Access' implementation of SQL contains many of the elements of SQL-92.

Basic SQL Syntax

A SQL SELECT command consists, at a minimum, of two parts—a field list and a data source—so that the most basic SELECT command looks like this:

```
select * from tblCar
```

Try typing the following command in the SQL View window:

select tvin, tmodel, tyear, nmileage from tblCar

and then clicking on the View button in the toolbar. You'll see the results shown in Figure 16-11.

16

You can also flip to Design view and see the graphical representation of the SQL SELECT statement that you typed in. Now that you've got the basic idea of how to enter and run a SQL command, it's time to explore the language.

Field Lists

The asterisk in the first SQL command described earlier is shorthand for "all fields," and it will pull all the fields in all the tables if the SELECT is using more than one table. You can also specify to select only certain fields. You do so by replacing the asterisk with a comma-separated list of fields that you want in the query. For example,

```
select tvin, tmodel, tyear, nmileage from tblCar
```

will produce a query with those four columns in the result set. This will pull only those four fields from the tblCar table.

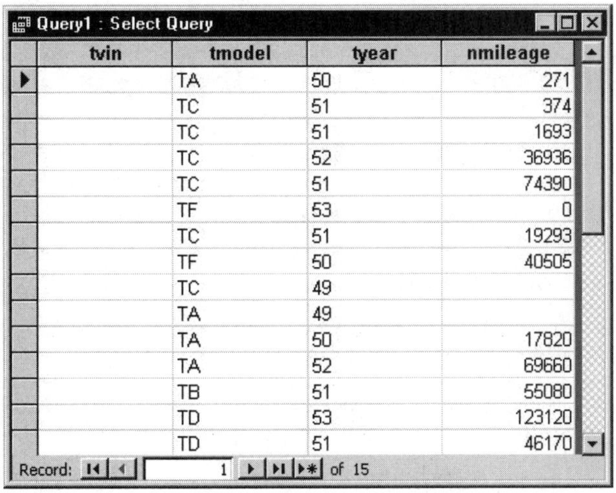

The resulting datasheet from the example SQL SELECT command

Figure 16-11.

Query1 : Select Query			
tvin	**tmodel**	**tyear**	**nmileage**
	TA	50	271
	TC	51	374
	TC	51	1693
	TC	52	36936
	TC	51	74390
	TF	53	0
	TC	51	19293
	TF	50	40505
	TC	49	
	TA	49	
	TA	50	17820
	TA	52	69660
	TB	51	55080
	TD	53	123120
	TD	51	46170

Record: I◄ ◄ 1 ► ►I ►* of 15

If you are pulling fields from more than one table, you can use just the field name, unless that name is present in more than one table. In that case, you need to precede the field name with the table alias. For example, if you were going to pull records from the Owner table but also wanted all the Dues records for each owner, you might want to also display the primary key values for each table. Since the Owner table's primary key (aidowner) is a foreign key in the tblDues table, it exists in both the Owner and Dues tables. Thus, it is necessary to specify it, like so (I'll get to the FROM and JOIN commands shortly):

```
select tblOwner.aidowner, tnamefirst, tnamelast, dpaid, camtpaid
  from tblOwner inner join tblDues
  on tblOwner.aidowner = tblDues.aidowner
```

Forgetting to include the "tblOwner" prefix will result in this message: "The specified field 'aidowner' could refer to more than one table listed in the FROM clause of your SQL statement." Don't worry if you run into this message now and then—everyone forgets the table descriptor. Of course, you'll have to fix your query before it will run.

Often you will want to pull all the fields from one table, but just a couple from another table. Instead of typing each field name, you can specify all the fields from one of the tables with the table alias and an asterisk, like so:

```
select tblOwner.*, dpaid, camtpaid
  from tblOwner inner join tblDues
  on tblOwner.aidowner = tblDues.aidowner
```

Even with a consistent naming scheme such as the one we're using in this book, field names are often terse and cryptic due to the naming conventions we've discussed. Accordingly, the result set of a SELECT may be hard to read, with strange-looking column headings. You may wish to use alternative headings with the AS keyword:

```
select tblOwner.*, dpaid as Paid, camtpaid as Amount
  from tblOwner inner join tblDues
  on tblOwner.aidowner = tblDues.aidowner
```

Notice the indenting of these last few commands. They would have been too long to fit on one line, but haphazard line breaks tend to cause more errors than a line that is neatly formatted. Depending on your personality and the amount of time you've got to fine-tune things, you may want to indent the AS part of the phrase so they line up, as shown next. If you're having trouble with syntax errors and can't find "that one missing comma," this may be a helpful technique to hunt the errant typo.

```
select tblOwner.*,
       dpaid    as Paid,
       camtpaid as Amount
  from tblOwner inner join tblDues
  on tblOwner.aidowner = tblDues.aidowner
```

You are not limited to field names in the field list clause of a SELECT command. You can also use valid Access expressions and functions.

Record Subsets

To filter out the records you don't want in your result set, use the WHERE clause. You've already seen it in the query window—here's where it is used in the SQL language. A WHERE clause contains an expression, an operator, and a value. For instance, to select all cars with over 50,000 miles on them:

```
SELECT * FROM tblCar where nMileage > 50000
```

You can use multiple WHERE clauses by appending them with an AND keyword. This command will return all TA model cars with over 50,000 miles on the odometer:

```
SELECT tmodel, nmileage FROM tblCar
  where nMileage > 50000
    and tmodel = "TA"
```

You can also test a column against a list of values. This list may take the form of a hand-typed string of discrete values, or of a result set of a second query. An example of the first type would be looking for rows in which the Model was either a TA or a TB like so:

```
select tmodel, nMileage from tblCar where tmodel in ("TA", "TB")
```

You can also use the NOT keyword to reverse the effect of an operator such as BETWEEN, LIKE, or IN. For example, if you wanted a list of all cars except the TAs and TBs, you could use the command

```
select tmodel, nMileage from tblCar where tmodel not in ("TA", "TB")
```

NOTE: SQL is case-sensitive, so a WHERE condition that uses an expression like *tModel = "TA"* will only catch those records in which the model was entered (or converted to) all uppercase.

If you try this same command with an OR instead of an AND, you'll see that nearly the entire table is returned. The only records that aren't included in the result set are those that don't satisfy BOTH conditions.

```
SELECT tmodel, nmileage FROM tblCar
  where nMileage > 50000
    or tmodel = "TA"
```

Aggregate Functions

You don't have to use SQL to return a collection of records. You may just want to find out how many records satisfy a given condition, or what the highest, lowest, sum, or average value is for a column. You can use one of SQL's aggregating functions to do so. The trick to remember here is that, even though you are, say, summing values for a group of records, the result set is just a single record that contains the value you were calculating. For instance, to find the average mileage of all cars, use

```
select avg(nMileage) as nAvgMileage from tblCar
```

This will produce a result set of one record that contains the calculated amount. You can do several aggregate functions at the same time, as long as they are all for the same set of records.

Subtotaling

We've seen that we can create a single record that contains an aggregate calculation for a query—for example, the total of all transactions between two dates. Often, however, we'd like subtotals as well—say, the average mileage for each model of car. We use the GROUP BY keyword to do so. Here's how:

```
SELECT tmodel, Avg(nMileage) AS nAvgMileage
FROM tblCar group by tmodel
```

16

Internally, SQL is creating a temporary table that contains all the fields in the field list as well as the grouping expression, but just for the records that satisfy the WHERE condition, like so:

```
tModel, avg(nMileage)
```

Obviously, this temporary table may contain multiple rows for each model. Then SQL performs the aggregation functions, creating a single row for each unique instance of the model. If the grouping expression isn't one of the fields in the list in the SELECT (which, in this case, it isn't), it simply isn't placed in the result set. Typically, however, you'd probably want to include the grouping expression or another identifier in the result set, or else you'd have a series of numbers with no descriptor—technically correct, but of no use.

Multitable SELECTs

As powerful as SQL is, it would be pretty useless if it only operated on a single table at a time. However, multitable SELECTs really bring out the power and elegance of using SQL in your programs. The JOIN and ON keywords are used to tell SQL (and Access) how to join two tables and produce a result set using data from both. However, a caveat or two is in order before I get into the specific syntax.

First, if you neglect the join condition, SQL will attempt to match every record in one table with every record in the other table. In other words, if tblOwner has 5,000 records and tblDues has 100,000 records, the query will take an extremely long time. The result set, if the query ever finishes, will have 500 million records. This will likely fill up the excess disk space and fray the nerves of the network manager in a hurry.

The second thing to know about joins is how SQL actually matches records. SQL will start from the child side of the relation, and find the matching parent. If the parent has no children, the parent record will be left out of the result set. In our example, owners without dues will be left out of the result set in the above query. This situation is called an *outer join* and can be handled with some additional qualifiers in the JOIN syntax.

The third warning about multitable SELECTs concerns joining three or more tables. SQL is not designed to handle a join of one parent and two children. For example, an owner may have several cars in the tblCars table, several transactions in the tblDues table, and several events in the tblEvents table. I've skipped the JoinEventOwner and JoinOwnerCar tables for simplicity. It is not possible to create a single simple SELECT command that will produce a result set that contains owners with their cars, dues transactions, and attended events at the same time. (You can do it with some advanced techniques that are beyond the scope of this book.) If you try it, you will end up with a result set from the parent and one of the children—whichever has more records. The query may seem to work, but the answer created will be wrong. I bring this up so you won't go bonkers trying to do something for which Access' SQL is ill suited. It would be better to create a series of queries, each of which just joined two tables.

Before getting into the nuts and bolts of all the keywords, here's what a simple outer join looks like:

```
select tblOwner.*, dpaid as Paid, camtpaid as Amount
  from tblOwner inner join tblDues
  on tblOwner.aidowner = tblDues.aidowner
```

This SELECT will produce a record set that only contains records in which there was both a parent and a child. You can use the LEFT OUTER JOIN and the RIGHT OUTER JOIN syntax to include all records, regardless whether there was a matching parent or a child on the opposite side. For example, the following command will produce all Owners, whether or not they have matching Dues records:

```
select tblOwner.*, dpaid as Paid, camtpaid as Amount
  from tblOwner left outer join tblDues
  on tblOwner.aidowner = tblDues.aidowner
```

Correspondingly, the following command will produce only those Owners who have matching Dues records, as well as any Dues records that are not attached to an Owner (tsk, tsk!):

```
select tblOwner.*, dpaid as Paid, camtpaid as Amount
  from tblOwner left outer join tblDues
  on tblOwner.aidowner = tblDues.aidowner
```

A full-blown implementation of SQL includes one more variation on the OUTER JOIN syntax, FULL OUTER JOIN, which would combine all parents and all children, and all records that were missing a partner from the other table. Access 2000 does not support the FULL OUTER JOIN syntax.

Controlling the Result Set: Order By

16

Records in a result set are presented in random order unless you use the ORDER BY keyword to control the order. Unlike indexes, which simply present a different view of the records but do not change the physical position, ORDER BY actually positions the records in the order that the ORDER BY field list specifies.

You can use field names or the number of the position of the column in the field list. This latter option is useful when you're using functions that create columns with an unknown name. You can also use more than one field as a tiebreaker in the event of duplicate values in the first column, but all ORDER BY fields must exist in the result set's field list. The default order is ascending, but you can override it with the DESCENDING keyword.

To sort a result set by model, and then by mileage within model, use

```
select tmodel, nmileage from tblCar
  order by 1, 2
```

Obviously, it's much safer to use the name of the field when you can, so that if additional fields are introduced into the SELECT, your ORDER BY clause still performs as intended:

```
select tmodel, tyear, nmileage from tblCar
  order by tmodel, nmileage
```

To sort the result set of a GROUP BY SELECT by the summed amount, use the column number of the aggregate function:

```
select tmodel, sum(nmileage) from tblCar
  group by tmodel order by 2
```

Controlling the Result Set: Distinct

In cases in which we are selecting a subset of the available fields in the source table or tables, it is possible to end up with a number of identical records. For instance, the Owner table may have more than one occupant of a household—the husband and wife may each be individually listed, or a parent and an offspring. But if you wanted a list of all the households in the table, you wouldn't necessarily want multiple copies of the same household. The

DISTINCT keyword eliminates all but one instance of duplicate records in the result set.

This is important: the DISTINCT keyword operates on the *result set,* which means just those fields in the result set, regardless of whether other fields in the original record would make two records in the result unique. This can be handy for determining values to use to populate a lookup table, for instance. Another reason to use the DISTINCT keyword is to find instances of typos in free-form text fields. For example, if the user has typed "10 Wethington Circle," "Ten Wethington Circle," and "10 Wethington Cir." as addresses for various members of the household, a SELECT of this sort would identify those errors.

Controlling the Result Set: Having

The SQL SELECT command has another keyword that many programmers confuse with the WHERE keyword—HAVING. While it sounds like it would perform the same function and, in fact, will do so, there is an important difference between WHERE and HAVING. While WHERE operates as a filter on the *table* to produce a filtered result set, HAVING operates on the *result set* to filter out unwanted results. For instance, the preceding result set listed each model and its average mileage. Suppose you only wanted the records with relatively high mileage? Here's a sample SELECT that would do the trick:

```
SELECT tblCar.tmodel, avg(tblCar.nmileage) AS AvgOfnmileage
   FROM tblCar
   GROUP BY tblCar.tmodel
   having avg(tblCar.nmileage) > 30000
```

I've only scratched the surface of the power of SQL SELECT, but given both the fundamental use of queries throughout Access and SQL's widespread use in database tools everywhere, it's well worth your time to become better acquainted with it.

CHAPTER 17

Advanced Form Techniques

hapter 5 gave you grounding in using forms. By now, you're probably hankering for more. In this chapter, I'll present advanced tips and techniques for creating forms, using controls on forms, and making forms perform special functions.

Advanced Form Tips and Tricks

Driving a car is fairly straightforward—there are just a few controls, and each has limited functionality. A software application, on the other hand, has a rich variety of forms and controls. Each is extremely flexible, usable for a wide range of purposes in many different situations. Accordingly, the learning curve for these objects is longer. Now that you're comfortable with the basics of building forms, I'll discuss a number of tips and tricks that will make your life easier and your form development faster and more enjoyable.

Selecting, Moving, and Positioning Controls

You've already seen that you can select a control by clicking it, and that you can use SHIFT-clicking to select more than one control. You can also select a group of controls that are in proximity by lassoing them. Click the mouse in a blank area of the form near the controls of interest, and then drag the rectangular grid created by the mouse cursor to partially or completely cover the controls, as shown here:

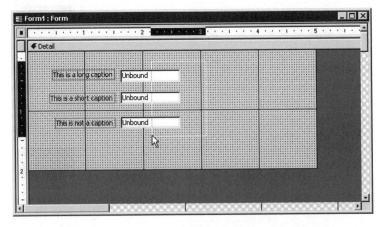

You can specify whether a control is selected when partially covered by the lasso by using the Selection Behavior options in the Forms Report tab in the Tools | Options dialog box.

Another clever way to select multiple controls in proximity is to use the ruler. Suppose you wanted to select all the controls in a horizontal band on the form. First, click in the vertical ruler, above the controls in question, so that a horizontal line appears across the form, as shown here:

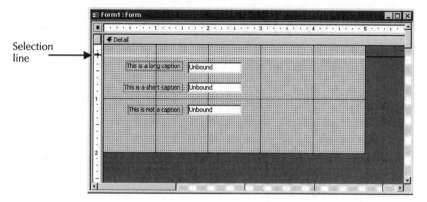

Selection line

Next drag the mouse down, so that the horizontal line splits into two, creating a selection band across the form, and the area highlighted on the form is depicted in reverse highlight in the vertical ruler, as shown next. Once you release the mouse button, all the controls in the selection area remain selected.

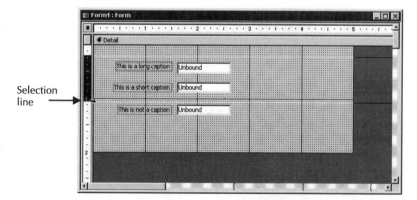

Selection line

You've already seen that you can move a control (and, for text boxes, its related label) by dragging the control with the mouse. Unfortunately, the cursor keys don't seem to work for minutely adjusting the position of a control. If you hold down CTRL, you can use the arrow keys to move a control in increments of approximately $1/100^{th}$ of an inch. You can also use Format I Align I To Grid to nudge the control to the nearest gridlines on the form, which is even easier than trying to eyeball tiny adjustments.

If you have Format | Snap To Grid selected, you may find it frustrating to deselect the command temporarily to make manual adjustments—and you don't have to. You can hold down CTRL to ignore the Snap To Grid setting when you want to align outside of the grid.

The Format | Size menu allows you to resize a group of controls in a number of ways:

◆ **To Fit**   This resizes all selected controls to fit the text within them. In other words, if a text box's control source is 25 characters long but the text box only displays 7 characters, resizing it "To Fit" will resize the text box to display approximately 25 characters. This isn't exact, because Access has to make a best guess at how wide 25 characters is going to be—and that answer varies depending on which proportional characters are used. You can use the Size property of each control to limit the number of characters that can be entered in the field.

◆ **To Grid**   This resizes all selected controls to the nearest gridlines on the form.

◆ **To Tallest**   This resizes all selected controls to match the height of the tallest control in the selection.

◆ **To Shortest**   This resizes all selected controls to match the height of the shortest control in the selection.

◆ **To Widest**   This resizes all selected controls to match the width of the widest control in the selection.

◆ **To Narrowest**   This resizes all selected controls to match the width of the narrowest control in the selection.

Resizing label controls when you've changed the caption can be a nuisance. To automatically size the label to match the caption, double-click any of the sizing handles except the upper-left handle.

Another visual attribute that you may want to fine-tune is the spacing between objects on your form. You can use the Format | Horizontal Spacing And Format | Vertical Spacing menu commands to automatically change the spacing. Both menu commands have the same three options: Make Equal, Increase Spacing, and Decrease Spacing. The first option is terrific for making the controls equidistant instead of having to calculate their positions manually. The other two adjust the space between the controls proportionally while maintaining their relative position.

Tab order is the order in which the focus moves when you tab from control to control. The tab order is determined by the order in which you drop controls on the form, but it may not be the order that the user is happy with. To change the tab order, right-click in the detail section of the form, and select the Tab Order menu command to display the Tab Order dialog box.

17

The Tab Order dialog box displays a list of controls in their original tab order. You can change this order in two ways. First, just choose the Auto Order button, and Access will change the order of the controls automatically, from top to bottom and from left to right when they are at the same vertical height.

You can adjust the order of each control individually by selecting a control, and then dragging it to its new position, as shown in Figure 17-1.

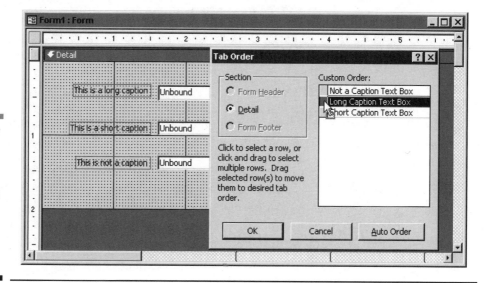

The Tab Order dialog box allows you to manually change the tab order of the controls on a form

Figure 17-1.

Form Properties and Events

Just as each control has properties and events, so does the form itself. While most of your work with forms will be involved with the controls' properties and events, there are some elements of display and functionality that are best handled on a form level.

Form Properties

To access the properties window, the form itself—not the detail, header, or footer band—has to be selected. You can do so by choosing Edit | Select Form, by clicking in the form window outside the form itself, by clicking on the Form Selector button (the gray rectangular button at the upper-left junction of the horizontal and vertical rulers), or by pressing CTRL-R.

There are 49 properties (not including form events), and it can be difficult to find a specific property, particularly when they're not listed in alphabetical order in the properties window. Thus, they've been divided into three categories that are more easily digested. There are 26 format properties, 10 data properties, and 13 "other" properties. Instead of listing every one of them, I'll discuss the most useful and important ones.

Format Properties

Here are some of the key properties you can use to control how your forms are displayed.

Caption   The caption of a form is the text that appears in the title bar of the form. You can set or change the caption of the property at run time to provide additional information about the status of the form, or to further identify the data on the form. For example, if you have a page frame on the form, you might want to display some identifying field, like name or ID number, in the title bar so that users can keep track of which record they are on while they navigate between pages of the page frame.

Default View   You can choose Single Form, Continuous Form, or Datasheet as the default view for the form.

Views Allowed   You can choose whether to allow the user to switch between Form and Datasheet view.

Scroll Bars   You can choose whether to display the horizontal, vertical, or both sets of scroll bars in a form.

Record Selectors You can choose whether to display the record selector—the gray bar that displays to the left of the record in Form view or the gray box to the left of each record in Datasheet view. This control has no use in forms that don't display data, such as informational or query dialog boxes, so you may want to hide it.

Navigation Buttons You can choose whether to display the navigation buttons at the bottom of the form. These controls have no use in forms that don't display data, so you may want to hide them.

Dividing Lines You can choose whether you want to display a line between each record of a continuous form.

Auto Resize You can choose whether to have a form automatically resized to display a complete record.

Auto Center You can choose whether you want the form to be centered in the application's main window when it's activated.

Border Style You can control the style of the form's border, choosing among None, Thin, Sizable, and Dialog Box. Each style controls a number of form appearance attributes.

◆ **None** This is used for splash screens, so that there is no visible border at all. This setting also automatically removes the title bar and all the controls that appear in the title bar, but it does not remove the record selector, the dividing lines, or the navigation buttons.

◆ **Thin** This is used for screens that are not resizable—the user can't drag the lower-left corner or select the Size menu command from the Control menu. You may use this setting for pop-up or "always on top" forms.

◆ **Sizable** This setting is most often used for day-to-day forms. All menu commands and controls are available, and you can customize the form as you need for specific requirements.

◆ **Dialog Box** This setting removes the Maximize, Minimize, and Resize menu commands from the Control menu and makes the border slightly thicker than the Sizable border style.

Control Box You can choose whether to provide a Control menu for the form. Since the Windows standards dictate the use of a Control menu for most forms, you should turn this off only for specific uses, such as splash screens.

Min Max Buttons   You can choose whether to enable the Minimize and Maximize buttons in the title bar of the form. You can choose to enable both buttons, just one, or neither. As with the Control box, disable either or both of the buttons only when absolutely needed.

Close Button   You can choose whether to enable the Close box in the title bar and whether to enable the Close menu command in the Control menu. This property also controls whether double-clicking the Control box will close the form. If you set this property to No, you must provide another method for the user to close the form.

What's This Button   To provide "What's This Help" in your application, you can display the What's This button in the title bar, as shown in Figure 17-2, by setting this property to Yes. You have to set the Min Max Buttons property to No to use this property. What's This Help allows you to create help topics for specific controls on the form. Selecting the What's This button and then a control will display help specific to that control. If there's not a help topic for that control, the form's help topic will be displayed; if there's not a help topic for the form, Access' native help will be displayed.

Picture, Picture Type, Picture Size Mode, Picture Alignment, Picture Tiling
These properties allow you to control the attributes of an image you want to use as the background of a form. The Picture property allows you to identify the file that will be used as the background, the Picture Type can be either Embedded or Linked, and the last three properties determine how the image will be sized if its dimensions aren't the same as the form's dimensions.

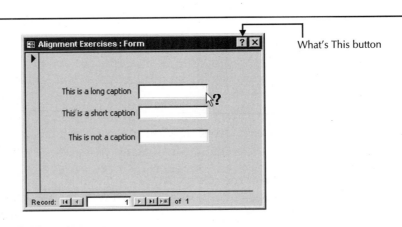

What's This button

Clicking on the What's This button in the title bar and then clicking on a control will display help specific to that control

Figure 17-2.

Data Properties
The following properties are especially useful for working with your data.

17

Record Source   This property is a database object or SQL statement that the form uses to populate the form's controls.

Filter   This property is the filter loaded automatically with the form.

Order By   This property is the sort order that is automatically loaded with the form.

Allow Filters   This property allows you to determine whether the records can be filtered during run time.

Allow Edits/Deletions/Additions   You can use these properties to control whether the user can add, edit, or delete records with the form. Note that a form's record source setting for these properties can't be overridden here. In other words, if the form's record source doesn't allow deletes, you can't allow them in this form by setting Allow Deletions to Yes.

Data Entry   You can set this property to Yes to allow users to add new records but not view or edit existing records. If set to No, the Allow Edits/Deletions/Additions properties settings are respected without any overrides.

Recordset Type   You can choose among Dynaset, Dynaset (Inconsistent Updates), and Snapshot. Dynaset creates a completely functional recordset that allows updating except when certain fields can't be updated, say, to the setting of referential integrity rules that restrict updates. Dynaset (Inconsistent Updates) creates a completely functional recordset and allows updating regardless of rules relating multiple tables. The Snapshot property doesn't allow any updating.

Record Locks   This property allows you to determine how locking is handled in the underlying record source—no locks, lock the record being edited, or lock all records in the record source. The first choice is also known as Optimistic locking, because Access optimistically assumes that it will be able to lock the record automatically when the user moves off the record or closes the form to save changes. This provides the best performance, but can also lead to problems if more than one user makes a change to the same data. The second choice is known as Pessimistic locking, since the record is locked as soon as the user starts to make a change. This guarantees that the user will be able to save his or her change, but at the same time can be restrictive for other users if the user leaves the record in Edit mode for a long time. The last choice, locking the entire table, is used in certain situations in which an operation can't allow changes to be made to any records until it's finished.

Other Properties

This section contains a grab bag of other handy properties you can use in creating your forms.

Pop Up, Modal   This property allows you to designate a form as either a Pop Up (it will remain always on top, regardless of what other forms are opened) or as Modal (retains focus until it's closed). A form set to be a Pop Up will be displayed on top of other forms—but it will not necessarily have focus, so the controls on the form with focus are still functional.

Cycle   This property allows you to control how TAB will work in a multirecord form. You can restrict TAB to cycle within fields of a single record, within all records on the form, or within all records. With the first option, when the user tabs off the last control of the current record, the focus is moved to the first control of the same record. With the second option, available only with multipage forms, when the user tabs off the last control on the page, the focus is moved to the first control on the next page. With the third option, the focus moves from the last control of the current record to the first control of the next record.

Menu Bar   You can tie a custom menu bar to a form by using this property.

Toolbar   You can tie a custom toolbar to a form by using this property.

Shortcut Menu   You can allow the use of shortcut (context) menus by setting this property's value to Yes.

Shortcut Menu Bar   If the Shortcut Menu property is set to Yes, you can tie a specific shortcut menu to the form with this property.

Help File, Help Context ID   You can use these properties to specify the name of a custom help file and a topic identifier for use with this form.

Allow Design Changes   You can use this property to control whether design changes can be made only in Design Mode or in Browse mode as well.

Form Events

Access has 32 different form events—which gives you a great deal of flexibility for reacting to a wide variety of specific events during the use of a form. As with properties, I won't go into all of them, but I will cover some of the more commonly used events.

17

On Current   This is code that runs when the focus is moved to a new record. You can use this event to run code that would initialize values for the new record.

Before/After Insert   This is code that runs before and after a record is added. You can use it to initialize values for a new record based on existing conditions when the record was added, and then to requery controls whose recordset may have been affected by the Insert.

Before/After Update   This is code that runs before and after a record is updated. You can use it to perform validations that involve multiple controls. Then you can use it to either accept or cancel the update based on the results of the validation, and also to requery controls.

On Dirty   This is code that runs just before a record is modified (but not saved). You can use this to check for certain conditions and then either allow or not allow the modification.

On Delete   This is code that runs when a record is deleted. This code is fired when the delete process is executed but before the record is physically removed. You could use this to restrict the deletion to certain sets of conditions, and to not even display the Delete Confirm dialog box if those conditions aren't met.

Before/After Delete Confirm   This is code that runs before and after a user confirms the deletion of a record. You can use the Before event to react to the results of the On Delete event, and the After event to perform actions after the deletion is actually performed.

On Open   This is code that runs before a form is opened. You can use this event to stop the opening of a form based on certain conditions.

On Load   This is code that runs when a form is loaded. You can use this event to perform certain operations when the form is loaded—note that you can't stop the form from opening like you can in the On Open event.

On Resize   This is code that runs when a form is resized. You can use this event to perform actions when the user resizes the form or when the form's size is programmatically modified. For example, you might change the caption of an "Advanced Options" button if the user resizes the form to display the advanced options controls.

On Unload   This is code that runs when a form is unloaded, but before it disappears from the screen. You can use this event to stop the form from unloading, such as when data hasn't been saved. This is triggered by selecting File | Close, by selecting the Control box Close menu command, by clicking on the Close box, or by closing the application or Windows.

On Close   This code is executed when the form is closed, but it can't stop the form from being closed like the On Unload command can.

On Activate   This is code that runs when a form is activated. You can use this to execute actions when a form receives focus and becomes the active form, and when there are active controls on the form.

On Deactivate   This is code that runs when a form is deactivated. You can use this to execute actions when a form loses focus. As with On Activate, use this when there are active controls on the form.

On Got Focus   This is code that runs when a form receives focus. You can use this event in lieu of On Activate when there are no active controls on the form.

On Lost Focus   This is code that runs when a form loses focus. You can use this event in lieu of On Deactivate when there are no active controls on the form.

Special Types of Forms

Access comes with two predesigned forms that can do a lot of grunt work for you. The *Message Box* form is used to provide one or more avenues of action to the user in a standardized format. The *Input Box* form is used to gather a single field of data from the user for later use.

The Message Box

You can use the Message Box form to stop a process and inform users of a situation, and then provide the user with the appropriate choices for continuing. This situation might be the conclusion of a process, when you would want to inform the users and have them continue the process, or the interruption of a process, when you would similarly inform the users and then terminate the process. You can also provide a choice to the users, allowing them to continue or stop the process, or to make a decision to go down one path of action or another.

17

The syntax of the Message Box function is initially straightforward, but can be expanded as your needs require. Only one parameter is required—the text that will appear in the body of the message box, as follows:

```
MsgBox ("This is a simple message box without any frills")
```

You can quickly add two more parameters. The first determines both the number and captions of the buttons on the Message Box dialog box and the type of icon, if any. The second parameter becomes the caption of the form and appears in the title bar. The following code displays a simple message box with a single OK button and a caption reading, "Simple Title."

```
MsgBox "This is a simple message box with a title", 0, "Simple Title"
```

The number used as the second parameter can consist of any number of values, according to the following tables.

Value of Second Parameter	Buttons That Display
No parameter	OK
0	OK
1	OK and Cancel
2	Abort, Retry, and Ignore
3	Yes, No, and Cancel
4	Yes and No
5	Retry and Cancel

Value of Second Parameter	Icon That Displays
16	Critical (stop sign)
32	Warning Query (question mark)
48	Warning Exclamation (exclamation mark)
64	Information (lowercase "i")

You can combine a value from both the first and second tables to display a certain combination of buttons along with the icon of your choice. For example, to display Yes and No buttons with a Question Mark, you would use a second parameter of 36.

You can also determine which button in the message box was pressed by turning the message box statement into a function and saving the result of the function to a variable you then react to, as shown in the following code:

```
intChoice = MsgBox( _
   "This is a simple message box with a title and some buttons", _
   3, "My Complex Title")
Select Case intChoice
Case 1
  lblWhatHappened.Caption = "The user pressed OK"
Case 2
  lblWhatHappened.Caption = "The user pressed Cancel"
Case 3
  lblWhatHappened.Caption = "The user pressed Abort"
Case 4
  lblWhatHappened.Caption = "The user pressed Retry"
Case 5
  lblWhatHappened.Caption = "The user pressed Ignore"
Case 6
  lblWhatHappened.Caption = "The user pressed Yes"
Case 7
  lblWhatHappened.Caption = "The user pressed No"
Case Else
  lblWhatHappened.Caption = "The user pressed Something Else"
End Select
```

See the Sample Message Boxes form in the source code for this chapter.

The Input Box

The Input Box dialog box is another of Access' prebuilt forms that you can use to quickly grab a value from a user. Figure 17-3 shows a sample form with a command button and a label. Choosing the command button calls an input box that requests a piece of information from the user, and then uses that information as the new caption for the label. In this figure, the command button was already chosen once, and the Input Box dialog box displayed is requesting another value, with a default value already filled in the text box.

The code in the command button's click event is as follows:

```
Dim strNameMovie As String
strNameMovie = _
   InputBox("What is the greatest movie of all time?", _
   "The Greatest Movie", "Top Gun")
lblNameMovie.Caption = strNameMovie
```

As you can see, the InputBox statement (or function) takes three parameters. The first is the message to display in the input box, similar to the Message Box function. The next two parameters, both optional, are the caption for the Input Box form and a default value that will be used to populate the text box in the Input Box dialog box.

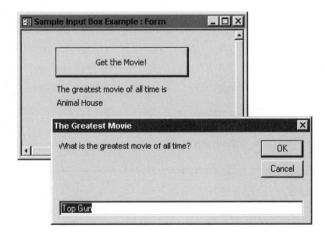

The Input Box dialog box allows you to quickly get a single field of input from the user

Figure 17-3.

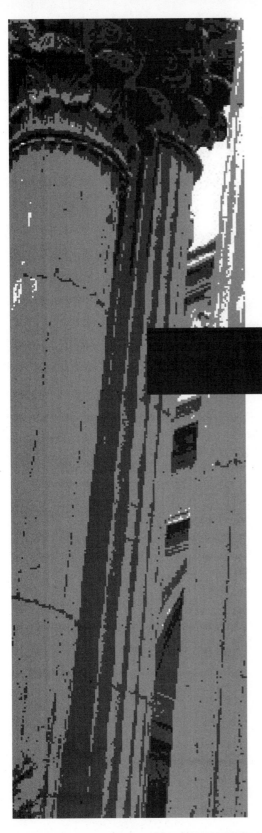

CHAPTER 18

Advanced Output Techniques

Chapter 6 introduced you to creating simple reports; but, as with forms, you're undoubtedly looking for more. While forms are useful, reports are much more so—because people want to extract the data they put into the application. A single method for entering data is often sufficient, but it's not uncommon to retrieve data in a variety of formats. In this chapter, I'll present advanced tips and techniques for the Report Writer and explore other mechanisms for getting data from Access.

Events and Advanced Properties

I covered the properties of the various sections of a report in Chapter 6, but there are more properties and a slew of events available to you. First, let's look at the events that occur during the execution of a report. To access these events, right-click either the report selector button (the gray button with the black square at the intersection of the report's horizontal and vertical rulers) or outside the report area but still in the report window to display the properties window.

Report Events

Just as you can control what happens before, during, and after the execution of a form, you can do the same with a report. It's not as obvious, because you generally don't think about interacting with a report as you do with a form. However, you can react to events that occur during the execution of a report, and you can cause certain actions to occur during the execution as well.

The first event is On Open, and it occurs as soon as you begin to execute the report. Remember that a report is based on either a table or a query. The report's On Open event occurs before the query is executed, as well as before the report is displayed or begins printing. You can use the On Open event to display a form that asks the user for parameters to be used when the query that the report is based on runs.

The next event that occurs during the normal execution of a report is the On Activate event. This event occurs when the report window becomes active, much like the On Activate event of a form. You can use this event to display toolbars or additional windows that work in concert with the report window, or to temporarily suppress the display of other elements in the application.

A report doesn't always execute normally. One situation you might run into is when the underlying table or query doesn't have any data. Some report writers just print the report without any records, keeping the headers, footers, and other nondata elements intact. Access will display "#Error" in the detail section of the report, and that's kinda ugly. It might even be awkward if the report were to print and the user were to submit it, thinking that the one page that printed comprised the entire report. You can use the On No Data event to execute an alternative action when there is no data in the underlying record source. For example, you might just display a dialog box indicating that, for the user to respond to.

The On Page event is executed after the page is formatted and just before the report is sent to the printer. You could use this to perform additional formatting or to otherwise tweak the report before it's printed, but I've not had a use for it.

The third event that may occur during the execution of the report is On Error. Obviously, this event occurs when a problem with the report causes the report not to be printed. This usually has to do with a failure between the report and its record source—if the query or table upon which the report was based isn't available or is gone. However, other run-time errors won't trigger this error; a calculation that divides by zero will just cause that expression to display an error. A problem with the printer will generate a Windows error, not an Access error.

Once the report has been completed, you can access the Close and Deactivate events. On Close could be used to shut the parameter-gathering form. On Deactivate could be used to close those toolbars or other objects that were displayed by the On Activate event. You could also use them to fire off a process now that the report has finished printing, although you would want to be careful to allow the user to verify that the report printed correctly.

Report Section Events

You can also react to events that pertain to specific sections of the report. These events are On Format, On Print, and On Retreat, although On Retreat isn't available in the page header or footer bands. To access these events, select one of the report's sections, such as the detail band or a group header band, and then right-click to display the properties window.

On Format is executed after Access has the data it needs, either by opening the table or by executing the query, but before the data is formatted on the page (and, obviously, before the page is printed). You can tweak the appearance of the section being printed with code in this event. For example, you might print certain items in a section based on the data that has appeared in the query that was run to support this report. You might also run calculations and collect data, such as using a counter to track how many records have been printed. You might use both of these to print the first and last entries that were printed on a page, such as in a phone directory or other such listing.

The On Print event occurs after the formatting has been finished but before the printing starts. On Print is fired for each instance of a section being printed. You would typically use this for reacting to or changing the data in a specific line on the report. As a result, you need to know what you can manipulate during a specific firing of the event.

When On Print is fired during a detail section, you have access to the data in the detail band. When it is fired during a group header section, you have access to the data in the group header band as well as the first record of data in the detail band. When it is fired during a group footer section, you have access to the data in the group footer band, as well as to the last record in the detail band.

You'll typically use the On Print event when you want to change the appearance of the report. You'll use the On Format event to change data that will show up in the report. Both On Format and On Print are executed after the Activate event of the report.

The On Retreat event is an odd piece of work; it is used when Access moves back to a previous section to adhere to a setting like "Keep Together With First Detail." For example, if the group heading has to stay with the first detail row, the group heading can't be printed on a separate page. However, until Access gets to the detail band, it won't know if it's going to have room to print the detail band on the same page as the heading band. If it finds out there's not enough room, then Access moves back to the group heading section, and On Retreat is fired as well. You will rarely use this, unless you are creating reports in which controls on the report aren't bound to data elements in a table or queries, and you have to manually keep the data and the report controls synchronized.

Special Report Properties

Report Writer has several properties that are only available at run time. These are pretty nifty tools to add to your repertoire:

18

◆ **MoveLayout**   Setting this to False will cause Access to keep the printing position as is—it's not advanced. This is somewhat similar to the old dot-matrix printers (or current ink-jet printers) in which you would withhold a line-feed so that you could make a second pass on the same line to overstrike or boldface a particular object.

◆ **NextRecord**   Setting this to False will cause Access to stay on the same record that was just printed.

◆ **PrintSection**   Setting this to False will inhibit the printing of a specific section. This is particularly handy to save development time for reports that need multiple variations of the same data. For example, suppose you need to produce "Detail Only," a "Detail and Summary," and a "Summary Only" report. Instead of creating three separate reports (yawn), create one report, prompt users for which of the three they want, and set the PrintSection properties to True or False depending on which report they selected.

◆ **FormatCount**   This property tracks how many times the On Format event has occurred for a specific section. This is useful information if you're using the On Retreat event, since On Format fires each time On Retreat fires. You may not want to execute the On Format event more than once, and FormatCount will help you do so.

◆ **PrintCount**   This does the same thing as FormatCount, except for the On Print event. As with FormatCount, you can use PrintCount to make sure that the code in the On Print event is only fired once.

◆ **HasContinued**   This property allows you to determine whether a specific section has been continued from the previous page. You can use this property to display (or hide) labels that indicate that a section is being continued from the previous page.

◆ **WillContinue**   This property allows you to determine whether a specific section will terminate on the current page or if it will continue to print on the next page. You can use the WillContinue and HasContinued properties to display or hide labels that indicate that a section will be continued on the next page ("Continued on next page...") or that it was continued from the previous page ("Continued from previous page...").

Additional Controls

Here are some additional controls you may find useful in your reports.

Page Break

You can manually force a page break to occur within a section by using the Page Break control. To set a page break between controls in a section, use the Page Break control from the Toolbox, just as you did with forms.

You can also create a page break at one end of a section or the other by setting the Force New Page property of a section. You can do this in a group header, a group footer, or in a detail section. Remember that each of these sections can be quite lengthy, so you might find it useful to print each section on its own page. For example, if a group header band contains a lot of information, you could break after it to list all the data for the group on a fresh page. The same goes for footers. And suppose that a detail band were actually a page in itself, like an invoice. You wouldn't want invoices for multiple companies to print on the same page, so you could set up each as its own page.

Images and Graphics

You'll often want to display more than just text and numbers. The Line and Rectangle controls are often used to visually break up sections of a report. You can change the Thickness, Border Style, and Special Effects properties of these controls. In addition, you may want to change the Back Style property of a rectangle from Normal to Transparent so that if you place a Rectangle on top of another control, the information in that control will be visible.

A Bound Object Frame is much like a Text Box control, except that it's used to display data in OLE fields, such as images, charts, and spreadsheets. An Unbound Object Frame, on the other hand, is used to display objects that aren't bound to underlying data. Rather, they would be used to display items such as bitmaps of logos. The object in the Unbound Object Frame can be edited from within the report.

If you don't need to be able to edit an object, however, a better choice for displaying images is the Image control. It requires fewer resources on the part of Access and Windows. The image (or other object) simply becomes a static chunk of data. If you find you later need to edit the object, you'll have to open and edit it in the program that was used to create the object, instead of doing so from within Access.

Providing Data to Your Reports

18

Throughout this chapter, as well as the introduction to reports in Chapter 6, I've consistently referred to a report's record source as being either a table or a query. As you become more comfortable with Access, you should gravitate toward using queries as the source for all your reports. In fact, let me go into more depth on the process you should use.

Remember that Access queries can contain information from more than one table at a time, including complex joins from multiple tables, and can even contain calculated fields. As a result, you should generate a query that contains as much data as possible, letting the Report Writer do as little data generation and calculation as possible, and relying on it to format and print data that already exists. There are several reasons for this.

First, it's easier to debug a report that's producing scurrilous data, since you can open the query and examine the raw data. If you rely on the report to do some of the intermediate calculations and you run into problems, you have several places to check—the data, the query, and the report—and it's much more difficult to document tricky expressions in a report than in a query.

Second, it's faster to develop and test a query, because you are just concentrating on the data. If you're working on a report at the same time, it's easy to get sidetracked from the data.

Third, you can potentially use the query for multiple reports, since all the data is there. I've created big queries that generate a result set whose members aren't all used by a single report, but many of whose objects are used in several reports. Instead of creating those elements over and over again, it was considerably easier to just create one query and pick which elements I needed for a specific report. Suppose the customer then asked, "You know how you have the XXX field on Report 2? Could you include it on this third report?" It was simple to drop a text box bound to the field from the query on to the report—instead of having to create a complex expression on the report.

Converting an Embedded SQL Statement to a Stored Query

To convert an embedded SQL statement to a stored query, open the report that uses the embedded SQL statement. Click the RecordSource property's ellipses in the Data tab of the report's properties window, and you'll see the SQL statement—displayed as a query. Select File | Save As | Export, and enter a name for the query. Close the Query window, and the report is based on a stored query, not an embedded SQL statement.

Finally, it's often faster to generate a query and then feed that query through the Report Writer, than to have a report slowly generate each page because it's having to do a lot of processing on each page.

This last point is worth expounding on. Reports based on stored queries (as opposed to embedded SQL statements) run faster, because Access creates and saves a *query plan*—a plan of execution that uses information about the data in the tables as well as the indexes on the tables that support the query. This plan is executed at run time. An embedded SQL statement must be compiled, a query plan built, and then the query executed—it's obviously slower. You also can't share an embedded SQL statement among reports.

Outputting Data to Other Formats

As I mentioned in Chapter 6, people don't always want a printed report when they want data from their application. Access allows you to output the data in your report to files using a variety of file formats. You can export to versions of Excel (Excel 97 or Excel 2000, or Excel 5–7), a simple text file, an .RTF file (viewable in Word and other word processors), and even to an Access .MDB file.

To export data using a report, select File | Export. The Export Report *<name>* To dialog box appears, as shown in Figure 18-1.

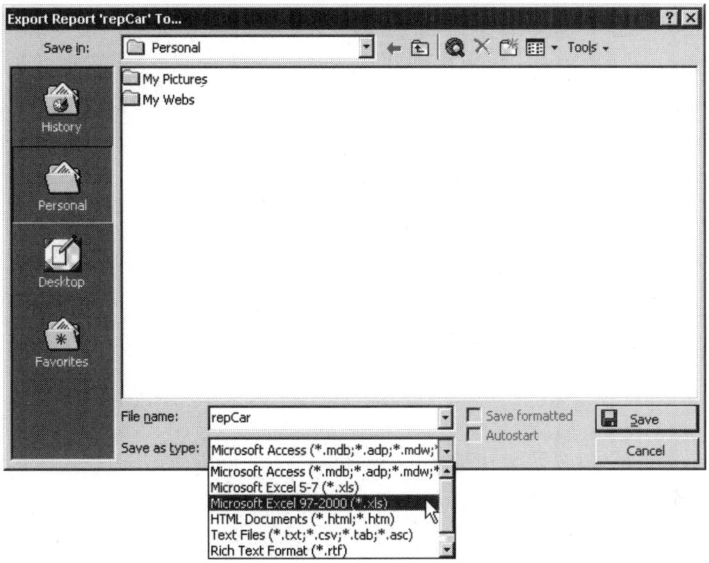

18

The Export
Report dialog
box allows you
to select which
type of file
format to
export to

Figure 18-1.

Choose the directory in which the new file will be saved, enter a name for
the new file you are creating, and select the type of file format you wish to
export to. Then choose Save. Note that if you save to an Access .MDB file,
you'll need to select an existing Access database—the report will effectively
be added to that .MDB file.

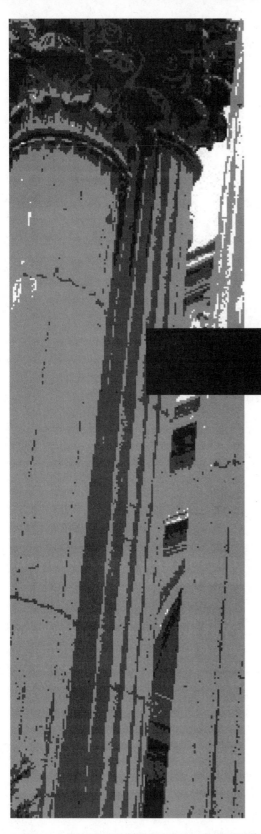

CHAPTER 19

Finishing Touches

Robert M. Pirsig wrote a book two decades ago about a man who went insane searching for a satisfactory definition of quality (*Zen and the Art of Motorcycle Maintenance*). While it's a fantastic story, I've always felt bad for the man in the book, because right around the same time, I came across a definition of quality that has stood the test of time for me. That definition is "fitness for use."

In other words, you can't tell whether an item has quality in and of itself—it has to be placed in the context of its use. A two-penny nail may have excellent quality—if you're going to use it to attach a sign to Fido's doghouse. The very same nail may be completely unacceptable if you're building a $10,000 couch.

The quality of an Access application, similarly, can't be measured just by looking at it. You have to consider what it's used for and who is going to use it. And if your application will be used in any environment but the most casual, or by users other than immediate family and close friends, you'll want to add some "spit and polish" to the collection of tables, forms, queries, and reports.

Suppose you were to walk into the home additions of two of your friends. It looks like one of them finished the room him- or herself, while the other one hired a contractor to do it. However, upon further questioning, you find out that both did the work themselves. What's the difference?

The answer is the finishing touches. One has cords hanging loose from the ceiling lights; the other doesn't. One has rough edges around the ceiling tiles; the other has each tile tightly in place. One has nails sticking out of the plaster; the other has dabs of wood glue covering each nail hole.

You can certainly play pool or watch the fights just as well in each place, but you wouldn't want to host a fancy dinner party in the room with all the rough edges. Same thing with applications—you wouldn't want to give a "90 percent finished" Access application to a customer or another department in your company.

What Makes Up a Polished Application?

A variety of components can help make your application more professional. These include

◆   **Custom help**   This is an HTML Help file that is included with your Access application. HTML Help is the third generation of help format. It features a two-pane window: the topic list and outline are in the left pane, and the topic contents are in the right pane.

◆ **Answer Wizard** This takes the form of Answer Wizard index files for the Office 2000 help system. You can include these (intended for rather static content) in an HTML Help file, and the Office Assistant can use these to answer "natural-language query" requests, in which the user can pose a question in their own words.

◆ **Application optimization** User perception of the quality of an application is in part formed by the "snappiness" of the application. Faster applications are perceived to be better. There are a number of tips and tricks you can use to speed up a completely functional Access application.

◆ **Error handling** Do you really want to let your users see those awful error messages that you've become so acquainted with? Of course not. A good error handler will not only shield your users from those errors, but also will allow them to gracefully decide between alternatives when an unexpected problem arises.

◆ **Security** More than one person, with varying requirements or abilities, may use the application. Including security features allows you to control which users can do what and will give your customer peace of mind.

◆ **Professional setup** You can give your users a Zip disk containing a bunch of files, but it's not the friendliest way to give them access to your application. All professional applications now include a setup routine that guides users through the installation of the application, prompting them to make their choices for various options. Your application should, too. The developer version of Office includes a Package and Deployment Wizard to help you do so.

◆ **Database maintenance** Things don't go wrong very often, but when they do, they tend to go really, really wrong. Providing the ability to compact and repair the databases that your application relies upon gives your users extra insurance—you hope they never need it, but it's nice to know it's there.

19

I've already covered error handling (Chapter 15), security (Chapter 10), and database maintenance (Chapter 10). In this chapter, I'll discuss the Microsoft Office Developer, HTML Help, the Answer Wizard, and application optimization. In the next chapter, I'll cover the Package and Deployment Wizard—how to prepare your Access application for deployment, sending it out to be installed by your users.

Microsoft Office 2000 Developer

To use HTML Help, the Answer Wizard Builder, and the Package and Deployment Wizard, you'll need Microsoft Office 2000 Developer (MOD). It contains all the components of Office Premium, plus a collection of tools to be used by developers for creating full-featured applications for each of the Office tools—such as Word, Excel, and of course, Access.

In addition to the three previously mentioned tools, it also contains a number of other tools that you may find useful:

◆   **Code Librarian**   This tool is a container that comes preloaded with a large variety of functions, subs, and HTML scripts. It can hold your own code snippets as well. Instead of trying to remember where you last used a piece of code, you can use the Code Librarian as a central repository for your reusable code. Very handy.

◆   **VBA Code Commenter**   This tool automates the creation of standard comment blocks for new procedures. The Code Commenter uses a template as the source for comment blocks. You can use the default template or create your own.

◆   **The VBA Error Handler**   This tool automates the inclusion of standard error handling into your procedures. One of the major pitfalls of Visual Basic is the lack of a global error handler—while not catastrophic, it's a huge pain to have to paste the same error handling code into every procedure in your app. The Error Handler will take care of some of the boredom involved in doing so.

◆   **VBA Multi-Code Import/Export**   This tool allows you to transfer multiple procedures with a single action. Exported modules are standard text files and use a CLS extension (class modules) or BAS extension (regular modules).

◆   **VBA String Editor**   This tool puts punctuation, including quotation marks, carriage return constants, and operators, into strings that don't contain them. Instead of wearing out your SHIFT key and trying to get every quote and ampersand correct, you can just type pseudo-English sentences, run the String Editor, and have the string formatted appropriately. It's not perfect (it can't handle nested quotes, for example), but even if it gets you 75 percent of the way there, it will save you a great deal of time.

◆ **WinAPI Viewer**   Making function calls to Windows can be confusing
and difficult because of complex syntax requirements. The WinAPI
Viewer allows you to automate part of the process. Much like Code
Completion in Visual Basic, you can use the Viewer to select an
object—together with the correct syntax—and paste it into your code
instead of trying to do so by hand.

◆ **Visual Source Safe**   This tool manages the source code in an
application that is used by multiple developers. Each developer working
on a project can "check out" a module from VSS, work on it, and then
submit it back to VSS, confident that no one else has made changes to the
same module. Formerly a separate application, VSS now comes with MOD,
and should be used by all developers. You can even use VSS as a single
developer, and store multiple versions of a project for later reference.

◆ **Agent Character Editor**   You know the little paper-clip character
that comes along for the ride with Office, offering help when it suspects
you're in a jam? This character is called an Office Assistant, and with the
Agent Character Editor, you can customize it, with different characters,
animations, and actions.

◆ **Data Access Components**   Microsoft's strategy for accessing data has
continually changed over the past few years—it's pretty much
impossible to keep track of each mechanism (and acronym) that's been
introduced. Office 2000 brings together several of these mechanisms
into a structure called *Universal Data Access*. The underlying foundation
is called *OLE DB* and provides a common interface to a variety of data
formats, including both relational and nonrelational data structures.
This interface is implemented through a series of components called
Data Access Components. If you're going to build Access applications that
do more than connect to MDB databases, you'll need to use these Data
Access Components to do so.

◆ **COM add-ins**   In Chapter 22, I'll discuss extending Access' user interface
by using controls other than those that come with Access. These controls
provide additional functionality that is not found natively in Access and
are called *ActiveX controls*. They are built by third-party vendors and
supplied to the developer marketplace as freeware, shareware, or for
purchase. You can also create ActiveX controls with Visual Basic, and then
use them in your Access applications (as well as other programming
environments that support ActiveX controls). In addition, you can build
COM add-ins that can be attached to your VBA code.

19

◆ **ActiveX controls**   As mentioned, you can use ActiveX controls with your Access applications to provide additional functionality. MOD comes with a whole raft of ActiveX controls—some of which work with Access and some that don't. I'll discuss these in more detail in Chapter 22.

There are even more pieces to MOD than just those included in this list, but this short briefing should give you an idea of what's available. I'll cover a few more in greater depth in the rest of this chapter and the next.

Installing MOD

MOD is a separate product from Access 2000 and consists of four CDs—one for the Office Development Environment (ODE) tools and three for the Microsoft Developer Network (MSDN).

Put the ODE CD in first, and you'll get an option to install Developer Tools or Developer Applications. Choose Developer Tools first. You can install all of them, or pick which ones you want from the following list:

◆ MSFT Data Access Components (Data Environment Designer, Data Controls, Data Binding Manager) connect your projects to external data sources in any VBA host application.

◆ Developer Add-Ins and ActiveX Controls, which are add-ins for creating setup programs, VSS integration, and other code management tasks. This also includes ActiveX controls for your use.

◆ MSFT Replication Manager consists of tools you can use to manage replicated applications through your organization (requires Access).

◆ MSFT VBA Add-In Designer (a template for creating add-ins for MSFT Office 2000 and other applications with support for COM add-ins).

Once the ODE tools are installed, you'll be prompted to install MSDN—which is the complete online documentation for MOD. It can take nearly a gigabyte if you install everything, but if you choose not to, be sure to open up the choices and select the MOD Documentation check box.

Once MSDN is installed, you'll be prompted to install developer applications, as shown in Figure 19-1. These applications are

◆ Visual SourceSafe 6.0

◆ HTML Help Workshop 1.2

◆ Answer Wizard Builder 2.0

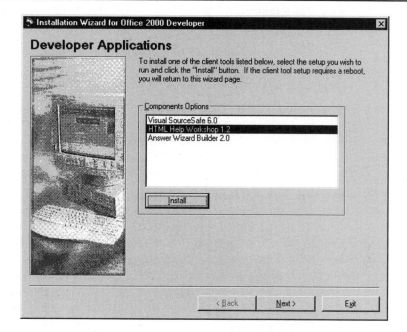

The third step of installing MOD will give you the choice of selecting one or more developer applications

Figure 19-1.

19

Click any one of these, and then choose the Install button. After installation is complete, you'll be returned to this screen so you can install another developer application.

Application Optimization

Unfortunately, there isn't a single button or menu command named "Make Application Go Faster" that you can execute. Nor is there a single hotspot where you should concentrate all your efforts. There are various areas in Access that can benefit from tuning in one form or another. These areas include (but are not limited to)

◆ Hardware and environment

◆ Design of databases and queries

◆ Design of forms and reports

I'll address each separately.

Hardware and Environment

Every application runs faster with newer rather than older hardware. Unfortunately, you can't just run out and buy a new computer each time you build an application. What should you have to run Access 2000, and what can you do to make best use of what you've got?

You should ignore the minimum suggested requirements for Office 2000 and, instead, regard the optimal suggested requirements as the minimum. In the past, Microsoft has stated minimum requirements as those needed to run the application—without considering the extra load that data or additional applications will place on the machine.

In general, you shouldn't worry about your processor speed as much as you should concentrate on getting enough RAM and a big hard disk with plenty of room to spare. You may also want to consider getting rid of utilities running in the background that you don't often use. Empty your Recycle Bin regularly. If you're of a mind to add software willy-nilly to your machine, you may want to consider keeping that practice to a minimum and uninstalling software that you no longer use.

Design of Databases and Queries

Many operations in Access depend on queries, including opening a form, running a report, or creating or executing a query in code. As a result, making your queries more efficient is an excellent use of your resources and will markedly improve results throughout your application. There are four parts to the execution of a query: definition, compilation, optimization, and final execution.

The SQL statement that defines the query is simply a text string—and it doesn't even have to have all its arguments in a strict order. Access' database engine, Jet, needs to break down that text string into its components, and this process is known as *parsing*. Once the string is parsed, Jet needs to figure out what to do with each piece, and how best to handle it. This is known as *optimization* and is the source of considerable effort on the part of SQL engine designers everywhere. In fact, the way that a database engine parses and optimizes SQL commands is widely considered one of the more valuable trade secrets that a software company owns, since a finely tuned optimizer makes their SQL product more valuable to their customers.

While a discussion of how Jet optimizes queries is beyond the scope of this book, some general considerations are worth mentioning:

◆ Queries that return smaller numbers of rows and columns are more efficient than larger queries. This is both because there is less data traveling across the network, and because there's a greater chance that the result can be stored completely in memory, instead of overflowing to disk. These two factors mean a query will execute faster if it's smaller. Consider limiting the number of columns in a query—clearly, a result set of four columns will take up less network traffic and memory than one that includes every column in every table, independent of how many rows are returned. The same goes for the number of rows—try to limit the number of rows requested to as few as possible.

◆ Similarly, try not to use complex expressions inside a query—the expression has to be evaluated for every row processed in the query. Better to return a result set and then manipulate it further. For example, instead of combining a series of fields in a query, pull each field separately, and then combine them after the query is finished. It's much more efficient to concatenate fields in a 40-record result set than in a 100,000-record query.

19

◆ Consider how to best normalize (and denormalize) your database structure. Generally, joins involving smaller tables execute faster than those containing more records. Instead of having one table that contains both Accounts Payable and Accounts Receivable (which can be done because the structures are identical), break it into two tables. You'll virtually never need to gather records from both AP and AR in one query, so there's no advantage to strictly normalizing here, and there's a significant advantage in keeping both tables half the size of the combined table.

◆ Jet compiles and optimizes a query the first time it's run, using information about the data in the database at the time it's run. Subsequent uses of the query simply run that previously compiled and optimized query. Clearly, that's tremendously efficient—no additional processing other than the actual execution of the query is necessary. If the dataset that the query operates on hasn't changed much, this is the way to go.

However, what if the database has changed drastically—for example, suppose one of the tables in the query has grown considerably larger, or that the indexes on the columns have been changed. The optimization strategy that Jet used the first time may no longer be valid on a table that now contains 25,000 rows, instead of the 158 rows it contained at first.

If you know that the data structures or contents have changed significantly, you can force Access to recompile (and thus, reoptimize) a query by opening it in Design view and saving it again.

◆ Since version 2.0, Access has incorporated a technology called Rushmore that uses a patented index-handling algorithm to speed up data access. To take advantage of Rushmore, you'll want to set indexes on every column that is used to join tables (the key columns, not every column in the table). Be careful that you don't add indexes to every column in a table; there is overhead associated with maintaining these indexes.

◆ You'll also want to add indexes on columns that you will want to sort on, since sorting also takes advantage of Rushmore. Again, consider which fields you *need* to sort on—do you really need an index on Phone Number?

◆ Use action queries instead of creating a record set and then writing code to process each record in it.

Design of Forms and Reports

Some of the same concepts discussed in the previous section apply to forms and reports:

◆ Obviously, if a form or report is based on a large query, it's going to take longer to load than if the result set is small. In client/server applications, the preferred technique is to ask the users for the record (or small recordset) they desire through a query mechanism, and then to present just that bit of data in the form. This same technique works on a LAN when the underlying data structure is large.

◆ Combo boxes and list boxes are wonderful additions to an application employing a graphical user interface. However, they can be dangerous—loading too many items into these controls can slow down the form response time considerably. Imagine if you had a half dozen combo boxes, each populated with 5,000 to 10,000 items. Not only would that slow down the form, but also your user would likely find it difficult to use a combo box or list box with that many items.

◆ Index on the first column that displays in a combo or list box, and don't include columns in the query that supports the control unless they're going to be used.

◆ It can be tempting to load a lot of controls onto multiple tabs of a page frame. I saw one application that consisted of a page frame with six tabs, and each tab held another page frame with anywhere from four to 12 tabs. There were over 1,200 controls on this one form. As you can imagine, even if the dataset populating this form were miniscule, it would have taken forever to load the form itself.

◆ Don't overlap controls on a form.

◆ Use the lightest-weight control possible. Image controls require fewer resources than unbound object frames. Consider hiding images and allowing the user to display them by pushing a button or selecting a check box, instead of forcing the image to be displayed for each record. OLE objects require significantly larger resources—don't use them unless the object *must* be able to be edited.

19

◆ Don't include fields (or records) in a query that won't be used in the form or report.

◆ Use expressions in your form or report instead of including them in the query. It's faster to concatenate fields from a single record in a query on a form or report than to have the query do all the work during the processing of the query. You'll want to weigh this technique with the additional load of maintenance—it's often easier to make a change in one query than in six forms or reports that rely on that query. Your mileage will vary according to your driving style and the current conditions.

◆ If you use a page frame, only bind data to the objects on the visible page when showing the form. Bind data to the objects on each subsequent page when that page is brought forward.

◆ Consider the trade-off between using memory to hide a form and experiencing the performance hit when the form is closed and opened again. There is no right or wrong answer—your particular situation will dictate what works best.

HTML Help Workshop

Watching the evolution of help systems over the years has been a particular fascination of mine. Most people have shied away from online help because, much like the printed matter that accompanies a product, it's traditionally been less than useful.

The technical tools we had available to build help systems suffered in a similar manner. Before Windows, help systems were a hodgepodge of constructs, each manufacturer doing their own thing. Windows helped standardize the way that online help was presented to the user, but help wasn't very helpful. Too often users were presented with an endless list of topics in no discernable order, and each topic page was a poorly formatted narrative that had too little relevant information.

This may even be your own impression. However, I'd like you to reconsider. The new standard for online help, Microsoft's HTML Help, is such an improvement over previous versions that I've come to depend on it both when accessing it for my own use and to present to my customers as part of the custom systems I develop for them. Indeed, I've won over more than a few skeptics; a demonstration of HTML Help has easily convinced them that the extra expense of online help will be well worth it.

What Does HTML Help Look Like?

Pressing F1 in any Office 2000 (or Visual Studio 6) application will display an example of HTML Help, as shown in Figure 19-2.

The HTML Help window displays a topic list in an Explorer-style view in the left panel and a selected topic in the right pane

Figure 19-2.

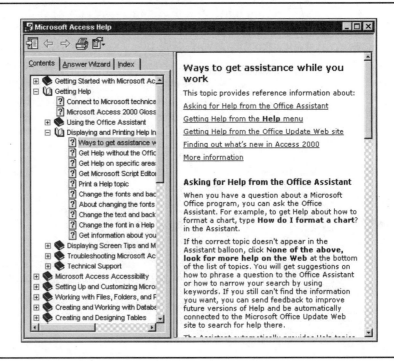

You can drill down through a hierarchy of topics in the left pane, clicking the plus sign to expand the list of available topics and the minus sign to close the list again for easier overall viewing. Selecting a specific topic heading in the left pane will display the topic contents in the right pane. So far, this looks pretty powerful, since the expanding and contracting Explorer view of topics is much more flexible and usable than the single list of topics provided in previous help systems.

For example, I routinely include four primary topics in my online help systems. First is an Introduction—sort of an "Executive Overview" of the system. Next is a User Guide—a list of major functions that can be performed by users, together with subtopics that are relevant to one of the major functions. One major topic might be "Printing," and underneath that, I'll list generic topics like "Setting up a printer" and "Using the Report Wizard," as well as instructions on producing specific reports. Another major topic in the User Guide would be "Security," and under that would be topics about setting up users, permission levels, passwords, and so on.

19

The third primary topic is a Reference Guide that describes the details of every form, operation, and report in the application that I'm delivering, as well as technical information about the tables and other data structures. The last primary topic is "Where to go for more help."

I view this first level of topics as equivalent to a single book that would be included in the system's documentation. The Introduction would be akin to "Read This First," for example. Each topic under a primary topic would be a chapter in the manual, and subsequent levels would correspond to major and minor headings in the chapter.

HTML Help has more to it than simply a great way to organize and present information. You probably already noticed that the left pane is actually a three-tab page frame, and the Explorer list of topics simply populates the first tab. The second tab allows you to look up information in the help system without knowing exactly where the information would be located. This Answer Wizard will be covered in "Answer Wizard Builder" later this chapter. The third tab allows you to enter one or more keywords and look up the associated topic in an index format.

The right pane, furthermore, is more than just a great big blob of dumb text. The topic pages act much like web pages on the Internet, complete with hyperlinks that will direct you to another help topic, as well as definitions for terms in the text. Icons, bitmaps, and other graphics, including screen shots, are often included in the text also.

Finally, the toolbar at the top of the HTML Help window allows you to perform some useful tasks. The first icon switches between Hide and Show and allows you to hide or show the left pane of the window. This is useful when you have limited room on your monitor and you want to be able to read the whole topic.

The next two buttons, Back and Forward, allow you to jump back and forth between topics you've visited, much like you can on the Web. The Print button allows you to print a topic from the help system. The Print dialog box that opens appears to be a standard dialog box, but there are several options in the bottom of the dialog box that you'll want to note. The check box on the left allows you to print all linked documents, while the check box on the right allows you to print a table of links (but not the contents of the pages themselves). Finally, the Options button gives you another access point to each of these functions.

Are you convinced that HTML Help is the greatest thing to hit help systems since context-sensitive help was devised? You can build your own help modules and include them with your Access applications, and the Microsoft Office Developer includes the HTML Help Workshop, a free tool that allows you to do so.

Building an HTML Help File

It is beyond the scope of this book to describe in complete detail how to use the HTML Help Workshop, but it makes sense to describe how it works and where to start.

HTML Help comes packaged as a single file with a CHM extension and can actually be run stand-alone—without needing to be attached to an application. If you do a search on your computer for files that end in .CHM, you'll undoubtedly find a number of them. As long as you have the proper HTML Help engine components installed, double-clicking on one of those files will display it just as when you pressed F1 in Access (or another application).

Which specific components (files, OCXs, and so on) are needed is a matter of debate, as the target has been moving ever since HTML Help was introduced in 1997. However, this is somewhat of a moot point. If you've got Internet Explorer 4.01 SP1 or later installed (you can check by selecting Help | About Internet Explorer in IE if you're not sure), you automatically have the proper components. Furthermore, when you distribute your .CHM file with your application, the Packaging and Deployment Wizard will automatically include the proper components with your application.

The HTML Help Workshop program takes one or more component files, such as HTML documents, graphics, and other files, and combines them into a .CHM file that you can distribute. You build a project file that acts as an organizer, point to your component files, add files like a table of contents and an index, and compile all of them into the .CHM file.

Fire up the HTML Help Workshop by selecting Start | Program | HTML Help Workshop | HTML Help Workshop, and you'll get an empty HTML Help Workshop window. Select File | New and choose a name for your project and a location for the HTML Help Workshop project to be located, as shown in Figure 19-3. I think this dialog box is somewhat confusing, since you're going to enter a name for the project and select a location at the same time. The name you enter will be used as the project filename; if you don't use the Browse button to choose a location, your project will be saved in the default HTML Help Workshop directory, wherever that may end up being on your machine. I prefer to keep a "help" directory under the root of my application directory, and locate my HTML Help project and all related files in that directory.

19

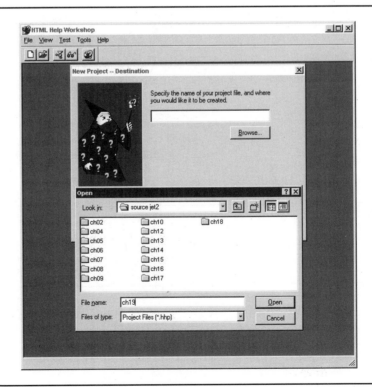

In the same dialog box, choose a name for your HTML Help project as well as a location

Figure 19-3.

You'll then be faced with an empty HTML Help project window. Your next step will be to add files to your project. Depending on where your help files come from, the tasks you perform for this will vary.

I usually write two Word .DOC files for an application. The first is the User Guide and the second is the reference section—also known as a "Functional Specification." Once they are finished (and the application is done), I'll split these files into multiple HTML documents (with .HTML extensions) using Word's Save As HTML or Save As Web Page features. Then I'll add these HTML files to the HTML Help project.

This is done by selecting the Add/Remove topic files button (second one from the top on the left side of the HTML Help Workshop window) to open the Topic Files dialog box, and then choosing the Add button to display the Open dialog box, as shown in Figure 19-4.

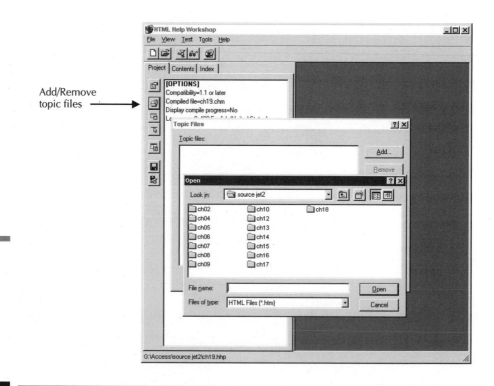

Add HTML
files to an
HTML Help
project
through the
Topic Files
dialog box

Figure 19-4.

Alternatively, you can create HTML files from within HTML Help Workshop by selecting File | New | HTML File.

Once you've added your files to the help project, you'll be able to create a table of contents, which generates the Explorer-style view in the left pane of an HTML Help window. You'll do this by selecting the Contents tab, giving a name to the table of contents file, and then adding headings and topics to the table of contents. Use the Insert A heading button to create headings for the table of contents. You can choose whether to attach a topic page to the header, as shown in Figure 19-5, as well as use the four arrow buttons to move the topic heading up or down in the list and shallower or deeper in the hierarchy.

19

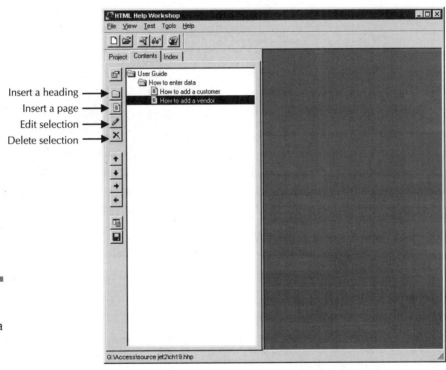

Use the Insert a heading button to add a topic to the help project

Figure 19-5.

Then use the Insert A page button to add topic pages to the help project. You can enter a phrase that will be used as the table of contents entry for the topic and also select an actual file that contains the contents of the help topic. The result is shown in Figure 19-6. As with headings, you can move a page around the table of contents outline as you desire by using the four arrow buttons.

Your third step, after creating the project file and adding a table of contents, will be to generate an index. Select the third tab, Index, and you'll see that the buttons on the left side of the window change yet again. Select the Insert a keyword button (with the key icon) to add a keyword. Once you've defined the keyword, you'll be able to select one or more files (and their help topics) to which the keyword is associated. When the user selects a keyword, the associated help topic will be displayed for viewing. If there is more than one associated help topic, a list of possible choices will be displayed from which the user can choose. See Figure 19-7.

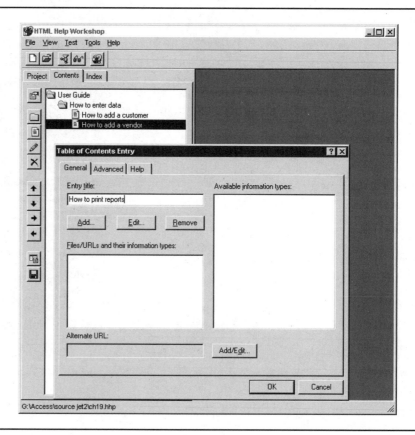

The Table of Contents tab contains entries for each heading and topic page

Figure 19-6.

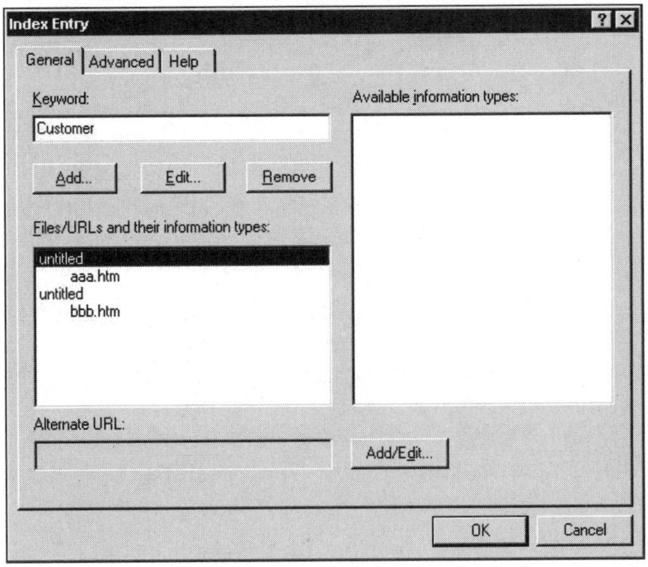

You can associate one or more help topics with a keyword

Figure 19-7.

You can use the Edit Selection button and the Delete Selection button (see Figure 19-5) to make changes to the keywords you've already added to your project.

The last step in creating an HTML Help file is to compile it. Selecting the Project tab will display the Save All Files And Compile button at the bottom of the column of buttons. This will save changes to all the files you've created or modified while working in the workshop, and then generate a .CHM file. You can have the Workshop display the progress of the compilation by checking the Notes and Progress check boxes in the Compiler tab of the Options dialog box that can be displayed by clicking the first button on the left side of the window.

Including HTML Help in Your Access Application

You'll need to do two things to include an HTML Help .CHM file with your Access application. First, you'll need to make sure it's packaged along with the rest of your application, and that will be covered in the next chapter on the Packaging and Deployment Wizard. The other thing you'll need to do is actually provide the ability for your Access application to call your help file when users press F1 or select a command from the Help menu.

The actual process is fairly complex and is explained in detail in the HTML Help Workshop online help. In brief, these are the steps you'll follow:

First, your Access application will make a call to help by setting the HelpFile and HelpContextID properties. If you want to simply have the same main help screen display whenever the user selects help, you can ignore the HelpContextID property, and just open the help file as specified by the HelpFile property. The page that is displayed by default is the selection you made in the Default Window drop-down combo box in the General tab of HTML Help Workshop's Project options.

More often, however, you'll want a specific help topic to display, depending on which form or report is open. This tailoring of a help topic to a specific module in the application is called *context-sensitive help*. You'll specify both the HelpFile and HelpContextID properties in each form or report that you want to call a specific help topic in your help file. The HelpContextID specifies the context ID of a topic in the help file specified by the HelpFile property.

You need to create a special header file that lists the symbolic IDs and numeric IDs for all the elements in a program for which you have context-sensitive help. Elements that don't have their own context-sensitive help topics will then automatically call the default help topic window.

Look under the topic "Context-Sensitive Help, guidelines for creating," in the HTML Help Workshop online help for specific and up-to-date details about matching topics. See the HTML Help API Reference for information about creating the header file and the code for context-sensitive help.

This discussion just briefly touches on using the HTML Help Workshop to build online help files for your Access application. I'd suggest you open the workshop and go through its help system to learn more about its myriad capabilities.

Answer Wizard Builder

Adding Answer Wizard index files to your Access application allows you to include extended help content either by using a custom HTML Help file or from a web site. These index files, with an extension of AW, allow natural-language queries to be answered with one or more plausible help-topic candidates. For example, instead of users having to look up "collation" under the Print help topic, they can simply type in a question like

"How do I print all the pages in a report at one time?" The Answer Wizard index file will locate topics that are likely to answer the question, and allow the user to select one or more topics to look for the answer. As help files get larger and more complex, this is an excellent way to help users find the information they need.

You use the Answer Wizard Builder to create these Answer Wizard index files. To start, select Start | Programs | Answer Wizard Builder, and select whether you want the Answer Wizard Builder to use a .CHM file (Compiled HTML Help file) or a web site.

You'll then be guided to create a series of questions and to map topics to those questions with the Answer Wizard Builder dialog box, as shown in Figure 19-8. It's not a trivial task to create and map this information, but it's well worth it for your users. I've found it useful to log questions that come into the help desk about a specific question, and then include those questions (and, of course, topics that include the answers) in the Answer Wizard index files for the next version of the system.

19

Building help files is not the most enjoyable part of building an application, but if you've kept careful notes and documentation during the development of the system, you'll have plenty of material to include, and the HTML Help Workshop and the Answer Wizard Builder will make short work of converting that information into useful online help files that your users will love.

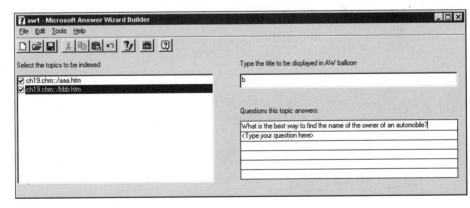

Use the Answer Wizard Builder dialog box to create questions and map them to help topics

Figure 19-8.

CHAPTER 20

Deploying Your Application

Bill Cosby, in one of his early comedy routines, once hypothesized that the act of graduating from a karate school was not, in and of itself, the goal of attending such a class. Rather, he said, "the goal is to get attacked." Similarly, while the design and development of an Access application is great fun, intellectually stimulating, and alternately frustrating and challenging, it is not a goal by itself. Your goal is to package your application in a deliverable form, to deliver and install it at your users' site, to train users so that they know how it works, and to have them successfully use it. This process is known as *deployment*.

It is beyond the scope of this book to discuss training and ongoing support and maintenance issues, but it is very much the purpose of this book—and specifically, this chapter—to show you how to package your application and how to install it at your users' location.

Packaging Approaches

Before you visit your customer's site to install the application, you need something to take with you. Different development environments provide a variety of mechanisms to build components that you deliver to your customers.

Low-level programming languages allow you to create a stand-alone executable (those files with EXE extensions) that is simply copied to the hard drive of the users' computers. The users run the program by executing the file, either by double-clicking on its name in Windows Explorer or by typing its name at a command-line prompt. Many users also set up a shortcut on the Windows desktop so that they can run the executable by clicking on the shortcut. Some installation programs will create this desktop shortcut automatically.

More sophisticated development environments provide tools, such as a setup wizard, to build an installation package, much like the one you used to install Office 2000. The developer uses this setup tool to specify a number of default parameters for users and creates a series of files that are delivered to users. The setup files may come on physical media, such as a series of floppy disks, high-density writable media like a Zip or SyQuest drive, or even one or more CD-ROMs. A SETUP program is either automatically run when the CD is placed in the CD-ROM drive, or the user can execute the SETUP program manually. Alternatively, the setup files may simply be provided electronically, through a web site or via e-mail—but the installation, via a SETUP program, is the same.

The installation routine that runs when SETUP is executed takes care of all the "behind the scenes" details, using the default parameters unless the users override them. The routine installs the entire program and any related data on the users' computers. This is actually quite a challenging and complex job, since, as applications are tightly integrated with Windows, it's not just a matter of copying files into a folder or two and then letting users have at it.

An Access application can include much more than just one or more .MDB files that contain the data, forms, queries, reports, modules, and so on. There may be ActiveX controls that need to be installed in the proper folder and registered with Windows. There may be online help, which consists of both the actual Help file and the help engine components, and those may need to be installed and registered with Windows as well. And, of course, there may be other files that aren't part of the .MDB file, such as external data files, bitmaps and other image files, and so on.

20

Distributing an Access Application—The Easy Way

You can distribute an Access application quite easily if the demands of your users aren't high. You can simply copy all the files that make up the application to a folder on the users' machine, and they can run the application just as you do.

However, there are several downsides to this approach. First, it assumes at least some familiarity with the process of copying files, setting up shortcuts, and other trivia that many users may not be equipped to deal with.

Second, the multitude of files in your application may make the delivery of the entire set awkward or difficult.

Third, it requires the user to own a copy of Access. If you're simply distributing your application to a friend, this may not be a significant hurdle. But if you intend to distribute the app to a larger, or geographically diverse, audience, this approach ranges from impractical to impossible.

Distributing an Access Application—The Professional Way

Access 2000, like many other development tools, has a setup wizard, the Packaging and Deployment Wizard, that enables you to create a professional installation package that you can distribute to individuals who don't own

Access themselves. This wizard is one component of the Office Developer Edition (ODE) that I introduced in Chapter 19.

How the Package and Deployment Wizard Works—The Steps You'll Take

You'll go through four steps in delivering your application after finishing the system itself. The first is to consider whether the users might have a copy of Access, and to make any necessary changes to the application itself. Second, you'll collect all the files that need to be distributed to your users. Third, you'll run the Packaging and Deployment Wizard to create the files to distribute. Finally, you'll deploy those files.

You don't have to be delivering a professional-quality application to thousands of users to take advantage of this mechanism. You may simply want to deliver this to a friend, and need to give him or her the whole shebang because he or she doesn't own Access.

Putting Your App Together

I've covered many of the pieces involved in assembling a complete application. There is much more than simply creating a few tables in a database, putting together some forms and reports, and perhaps marking one form to be a switchboard. A complete application includes an error handler, security, data maintenance, online help, and so on. However, it doesn't even stop with these components. You'll also want to determine whether your user has a copy of Access, and if not, include a copy of the Access 2000 Run Time, as well as configure your software to run in this environment.

The Access 2000 Run Time

The Access 2000 Run Time is a separate set of components that you include with your application so that it can run without Access itself being installed. Users will be able to use your application just as if they were running Access, but they will not have the ability to modify pieces that you don't want them to change.

In addition to not being able to modify the application, your users will have no access to some standard Microsoft Access features. For example, an application running in Run Time mode doesn't display the main Database window.

For this reason, you'll want to test your application by running it in Run Time mode. You can do this in two ways. Either you can install the entire application on a machine without Access, or you can simulate the Run Time environment on your development machine. The second approach is preferable because it's less work (you don't have to have a second machine available), and you can take advantage of debugging tools on your development machine that you wouldn't have available on a machine without the Access development environment.

Simulating the Microsoft Access Run Time Environment

To simulate the Run Time environment, you can pass the /runtime parameter to the command that starts Access, and Access will behave as if only the Run Time were installed. To do so, you can execute your application with the Run command, but a better way is to create a shortcut on your desktop that includes the /runtime parameter. This way you can run Access in development or Run Time mode simply by selecting the appropriate desktop shortcut.

First, create a shortcut to Microsoft Access. (If you haven't done this before, right-click the desktop, select New | Shortcut, and point to MSACCESS.EXE using the Browse button. MSACCESS.EXE should be found by selecting Program Files | Microsoft Office | Office.)

Next, right-click the shortcut, select the Properties menu command, and select the Shortcut tab in the Properties dialog box. In the Target text box, type the path to the database that you want to open, and add the string "/runtime" after the database path. For example, the following string in the Target text box runs Access normally. Note that the quotes around the string are needed because of the spaces in the string.

```
"C:\Program Files\Microsoft Office\Office\MSACCESS.EXE"
```

The following string will open the MG CLUB database in the APPS folder on drive F:

```
"C:\Program Files\Microsoft Office\Office\MSACCESS.EXE"
  "F:\APPS\MG CLUB.MDB" /runtime
```

20

Differences Between Full Microsoft Access and the Run Time Environment

Applications written in languages like C++ or Visual Basic can be compiled to a single executable (.EXE) file that contains all the components needed for execution. Access applications, on the other hand, can't be compiled into an .EXE file at all. Instead, the Run Time environment acts as a foundation upon which the MDB can be used. It is transparent to users how these two components interact. In fact, depending on how you designed the user interface of your system, users may not even be aware that they are running an Access application.

However, the Run Time environment is not identical to the native Access environment that you develop in. Here are some of the primary differences:

◆   Users do not have access to the Database or Macro windows.

◆   All Design views are hidden.

◆   Access to the Visual Basic for Applications environment or Visual Basic IDE is restricted.

◆   You can add your own custom toolbars to your application, but native Access toolbars aren't available.

◆   A variety of specific menu commands (both on the main Access menu and various shortcut menus) are unavailable, along with certain keystroke combinations.

◆   Errors will shut down the application (instead of returning to the interactive environment that you use to develop). As a result, you need to provide a custom error handler.

The Run Time Licensing Key and Microsoft Access

One action that occurs when your application is installed on your users' machine with the Access Run Time is the creation of a license key in the Windows registry. This key is checked by both Access and the Run Time module. If Access is being started in Run Time mode, the key is checked to determine whether to allow Run Time mode. If your application is run with a Run Time module, it determines whether to allow the application to run. If the key doesn't exist and Access isn't installed on the machine, the application won't run.

Securing Your Application if Users Have Full Microsoft Access

What if you distribute your application with the Access Run Time, but one of the users receiving the application already has Access installed on his or her machine? You may be wondering if that user can get at your application by opening it with Access instead of running it with the Run Time. Unfortunately, the answer is yes, unless you've taken measures to secure your database.

First, if you provide mechanisms to start the application, be sure to include the /runtime parameter with each mechanism. This way, the Run Time module is invoked even if your users have Access installed, preventing inadvertent use of Access instead of the Run Time module. However, this still won't prevent users from opening your database from Access.

Secure each object in your database as described in Chapter 10. This will ensure that your users can't modify them even if they open your database in Access. Be sure to create your own workgroup and give it your own workgroup ID—don't use the default provided with Access.

Eliminate all menus, toolbars, and other actions that you haven't created yourself. This will prevent your users from inadvertently gaining access to a component in Design view, for example. It will also prevent users from viewing code in a module, which may be important if you have proprietary algorithms or other confidential information in your VBA code.

Set the AllowBypassKey property to False to disable the SHIFT key. This will prevent clever users from bypassing startup components, such as a startup form, an AutoExec macro, or other startup properties. Note that this will also prohibit you from doing the same thing. I get around this by keeping a file with an unusual name in the root folder of my development drive, and checking to see if that file exists. If the file exists, the AllowBypassKey property is set to True; otherwise the property is set to False. A name like "ACCESSDEV.WHIL" in the root reminds me that this is the "development mode flag file" so I don't accidentally erase it myself, but it's also unusual enough that users won't have it on their machine. The contents of the file don't matter—just the existence of the file itself.

Along the same lines, you'll want to watch out for properties that could give your users access to components to which you don't want them to have access. For example, setting AllowBreakIntoCode to False will prohibit users

20

from opening a module window in the event an error isn't trapped. Setting AllowToolbarChanges to False will prohibit users from modifying the toolbar and/or menu. And setting AllowSpecialKeys to False will prohibit users from opening the Database window, Immediate window, or pausing execution of a VBA module or a macro.

Be sure to save your database as an .MDE file, as discussed in Chapter 10. In addition to securing any Visual Basic code, doing so will reduce the size of the database file, thus improving performance.

Installing the Access Run Time

The Access Run Time module is not automatically installed on your development machine, even when you install the Microsoft Office Developer components. You'll need to copy the contents of the Access RUNTIME folder on the MOD CD to the following location on your machine:

```
\Program Files\Microsoft Office\ODETools\V9\Runtime
```

If you don't, you'll be prompted for the MOD CD each time you want to include it in an Access application you are setting up with the Package and Deployment Wizard.

Packaging Your Solutions

Once you've finished programming your application, you'll need to assemble all the files that will be used in the application. These files will be put into a "package"—one or more .CAB files that contain compressed versions of your database and all other files that are needed by the application (such as the Access Run Time module). These other files may include components like third-party .DLLs, ActiveX controls, help files, graphics and images, and so on. Remember that your application may even rely on secondary .MDBs that contain common source code or other components. You may also need to create dependency files for your application. (See the following section, "The Packaging Process.")

The Packaging component of the Package and Deployment Wizard creates these packages.

The Packaging Process

To create a package, you'll first need to identify and gather all the files that you will have to distribute to your users. I've found it useful to create three separate folders for an application. The first folder contains all the files required during the development of the actual application—.MDBs as well as any ancillary files. This is also where any documentation I use during the project goes.

The second folder contains a copy of the files that need to be distributed. An ActiveX control may need to be in your WINDOWS\SYSTEM folder for you to use it during development, but you may need to include a second copy of it with the actual files to be distributed.

The third folder contains a copy of the package that is created by the Packaging and Deployment Wizard. These files are the actual files that are delivered to your users, either electronically or on physical media such as disks or CDs.

20

IN DEPTH

Structuring a Development Directory Tree

My development directory consists of a series of folders, one for each customer of mine. Under each customer folder, I have separate folders for each project or application I am working on for that customer. I also have a separate folder for general information that is specific to that customer as well.

Under each project folder, then, I have five more folders. The first is for the documentation for the project. The second is for the help files for the application—this may include image files that get incorporated as screen shots, multiple .HTM files that get included as topics in HTML Help, and, of course, the final .CHM file. The third through fifth have already been described: the actual development folder, a folder for files to build from, and a folder with the files to distribute.

For example, for Galactica Corp, I'm working on two projects, the CUSTREP project and the TAKEOVER project.

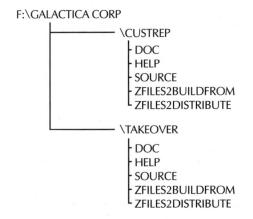

```
F:\GALACTICA CORP
        ├─────────────── \CUSTREP
        │                 ┝ DOC
        │                 ┝ HELP
        │                 ┝ SOURCE
        │                 ┝ ZFILES2BUILDFROM
        │                 └ ZFILES2DISTRIBUTE
        │
        └─────────────── \TAKEOVER
                          ┝ DOC
                          ┝ HELP
                          ┝ SOURCE
                          ┝ ZFILES2BUILDFROM
                          └ ZFILES2DISTRIBUTE
```

Using common names for each of these helps me keep organized and able to move between projects quickly and easily, without having to remember specifics such as folder names. I've included a "Z" at the beginning of the last two folders so they stay in alphabetical order in Explorer. It's also the order in which they will be used. DOC comes first because all correspondence—including that which starts the project—goes in there. Next come HELP and SOURCE—created and maintained simultaneously. Finally, near the time I'm ready to ship, the last two folders come into play.

Once you've got all the files assembled in the ZFILES2BUILD folder, create dependency files if necessary. You can do this with the Packaging and Deployment Wizard as well.

Next, determine where you want to install each file that you're going to distribute. You will probably want to create your own folder for your application—either in PROGRAM FILES or in your own folder—but place files like .DLLs and .OCXs in the Windows System folder. If you are including files from a third-party vendor, you may need to manually search for all the files from that vendor.

Then run the Packaging and Deployment Wizard. It will lead you through the selection of all files and create a SETUP.EXE file, together with one or more .CAB files.

Dependency Files

Just as man does not live by bread alone, many applications require more than Access to function. A *dependency file* contains information about the files that are required for an application or a component of an application to function. For example, an ActiveX control that you use in an application may actually consist of more than just an .OCX file. It may need a second .DLL or a .LIC (license) file. The .OCX file probably needs to be registered in the Windows Registry as well. The .DEP file that comes with the ActiveX control will include information about all the files that are required for that .OCX file to operate and how they are to be registered.

20

The Packaging and Deployment Wizard will look through the .DEP files of each component you include in your application and notify you if any pieces are missing.

The Packaging and Deployment Wizard

The Packaging and Deployment Wizard comes with Microsoft Office Developer. You have to install it as an add-in, but it's not an Access Add-In, as you might suspect. Thus, it won't show up as a result of choosing Tools | Add-Ins from the Access main menu.

Instead, you'll need to open the Visual Basic Editor by selecting Tools | Macro | Visual Basic Editor. From the VBE menu, select Tools | Add-Ins | Package and Deployment Wizard.

NOTE: If this is the first time you've run the Package and Deployment Wizard, you'll need to add it to the Add-Ins menu. Select the Add-Ins Manager, select the Package And Deployment Wizard, and check the Loaded/Unloaded option. You may want to keep Load On Startup checked so that the add-in appears in the Add-Ins list from then on.

Select "Package" on the first screen of the wizard, and then follow the steps until the wizard notifies you that you have finished. Be sure to select the ZFILES2DISTRIBUTE folder or whatever location you've chosen for the files you'll send to your users.

Once you've created your distribution files, you'll want to place those files on the appropriate distribution media, such as physical media like floppies or CDs, a shared folder on a network, or a web site. Run the wizard again, and select the Deploy option to do so.

If you have to go through multiple rounds of beta testing for your application, you may find that you enter the same information over and over again. You can save, view, and manipulate these scripts through the Manage Scripts option in the wizard.

PART IV

Advanced Capabilities

CHAPTER 21

Client/Server
Techniques

Up to now, you've used Access as a file-based system. This means that the data is stored in a file on your computer, or on another computer that you have access to on a local area network. There are pros and cons to this approach. Ease of development and low cost are two primary reasons that file-based systems are commonly used. As you've seen in the first 20 chapters of this book, it's relatively easy to create an Access application, and other than owning a copy of Access 2000 and Microsoft Office Developer, there's no additional software cost involved.

However, there are some downsides to this approach as well. One downside has to do with scalability. An Access application may work well for a single user and, depending on how heavy the usage is, for several users at a time. But once the load moves past 10, 20, or 50 users, performance will suffer to such a point that the application becomes unusable. Additionally, there are some applications in which the data is of such importance that it must be stored in a secure container, and limited access to it is rigorously enforced.

A client/server application structure satisfies these two requirements—a higher number of users and data security. Naturally, there are trade-offs. A client/server application is more complex to develop and generally is more expensive, as a client/server database often includes a license fee for each user in addition to the initial cost of the software. Given the costs involved in the development of the application, however, these costs can be insignificant.

A client-server application structure involves a "front end" that runs on the user's computer and a "back end" that runs on a separate computer. The front end includes the user interface, such as forms and reports, and modules, written in VBA, that contain business rules that enforce the logic of the application. The back end holds the data, as well as rules and triggers that control access, enforce security, and ensure that the data that gets into the database is correct.

Since you're used to seeing an Access application in which the data is stored in the same MDB as the forms, reports, and modules, you may be wondering how Access works with a client/server architecture. The answer is that you use a different type of Access file—a project, with an .ADP extension—both to hold your user interface and to connect to the back end. You can use a variety of back ends, but often Microsoft SQL Server is the tool used as the back end.

Creating an Access Project

A project provides access to a back end such as SQL Server through a new database architecture from Microsoft called OLE DB. OLE DB provides a single common interface to a variety of back-end databases and data sources, including relational data (like the tables you use in Access), text files, ISAM files, e-mail files, spreadsheets, and binary files like images, sounds, and movies.

The project can only contain forms, reports, modules, and other user-interface or business objects. It can't contain any data-oriented objects, such as tables or stored procedures. These are stored in SQL Server.

To create a project, you need to have access either to a SQL Server database (version 6.5 or later) or to a Microsoft Data Engine (MSDE) database. SQL Server 6.5 requires NT 4.0 and SQL Server Service Pack 5 or later. SQL Server 7.0 requires NT 4.0 and NT Service Pack 4 or later, or Win95. MSDE requires NT 4.0 or Win95. The Microsoft Data Engine will be discussed later, in the "The Microsoft Data Engine (MSDE)" section.

21

Select File | New, click the General tab of the New dialog box, and select Project (Existing Database). In the File New Database dialog box, select a location in the Save In text box and enter a name in the File Name text box. Be sure that "Microsoft Access Projects" is displayed in the Save As Type combo box. Finally, click the Create button.

The Data Link Properties dialog box will display, as shown in Figure 21-1.

Make sure the Connection tab is displayed, and then enter or select a server name, choose which type of security (and any appropriate parameters), and choose the database that you want to connect to on the server. The default server name for MSDE is the name of your computer and the default logon ID is "sa" (for "system administrator"). The name of your computer is displayed in the Identification tab of the Network applet found in the Control Panel.

OLE DB allows you to use this same Data Link Properties dialog box to connect to all sorts of data sources. For example, if you had the appropriate OLE DB drivers, you would see additional servers and databases in the various controls in the dialog box. OLE DB provides one consistent interface to widely disparate types of data. Of course, each OLE DB provider (data source) defines specific connection parameters. SQL Server requires a server name and location, and a user name. Entering security information is optional. Other providers may require different information.

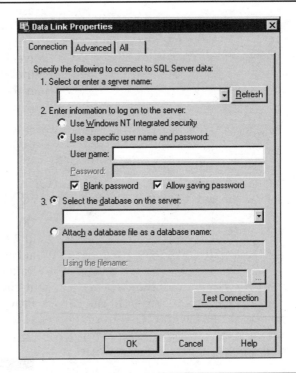

Use the Data Link Properties dialog box to create a connection to a back end

Figure 21-1.

Using an Access Project

There is very little difference in the techniques you use while creating a file-based Access application and one that uses SQL Server as a back end. The process of creating forms, reports, and modules is pretty much the same in both cases. Some of the user interfaces—dialog boxes, drop downs, and so on—are slightly different, but the concepts—databases, tables, fields, and so on—are the same. There are also a number of wizards that can help guide you through your first few forms and reports. The interface for handling the data, of course, is completely different. You use the SQL Server design tools to create, edit, delete, and view tables, stored procedures, and other database components in SQL Server.

Changing Connections

You might want to change connections for your project for a variety of reasons. For example, you might be using the same application to connect to multiple databases, each for a separate business. Instead of keeping the records for all the companies in one database, you would create multiple (but identical) databases, and then switch from "Company A" to "Company B" as needed. Another example would be during development. You might use one database for testing, and another to hold live data. A third reason would be to switch servers. In the event that the machine holding your database failed, you might want to be able to simply switch the connection to a second, backup, server.

To switch connections for an Access project, select File | Connection. This will bring up the Data Link Properties, and you can select a different server or database as desired.

Installing Additional OLE DB Providers

When you install Office 2000 or Access 2000, the OLE DB providers for Microsoft Jet 4.0 and for SQL Server 6.5 and 7.0, as well as for ODBC Drivers and Oracle, are automatically installed. You can see which providers are installed on your machine, by selecting a Data Link file (with a UDL extension) in Windows Explorer, then right-clicking and selecting the Properties menu command to display the Provider tab of the Data Link Properties dialog box, as shown in Figure 21-2.

21

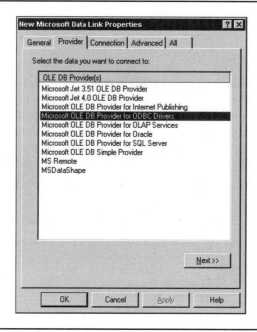

The Provider tab of the Data Link Properties dialog box displays all the OLE DB providers that are installed on your machine

Figure 21-2.

If you don't have an existing Data Link file, you can right-click in Explorer and select New | Microsoft Data Link, and a new, empty Data Link file will be created in the current directory. Then open its Properties dialog box as just described.

The Microsoft Data Engine (MSDE)

You may not always have access to SQL Server during the development of your Access client/server application. For example, you may not be connected to the network that has the SQL Server box. Or the SQL Server box itself may be down. Or it may be inconvenient to have a copy of SQL Server running on your local development machine for you to work with during these times. You can use MSDE to provide local data storage that is compatible with SQL Server 7.0, or to provide a remote data storage mechanism. It is designed to run on computer systems that don't have the horsepower to run SQL Server, such as individual development machines and small servers. The data engine for MSDE is the same as the one that SQL Server is based on, so applications will run on both transparently.

There are a few limitations, of course—a file can be no larger than 2Gb with MSDE, and it doesn't support some high-end features like symmetrical multiprocessing on non-NT operating systems. Also, MSDE isn't automatically installed when you install Office 2000 or Access 2000.

You'll need to run SETUPSQL.EXE, found in the SQL\X86\SETUP folder of your Office or Access CD-ROM. You may also want to take advantage of the additional help files found in the WINDOWS\HELP folder: REPLQIZ.CHM (Replication Wizard Help) and ENTMGR.CHM (SQL Server Enterprise Manager Help). Once you've got it installed, you'll need to start the SQL Server Service Manager if you're running Win9x. Click the Start/Continue menu command after double-clicking on the MSSQLServer icon on your taskbar. You can select the Auto-Start Service When OS Starts check box in the SQL Server Service Manager dialog box if you want MSDE to start each time you boot your Win9x machine. MSDE will automatically start on NT.

Rethinking the User Interface for Client/Server Applications

The fundamental difference between file-based applications and client/server systems is that you don't have access to the entire database at once. When you open a table in an Access MDB, you are physically connected to the file and can move back and forth through that file nearly instantaneously. The only bottleneck is the speed of the hardware that moves data from a file to the memory in your computer—either the local data bus or the network cable.

Contrast this with the architecture of a client/server system. When you open a client/server application, you'll make a request for some data from the back end. That request has to navigate over the network (just like a file-based system), but then the back end has to process the request, find the data, perform any processes (validating security, for example), and send the requested data back over the network wire. This is radically different—because the "transaction" is then terminated. The client/server system has sent the application a chunk of data—the application isn't directly connected to the data file. Thus, if the user wants the "next record" in the database, the application makes a second request, which the back end must then process as it did the first request. With a file-based system, the application is already in the data file, and its record pointer merely changes position.

This means two things. First, you want to limit the amount of data that you are bringing back from the server, over the network, and then to the application. If your database contains 10 million records, you don't want to request all 10 million records. Instead, you want to bring down as few records as reasonable, and then structure your application to work with that small recordset.

21

What does this mean to your user interface? When you create a form, you will likely not allow users to navigate back and forth through the entire table. Instead, you should create a generic query form that asks users for a parameter that describes the range of records to be brought back from the server. For instance, you might have them enter a Vehicle Identification Number (VIN), or ask for a Make, Model, and Year, instead of just displaying the entire Automobiles table.

Alternatively, you could define a filter in the ServerFilter property of a form or report, or modify the FilterLookup property of a Filter By Form and Server Filter By Form window.

You can also limit the number of records brought back if the request, even after being narrowed down, would generate too large a load. Use the MaxRecords property to set this limit.

Second, consider how the user is going to make requests. You might be rather flip about working with multiple files and updating controls on various forms "on the fly" in a file-based system, since the data is all right there for you to work with. On the other hand, you wouldn't want to refresh a control on your form from a table in a client/server database. Each time you did so, your application would have to send the request down the network wire and have the back end process the request and send back the entire dataset. If you did this several times for a single form, the performance of the application would suffer greatly, and users wouldn't stand for it.

There is a third issue, not directly part of the architecture, but closely related. You'll want to think about where to put the logic that controls how your application works. In a file-based application, you would ordinarily use programming code, such as macros and VBA code modules, to contain the rules that enforce what data can be entered into your application and how the various components talk to each other.

In a client/server application, you can create programs called *stored procedures* that are part of the back end and are executed whenever certain events occur or are executed by certain events. These stored procedures are compiled and executed on the server, and thus are generally quite fast. For example, you could create a stored procedure that limits the type of data that is entered into a table, or that references and updates other columns in the table based on data in an update. A special type of stored procedure, called a *trigger*, automatically executes when you update, insert, or delete data.

However, sometimes stored procedures don't execute. They may also fail, based on some predetermined condition. For example, a user may choose to purchase an automobile in the list of cars for sale. However, if he or she brings down the list of available cars, and then goofs around for a while before making his or her decision, the automobile might have been sold to someone else in the meantime or the price might have changed. Or perhaps the user simply enters an incorrect value that is rejected by a stored procedure on the server. It is often difficult to get useful error messages from the back end and then translate them appropriately so that users can understand what happened—and what they should do about it.

An alternative that I recommend is to keep as few business rules in stored procedures as possible, leaving that chore to the front end, where interaction with the user is much friendlier. Use the front end you are building in Access (and VBA) to hold your business logic and rules that validate and control how your data is handled. Use the stored procedures on your back end as an "enforcer of last resort"—to absolutely, positively, make sure that no bad data gets into your database. For example, you might write code that generates unique customer ID numbers, and then use a stored procedure to enforce uniqueness. This way you can be sure that every Customer ID number will be unique, even if your code failed.

Optimizing Access Applications with a SQL Server Database Back End

Many of the same rules you use to design file-based Access applications apply to client/server applications that use SQL Server. For example, normalizing appropriately, indexing on fields that are used in a filter, using sort and join operations, enforcing referential integrity, and using the correct data type for each field all contribute to the general cause of improved database performance. Regularly compacting your database will save on disk space and optimize your indexes for improved performance as well.

Try to minimize the amount of data that has to be brought back from the server until the user really needs it. For example, if the user asks for the invoices for a customer in April, you just bring back the April invoices—you don't include the May invoices "just in case." Similarly, you will want to minimize the amount of data displayed on a form until the user needs it. Don't populate controls with lists of data until the user has made the appropriate choice that makes that population appropriate. For example, if the user is entering a name and address, don't populate the "State" table until you determine which country the user is in. Why fill the control with all the Mexican states only to find out the user is entering a Canadian address?

21

Consider a "More" button that displays details for a record. For example, for an automobile, you may only need the Make, Model, Year, and VIN. Don't bring up the serial numbers, manufacturing attributes, owner information, previous owner history, and service records until requested.

Create a special form or set the DataEntry property of a form to Yes if you are creating a heads-down data-entry form. Access won't display existing records in the recordset and will open the form faster. When it comes time to update the back end, use SQL UPDATE to commit changes to multiple records at a single time, instead of processing the records one at a time. The back-end engine will be more efficient at this type of operation.

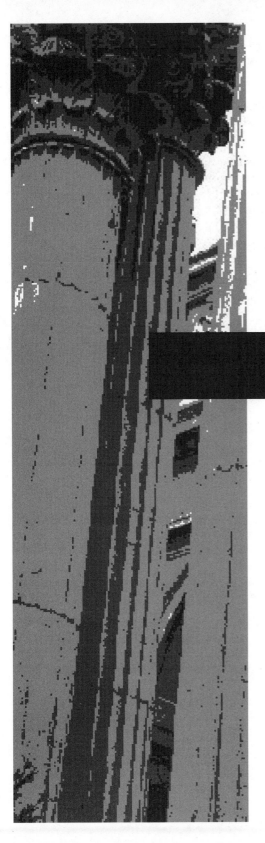

CHAPTER 22

Using ActiveX Controls in Your Access Application

One of the cornerstone philosophies driving the development of Microsoft products through the late 1990s and into the 2000s is the concept of software components.

In the early days of computers, programmers wrote huge, monolithic programs for a specific company. As the industry developed, programs were written for applications that many companies could use; sometimes those programs were then customized for each company. Eventually these programs became powerful enough and flexible enough that the same program could be used by many companies without modifications. However, they all shared the common trait of being a single, huge program.

As a result, if a second program needed the identical functionality of the initial program, one of two things would happen:

◆ Programmers of the new program wrote a brand-new routine either because they didn't know about the existing routine in the first program, or because they knew about it but felt they could do it better.

◆ Programmers copied the first routine into the second program and made any necessary changes so that it fit in the second program.

These practices were bad ideas. The first practice was bad both because it was a waste of time, and because the first routine had likely been tested and used enough that the bugs had been worked out. The new routine was subject to all the problems that new code often carried. It was also a bad idea because if a change in the business process required a change in that functionality, changes in both routines needed to be made—and the changes would have to be different, because the routines were different.

The second practice was bad because if one of the programs were modified, the second would either have to be modified as well or the initially identical functionality in each program would begin to diverge. More often than not, bugs that were found and fixed in the routine in one of the programs were not fixed in the other.

In the early 1990s, Microsoft and other companies began to implement a mechanism for providing reusable programs that is now known as *ActiveX*. The functionality of a program was broken out into components that could then be reused by other programs. "Write once, use many times" was the mantra that was preached by the ActiveX disciples. For example, suppose a word processing program needed a spell checker. Instead of tightly binding the routines for the spell checker into the word processing program, programmers would create the spell checker as a separate program. Other applications that also needed a spell checker could then use that same spell checker.

This had a number of advantages. First, programmers saved time by writing the spell checker only once. In addition, the spell checker would contain a single public interface that many applications could use in the same manner. Second, the spell checker could be made very robust and powerful, since the programmers were intentionally writing it to be used by many applications. If, instead, the programmers for each application were to write their own spell checker, the results probably would have been inferior. Third, once the spell checker was made available, programmers could add it to each of their applications. Since it was the same spell checker each time, they knew how to work with it. Finally, users would only have to learn one spell checker—not a different one for each application they used.

Another example of a common component that could be used across many applications is the File | Save dialog box that you use when opening a file in a Windows application. Before Windows, each application used a different mechanism to save a file; one program used the File | Save command from a menu, another used the F3 function key, and yet a third used the CTRL-S keystroke combination. Now virtually every Windows program uses the same File | Save dialog box, and all the benefits just listed accrue.

22

In fact, as Windows applications became more powerful and users became more sophisticated, software developers invented new controls that provided additional functionality throughout the programming environment. These ranged from types of controls that an application developer could include on a form (in addition to the standard tools that their tool provided) to full-blown mini-applications like spell checkers, e-mail programs, and faxing tools.

The underlying mechanism, however, was always the same. An ActiveX control, consisting of a file with an OCX extension (and possibly some additional files), was placed in the WINDOWS\SYSTEM or WINNT\SYSTEM32 folder (or another folder). That file was "registered" with Windows, and then all development tools on that computer would know about and could use that ActiveX control. Access developers, like those who develop applications in Visual Basic, Visual FoxPro, and Visual C++, can take advantage of ActiveX controls that are installed on a computer. In this chapter, I'll discuss how to find out which ActiveX controls are on your computer, how to put them on a form (and thus include them in an Access application), and some caveats about ActiveX controls.

What ActiveX Controls Do I Have Access To?

There are four ways that ActiveX controls may "find their way" onto your machine. I use this term purposely; unlike applications that you buy and install yourself, ActiveX controls often seem to just show up, because they are often installed behind the scenes when you install other programs.

First, Access 2000 itself ships with one, the Calendar Control, a much improved and graphical method of entering and displaying dates. A second source is the Microsoft Office Developer, which ships with a whole raft of ActiveX controls. A third way is through other programs. If you install another application—particularly a development tool—it likely will come with its own set of ActiveX controls.

The final way is to buy your own from any of a huge number of third-party vendors. If you're willing to work a bit, you can search the Web for "ActiveX controls." The last time I did so, I found 61,000 hits. You could also determine which ActiveX controls are installed on your system (I'll discuss how to do this in the next paragraph), determine who the vendors of those controls are, and then contact them for lists of other controls that they make. Or you could simply pop over to http://www.vbextras.com, which has been a top-notch third-party reseller of ActiveX controls for years.

So what ActiveX controls are already on your system? To find out, all you need to do is select the Insert | ActiveX Control menu command. The Insert ActiveX Control dialog box, as shown in Figure 22-1, will be displayed.

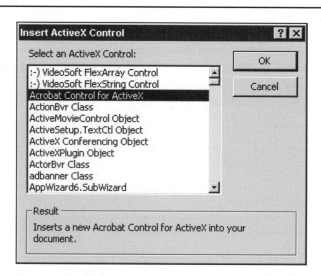

The Insert ActiveX Control dialog box displays a list of all the registered ActiveX controls on your machine and allows you to place one on a form

Figure 22-1.

Alternatively, you can open a form and then click the More Controls button in the Toolbox, as shown in Figure 22-2. It will display a pop-up menu with every ActiveX control that's registered on your machine. This method can be awkward since, as a developer, you are likely to have many ActiveX controls registered on your machine, and the pop-up menu becomes far too cumbersome to navigate with hundreds of choices on it.

22

More Controls ———

The More Controls button on the Toolbox displays a pop-up menu of all the registered ActiveX controls on your machine and allows you to place one on a form

Figure 22-2.

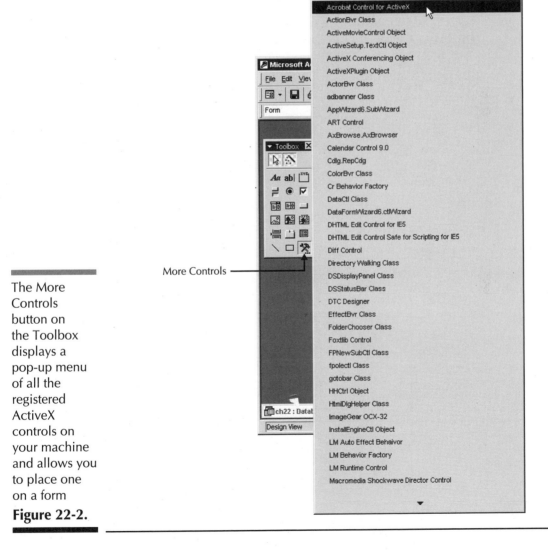

The list of ActiveX controls that you see isn't always the most useful. The text that displays is controlled by the vendor of the control and, thus, the descriptions vary. Some descriptions include the name of the vendor and the full name of the control; others simply list an abbreviated name of the control. It can be difficult to match the name of the product on the box that you bought with the name in the list of ActiveX controls. Here's a tip to help you make sense of this list.

If you select Tools | ActiveX Controls, you'll see the ActiveX Controls dialog box, as shown in Figure 22-3. At first glance it may seem similar to the Insert ActiveX Controls dialog box in Figure 22-1. However, this dialog box isn't used to add a control to a form. Instead, it allows you to do two things that the Insert dialog box doesn't. First, you'll see that the folder location and filename of the highlighted ActiveX control are displayed below the list box of controls. This can be handy for chasing down more information about the control. For example, if you right-click that .OCX in Windows Explorer, and select the Properties menu command from the shortcut menu, you'll get a dialog box with one or more tabs that describe various attributes of the control. For instance, the ART32X.OCX from AccuSoft has a General tab and a Version tab, as shown in Figure 22-4. The Version tab has all sorts of useful information that you can take advantage of if you're trying to determine who the manufacturer is, what the version of that file is, and so on.

The ActiveX Controls dialog box displays both a list of available ActiveX controls and the location and name of the highlighted ActiveX control .OCX in the list

Figure 22-3.

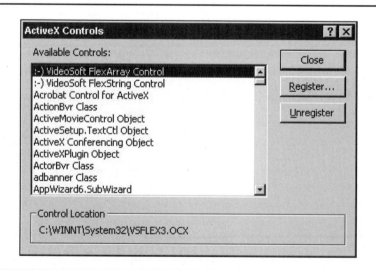

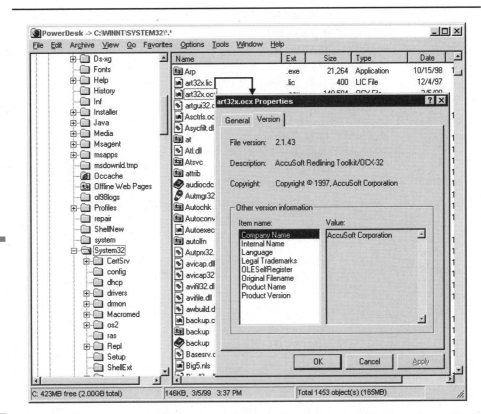

Many ActiveX
controls have
a Properties
dialog box
that provides
information
about the
vendor of
the control

Figure 22-4.

Second, this dialog box allows you to "register" the control with Windows. Windows 9*x* and Windows NT both maintain a file, called the *Registry,* that contains information about how Windows is set up and configured to run on the specific machine as well as with other software on the machine. The Registry is the replacement for the .INI files used in Windows 3.*x*.

The Registry contains information about each ActiveX control that is installed on the machine and available to be used with applications. However, simply copying an ActiveX control onto a machine doesn't register it with Windows. Normally, the installation program for an ActiveX control will automatically enter that information—register it—in the Registry. If the control you want to use isn't listed in the Insert ActiveX Control dialog box or the More Controls pop-up menu, you need to first make sure that the files that comprise the control are on your computer, and then you need to register the control.

When you click the Register button in the ActiveX Controls dialog box, you'll be presented with an Add ActiveX Control dialog box that looks much like a File | Open dialog box. You'll need to navigate through the various folders, locate the .OCX file for the control you want to register, and then choose OK. The control will then be displayed in the list, and you'll be able to use it in your Access applications.

How do you know where the control's files are? Unfortunately, the short answer is that you often don't automatically know. You can't assume that all .OCX files are going to be located in WINDOWS\SYSTEM or WINNT\SYSTEM32. For example, I've got OCX controls located in the following folders on my C drive:

```
WINNT\SYSTEM
WINNT\SYSTEM32
Program Files\Web Publish
Program Files\Microsoft Visual Studio\VB98\Wizards
Program Files\Microsoft Visual Studio\Common\Tools\VCM
Program Files\Microsoft Office\Office
Program Files\Common Files\Microsoft Shared\Repostry
Program Files\Common Files\Microsoft Shared\MSInfo
```

This is only a partial list—there are about 40 different folders I've found .OCXs hiding in.

Fortunately, you'll not often need to manually register a control unless you've specifically been given a set of files from a vendor. In those cases, the vendor will tell you where to copy the controls.

Finally, you can use the ActiveX Controls dialog box to unregister a control. Why might you want to do this? Remember, registration means that information about the control is placed in the Registry. If you need to delete the control from your machine, you wouldn't want information about it to stay in the Registry. Other programs could assume that the control still exists and try to use it, with all sorts of potentially horrible results. Thus, *before* you delete an .OCX (and its related files), be sure to unregister it with the ActiveX Controls dialog box.

Using an ActiveX Control on an Access Form

Getting started with ActiveX controls on an Access form is reasonably straightforward. It's simply a matter of creating (or opening) the form and then dropping the desired control on the form, either by selecting the control from the pop-up menu that displays from the More Controls button, or by selecting the Insert | ActiveX Control menu command.

Note that, unlike Access' native controls, not all ActiveX controls have a visual component to them. For example, the AccuSoft Redlining Toolkit (ART) control I used as an example in Figure 22-4 doesn't have a visual component. It's designed to be used in combination with another control—AccuSoft ImageGear—that displays images such as JPGs or GIFs. Once an image is displayed in the ImageGear control, the ART control displays a toolbar that provides the ability to temporarily annotate the image, much like John Madden drawing lines and circles on a TV screen during a football broadcast. The toolbar doesn't show up on the form in design mode—just a small button with a caption of "ART" to let you know that the control is part of the form now.

Once the control is on the form, you'll work with it much like the native Access controls. You'll set properties and call methods, and perhaps even write code that is executed when certain events intrinsic to the control are executed.

How do you know what properties and methods a control has? First of all, you can look at the Properties window. Right-clicking on the control will display a Properties window with the standard Format, Data, Event, Other, and All tabs. You can easily guess that the Value property holds the current value of the control—such as a URL for a hyperlink control or the highlighted date in a calendar control. Similarly, the Caption property would be a text field that allows you to display a helpful description on the control for the user at run time. It's pretty easy to figure out what the On Got Focus and On Lost Focus events will do.

22

Most controls also come with documentation—either online in the form of a text (.TXT), Windows Help (.HLP), or HTML Help (.CHM) file—or printed and included in the package. Often you can simply guess at what properties do by experimenting. Determine what the default value is, change it, and see what happens when you run the form. For events, try including a message box like "The *XXX* event is now firing" to determine when an event is executed.

Let's use the Microsoft Calendar Control (the formal name is "Calendar Control 9.0") as an example, since it's available with Access. First, you'll have to install it from the Access 2000 CD, because it's not automatically installed. Once it's installed, create a blank form and drop the control on the form. When you open the Properties window, as shown in Figure 22-5, you'll see some old favorites and some new properties that are obviously specific to the Calendar Control.

If you click the Other tab, you'll see all sorts of goodies. For starters, the Value property is the currently selected date in the calendar, and the Day, Month, and Year properties are the individual components of that value. The MonthLength property can be set to Short or Long, and it controls

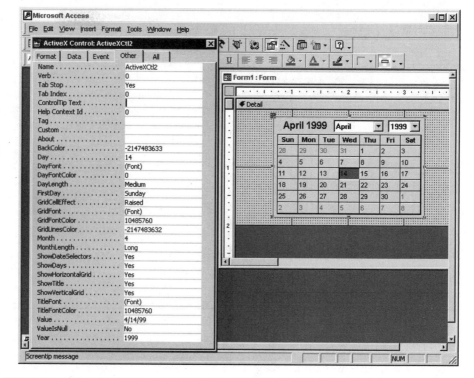

The Properties window of the Calendar Control contains both properties common to many controls and properties specific only to the Calendar Control

Figure 22-5.

whether you see "Apr" or "April" above the calendar. The ShowDateSelectors property controls whether the Month and Year combo boxes are displayed. The ShowDays property controls whether the days of the week are displayed above the grid of days. The ShowTitle property controls whether the name of the month and the year of the displayed month are shown above the grid as well. You can even control which day of the week is used to start out the week—if you pick "Tuesday" for the FirstDay property, the columns will run from Tuesday through Monday.

A typical use for the Calendar Control is to allow the user to graphically enter a date instead of typing the date into a text box. For example, you could provide a text box that allows the entry of a date and a button next to it to allow the user to display the calendar control, as shown in Figure 22-6.

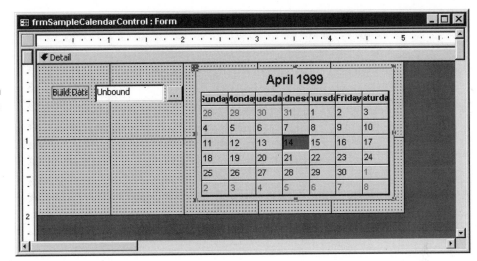

Clicking on the Ellipses button next to the Build Date text box will display the calendar control during run time

Figure 22-6.

22

When the user selects the Command button, the following code will execute, displaying the Calendar Control:

```
Private Sub Command5_Click()
ActiveXCtl2.Visible = True
End Sub
```

Once the user has selected a date, the control will lose focus, causing the selected date in the control to be placed back in the text box:

```
Private Sub ActiveXCtl2_LostFocus()
Text3.Value = ActiveXCtl2.Value
End Sub
```

Finally, once the text box receives focus again (there are only three controls in this example), the Calendar Control is hidden again:

```
Private Sub Text3_GotFocus()
ActiveXCtl2.Visible = False
End Sub
```

This example doesn't bind the text box to a field in a database table, nor does it do any validation. For example, you might want to set the initial value of the calendar control to today's date if the text box were left empty, and to set it to the date of the text box if there were already a date in it. Your choices depend on the functionality that your users want to have.

Caveats in Using ActiveX Controls

First of all, as the saying goes, "Interchangeable parts aren't." It's terribly complex to create a control that can truly work with every kind of Windows development tool. The tools are so varied that it's impossible for an ActiveX control to provide a single common interface that can be used efficiently and reliably by all of them. As a result, many ActiveX controls do not work with one or more tools. The creators of ActiveX controls are generally small programming shops, so they don't have the resources to test their controls with all the development tools out there. Thus, they'll likely be able to tell you whether their control will work with some of the more popular applications, but not all of them. Since Access is in wide use, it's highly likely that a well-built ActiveX control will work—but there's no guarantee short of trying it yourself. Even if the manufacturer states that their control is compatible with Access, it's possible for you to come up with a specific implementation that they haven't tested—or even thought of—and thus you could run into problems.

The second issue to be aware of is that documentation is often incomplete or just plain wrong. The interface that an ActiveX control presents to the programmer, while much simpler than providing raw source code to the control, can still be complex, with many properties and methods to be used in various situations. It's not uncommon for a useful control like a grid or an outliner to have dozens of properties and as many methods for the various pieces.

Given that many controls are written by small shops on limited budgets, it's likely that the shop shipped the control as soon as they felt it was stable and reliable enough for the market—regardless of the state of the documentation. So what probably happened was that one of the programmers whipped up a few pages of reference for the control, threw together a couple of simple sample uses, and spell-checked and proofread it during the final build of the control.

Don't be surprised when you feel the documentation you get with a specific control is sparse. Go to the manufacturer's web site, and see if additional information has been posted or if they host an e-mail or chat session where users can share tips and tricks.

The third problem, and definitely the biggest, involves the fact that these are all supposed to be common controls, and thus they are all installed in the same folder. However, just as with your own Access application, these controls are regularly updated, and different versions aren't always compatible with each other. This has serious ramifications if two different applications use the same control, but are shipped with different versions. Let's look at what happens.

Suppose Application 1 ships with version 3.2 of an outliner control. That control is installed in the WINDOWS\SYSTEM or WINNT\SYSTEM32 folder, and the application runs fine. A few weeks later, the user installs Application 2, which happens to also use that outliner control. However, Application 2 uses an older version of the outliner control, version 3.011. If the install program isn't careful, and it often isn't, version 3.011 overwrites version 3.2. The bug fixes and additional features that were included in the control between version 3.011 and version 3.2 are no longer available, and Application 1 starts misbehaving.

What to do? You could install Application 1 again. It would install version 3.2, but that risks breaking Application 2, because it's possible that the functionality of part of version 3.2 is now different from 3.011. Clearly, this can become a bad situation, with the users stuck in the middle. Each manufacturer claims their application has to have their version to work properly, and the manufacturer of Application 2 won't have a new version of their program that uses 3.2 for some time. By then, of course, the manufacturer of Application 1 will probably have upgraded to version 3.48 of the control.

22

A previous implementation of ActiveX controls was formerly known as .DLLs (dynamic link libraries), and they too suffered from this problem. Although the name (ActiveX) and extension (OCX) have changed, this problem is still referred to as "DLL Hell." There isn't a good solution yet, although some applications have begun to ship with their own controls placed in their own private folder—which, of course, negates the whole idea of sharing components.

The last issue involves deployment. Different installers work differently, and they also vary according to the specific .OCX. Some installers automatically detect which ActiveX controls are used in an application and grab the appropriate copies directly from the WINDOWS\SYSTEM or WINNT\ SYSTEM32 folder. Other installers aren't as clever—you'll need to copy the ActiveX control to the folder that contains all the files that you want to include as part of the package you are using to create a deployment package. It gets trickier, however, because some ActiveX controls aren't made up of a single .OCX file. They may require additional files that provide supporting functionality. Unfortunately, those files may not be named in a fashion that makes it obvious that they're part of the OCX package. The documentation may include information about which files needed to be distributed, but it may not. And there may or may not be information about dependency files as well. Remember what I just said about lack of documentation?

I'm not trying to scare you off from using ActiveX controls—far from it. ActiveX controls can provide functionality that you can't get any other way. That functionality enriches the users' experience such that their productivity and the usefulness of the application soar. But nothing comes free. Be aware that the promise of component software is not fully realized, and that you can expect to run into some challenges when integrating ActiveX controls with your application.

CHAPTER 23

Connecting with Other Applications: Using Automation in Your Access Application

You may very well want to connect your Access application to another application in some fashion. For example, you may want to share data. Or you may want to modify the functionality of that application if it's really robust, knowing that to duplicate that function in Access would be very time-consuming—and probably less functional. So, just as with ActiveX controls, you need to expand your horizons and take advantage of the talents locally instead of outsourcing to a new, expensive, and possibly out-of-date tool.

You might want to connect to another app and get that data. If that app's data is in a particular encrypted format, you may need to use that app to open the data file, instead of going after the data file yourself.

You might want to take control of that application and, essentially, use it as an extension of your application. If Word can produce nicely formatted letters with fonts, images, and so on, why not do that part of the job while you direct Word from Access?

Or, you may have another application or program that needs to get at Access data now and then.

While each of these needs is different, they all fall under the same general topic of "Automation." In this chapter, I'll discuss two specific techniques: DDE (Dynamic Data Exchange) and Office Automation.

Dynamic Data Exchange (DDE)

As its name suggests, DDE is a standard mechanism through which two Windows applications can share data. The purpose of DDE is to allow an Access application to request data from another application, such as Excel, or to allow another application, such as Word, to request data from Access.

In both cases, the application requesting the data is known as the *client* and the application providing the data ("serving" it to the client, as it were) is known as the *server*.

DDE has fallen out of fashion over the past few years as automation techniques have become more powerful and reliable. In some cases, however, DDE may still be all you need.

Much as you connect an Access application to a back-end database in a client/server system, you create a "conversation" between a DDE client and its server. This conversation is established on a data file in the format that the server application supports, or on the "System" topic that supplies information about the actual application running on the server.

Much like a conversation between humans, the existence of the conversation allows information to be transferred between the two parties. However, once the conversation has begun on a specific topic, only data relating to that topic can be transferred. This is one of the reasons that DDE isn't as widely used—imagine if you had to hang up and call again if you wanted to start talking about a different subject.

You open a DDE channel with the DDEInitiate function, specifying the database filename as the topic of conversation. Then you use the DDEExecute function to move data from the server to the client. The DDEExecute function recognizes several Access commands that can be used by the client to request specific actions from the server. For example, you can use the name of a macro in the current database or a Visual Basic action using a valid DoCmd method.

The client application will use DDERequest to request text data from the server, DDEPoke to send data to the server, DDETerminate to close the current channel, and DDETerminateAll to close all open channels.

The following example uses Microsoft Word as a client to request data from an Access database. This code is a Word VBA module and requires Access to be running to execute successfully.

23

```
Sub GetAccessData()
' open the conversation using the System topic
iChannelSys = DDEInitiate("MSAccess", "System")
' assumes your Access database is in the root of drive E
DDEExecute iChannelSys, "[OpenDatabase E:\MG.MDB]"
' run the New Cars query in the MG database
iChannelCars = DDEInitiate("MSAccess", "MG.MDB; QUERY New Cars")
' plop the results into a string variable
sDataResults = DDERequest(iChannelCars, "All")
' close both channels and the database in order to conserve resources
DDETerminate iChannelCars
DDEExecute iChannelSys, "[CloseDatabase]"
DDETerminate iChannelSys
End Sub
```

You can find more information about DDE, the specific topics used by DDE, and related information by searching in online help under "DDE."

Automation

Automation has gone through a number of phases over the years. Its progenitor was DDE, but it was reborn on its own around 1995 as OLE (object linking and embedding). OLE was a technology in which an object in one application, such as a bitmap or a chart, could be used by another application. Developers had two choices when deciding how the object and application would be connected.

The first choice was to embed a copy of the object in the second application. Selecting the object automatically loaded the application from which that object had originally been created. For example, embedding a Paintbrush bitmap in a Word document and then selecting the bitmap would load Paintbrush for on-the-spot editing and modification. The only downside was that the editing was done on that specific copy of the object—not on the original source file.

The second choice was to simply include a link to the file of the object. This method kept the size of the master file considerably smaller, but the risk was that the links could be broken if some but not all of the files in the collection were moved.

Around the same time, the precursor to ActiveX controls, OLE controls, came into vogue, and were eventually renamed "ActiveX controls." OLE was succeeded by OLE Automation, which was then renamed, simply, "Automation." Both moves were made primarily to reduce the perceived dependency on Microsoft, as OLE was viewed as a proprietary technology, while the "ActiveX" moniker has been made more open so that it would be embraced by the entire industry.

Automation, then, is the process of having one application control another, again in a client/server relationship, with the client requesting data from the server. Suppose you had Access making requests to Excel for calculated values, taking advantage of Excel's superior financial acumen. In this scenario, Access is the client and Excel is the server, even though Excel may never have been seen in the process. In another case, Visual Basic might be the client, making calls to Access to send output to the Access Report Writer. The use of Excel in the first situation and Access in the second situation are invisible to the users—they only know they're running, respectively, Access and a Visual Basic application.

Not all applications can act as both a client and a server, and the documentation for an application will have to answer that question for you.

In the case of Access, fortunately, you can use Access as a client or as a server, depending on your needs.

The fundamental concept behind automation is the use of objects. In your client application, you'll create an object reference to the server application, and then make calls to that object using methods of that application. These methods are often either macros or application commands.

For example, in a VBA module in an Access client application, the command

```
Set oExcelApplication = createobject("Excel.application")
```

will create a reference to the Excel application object. This is simply a reference to the object—it hasn't activated Excel. You can't see Excel in the taskbar, for example, if you task switch in Windows. If you wanted to create a reference to a new Excel worksheet, you'd use the command

```
set oSheet = createobject("Excel.sheet")
```

Again, Excel is not visible. You can now control the application (Excel itself) or the specific worksheet with additional commands that are germane to Excel. For example, the following code would create a mini-spreadsheet of data in the upper-left corner of the worksheet:

23

```
osheet.cells(1,2).value = "January"
osheet.cells(1,3).value = "February"
osheet.cells(1,4).value = "March"
osheet.cells(2,1).value = "Sales"
osheet.cells(2,2).value = 100
osheet.cells(2,3).value = 200
osheet.cells(2,4).value = 300
```

Suppose, however, that you wanted to activate an existing automation object (and create a reference to the object). You would use a command like so:

```
oSheet = getobject("d:\worksheets\mysheet.xls")
```

You can also call methods of objects in a similar fashion. For example, to add a workbook to an Excel object, you would use a command like so:

```
oExcelApplication.Workbooks.Add
```

Be careful about how various servers are treated in automation. In particular, you'll want to determine if an application is already running, so that you don't accidentally start up a second instance. However, this is not as clear-cut an operation as it seems, because different applications behave differently when automation clients call them. For example, if you use three CreateObject commands with Word 97 as a server, you'll get three references to a single instance of Word. On the other hand, if you use three CreateObject commands with Excel 2000 as a server, you'll get three separate instances of Excel. (And you thought only *users* did that sort of thing!)

As a result, you'll want to know how to determine if an application is running, but that technique will vary according to which server you're working with. If you're strictly using Excel, you could use GetObject to attempt to retrieve an existing reference to the server application. If you're successful, then obviously Excel is already running. On the other hand, this won't work with Word because of some internal issues with how Word functions. One work-around I've used has been to attempt to establish a DDE channel with Word from Access. If that action is successful, then Word is running. You'd want to immediately terminate the link, of course, since you're just using DDE to test the waters.

Each application works differently, and you'll simply have to consult the documentation or test it yourself.

This issue is important because automation is resource intensive—indeed, even on fast machines, it can drag. When you consider the individual requirements of Access, Word, Excel, PowerPoint, and so on, you'll find that a 64MB machine with a 200MHz or better processor is not an unreasonable expectation. If you intend to run several complex applications at once, you will probably want even more. And if you're thinking "that would never happen," you might want to rethink your position. I've found that once people start actively using automation, they discover whole new worlds of functionality. For example, a natural extension of database management is to map the data and to e-mail or otherwise communicate it to large lists of customers or prospects. Both can be extremely demanding. Of course, the patience level and tolerance of your users will be the ultimate arbiter of hardware requirements.

The most difficult part of using automation is learning the syntax of the commands that you are going to use in VBA to drive the server application. I've already shown you how to open a worksheet and how to enter data into cells. But how did I know what those commands were?

You can begin spelunking through an object's properties and methods by using its *object libraries*—a list of all the properties and methods that are available to the external world. You can use the Object Browser to do so as soon as you've created a reference to the object you're interested in inspecting.

To create a reference, open a Code window—an empty module will do fine. Then select Tools | References from the Visual Basic for Applications menu to display the References dialog box, as shown in Figure 23-1.

Find the object that you want to work with—in Figure 23-1, it was Excel 9.0 (from Office 2000)—and check it. Then select the OK button.

Now that a reference to the object has been made, you can open the Object Browser. You can just press F2, or select View | Object Browser, or select the Object Browser button in the toolbar if you've got a Code window open. The Object Browser consists of two panes. The left pane lists the various objects available in the application you're inspecting, such as "Application," "Workbook," and "Sheets." By selecting a specific object, you display a list of properties and methods in the right pane of the Object Browser window, as shown in Figure 23-2.

23

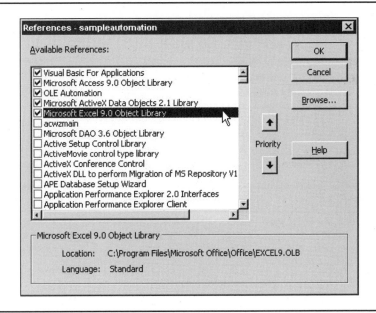

The References dialog box is brought forward from the VBA Tools menu

Figure 23-1.

The Object
Browser
displays
objects
available for
inspection in
the left pane,
and the
properties and
methods of the
selected object
in the right
pane

Figure 23-2.

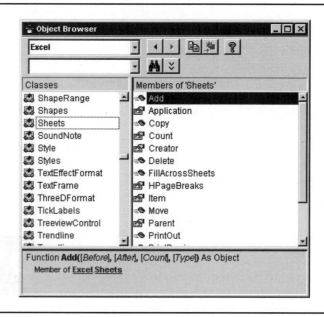

Once you've got a list of properties and methods, it's a matter of trial and error, or being lucky enough to find documentation on the specific application you're interested in working with. Some applications that you'll want to work with as a server have their own built-in macro recorders, which can be used to document the steps you want your client to perform. The resulting macro can often be examined to determine which properties and methods you will want to duplicate in your own client procedure.

You can also control Access from other applications. You can find Access' object model documented in Access Help, and you'll want to examine it thoroughly before starting to program your client to make requests of Access. Unfortunately, Access does not have a Macro Recorder like Excel and Word, so you'll have to rely on trial and error with the objects listed in help and examined in the Object Browser.

Automation is a flexible and powerful technique for making multiple Windows applications work nearly as one. The trick to making automation succeed, even more so than with other aspects of Access programming, is to take one step at a time and make sure each function operates as you expect before starting on the next one.

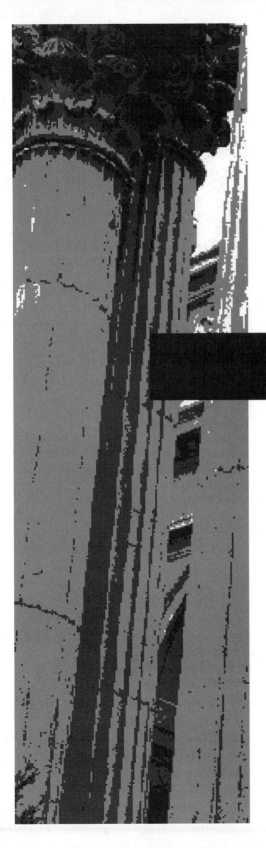

CHAPTER 24

Working on the Web with Access 2000

Access 2000 has a number of features to make working with the Internet easier and more natural. But before I discuss those specific tools, let's consider why you should even include the Internet in your application development. "After all," you might say, "I'm just building an application for myself (and perhaps a few coworkers). I'm not building a big fancy web site for people to shop on."

That may be true, but you're missing the point. In terms of application development, the Internet is simply another mechanism for distribution of and access to your application and its data, and for expanding the reach of your application to include additional information. Just as local area networks allow users to share data and applications throughout an office or a company, the Internet can allow you to share information from your application with the world. Furthermore, as a vast storehouse of information, the Internet provides a "location" for including additional information in your application.

If it hasn't already, the Internet will have a huge impact on the way you will do development in the future. You need to plan for it now.

Access 2000 has a number of features that allow you to integrate your application, in varying degrees, with the Internet, including

◆ The Hyperlink field type allows you to store URLs (uniform resource locators) and UNCs (uniform naming conventions) in a table and attach a different one to each record. You could use this to include home pages for individuals or companies, or to attach relevant web sites relating to content or topics for a record.

◆ You can save reports in HTML format so that they can be viewed through a browser—both on an intranet and the Internet.

◆ *Data Access Pages* are web pages that you can use to maintain (view, add, edit, or delete) data in an Access MDB or in a SQL Server database.

Hyperlink Field Type

As you learned in Chapter 3, when you create a table in an Access database, you can specify the type of data for each field. The Hyperlink field type allows you to store URLs and UNCs in a table in a native format friendly to URLs and UNCs, instead of using a string data type and then having to massage the data when you want to use it.

A *URL* is the name of a web site or page, and it takes the format http://www.*yourwebsite*.com. The *UNC* is a generic way of referring to the location of a file or folder, and it takes the format *SERVER**SHARENAME*\ to refer to that entity.

This is handy when you want to attach a different URL or UNC to each record in a table. For example, in an address book, you might want to include the home page of the individual; for a company, you could include the company's web site URL. In the MG database we've been using, you might want to have a specific page for each car in the automobile registry that includes photos and stats about the car. Instead of forcing a user to navigate through a maze of pages to get to a specific car, you could include the URL of the page for each individual automobile.

To use a Hyperlink field type, create the field and assign it the Hyperlink data type as you would assign any other data type to a field. Then open the table in Datasheet view, right-click the field containing the hyperlink field, and select the Hyperlink menu command, as shown in Figure 24-1. Selecting the Edit Hyperlink menu command from the Hyperlink drop-down menu will display the Insert Hyperlink dialog box, as shown in Figure 24-2.

The Insert Hyperlink dialog box is full of options for automatically inserting many different kinds of data.

24

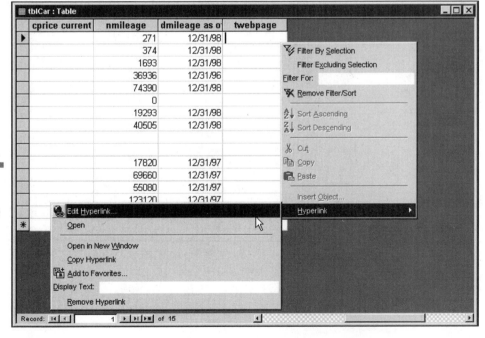

Select the Hyperlink menu from the field shortcut menu to modify the hyperlink data in a field automatically

Figure 24-1.

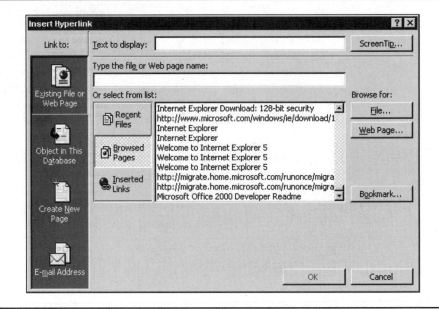

The Insert Hyperlink dialog box allows you to automatically insert a hyperlink by navigating to it through a variety of mechanisms

Figure 24-2.

First of all, you can choose what type of object you want to link to. Your choices are an existing file or web page, an object in the current database, or an e-mail address. You can even choose to create a new page from scratch.

If you choose Existing File Or Web Page, more choices appear. You can display either the URL itself or descriptive text. The description "http://www.ebs100.com/wwdefault" may not be useful information in a database, but "The Ultimate Car Price Database" would be. If you select a URL that has a title in the web page, that title will be displayed in the Text To Display text box, as shown in Figure 24-3.

You can select a file or web page name in many different ways. You can manually enter a filename or web page name in the text box in the middle of the dialog box. You can select it from a list, and choose what type of list you want to see—Recent Files, Browsed Pages, or Inserted Links. Finally, you can also browse using the File and Web Page buttons. You can even grab a bookmark from the existing document.

If you choose Object In This Database, you'll get an Explorer-style view of all the possible objects in your database, as shown in Figure 24-4.

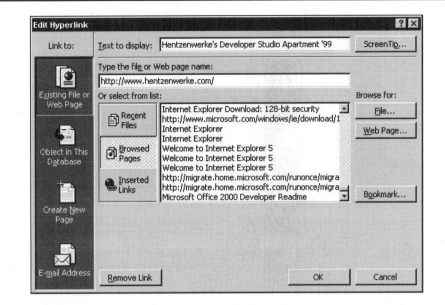

The Text
To Display
text box is
automatically
populated with
the title of a
valid web page

Figure 24-3.

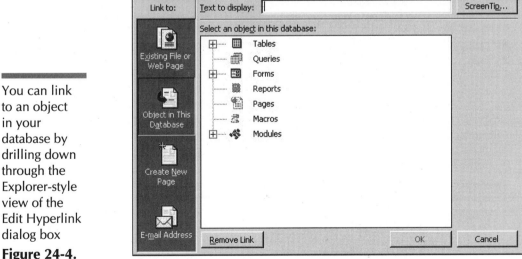

You can link
to an object
in your
database by
drilling down
through the
Explorer-style
view of the
Edit Hyperlink
dialog box

Figure 24-4.

24

If you choose E-mail Address, you can select from a list of recently used e-mail addresses, or enter some other one. I'm a little curious why there is no Browse button for selecting an e-mail address out of, say, Microsoft Outlook or whatever e-mail program is currently installed; I imagine that will appear in a future version. You can enter your own text to display instead of a possibly cryptic e-mail alias, as shown in Figure 24-5.

Once you've inserted the hyperlinks for the appropriate records, your datasheet should look like Figure 24-6.

Saving Reports as HTML

Most of the people who interact with an application are only interested in getting data out of the system. Relatively few are involved in entering and editing the data. The Web provides a mechanism to distribute reports in a rapid, efficient, cost-effective manner. You can create reports that can be published on the Web very easily with Access 2000. It's simply a matter of saving the results of a report to a file in a format that's readable by web browsers.

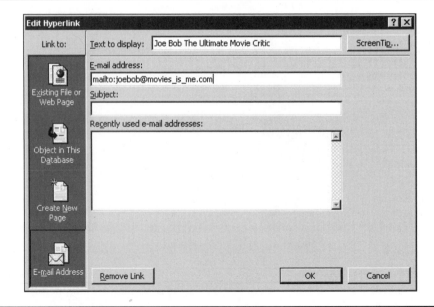

You can insert a hyperlink to an e-mail address and provide a user-friendly description of the address

Figure 24-5.

The Datasheet view of a table with hyperlinks to both URLs and e-mail addresses

Figure 24-6.

	cprice current	nmileage	dmileage as o	twebpage
		271	12/31/98	Hentzenwerke's Developer Studio Apartment '99
		374	12/31/98	Joe Bob The Ultimate Movie Critic
▶		1693	12/31/98	
		36936	12/31/96	
		74390	12/31/98	
		0		

Record: |◄| ◄| 3 |►|►|►*| of 15

First, select the report whose results you want to publish on the Web. Select File | Export to open the "Export Report <*name*> As" dialog box. Choose HTML Documents in the Save As Type combo box, as shown in Figure 24-7, rename the file to be created, and choose the Save button.

You will be prompted to choose an HTML Template, but you are not required to. Select a Template or choose Cancel, and your HTML-formatted report will be saved in the folder you chose. It is now viewable through a web browser, and you can put it on your web site, publish it on your intranet, or do whatever else you need to do.

24

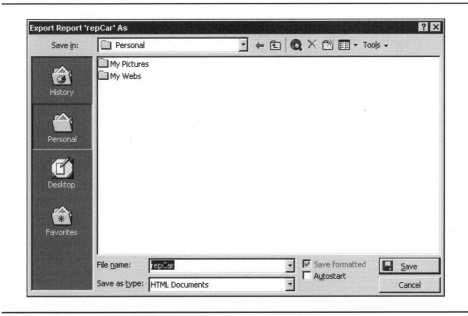

Select HTML Documents in the Export Report dialog box

Figure 24-7.

Data Access Pages

A Data Access Page is a new type of object in an Access database that allows users of your application to maintain (view, add, edit, delete) data in an Access MDB or a SQL Server database over the Web.

You can create pages that are used to maintain data in a fashion similar to that of your Access forms as well as to simply display data, much like your Access reports do. Data Access Pages that display data are not the same as exporting an Access report to an HTML document as discussed in the previous section. You can even store HTML markup tags in specific fields in your tables and use them to display HTML-formatted text on a Data Access Page.

Creating and using a Data Access Page is much more straightforward than it may seem at first—Microsoft has provided a lot of horsepower behind the scenes. Essentially, you just create a Data Access Page using any of the same techniques you use to create an Access form, but when you save the Data Access Page, an HTML page is saved outside of the .MDB file. (There's also a Data Access Page object in the Access database, in case you were wondering.) Then you simply open that external HTML page through a browser such as Internet Explorer 5. The Data Access Page contains the necessary information to make the connection to the database (either in Access or in SQL Server) so that the page can get to the data.

NOTE: If you move your data, you'll have to rework the Data Access Page, because the entire hard-coded path to the database is included in the connection string. For this reason, there is no source code included with this chapter. The Data Access Page would reference an .MDB stored deep in the subfolders on my machine, and it wouldn't be prudent to assume that you've got the same folders on your machine.

Let's walk through a simple example to see how to create and publish your own Data Access Page.

First, open your database and select the Pages button under the Objects bar. Next, decide which mechanism you want to use to create a Data Access Page. The wizard is fairly straightforward, although it's limiting once you want to do anything other than basic data entry into fields.

To create a Data Access Page in Design view, just click the Design toolbar button or double-click the Create Data Access Page In Design View object in the right tab of the Database window. You'll get a Design View window like that shown in Figure 24-8.

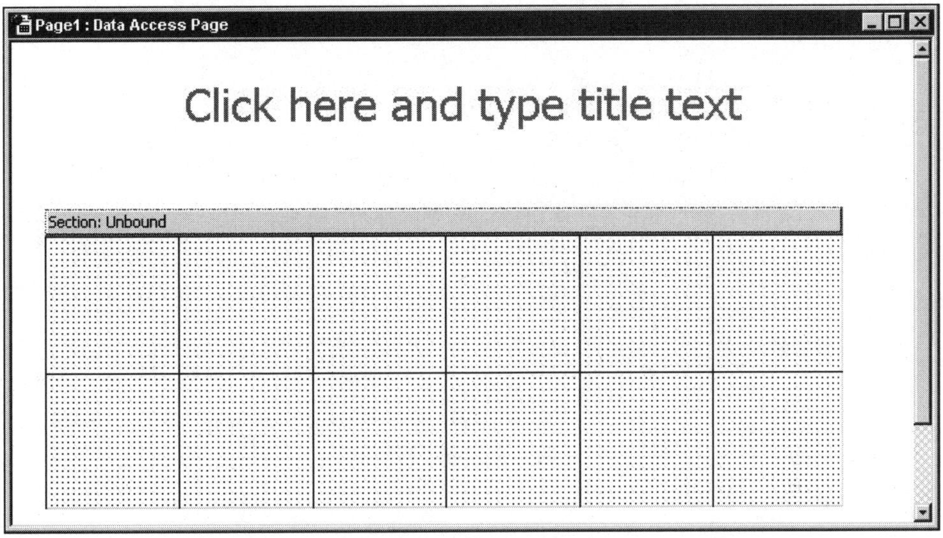

Page1 : Data Access Page

Click here and type title text

Section: Unbound

The Design
View window
for a Data
Access Page
looks and
works much
like the Design
View window
of a standard
Access form
Figure 24-8.

The next step is to drop controls onto the Data Access Page and set their
properties, much like you did with Access forms. There is a wider variety of
controls that you can use with Data Access Pages, as shown by the five
additional controls in the Data Access Pages Toolbox in Figure 24-9.

24

The Data
Access Pages
Toolbox
contains a
wide variety
of controls
for use with
web pages
Figure 24-9.

For example, the following controls are available to be dropped onto a Data Access Page:

Bound HTML
Scrolling Text
Office Pivot Table
Expand/Contract buttons
Record Navigation toolbar
Office Chart
Office Spreadsheet
Bound and Unbound Hyperlinks
Hotspot Image
Movie

Access form controls that are not available with Data Access Pages include Toggle Buttons, Bound and Unbound Object Frames, Tab Control, and Page Breaks.

The third option is to edit a web page that already exists. While powerful, this option should be kept until last unless you are already comfortable with web page design and creation.

Once you've placed your controls on the page, you'll want to tie the page to some data. This is probably the most obscure step in the process, but it isn't too hard. Select the Unbound section of the Data Access Page, as shown in Figure 24-10, right-click so you can select the Properties menu command, select the Data tab, and pick the desired RecordSource. Once you've done so, you'll be able to set the Control Source for data-bound controls. After you do that and set any other properties you like, your page is ready for publishing.

Save your Data Access Page, and you'll be greeted with the Save As Data Access Page dialog box. Access will save a Data Access Page object in your database separately (and automatically). This function creates an HTML page that you'll use as part of your web site. Select the name of the page and the location, choose the Save button, and you're all set.

Note that while you won't want to move the database, you can move the Data Access Page anywhere, as long as access to the original database isn't restricted. Thus, you might want to save all your Data Access Pages in a single "Working Copies" folder until you've finished, and then hand them all over to the person in charge of the web site.

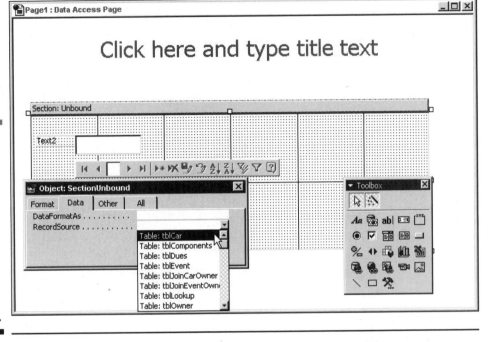

You can bind a data access page to a data source by selecting it through the RecordSource property in the Unbound section of the page

Figure 24-10.

Conclusion

24

Access 2000's web-related features make it easy to provide wide-ranging access to your Access applications. Even if you're not planning on using these features now, it's good to keep them in mind. More than likely, you will run into users or customers who will suddenly pop out with "Can we put this on the Internet?" with no advance warning. You'll then be glad that you're prepared.

Index

NOTE: Page numbers in *italics* refer to illustrations or charts.

A

Access 2000
    See also databases
    ActiveX controls, 435-448
    advanced form techniques, 363-377
    advanced queries, 341-362
    Automation, 449-456
    building applications, 285-301
    client/server techniques, 425-433
    collections, 257-264
    Control menu, 7
    customizing environments, 8-12
    databases overview, 17-53
    datasheets, 55-76
    debugging, 303-324
    deploying applications, 411-422
    described, 4-5
    designing applications, 267-283
    designing databases. *See* normalization
    dialog boxes, 5, *6*
    error handlers, 325-339
    forms, 109-150, 363-377
    interface, 5-16
    Internet and, 457-467
    macros, 177-208
    maintenance, 244-246
    menus, 7, 230-239
    as object-based tool, 258-259
    output techniques, 379-387
    overview, 4-5
    queries, 79-107
    refining applications, 389-409
    reports, 151-175
    Run Time component, 414-418
    ScreenTips (ToolTips), 7-8
    security, 246-255
    title bars, 7
    toolbars, 7-8, 239-241
    VBA (Visual Basic for Applications), 209-227
    worksheets. *See* datasheets
Access CurrentDb( ) function, referencing workspaces and databases safely, 264
Action column, macros, 179
action form controls, 117-118
    command buttons, 118
    page breaks, 118
    sub forms, 118
    tab controls, 118

N

O